WOMEN
AND THE
GREAT
HUNGER

Published by:
Quinnipiac University Press
275 Mount Carmel Ave
Hamden, CT 06518-1908
www.quinnipiac.edu
for

Ireland's Great Hunger Institute
www.qu.edu/institutes-and-centers/irelands-great-hunger-institute/

ISBN: 978-0-9909454-2-0

Cover Image : Cottage Interior, Claddagh, Galway, 1845 by Francis William Topham
Designed by Cindy O'Dell
Printed by Paladin Commercial Printers

Women and the Great Hunger

Christine Kinealy

Jason King

Ciarán Reilly

editors

Table of Contents

Acknowledgements

The editors would like to thank the 17 contributors to this volume, each of whom has provided a unique and original insight into the largely untold story of women during the Great Famine, and the multiple legacies of the tragedy.

The initial inspiration for this volume was a gathering of scholars at Quinnipiac University, hosted by Ireland's Great Hunger Institute and facilitated by Lynn Bushnell and Charity Kuchyt. The project quickly gathered its own momentum and revealed the richness and depth of research currently being carried out on women and famine. The essays in this volume represent a small part of this work.

Many librarians and archivists - from Canada to Australia - have given assistance and guidance to the contributors to this publication. We thank them all for their time and expertise. Particular thanks are due to Dr. Alan Delozier of Seton Hall University, Robert Joven of the Arnold Bernhard Library and Jim Callery of Strokestown Park in Roscommon. We also are grateful to the various copyright holders who granted permission for us to use the various images in this book. Other individuals and institutions have assisted in various stages of production. The Centre for the Study of Historic Irish Houses and Estates at Maynooth University, in particular Professor Terence Dooley, facilitated the research into the chapter presented by Dr. Ciarán Reilly. A number of people at Quinnipiac University assisted in preparing the book for publication, in particular, Donna Pintek and Cynthia Greco.

Families are often the unsung heroes of supporting scholars in the process of transforming ideas into the written word, and the written word into a book. The editors would like to pay particular tribute to: Michael, Carol, Siobhán and Ciarán; Tara, Donnacha and Odhrán; and Kerry, Aislinn, Nathalie, and Fergus. They make everything not only possible, but worthwhile.

Christine Kinealy

Jason King

Ciarán Reilly

Introduction

"This expertise is hard won": women and the Great Hunger in Ireland

Christine Kinealy, Jason King and Ciarán Reilly

In 1991, Margaret Ward chastised a number of leading Irish historians for writing histories that were "strangely women free." The appearance shortly afterward of the much-anticipated *Field Day Anthology of Irish Writing*, which also was overwhelmingly woman free, ignoring both pivotal feminist texts and momentous women writers, confirmed Ward's accusation. When challenged, Seamus Deane, editor of the *Field Day Anthology*, was repentant and promised a further volume to correct the omission. In fact, two further volumes were produced that were dedicated to women and their writings, although they did not appear until 2002.[1] Both volumes were well-received. However, as Catriona Crowe observed: "This expertise is hard-won; battles had to be fought, and still have to be fought, to secure for women's history, and women's studies in general, the resources and the status they deserve in the academy."[2] In the intervening years, despite some attempts to "write women into Irish history," the historiography remains sparse. In the area of the Irish Hunger,[3] which has been the subject of extensive scholarly research since 1994, women remain largely absent from the narrative. This volume will go some way to correcting that absence. More importantly perhaps, it will throw some light on the multiple resources that are available to researchers interested in exploring the role of women during the Great Hunger.

Since the publication of Margaret Kelleher's *The Feminization of Famine: Expressions of the Inexpressible?* (1997), critics have tended to examine the portrayal of Irish women as signifiers of dearth and hunger. They often emphasize their role in famine representations as "bearers" rather than "makers" of meaning. According to Kelleher, "the famine victim herself may possess an allegorical function, embodying the fate of mother earth, the mother/land, even nation... figuring both the crisis of famine and society's survival."[4] Stuart McClean contends that these allegorical female representations of Famine Ireland are "contrastively defined" against a "(male) realm of historical agency and national struggle" in which women's actual experiences of the Great Hunger seem ahistorical.[5] Other scholars, including Sarah Goss, George Cusack, Marguérite Corporaal and Melissa Fegan, have built on Kelleher's pioneering work, largely in the field of literary representation. Indeed, while many contemporary depictions of the Famine have been dominated by female imagery, the involvement of women in other ways (e.g., as landowners, as relief-givers, as law-breakers, or as providers for the family) has received little attention.[6] This book asks: how did women experience—and shape—the tragedy that unfolded in Ireland between 1845 and 1852?

Women and the Great Hunger in Ireland breaks new ground in its emphasis on ordinary women's agency, experiences, interpretations, and eyewitness perspectives of the Great Hunger and Irish Famine migration from a wide array of newly discovered and under-utilized archival sources. It also acknowledges innovative female scholarship on the Irish Famine that has been overlooked in the historiography. As Christine Kinealy notes in the opening chapter, Cecil Woodham-Smith's

The Great Hunger (1962) was often dismissed until recently as the work of a non-professional historian; yet it "was more thoroughly researched than any previous book on the Famine and, indeed, than many that eventually followed. The use of local, national and international archives set a benchmark for research that few Famine historians have matched." Kinealy and fellow editors, Jason King and Ciarán Reilly, seek to build on Woodham-Smith's work and to meet the standard of archival scholarship that she set.

Women and the Great Hunger in Ireland aims to recover women's voices about the Great Hunger from across the social spectrum on both sides of the Atlantic. The diversity of women's voices that emerge in the pages that follow reflects the Famine's sheer devastation as well as their resilience in response to the blight. At the bottom of the social hierarchy were the cottiers and landless laborers, who were mostly illiterate and left relatively little trace of their existence. Ciarán Reilly has discovered petitions written on behalf of cottier tenants in the Strokestown Park House in Roscommon and the Lucas-Clements archives in Cavan that attest to the divisive impact of the Great Hunger on vulnerable families. A case in point is the Strokestown "Petition of Widow Kilmartin, 14 July 1848" in which she complains that "the morning after my husband was buried his father and sister came... to put me out for nothing." Gerard MacAtasney has unearthed the testimony of Jane Corbett in Carrick-on-Shannon, who witnessed "children dying in the streets and older persons on the roadsides and in fields" on 19 May 1847. Gerard Moran notes the sad story of Jane Kelly, who received assistance to emigrate after residing for five years in the Mountbellew workhouse, only to find herself incarcerated in 1857 in a Canadian lunatic and idiot asylum for decades to follow. "It is difficult to trace the lives of most of these emigrant girls" like her, he suggests. "As orphans, they ended up in unknown destinations in North America, often untraceable by family and friends." Yet they can be glimpsed in passing in the meticulously documented annals of the Grey Nuns who cared for Irish Famine migrants in the fever sheds of Montreal and in institutions they created for their support. As Jason King observes, Famine Irish widows and orphans under the care of the Grey Nuns were encouraged to be mutually supportive and to "endeavor to help one another" in a spirit of female fellowship that found lasting expression in a network of autonomous female-led institutions the Sisters created to shelter vulnerable migrants who had nowhere else to turn. These women's voices attest to both the sundering of familial bonds and this spirit of female fellowship under extreme duress.

Even less perceptible are the voices of children of the Great Hunger that emerge in the margins of these studies. The plight of orphaned children was seared in the memory of those who bore witness to their suffering. As King observes, the Sisters of Providence recorded the spectacle of weeping "little children, who were still clasped in the arms of mothers who had died during the night" in Montreal's fever sheds. Reilly has uncovered the petition of Alice Donnocho, who lamented that "my children are almost starved to death so I beg your honour will take pity". Moran and Reilly both note recurrent patterns of child desertion in Irish workhouses during the Famine period. "As the family was segregated on entering the workhouse, for a long time the children were not aware they had been abandoned," Moran contends. These chapters also point to a further under-researched area in Irish famine studies: its impact on children.

A theme of many chapters is how women's involvement during the Famine and its aftermath was characterized by multiple and varied layers of public engagement. This often was manifested in unexpected ways. Cara Delay's chapter, in which women emerge simultaneously as both victims and as heroic figures, points to the complexity of their experiences. Through her examination of how women—the "meddlers" of her title—interacted with authority figures in the churches, she shows them as people with agency, not simply as passive victims.

Daphne Wolf investigates some of the themes of agency explored by a number of other authors. She does so by looking at the issue of clothing—or lack of—during the Famine. In both Wolf's chapter, and MacAtasney's micro-study of women in Leitrim, we learn of people who are "nearly naked," and thus unable to engage in basic activities that might ensure their survival. The issue of self-esteem is also explored. Wolf contends that "lack of clothing in a time of extreme want constituted a unique level of dispossession." The need for clothing by the poor into 1848 and 1849 is a grim reminder of the longevity of the crisis. The provision of clothing, bedding, medicine and fuel are areas in whichprivate philanthropy exposed the deficiencies of the British government's relief policies. In many instances, it was women who stepped up to fill this vacuum, although this is an area that would benefit from more local research.[7]

During one of her many press interviews, Woodham-Smith praised the "stead-fastness of women" during the Famine. Four individual women are singled out for special attention in this volume: Asenath Nicholson, Frances Cobbe, Jane Elgee Wilde and Hester Catherine Browne. American-born Nicholson defied many conventions; travelling to Ireland alone and traversing the country initially to find out about the poor and then, following the failure of the potato, to provide direct relief. She proved to be a perceptive eye-witness who left full accounts of her journeys. According to her biographer, Maureen Murphy, Nicholson was more than an educator; she regarded Irish schools as a "litmus test" of how the poor were treated. She viewed education as a potential vehicle of escape from poverty and starvation. Indeed, Murphy's chapter builds on her comprehensive biography of Nicholson, *Compassionate Stranger: Asenath Nicholson and the Great Irish Famine,*[8] to explore how "her most poignant accounts of suffering were those of the children she met in schools."

Like Nicholson, Frances Cobbe was outspoken on many social issues of the day, including Abolition, which provided one of the few accepted outlets for women to emerge into the public sphere.[9] Cobbe, however, occupied a place in Victorian public discourse that was rarely granted to her gender. Regardless of recent interest in Irish-born Cobbe, she is seldom viewed through an Irish prism, something that Maureen O'Connor seeks to rectify. Like Nicholson and Speranza, Cobbe was a witness to the Famine, although her response was more muted and mediated. Her experiences, nonetheless, shaped her subsequent views and writings on the Anglo-Irish ascendancy—the class from which she was drawn.

Similarly, Speranza (also known as Jane Francesca Elgee, or Lady Wilde) was born into the Anglo-Irish ascendancy. She sought in her verse to convey the devastation wrought by the Great Hunger as well as the despair of parents who deserted their offspring, because they could "not stay and listen to their raving, famished cries." According to Amy Martin, Speranza did not attempt to give voice to afflicted children, but to render their voicelessness in poetic form. She repeatedly emphasizes the figure of the stricken child incomprehensibly suffering from the effects of hunger as a personification of what Martin terms a "poetics of dehumanization." Speranza was widely acclaimed for her representations of victims of the Famine and even regarded after her death in 1896 as Ireland's "National Poetess of the century", but her literary reputation subsequently fell into decline and was eclipsed by that of her son, Oscar Wilde. Nevertheless, "she remains an important eye-witness to, and champion of, the Irish poor during the Great Famine," suggests Matthew Skwiat. Both Martin and Skwiat have begun to re-evaluate Speranza's legacy as Ireland's "national poetess" who registered the inchoate cries of the children of the Great Hunger in her extraordinary verse.

Just as women feature prominently in the imagery and iconography of the Famine, they are also conspicuous in the folklore of the catastrophe. Indeed, as Patricia Lysaght has argued, they are frequently represented in folklore for their benevolence and good will. Here, in particular, the horror stories of the Famine are counter-balanced with the generosity of women.[10] Eileen Moore Quinn's chapter on the "lore" of women immigrants on culture in New England, reminds us that the impact and memory of the Famine were not confined to the island of Ireland. She explores the transmission of oral traditions through the words and expressions passed down by immigrant mothers and grandmothers to their children, but more particularly the women. Her chapter reveals how Irish women in New England, in post-Famine decades, utilized and adapted memories and the language of survival as a resource when abroad.

Reflecting recent developments in historiography, the chapters in this volume are multidisciplinary and employ different theoretical and methodological approaches. The utilization of new approaches, made possible by recent medical advances, is evident is Oonagh Walsh's groundbreaking chapter on "The Great Famine and Epigenetic Change in Ireland." In it, she explores the possible link between the physical and psychological stresses of the Great Famine, and the chronic health conditions experienced by a substantial proportion of the Irish population in the post-Famine years. In particular, it examines the question of whether the exceptionally high levels of mental ill-health, as well as raised levels of cardiovascular disease in particular, are linked to the nutritional deprivation of the Famine years. It further complicates the question of when can the Famine be said to have ended, and how little we still know about the legacies of this tragedy. Indeed, Walsh explores how the children of the Great Hunger continued to suffer its effects long after the blight had passed.

The final chapters bring together new voices and new ways of understanding this topic. They also suggest alternative ways of making famine history more accessible to a wider audience. Just as Jason King's chapter uncovers and pays tribute to the role of the Grey Nuns of Montreal in saving the lives of many fleeing Irish in 1847, Turlough McConnell reveals the story of another religious order—the Sisters of Charity—who saved the lives, and souls, of Catholic immigrants to New York. In 1846, Mother Angela Hughes, sister of the Tyrone-born Bishop John J. Hughes, arrived in the city to found St. Joseph's Half Orphan Asylum for children. As the Mission spread, the Sisters helped to create the country's first system of free parochial schools and social services. Like the Grey Nuns in Montreal, they created female-led institutions and social infrastructure to help care for the Famine Irish in New York. McConnell helps to rescue the intrepid Angela Hughes from the shadows of her more famous brother.

If women's agency is a central contention of a number of chapters, lack of choice is a theme of Rebecca Abbott's examination of the 4,000 young women who took part in the Earl Grey emigration scheme to Australia. Self-identified as orphans, these teenagers travelled thousands of miles into the unknown. Many found husbands and they had, on average, seven children each. Only a small number (as few as two) ever returned to Ireland. Through interviews with their descendants, Abbott recovers the contribution of these pioneering women to Australian history. Their legacy includes descendants who now comprise a significant portion of Australia's population, descendants who are proud to claim "Earl Grey Girls" as their forebears.

In general, landowners have been criticized for their lack of compassion and generosity to their tenants during the Great Hunger. Even the Society of Friends, eye-witnesses to so much suffering, were repeatedly critical of the landowning class, but most especially absentee landowners.[11] The role of female landowners has received little attention. Recent research, however, suggests a variety of responses; the famous Maria Edgeworth, for example, despite being an octogenarian, was active in obtaining and providing relief to her tenantry.[12] The chapter by Sandy Letourneau O'Hare and Robert Young adds both to the interdisciplinary nature of this volume, and to the ways in which previously hidden histories can be made visible. The Lady Sligo Exhibition, which was first displayed at Quinnipiac University and then travelled to Westport House in Co. Mayo, challenges traditional perceptions of landowners during the Famine. Based on a collection of 200 family letters, most of which were written by Lady Sligo, the exhibition tells the story of one family—the Brownes of Westport House—who were pro-active in obtaining relief for their tenants. The exhibition also rescued this eponymous matriarch from obscurity, suggesting that the role of Anglo-Irish women of the ascendancy class is multifaceted.

Constance and Eva Gore-Booth were born into the ascendancy, but had formative experiences in alleviating hunger and providing relief for tenants during the forgotten famine in 1879-1880 that helped shape their political temperaments as some of the most influential and radical women in 20th-century Ireland. In her afterword, Ruth Riddick reflects on their legacy and offers closing remarks that are both personal and provocative. She too explores issues of culture, power, personal agency, and self-esteem, but in the context of the late 20th century. Her words are a reminder of how far the women's movement has come in a relatively short time, while showing us simultaneously the stuttering steps that brought us to this place. It is also a call not to be complacent—thus bringing us back to our opening quote by Catriona Crowe. It is no coincidence that Riddick was a contributor to the Field Day anthologies that were devoted to women's writing.

Ultimately, *Women and the Great Hunger in Ireland* recovers the voices of the most vulnerable female cottiers and caregivers of stricken emigrants in the fever sheds of Montreal, destitute orphans and their descendants in North America and Australia. It also sheds new light on the role played by more prominent and affluent women in alleviating suffering, who have largely been invisible in scholarship on the Great Hunger. The richness and variety of the chapters that follow provide a signpost to areas that could be further researched or, indeed, retold. Much of the writing is based on consulting little used sources or applying new methodological approaches. Utilizing primary sources to retell history in the form of exhibitions, films and new media is a theme that underlines the final chapters. Overall, these developments suggest the vibrancy of Famine studies on both sides of the Atlantic. *Women and the Great Hunger in Ireland* makes an important contribution not only to the historiography of the Famine, but also to the future of history in the age of trans-media historical storytelling.

Endnotes

[1] Various eds., *The Field Day Anthology of Irish Writing*, vols 4 & 5 (Cork: Cork University Press, 2002). Ruth Riddick's LIP pamphlet, The Right to Choose: Questions of Feminist Morality is included in the Anthology. See also the Postscript.

[2] Catriona Crowe, "Testimony to a flowering," *The Dublin Review*, issue No. 10, Spring 2003: https://thedublinreview.com/testimony-to-a-flowering/ Accessed 4 March 2016.

[3] There are a number of ways of referring to the tragedy that occurred in Ireland in the late 1840s: The Great Famine, The Great Hunger, and The Bad Times, being some of the most commonly used. The Great Hunger tends to be more frequently used in the U.S., while in Ireland The Great Famine is more prevalent. Both descriptions are used this volume, reflecting the transatlantic nature, and personal preferences of the authors. Further discussion of these titles are also explored in Chapter One.

[4] Margaret Kelleher, *The Feminization of Famine: Expressions of the Inexpressible?* (Cork: Cork University Press, 1997), pp. 6, 8.

[5] Stuart McClean, *The Event and its Terrors: Ireland, Famine, Modernity* (Stanford: Stanford University Press, 2004), p. 138.

[6] William Carleton's *The Squanders of Castle Squander* (1851/1852), written in the final stages of the Famine, goes beyond seeing women simply as spectacles of starvation, although it tends to be less well known than Anthony Trollope's *Castle Richmond* (1860). For more on the literature see, Christopher Morash, *Writing the Irish Famine* (Oxford, Clarendon Press, 1995).

[7] See Maria Luddy, *Women and Philanthropy in Nineteenth-Century Ireland*. London: Cambridge University Press, 1995. Christine Kinealy. *Charity and the Great Hunger in Ireland. The Kindness of Strangers* (London: Bloomsbury, 2013).

[8] Maureen Murphy, *Compassionate Stranger: Asenath Nicholson and the Great Irish Famine* (Syracuse: Syracuse University Press, 2015).

[9] Clare Midgley, *Women Against Slavery: The British Campaigns, 1780-1870* (London, Routledge, 2004).

[10] Patricia Lysaght, 'Perspectives on women during the Great Irish Famine from the oral tradition' in *Béaloideas*, 64/65 (1996-1997), p. 77.

[11] Society of Friends, *Transactions of the Central Relief Committee* (Dublin: Hodges and Smith, 1852), pp 188, 212-16.

[12] Kinealy, *Charity and the Greater Hunger,* chapter 7.

⌘

Chapter One

"Never Call Me a Novelist": Cecil Woodham-Smith and *The Great Hunger*

Christine Kinealy

The Great Hunger, written by Cecil Woodham-Smith and first published in 1962, retains a freshness and energy that belies its age. The same could be said of the author. It is hard to see her as somebody who was born during the reign of Queen Victoria, who attended Oxford University but, because of her gender, could not graduate, and who, for the same reason, was not eligible to vote in a general election until she was aged 32. Also as a young wife and mother, married to a successful solicitor, the expectation was that Cecil would not work outside the home. These were the restrictions on any intelligent educated middle-class woman in the early decades of the 20th century, and they help to explain the unusual and circuitous path that led to the writing of *The Great Hunger*. They also may help to explain why the reaction to this book, especially within the male-dominated academic community, was not always welcoming.

Cecil Blanche Fitzgerald was born in south Wales in 1896. Her father was Colonel James FitzGerald, an officer in the Indian Army. The FitzGeralds were members of the Church of England. Cecil attended The Royal School for Daughters of Officers of the Army in Bath; she later claimed that she had been expelled for taking unauthorized leave.[1] Between 1914 and 1917, she studied at St. Hilda's, a constituent college of the University of Oxford, where she took her final examinations in English. However, women were not permitted to be members of the University until 1920, and so she did not graduate until 1926.[2] Socially also, women were segregated from the men students and they were strictly chaperoned. A 1909 regulation stated:

> It is a rule well understood by women students, that attendance at College lectures is not to be made an excuse for conversation inside or outside the lecture-room. There is also a general rule that young students do not go alone to College lectures.[3]

Cecil's time at Oxford coincided with the First World War and the Easter Rising. She expressed sympathy with the latter, while recognizing that, in Britain, the Rising "had made pro-Irish sentiment unpopular even in normally tolerant university circles."[4] In later interviews, she spoke of being involved in the 1920s as a very junior member of the Irish Society for Self Determination.[5]

After leaving Oxford, Cecil worked as a copy writer in a London advertising agency, where she remained for over 10 years.[6] In 1928, she married a successful London solicitor, George Woodham-Smith. It was a long and a happy marriage, which produced a son, Charles, and a daughter, Elizabeth.[7] As was the tradition, Woodham-Smith did not work outside the home. However, during this period, she wrote at least three romantic novels, using the pseudonym, Janet Brown.[8] This phase of her writing career was not referred to in her later interviews. Her move to historical writing came when her two children commenced at boarding school.[9]

Woodham-Smith witnessed two world wars. During the second, she took her young children out of London to Hampshire for safety. It was at this time that Woodham-Smith was challenged to write a book about Florence Nightingale, a long-standing interest of hers.[10] Following nine years' research, which included researching in family and previously unpublished papers, Woodham-Smith's first scholarly publication appeared. The publication met with both critical and commercial success. It was also awarded the James Tait Black Memorial Prize for Biography; an honor that was bestowed by the University of Edinburgh. Woodham-Smith later said of this book, "I wrote it to see if I could write. I found that I could."[11] Regardless of the acclaim that greeted *Florence Nightingale*, Woodham-Smith was still being pigeon-holed by her gender. She frequently was asked if she would consider writing a novel—a question she "deplored." Her response was, "There's room for a woman who doesn't write a novel, don't you think?"[12] The success of *Florence Nightingale* led Woodham-Smith to her next topic, the Crimean War. Her second book, *The Reason Why,* was shorter than the first (400 pages compared with 288 pages).[13] Researching on Lord Lucan, one of the commanders of the disastrous Charge of the Light Brigade, consolidated her interest in next writing about the Great Famine. *The Reason Why* was also successful, it even being praised by the Duke of Edinburgh at a weekend gathering to commemorate the Battle of Baklava. Woodham-Smith was one of the guests and she presented the Duke and Queen with a copy of her publication.[14]

Woodham-Smith began researching the Famine in 1953, although she claimed that she "had had the story in her head for far longer than that."[15] Three years into her research, the long-awaited *The Great Famine, Studies in Irish History* by historians, R.D. Edwards and T.D. Williams appeared. The back-story to the writing of *The Great Famine* has been eloquently retold by economic historian Cormac Ó Gráda.[16] The publication was a pet project of *An Taoiseach*, Éamon De Valera, who wanted a scholarly book to mark the 100th anniversary of the appearance of the potato blight. As encouragement, the contributors were given a generous subvention of £1,500. Despite this financial support, the publication did not appear until 1956 (11 years late) and was half of the size of the volume promised.[17] Also, rather than providing a complete overview of the Famine, the book comprised of a series of chapters of uneven quality (some did not have references). The two editors and the seven contributors were all men.[18] The delays and vicissitudes which accompanied the writing of *The Great Famine* provide a number of insights into Irish academia and their interest in the Famine in the middle of the 20th century. Inevitably, perhaps, the academic community greeted the book positively.[19] Indeed, even a review by Woodham-Smith praised *The Great Famine*, noting its "justice and generosity" and "sober scholarship."[20] She pointed out, however, that it had no narrative, no conclusion, and certain topics—population, culpability and mortality—had been avoided. Nonetheless, she acknowledged that, "No more valuable contribution to the study of Irish history has been made for many years."[21] Perhaps the most damning criticism of *The Great Famine* was made by one of the editors, Dudley Edwards, who predicted privately that the volume would have the feel of "dehydrated history." In contrast, he believed that Woodham-Smith's writing possessed the "ability to be on fire."[22]

Following the pattern established in her two earlier books, Woodham-Smith researched papers held both in public record offices and in private ownership. Her early investigations commenced in Britain and Ireland, but later extended to many depositories in the U.S. and Canada. Indeed, one of the enduring strengths of her research is the time that she took to demonstrate the importance of Canada as a refuge for the fleeing Irish and to show that Famine mortality was not confined to Ireland, as the mass graves along the St. Lawrence River testified. Woodham-Smith's attention to the historic relationship between Canada and Ireland was subsequently marshalled as an argument for Ireland's need to be involved in "Expo 67" to be held in Montreal.[23]

Woodham-Smith used the workhouse records in Co. Mayo—one of the poorest regions in Ireland—as a case study. Although workhouse records had survived for most of the 163 Irish Poor Law Unions, they had rarely been consulted by historians. In the 1950s (and the decades that followed) many of these records were neither appropriately stored nor catalogued.[24] Woodham-Smith recalled:

> When I arrived in Castlebar in December 1953 no one regarded the books as of any significance. They were stacked up in a loft, approached only by a ladder. They had been nibbled by mice and were covered with the dirt of years and the droppings of birds, and my husband and I had to use electric torches to identify the volumes with which I was concerned ....[25]

In an effort to preserve them and make them more accessible, the records were moved to the National Library in Dublin.

Researching and writing *The Great Hunger* took far longer than Woodham-Smith had anticipated. In 1955, she was questioned about her completion date by the wife of an unidentified historian, who also seemed to be writing on this topic. Woodham-Smith responded, "1958 or even 1959," adding, "and [I] hope that would not conflict."[26] She also explained that she was writing from Devon "where I am for a few days with my daughter and her children building sand castles and catching shrimp."[27] In June 1958, the research was still not complete and Woodham-Smith informed the *Irish Times* that she expected her book to be finished in 18 months. She also revealed that, with the help of the Agricultural Research Unit, she was attempting to grow a lumper potato. At that stage, she had completed five years of intense research, leading the paper to assert, "As a historian, she is no less thorough than Mr. Taylor."[28]

Whilst researching the book, Woodham-Smith also was giving lectures on various aspects of the Famine. In 1958, she broadcast a lecture for the BBC on the topic of Alexis Soyer, the French celebrity chef who devised both a recipe and a method of feeding mass numbers in the soup kitchens.[29] The program was well received on both sides of the Atlantic, with the American magazine, *Harpers*, publishing it in its September edition.[30] The following year, however, she turned down a number of lecturing opportunities due to recurring influenza and bronchitis. Woodham-Smith's main concern was the delay it was causing her writing.[31] In July 1959, she confided in Major Ingrim (who was assisting her research), "I am worried about this book and don't seem to be making the progress I should like."[32] Three months later, when asked by the BBC to talk about her hobby of collecting china, she declined on the grounds, "I am in the middle of a book which is proving most difficult and exacting and I must stick to it until it is at least nearly finished."[33] The following month, when asked by Henry Hudson to write an article for the *Times*, she again declined, explaining, "I am working very hard indeed on my new book which is more complicated and difficult than anything I have attempted before and I am already behind with it. Unfortunately, I work slowly ..."[34] These comments demonstrated that, regardless of her experience, she was struggling with the subject matter, and that her deadline for completion was still not clear.

Less seriously perhaps, the book was also affecting Woodham-Smith's personal life, as a part of the glittering London social scene. In May 1960, she was informed by St. James's Palace that she was not going to be sent a ticket for Royal Ascot (a prestigious horse-race) as she had not attended for the previous three years. Woodham-Smith replied with an apology: she had been preoccupied with writing her new book, but promised that if she was sent a pass, she would attend.[35] News concerning the delays in completing *The Great Hunger* even reached Dublin. In June 1960, R.D. Edwards of UCD sent a personal letter to Woodham-Smith thanking her for renewing her subscription to the Irish Historical Society. He also took the opportunity to ask:

> How is your book on the Famine getting on? I heard rumours that you had lost interest, but was not prepared to believe. Best wishes to your husband and family.[36]

As her response to lecture at the Royal Society of Literature in the same month showed, Woodham-Smith had far from lost interest. While thanking the Society for their "flattering" invitation, she declined, on the grounds that "I am struggling with the last quarter of a book and have made up my mind not to accept any outside invitations however attractive until it is finished."[37] In mid-1961, buoyed by time spent in the south of France for health reasons, Woodham-Smith was back on the lecturing circuit. She agreed to speak at Bedford College, part of the University of London, "on some aspects of the Irish Famine."[38] In 1959, the college had asked her to be a governor but, for health reasons, she had requested them to postpone the offer for a year.[39] Bedford College had been founded in 1849 as the first higher education college in the United Kingdom for the education of women.[40]

The success of Woodham-Smith's publication gave her a public profile that was unusual for women. In the late 1950s, for example, a painting of her was displayed in the Royal Academy in London.[41] Her success also meant that she received many offers to lecture and to write. Asked if she would write a biography of Ramsey MacDonald, she declined, explaining, "My period is a small one, the middle of the nineteenth century, and I would not feel able to go outside it."[42] Her views of her own limitations were again evident in October 1960 when she responded to a request to contribute to a funny cookbook to be published in the U.S. entitled, *Artists and Writers Cook Book.* She refused on the grounds that, "I have no qualifications as a writer of humour."[43] Just as revealing was her reluctance to write book reviews. When turning down an offer from *Time and Tide* in 1961, she explained, "I don't, in fact, much enjoy reviewing, perhaps because I have no gift or facility and hate finding fault."[44]

Despite being preoccupied with completing *The Great Hunger*, Woodham-Smith found time to support social issues close to her heart. In 1958, she and a number of other prominent British women wrote a letter to the *Times* supporting the Wolfenden committee's recommendations on homosexuality; namely, that homosexual behavior between consenting adults in private should no longer be a criminal offence.[45] In early1961, she was invited by Victor Gollancz from the National Committee for the Abolition of Capital Punishment to be on the platform of a rally. She immediately responded that she would be glad to attend.[46] Woodham-Smith was also a supporter of the Irish Society for the Prevention of Cruelty to Children, making time to attend its meetings when in Ireland. While praising women, she explained that she could not bear to see children suffer: "in this connection Irish mothers are quite remarkable in the sacrifices they make for their children."[47]

Woodham-Smith was a formidable researcher but, in days when pencil and paper and on-site visits to archives were the main tools of the historian, Woodham-Smith was fortunate that she could augment her own research with external—and expert—assistance. In London, she was assisted by a relative, Phyllis Woodham-Smith, and she consulted with multiple academics and experts to both advise and assist her. On the question of Famine epidemics, for example, Woodham-Smith sought expert advice, writing to Sir Charles Dodds CBE in Middlesex Hospital on this issue. She also inquired from him as to where the best place was to view large-scale pictures of lice.[48] In the book's acknowledgements, various members of the Wellcome Foundation were thanked.[49]

Woodham-Smith's most gifted, and perhaps surprising, mentor was R.B. (Robert Brendan) McDowell. McDowell was originally from Belfast, which Woodham-Smith regarded as "perfect" in giving balance to her interpretation.[50] He was also a self-professed Unionist and supporter of the British Conservative Party, who had little patience with what he regarded as "the fatuity of extreme nationalism."[51] In 1940, McDowell had published a letter in the *TCD Miscellany* saying that unionists in the South should, "Never fail to emphasize Ireland's connection with that great civilization from which she has derived so much and which is, perhaps, the last hope of humanity in our time."[52] McDowell had written a chapter on Ireland on the eve of the Famine for the Edwards and Williams volume for which he had received "a substantial cheque."[53] The strange coupling, of the neat and elegant Woodham-Smith, and the eccentric and disheveled McDowell, worked well. One of their frequent meetings in the Gresham Hotel in Dublin was observed and described thus:

> Seated at a table in a quiet corner, Mrs. Woodham-Smith would have the professor on one side and her secretary on the other side, making notes from time to time. Presumably answering an interesting question, Professor McDowell might burst forth with a torrent of words, often waving his hands around. Eventually there might be a complete lull in the conversation and after a while it would be realized he had fallen asleep. Later, he was likely to burst back to life, continuing where he had left off.[54]

In addition to helping with research, McDowell spent three days at the beginning of December 1961 working with Woodham-Smith on the typescript.[55] Privately, George, her husband, paid McDowell undisclosed amounts of money for his assistance, which the historian described as being "too generous."[56]

McDowell took his duties as a researcher and mentor seriously. In early 1962, when Woodham-Smith was thinking about choosing suitable images, McDowell visited the National Gallery and the National Library on her behalf. He advised her, "The *Illustrated London News* drawings are bad but have a rude authenticity." He thought that William Thackeray had created some Famine drawings, which he was going to research further.[57] When Dublin yielded little of artistic merit, McDowell visited Belfast, but found nothing in the art galleries there.[58]

McDowell returned to London in early 1962, he informing George in advance:

> I need scarcely say how much I am looking forward to seeing you both. I enjoyed immensely discussing the Famine with Cecil on my last visit and I am convinced her book is going to be a most important contribution to nineteenth century British history. I am sure she is feeling the strain and even perhaps becoming a little tired of the familiar typescript, but the result will be I am sure very worthwhile.[59]

When Woodham-Smith submitted the first draft of her manuscript to Hamish Hamilton in November 1961, she warned her editor, Roger Machell, that some of the individual quotes, and the book itself, were overlong. His response, after reading it, was that the book was "a masterpiece, fully justifying the nine years work you have put into it."[60] Woodham-Smith, in turn, was clearly relieved:

> Your letter gave me the utmost immense pleasure to read I nearly burst into tears, and it was angelic and sympathetic of you to write ... thank you for your letter which I can hardly believe is true.[61]

Following Jamie Hamilton's (the owner of Hamish Hamilton) reading of the typescript, cuts of 20,000 words were suggested to bring it down to 175,000 words.[62] He also suggested that Woodham-Smith include an appendix (a literary device that she did not favor) in order to capture some of the procedural details regarding relief.[63] In the final version, two appendices were included—one focusing on Charles Trevelyan and Charles Wood and the other on the Young Irelanders.

In the early months of 1962, as she neared completion, Woodham-Smith worried about her citations being accurate, who should be acknowledged, and who should receive free or review copies.[64] She recommended that the three main Irish newspapers (the *Irish Independent, Press* and *Times*) should each receive a copy. Privately, however, she described the *Times* as "the paper of the ascendancy, Protestant, fishing, shooting, hunting." [65] In regard to illustrations, she suggested they should include Robert Peel, Daniel O'Connell, John Russell, Queen Victoria and:

> Then above all there is Trevelyan. I feel a certain hesitation in asking the family to lend a portrait or portraits, when I am going to be so nasty about him ... they are very touchy as a family.

Her solution was to ask her editor, Machell, to make the request on behalf of the publishing house.[66] However, the portrait of Trevelyan that was eventually used came from the National Trust. Its location also prompted some discussion, when the publisher suggested that it should be used as a frontispiece. Woodham-Smith disagreed, on the grounds that, "I don't think we want to throw any extra emphasis on the English administrative aspect."[67] At this stage, Woodham-Smith was thinking about the cover and was considering using a painting by a woman artist. She informed McDowell that she favored a painting by Lady Butler for the cover on the grounds that, "it expresses forcibly the essence of the subject."[68] Lady Butler (née, Elizabeth Thompson, 1846-1933) was an interesting choice. Butler was English-born and her connection to Ireland had come through marriage in 1877 to an Irish Catholic. A honeymoon in Co. Kerry had consolidated her husband's sympathy for the Irish poor and awakened hers.[69] When visiting again 11 years later, she witnessed the painful aftermath of an eviction in Co. Wicklow, and this became the inspiration for her painting, "Evicted." The painting centered on a beautiful, but heartbroken, woman amidst the ruins of what had been her cottage. It had been displayed in the Royal Academy in London in 1890, but did not sell. Nonetheless, it clearly made an impact; the Prime Minister, Lord Salisbury, joked that its "breezy cheerfulness" made him want to be part of an eviction. In the end, a water-color version of this painting was used on the first British edition of *The Great Hunger*.[70]

In March 1962, Woodham-Smith was asked to give a lecture in the Royal Society of Literature in London. She responded that she was "delighted to accept," but requested that they postpone it until the end of the year. Her explanation was the same as the one that she had been offering for a number of years—*The Great Hunger*: "I am now in the last throes of completing a new book, which is to come out in the autumn, and I do not feel I can undertake anything until it is safely in the printers hands."[71] The organizers were delighted with this response informing her, "we have had so many requests from our members for a lecture from you, and I do hope that some time you will be able to give us this great pleasure." Woodham-Smith was offered a fee of 15 guineas and told she could lecture on a topic of her choice.[72] Woodham-Smith's conditions were that she would speak for an hour—but that she preferred not to take any questions.[73]

The Royal Society lecture finally took place on 16 November 1962, four days after *The Great Hunger* had been released. Woodham-Smith spoke on "The Founding of Irish America." The meeting was presided over by a fellow historian, Professor Robert William Greaves, of Bedford College. He, however, had not been the first choice. Woodham-Smith had privately suggested that the historian Cicely Veronica Wedgwood be asked to fill this position. The women had lectured together to the Royal Society. Wedgwood had been a substitute for the historian Hugh Trevor-Roper, a friend of Woodham-Smith, who had had to pull out.[74] Woodham-Smith's choice of Wedgwood is perhaps suggestive of how she viewed herself in terms of her own writings and her gender. Wedgwood (1910—1997), a historian of 16th- and 17th- century English history, specialized in writing biographies and narrative histories. Like Woodham-Smith, her books were widely read.[75] According to the *Economist*, "she had a novelist's talent for entering into the character of the giants of history," an approach similar to that of Woodham-Smith and for which Wedgwood was unapologetic.[76] Wedgwood had studied at Bonn University and graduated from the University of Oxford, with a First Class degree in Modern History. From 1962 to 1991, she was a "Special Lecturer" at University College, London.[77] Significantly, Wedgwood used only her initials, C.V. when publishing, as a way to disguise her gender, believing that women were not taken seriously as historians.[78] During her long life, Wedgwood was prolific, but one of her obituaries suggested that she would have written more on the Civil War, but was "probably discouraged, if not intimidated, by the envenomed controversy with which academics surrounded the subject" and "the rudeness with which academics treated each other over it, when she herself was always courteous and lady-like."[79] The experiences of Wedgwood provide an insight into the academic world that Woodham-Smith had been thrust into by her publications. Both Mary O'Dowd and Nadia Clare Smith have concurred that by the 1950s, Irish history was a "male preserve,' with female historians not fitting into the dominant orthodoxy of a "(masculine) scientific, objective, impartial history."[80]

As it turned out, Wedgwood was unavailable to chair the lecture. This presented the organizer with a problem, she informing Woodham-Smith:

> .... I have been trying to think of Irish fellows with an historical flavor, or historical fellows with an Irish flavor. Without much success. Our Irish fellows tend to be poets and not historians! I suppose Monk Gibbons wouldn't do? I know he is not a historian but he is very Irish, often in London, and greatly admires women historians![81]

In her place, Woodham-Smith suggested that another woman be asked, her good friend, the Irish novelist, Elizabeth Bowen. Bowen also declined as she was travelling to the U.S.[82] Although Greaves was not the first, or even second, choice, Woodham-Smith declared that she was happy with this arrangement. In the event, he proved to be an accomplished chair. He described *The Great Hunger* as being "widely acclaimed as a valuable contribution to Irish history" and complimented Woodham-Smith for her nine years of extensive research and her thoroughness, adding that whenever he visited the British Museum or the Public Record Office, he found Woodham Smith was already there. He concluded by saying that she was able to "write history so that it could be read by people who were not historians."[83] Woodham-Smith kept the relevant press cutting of this lecture in her private papers. Even more tellingly, after returning home that evening, with her trademark graciousness, Woodham-Smith wrote to the organizer:

Thank you so much for those delicious drinks. I am always so nervous when I have to speak that I need reviving afterwards, and I was most grateful. I am so glad that you think it went off well; the audience certainly was an excellent one. With best wishes, Cecil.[84]

The release of *The Great Hunger* on 12 November 1962 was marked with a cocktail party at theNational Book League in London. Among the 97 guests were Lord and Lady Lucan.[85] During the Famine, Lord Lucan's ancestor had achieved a grim notoriety for carrying out wholesale evictions, he even being criticized in the House of Lords for his cruelty.[86] Woodham-Smith had written critically of Lord Lucan's cruelty to his tenants in her previous book, *The Reason Why*.[87] The origins of the title of Woodham-Smith's new book is unclear, but it may have been chosen as an attempt to differentiate itself from the Edwards's volume and Canon O'Rourke's *History of the Great Irish Famine* (1874), rather than any reluctance to use the word, "Famine."[88] Until this time, the phrase, "The Great Hunger," had only occasionally been used to describe the tragedy,[89] for example, in the *Connacht Telegraph* on 10 December 1927. The poet, Patrick Kavanagh, however, believed that he had first coined the phrase "*an gorta mór*" for his book of poetry "The Great Hunger (1942)." Moreover, he claimed that Woodham-Smith, "had 'ruined' his title by using it for her 1962 study."[90] Although, therefore, she was not the first to use this phrase, this publication undoubtedly popularized it.[91]

A few days after the London launch, Woodham-Smith traveled to Ireland for a post-publication book launch.[92] George was ill, so she had to travel alone. She was particularly daunted by the thought of hosting the party without her husband's support, confiding in Machell, "I only hope I don't drink too much."[93] Among the 40 guests who attended the Dublin party were Professor Delargy of the Folklore Commission, Professor Dudley Edwards and his wife, R.B. McDowell, K.B. Nowlan, and Lord and Lady Wicklow.[94] While there, she undertook a long interview with the *Irish Independent,* from her penthouse suite in the Gresham Hotel.[95] In the course of it, Woodham-Smith paid tribute to her own gender during the Famine, "If one thing stands out more than any other, in this terrible history of courage and endurance, it is the steadfastness of Irish women." The title of the article was a quote from Woodham-Smith, "Never call me a Novelist," the journalist explaining:

> Not a novelist but a historian, Mrs. Woodham-Smith nevertheless brings the drama of created characters to her real-life record, imbuing the facts objectively collated with an unmistakably subjective compassion and sympathy.
>
> It is this conjunction of intellectual detachment and sensitive understanding of humanity which gives to her books the excitement of the novel which she so flatly repudiates.[96]

Perhaps, then, it was no coincidence that in the final exam for history in University College, Dublin, in 1963, "history students encountered as the essay topic of a final exam the dismissive proposition, "The Great Hunger is a great novel."[97] Such unworthy tactics to undermine Woodham-Smith's work can be viewed as what Ó Gráda has described as "undoubtedly an element of sour grapes in the Irish historians' reaction."[98]

While in Dublin, Woodham-Smith was told the good news that one Dublin bookshop had sold 50 copies of her book in one day and, during the course of the interview, copies were brought to the room for her to sign.[99] Sales in Ireland continued to be buoyant; by June 1963, over 80,000 copies had been sold and plans were being made for French, Swedish and German translations.[100] The book was fifth in the U.S. Non-Fiction list, and still climbing.[101] Already, a paperback version of *The Great Hunger* was being produced. By April 1964, over 150,000 copies had been sold.[102] For three months, *The Great Hunger* had topped the best-sellers lists in both fiction and non-fiction in Britain. According to Woodham-Smith, it was being read by two groups of people there—those who could not understand why the Irish hated the English and those living in Britain with Irish connections. Neither group had tried to exonerate the British government, the author explaining, "the English are basically a very nice race, whatever else they may be, and they recognize the truths of the event." [103]

Woodham-Smith was frequently described as being English, which she detested. In the wake of writing *The Great Hunger*, however, her Irish roots were frequently alluded to, particularly her connections with Lord Edward FitzGerald and Silken Thomas. There was even a suggestion that her family in Ireland had connections dating back to Strongbow, to which she responded in her trademark self-deprecating way, that such information "everybody accepted without trying to prove or discount it."[104] In terms of her own identity, however, she was unequivocal:

> I am a Fitzgerald, a descendant of the Fitzgeralds of Leinster, and I am very proud of it. Granted, my father was living in Wales when I was born, but I insist that I am Irish.[105]

Woodham-Smith's personal appearance was frequently referred to by interviewers; one *Irish Independent* reporter describing her as a "small elegant woman, whose porcelain fineness covers a mind of tempered steel."[106] Another interview opened by saying that "for one so tiny," her scholarly output was amazing.[107] The *Irish Times* referred to her as, "a slender white haired woman with a thin high-boned face and laugh lined."[108] A few months later, when lecturing in Castlebar, she was described as "frail and indomitable."[109] A nominal admission fee of two shillings was charged for this lecture, with all of the proceeds going to the "Freedom from Hunger" campaign.[110] Far more money than anticipated was collected, a local newspaper explaining, "the lecture had obviously eaten into the hearts of the people."[111]

While the response to *The Great Hunger* was overwhelmingly positive, there were some public wrangles. Within a few weeks of release, Woodham-Smith was embroiled in a dispute with the Council in Mayo. To preserve the local workhouse records, she had arranged for the 520 surviving ledgers to be sent to the National Library. A local lawyer complained that the council had not been consulted and demanded their return to Mayo.[112] The public dispute was ended when the local council issued a press statement saying they had agreed the books could go to the Library on loan and the Library had paid the transport costs.[113] A review in the *Irish Independent*, written by Donal McCartney chastised Woodham-Smith for using Swineford, with an "e", when referring to the town and workhouse. Woodham-Smith responded by referring to contemporary documents where her spelling was used. McCartney admitted that the author was correct.[114] Not all differences were settled so amicably. Privately, Woodham-Smith was snubbed by Jenifer Hart, who had written about Trevelyan's role at the Treasury in 1960.[115] It appeared that Woodham-Smith had not acknowledged Hart's work; something that was corrected in later editions. Nonetheless, Hart refused to meet with Woodham-Smith when the latter visited Oxford in 1964.[116]

A tetchy public dispute also arose over Woodham-Smith's description of Thomas Francis Meagher, as being pro-slavery. When this was pointed out, Woodham-Smith issued an apology in the *Western People* and promised a correction.[117] The mistake was corrected in the second impression with Meagher correctly being given his role in the Union army.[118] However, Woodham-Smith's offer to correct the mistake in subsequent impressions, led to further public criticisms, this time led by Aidan Clarke of Magee College, Derry, who asserted:

The danger of making unacknowledged alterations in a reprint is perhaps sufficiently illustrated by the correspondence, but Mrs. WS has not only violated a convention of scholarship, she has also made nonsense of bibliographical terms; a reprint in which alterations have been made, however slight, is not properly speaking a new impression, but a new edition.[119]

Clarke's criticism set the tone for some later academic criticisms that focused on style rather than content. These criticisms may have informed Woodham-Smith's article, written for *The New York Times* in May 1963, and entitled, "No Mistake about it, the Historian is a haunted man."[120] Its opening sentence set the tone, "Writing history is nervous work, thanks to the vigilance of other historians." She further explained, "The historian can be certain that no error will pass unnoticed."[121]

Inevitably, *The Great Hunger* was compared with the earlier Famine book. One favorable review in Ireland pointed out:

> While the Great Famine remains an impressive and immensely valuable contribution to the study of one of the most decisive events in Irish history since the battle of Kinsale, it cannot be overlooked that the book inevitably suffers from a certain 'compartmentalization'. The result of its multiple authorship ... when one has read Mrs Woodham-Smith's account of the Great Hunger and returns to consult *The Great Famine*, the disproportion of treatment in the latter volume at once becomes apparent.[122]

The Great Hunger was admired by President Éamon de Valera. The 81-year-old president attended a lecture given by the author in Dublin in November 1963. *Fianna Fail* politician, Donogh O'Malley, proposed a vote of thanks to Woodham-Smith, and claimed that *The Great Hunger* had made a greater impact in Ireland than any other historical book. Less tactfully, he added that in England, "it had given the general public a knowledge that horrified them, and made them realize why the Irish disliked the English."[123] Woodham-Smith, in turn, was an admirer of de Valera. George, her husband, tried to obtain a "Talking Book" copy of *The Great Hunger:*

> to give it to Mr De Valera who, although he can see enough to get about, is now unable to read. He has had 'The Great Hunger' read aloud to him. Dev has been a hero to Cecil for more than 40 years.[124]

An audio copy was delivered to De Valera via the Irish embassy as a gift from the author.[125]

A number of American universities offered honorary doctorates to Woodham-Smith, but she declined. In 1964 though, she accepted an honorary D.Litt. from the National University of Ireland.[126] The introductory address was made by Dr. Michael Tierney, President of UCD.[127] He described Woodham-Smith as, "one of the most distinguished writers in the English language today and belonging to a class of historical writers whose exemplars have been McCauley, Carlyle, Froude and Freeman." He went on to say:

> Her last work, *The Great Hunger*, has received the praise of the world. By this book in particular, she has shown herself to be not only a great historian and a great writer, but also a great benefactor to Ireland. She has done our people an immense if painful, service by demonstrating with a wealth of detail the full-horror of the man-made chaos from which our modern Ireland has emerged.[128]

Woodham-Smith was the only woman to be so-honored that year.[129] President de Valera, chancellor of NUI, attended. He also hosted a lunch at *Áras an Uachtaráin* in her honor, inviting in addition, "his old comrades Jim Ryan, Frank Aiken, Sean T. O'Kelly, and their wives."[130] Again, Woodham-Smith was the only woman to be recognized in her own right, and not simply as a wife. The following year, Woodham-Smith accepted an honorary doctorate from St. Andrews University in Scotland.[131] In 1967, she was made an Honorary Fellow of St. Hilda's College, Oxford.[132]

For the most part, the academic reception to *The Great Hunger* was positive, although the exceptions set the tone for later, negative assessments. An early endorsement came from Conor Cruise O'Brien, an Irish historian and diplomat, who served as the vice-chancellor of the University of Ghana between 1962 and 1965. His praise for Woodham-Smith was generous, he claiming:

> Her just and penetrating mind, her lucid and easy style and her assured command of the sources have produced one of the great works not only of the nineteenth century Irish history, but of nineteenth century history in general.[133]

Privately, O'Brien believed that the book held lessons for all colonized peoples. In a personal letter, he informed Woodham-Smith that:

> When I saw President Nkrumah yesterday, he had on his desk a copy of 'The Great Hunger'. He started talking about it immediately, with great animation. He said he was half way through reading it for the second time. It was quite clear that it had made a very strong impression on him, and I think, by the way he talked, that it had the effect of extending the range of his imaginative sympathy beyond the frontiers of Africa and of the colored world generally.

> If so, this is, in its way, an important historical event. He is, beyond doubt, the most representative tropical African leader today, and things that change his mind tend thereby to inflect the course of thought and action in Africa.[134]

In later years, O'Brien would become closely associated with the "revisionist" interpretation of Irish history, which opposed overtly nationalist views of Ireland's past.[135] In the 1960s, however, his politics were more left-leaning and clearly sympathetic to Woodham-Smith's interpretation.[136] O'Brien's change of heart is, perhaps, a microcosm of the wider ideological divisions that took place in Ireland following the onset of the "Troubles," during which time *The Great Hunger* became part of a contested history.

Inadvertently, *The Great Hunger* became bogged down in a number of controversies which proved to be both enduring and damaging. One of the less palatable outcomes was a number of *ad hominem* attacks on Woodham-Smith. In some reviews, the Irish Famine was compared with the Holocaust—the later tragedy still being part of a living memory. This comparison was expressed by the Irish writer Frank O'Connor, in a review in the *Irish Times*:

> I had read only a few of the conscientious memoranda of Sir Charles Edward Trevelyan when I began to be troubled by an impression that I had read something like them in another connection. It was some hours later when the name flashed across my mind – Eichmann ...

> For reasons which the author cannot explain, and which, perhaps, no civilized human

being could explain, a majority of Englishmen hated the Irish as a majority of Germans hated the Jews, and would not oppose a policy of extermination.[137]

Two well-respected historians drew similar conclusions. D.W. Brogan of Peterhouse College in Cambridge, writing for *The New York Times* stated: "Mrs Woodham-Smith cites documents that would have given credit to a *Sturmbannfuhrer* ...There were, of course, no gas ovens. Typhus was nearly as effective."[138] *The Great Hunger* was also reviewed by A.J.P. Taylor, who was then lecturing at Oxford University. His review appeared in the *New Statesman* and was entitled "Genocide." Taylor wrote, "When British forces entered the so-called 'convalescent camp' at Belsen in 1945, they found a scene of indescribable horror...Only a century before, all Ireland was a Belsen ...."[139] Taylor's review, in turn, drew criticism from Leopold Woolf, a Jewish intellectual, who criticized Taylor for making this comparison. It is unlikely that Woolf ever read *The Great Hunger*, but the two men were already antagonists who had disagreed over Taylor's interpretation of the Second World War.[140] Taylor's review, therefore, provided a forum to continue this argument. Following a number of angry exchanges, with Woodham-Smith's book as the unwitting target, the *New Statesman* declared that it would print nothing further on this matter. At this point, an unexpected champion appeared in the form of the writer, Brendan Behan. In a letter written in December 1962, and addressed to Woolf, care of the *New Statesman*, he stated, "Now, it seems I am getting into form after reading 'The Great Hunger' by Cecil Woodham-Smith, for it tore the heart out of me."[141] He added:

> Mr Woolf ... Let me tell you straight, if you join in the controversies of the simple annals of the Irish poor, you must put up with the simple manners of their descendants.
> You seem to think that Mr Taylor's and Miss Woodham Smith's [sic] views of the so-called Irish Famine in some ways lessen the horror of the later Belsen.
> I say so-called because there was enough corn and cattle exported from Ireland in so-called Black '47 than would have fed the population ...

The letter was never published; the editor explaining that correspondence on the topic had closed on 21 December 1962.[142] Further support for both Taylor and Woodham-Smith came from another lecturer from Oxford, J.M. Hinton, in the *New York Review of Books*.[143] He averred, "Mr. F. H. Hinsley calls it a 'gaffe' when A.J.P. Taylor says that in the Great Famine all Ireland was a Belsen. I was with a Quaker relief unit at Belsen, and I have read Miss Woodham-Smith's book about the Irish famine. I see no 'gaffe'."[144] Possibly anticipating that accusations of extermination and genocide might be levelled against the British government, Woodham-Smith had, in fact, already addressed these topics in *The Great Hunger*:

> The British government has been accused, and not only by the Irish, of wishing to exterminate the Irish people, as Cromwell wished to 'extirpate' them, and as Hitler wished to exterminate the Jews. The eighteen-forties, however, must not be judged by the standards of today; and whatever parsimony and callousness the British government displayed towards Ireland was paralleled seven years later by the treatment of their own soldiers which brought about the destruction of the British Army in the Crimea.[145]

One of the most damning reviews of *The Great Hunger* was made by Irish historian, F.S.L. Lyons, which did not appear until 18 months until after the book was published. He explained, "there is a good deal to be said for waiting until the tumult and the shouting have died a little before subjecting a best-seller to a calmer and more critical appraisal."[146] Interestingly, Lyons had reviewed *The Great Famine* shortly after its release and had been fulsome in his praise for it.[147] He was less generous in his second review:

... to the serious historian, *The great famine* is the touchstone by which *The great hunger* must be judged. Mrs Woodham-Smith is herself aware of this and acknowledges her debt in her preface ... but the appearance of this second study in a field where so much distinguished work has already been done, raises two questions for the critic. First, given the existence of *The great famine* was *The great hunger* really necessary? And second, if it was necessary wherein lies Mrs Woodham-Smith's distinctive contribution?

Lyons then paid tribute to Woodham-Smith's skills as a writer and a researcher, but this praise was followed by a blistering attack on her ability as a historian, which was not simply about the book, but was churlish and personal:

Why then does one come from it – as in the end one does—with a sense of dissatisfaction, almost of disappointment? The answer, I think, may be that Mrs Woodham-Smith's narrative runs too smoothly, it is limpid as a pool is limpid—it lacks depth. Or perhaps one should put it another way and say that it lacks self-awareness, that lurking nagging uneasiness – which is the hall-mark of the true historian—that, however prolific his sources, there are still problems to be solved and much that remains untold. That is what one means, presumably, by the necessary humility of the scholar. I do not, I confess, see very much of that humility here.[148]

Lyons concluded his long review with a play on the title of Woodham-Smith's previous publication, by opining, "Students will go to *The great hunger* to find out what happened in the starving time and how it happened. But they will still turn to *The great famine* to know the reason why."[149] Three decades later, Ó Gráda criticized this uneven treatment of the two books, commenting that Lyons':

... remarkably indulgent review of Edwards and Williams bears comparison with his delayed, rather snide reaction to Woodham-Smith. His belated review of The Great Hunger in Irish Historical Studies made several valid points, but there was also a great deal of nit-picking, and in one important respect at least, Lyons stands accused of double standards.[150]

Regardless of—and perhaps in part, because of—these controversies, *The Great Hunger* continued to sell well and to be reprinted. At the beginning of 1973, 10 years after its publication, Woodham-Smith had earned £67,743.79 in royalties.[151] At this stage, a new paperback was in preparation. Knopf were the publishers, Hamish Hamilton having been sold in 1965.

The controversies regarding *The Great Hunger* did not go away and, indeed, intensified with the next generation of revisionist historians. In 1994, when reviewing three books about A.J.P. Taylor, Roy Foster, an Irish historian based in Oxford University, suggested that Taylor had written "his most black-and-white history in the form of *New Statesman* reviews." Foster cited the example of the review of *The Great Hunger*, criticizing Taylor for seeing, "the Irish Famine, for instance, as English "genocide," explaining the revolution 60 years later."[152] Foster had made his own disdain for Woodham-Smith and her work clear in a provocative article written in 1986 entitled, "We are all revisionists now." In it, he had patronizingly referred to Woodham-Smith as a "zealous convert," suggesting:

The slightly blasé and skeptical way in which many Irish people view the institutionalized pieties of Irish history is not echoed in Irish communities abroad; nor does it appear in influential popular histories written by zealous converts like Cecil Woodham-Smith.[153]

Why did Woodham-Smith and her book provoke such strong reactions? For historian Elizabeth Malcolm, the answer was partly gender: "An English woman and amateur historian bringing a more engaged approach ... was clearly resented by Irish male professional historians bent upon turning their discipline into a science."[154] Peter Gray, who has written extensively on the Famine, offered a different explanation: "The academic hostility [to *The Great Hunger*] owes something to A.J.P. Taylor's provocative review likening Famine Ireland to Belsen in 1945."[155] This explanation suggests that the book was disliked—because some reviewers chose to compare the Great Hunger with the Holocaust ... but, if this was the case, how valid is it to judge a book by its reviews? Moreover, in the 21st century, how acceptable is it to continue to define Woodham-Smith by her gender and status? The ground-breaking *Atlas of the Great Irish Famine* published in 2012, for example, described *The Great Hunger* as "the work of the non-academic woman historian ..."[156] None of the other contributors, including the other Famine historian John O'Rourke, are described by their gender and (non) academic affiliations.[157]

Immediately upon completing *The Great Hunger*, Woodham-Smith had started working on her next project—a two volume biography of another woman, Queen Victoria. She estimated that it would take 10 years to complete.[158] While writing the first volume of what would prove to be her final book, Woodham-Smith returned to Ireland often, especially to the west. Dogged by increasing poor health, she saw Ireland as somewhere that she could recuperate and be at peace.[159] Her gratitude to those who had assisted her while writing *The Great Hunger* did not diminish with time: in 1966, she bequeathed Daniel MacDonald's painting, *An Irish Peasant Family Discovering the Blight of their Store*, which had first been exhibited in 1847, to the Irish Folklore Commission in Dublin. She had purchased it at Christies and presented it to the Folklore Commission in recognition of their "very great help."[160] Woodham-Smith's interest in Irish politics also continued. In December 1973, while commenting to a friend on IRA "atrocities," she added, "The tartan gangs have turned the Irish situation upside down and I notice that Mr. Paisley has prudently retired."[161]

Cecil Woodham-Smith died on 16 March 1977, aged 80. The Royal Society of Literature's Obituary described her as:

> ... one of the most gifted biographers and narrative historians of her generation. Though she never lived in Ireland she set great store by her Irish ancestry and during her time at St Hilda's College, Oxford, her pro-Irish sympathies were very much in evidence; more than 30 years later these sympathies were directed into her most somber and relentless work, the Great Hunger.[162]

Similarly, the London *Times* wrote:

> Cecil Woodham-Smith was one of the most gifted biographers and narrative historians of her generation. She displayed an attention to detail, a flair for story-telling, and an historical and human intelligence that set her work apart ... In life, as in scholarship and literature, Cecil Woodham-Smith was a perfectionist, content only with the highest standards. A good lecturer and most entertaining in conversation, she was sharply witty in speech, but sympathetic and generous in action, especially to her fellow writers and to young people.[163]

There was little in Woodham-Smith's life-style to suggest that she would find herself at the center of a row over Irish history that would persist for decades, or that she would become a champion to Irish nationalists and a scourge of revisionists. She was born in Wales, to a military family who, on both sides, had served as officers in the British army. She and her husband were wealthy and mixed in an upper-class milieu in London, which included the Royal Family. Her social activities were reported in the columns of the *Times*.[164] In 1960, she had been awarded a CBE by Queen Elizabeth II, for services to the British Empire. When she died, her estate was valued at almost £100,000.[165]

Moreover, Cecil Woodham-Smith was no ordinary historian. She had no formal training, never worked within an academic institution, and had given up her career following marriage: a move that was typical, and often compulsory, in the 1920 and 1930s. Her family wealth (to which she contributed a substantial amount) meant that when writing *The Great Hunger* she had the support of a maid, a secretary, a chauffeur, and a personal assistant. Her circumstances also meant that she could work on this project full-time, the intermittent delays being caused by periods of ill health. Additionally, it meant she could afford frequent research trips to Ireland and North America. The outcome was a book that, regardless of any limitations, was more thoroughly researched than any previous book on the Famine and, indeed, than many that eventually followed. The use of local, national and international archives set a benchmark for research that few Famine historians have matched. Woodham-Smith was an accomplished historian who refused to be defined—or confined—by place of birth, social class or gender. Her contributions to Irish history are immense.

Endnotes

[1] Elizabeth Longford, "Smith, Cecil Blanche Woodham (1896–1977)," *Oxford Dictionary of National Biography* (Oxford UP, 2004), p. 1.

[2] Cecil Blanche Woodham Smith, née Fitzgerald, Archive of St. Hilda's College:
www.st-hildas.ox.ac.uk/index.php/history/histearly.html
Accessed 19 May 2013.

[3] Ibid. Women over 30 gained the right to vote in UK elections in 1918; this was extended to women over 21 in 1928.

[4] *Irish Independent*, 23 Nov. 1962.

[5] Ibid. The Irish Self-Determination League of Great Britain had been founded in London in 1919. By 1921, it reached its maximum membership, which was 38,726. See, Peter Berresford Ellis, *The Irish Self-Determination League of Great Britain, 1919-24*:
www.irishdemocrat.co.uk/features/isdlgb-1919-24/
Accessed 26 Nov. 2015.

[6] *Irish Independent*, 23 Nov 1962.

[7] Their affection is evident in all of their correspondence. What is less well-known is that Cecil had had an earlier marriage to Frederick W. Taylor in London in 1920:
https://familysearch.org/search/collection/results?count=20&query=%2Bgivenname%3Acecil-%20%2Bsurname%3AFitzgerald-%20%2Bmarriage_place%3A%22St%20Pancras%22-%20%2Bmarriage_year%3A1919-1922-&collection_id=2285732
Accessed 13 Dec. 2015.

[8] They included *April Sky* (1938), *Tennis Star* (1939) and *Just off Bond Street* (1940):
www.jrank.org/literature/pages/6264/Cecil-Woodham-Smith-%28Cecil-Blanche-Woodham-Smith%29.html
Accessed 2 June 2011.

[9] Longford, *DNB*, p. 1.

[10] *Irish Independent*, 23 Nov. 1962.

[11] Cecil Woodham-Smith, *Florence Nightingale, 1820-1910* (London: Constable, 1950).

[12] *The New York Times*, 4 March 1951. The name of later editions varied.

[13] Cecil Woodham-Smith, *The Reason Why: the Story of the Fatal charge of the Light Brigade* (London: Constable, 1953).

[14] "Queen and Duke Spend Weekend at Barnwell," *Northampton Mercury*, 26 Nov. 1954.

[15] *Irish Independent*, 25 Jan. 1963.

[16] Cormac Ó Gráda, "Making History in the Ireland of the 1940s and 1950s: the Saga of the Great Famine," in *The Irish Review* (1992), 87-107.

17 Ibid.

18 R. Dudley Edwards and T. Desmond Williams (eds.), *The Great Famine: Studies in Irish History, 1845-52* (Dublin: Browne and Nolan, 1956).

19 Kevin Whelan, "The Revisionist Debate in Ireland," in *Boundary* 2, 31, 1 (2004), 179-205.

20 Woodham-Smith, "The Harvest was Death," *The New York Times,* 4 Aug. 1957.

21 Ibid.

22 Ó Gráda, *Making History,* pp 101, 107.

23 *Irish Independent*, 3 March 1966.

24 In the early 1980s, the workhouse records for counties Donegal, Dublin, Kerry, Wexford and Meath, remained uncatalogued and not always appropriately housed. The Mayo records were in the NLI while PRONI had collected most of the records for Northern Ireland. Little had changed by 2016.

25 Woodham-Smith to County Manager, Castlebar, Co. Mayo, 29 Nov. 1962, Letters of Cecil Woodham-Smith, Mayo Co. Library.

26 Woodham-Smith to Mrs. Monsell (she has not been identified), 28 July 1955, MSS ad, 9437/10/1, the Archive of the Royal Society of Literature (RSL), GBR/0012/MS RSL, Department of Manuscripts and University Archives, Cambridge University Library.

27 Ibid.

28 *Irish Times*, 28 June 1958. The reference is to A.J.P. Taylor, a historian and public intellectual.

29 BBC to Woodham-Smith, 11 July 1858. She was paid 18 pounds, 15 shillings for this appearance, Box 16, File 2, Howard Gotlieb Archive, Boston University. For more on Soyer see, Christine Kinealy, *A Death-Dealing Famine. The Great Hunger in Ireland* (London: Pluto Press, 1997).

30 Miss Wood to Woodham-Smith, 9 Aug. 1958, Box 16, File 2, Boston.

31 Ibid., Letter from George Woodham-Smith on behalf of Woodham-Smith, 9 Feb. 1959.

32 Ibid., Woodham-Smith to Major Ingram, 14 July 1959.

33 Ibid., Woodham-Smith to BBC, 5 Oct. 1959.

34 Ibid., Woodham-Smith to Henry Hudson, *Sunday Times*, 11 Nov. 1959.

35 Ibid., Woodham-Smith to St. James's Palace, 25 May 1960.

36 Ibid., R.D. Edwards, UCD, to Woodham-Smith, 30 June 1960.

37 Woodham-Smith to Miss Paterson, Cambridge, 7 June 1960, Archive of RSL.

38 Woodham-Smith to Bedford College, 11 May 1961, Box 16, File 4, Boston.

39 Ibid., 22 Oct. 1959.

40 The University of London:
www.british-history.ac.uk/vch/middx/vol1/pp345-359#h3-0002
Accessed 10 Dec. 2015.

41 Royal Academy Summer Exhibitions 1939 to 1959, *Catalogue of paintings and other works by Anthony Devas*: R55, Mrs Cecil Woodham-Smith, 1956, Oil, RASE 1957 Cat. No.: 236:
www.devas.org.uk/adevaslst.html
Accessed 11 Feb. 2015.

42 Woodham-Smith to Frederick Muller Publishers, 8 Sept. 1858, Box 16, File 2, Boston.

43 Woodham-Smith to Roger Machell, Editor, Hamish Hamilton, 20 Oct. 1960, Box 16, File 4, Boston.

44 Ibid., Woodham-Smith to *Time and Tide,* 6 March 1961.

45 *Times*, 19 April 1958.

46 Victor Gollancz, National Committee for the Abolition of Capital Punishment, 6 April 1961; Woodham-Smith to Gollancz, 10 April 1961, Box 16, File 4, Boston.

47 *Irish Independent*, 1 June 1963.

48 Woodham-Smith to Sir Charles Dodds CBE, 6 March 1961, Box 16, File 4, Boston.

49 Acknowledgments, Cecil Woodham-Smith, *The Great Hunger* (London: Hamish Hamilton, 1962), p. x. Later paperback editions did not include any acknowledgements, for example, Woodham-Smith, *The Great Hunger* (New York: Signet, 1964) and Woodham-Smith, *The Great Hunger* (London: New English Library, 1979).

"NEVER CALL ME A NOVELIST": CECIL WOODHAM-SMITH AND *THE GREAT HUNGER*

50 Woodham-Smith to Jamie Hamilton, 5 Dec. 1961, Hamish Hamilton Archive: DM1352, University of Bristol.

51 "Colourful historian of Ireland and stalwart of Trinity College Dublin: R.B. McDowell Obituary," *Guardian*, 14 Sept. 2011. McDowell was a supporter of the British Conservative Party and helped to bring leading Conservative politicians including Enoch Powell and Keith Joseph to TCD, R. B. McDowell, *McDowell on McDowell: A Memoir* (Dublin: Lilliput Press, 2012), pp.162, 98-100.

52 Ibid., p. 100.

53 Ibid., p. 110.

54 Christopher Sands in *Irish Times*, 16 Sept. 2011.

55 Cecil to Fred Muller Publishers, 2 Dec. 1961, Hamish Hamilton Archive.

56 Brendan Mc Dowell (TCD) to George Woodham-Smith, 21 Feb. 1962, Box 5, file 3, Boston.

57 Ibid., McDowell to Woodham-Smith, 18 Jan. 1962.

58 Ibid., 4 Feb. 1962.

59 Ibid., McDowell (TCD) to George Woodham-Smith, 21 Feb. 1962.

60 Roger Machell to Woodham-Smith, 1 Dec. 1961, Hamish Hamilton Archive.

61 Ibid., Woodham-Smith to Machell, 2 Dec. 1961.

62 The half Scot and half American, Jamie Hamilton, founder of Hamish Hamilton in 1931, also published J.D. Salinger, Jean Paul Sartre, Truman Capote and historians A.J.P. Taylor and D.W. Brogan: http://fivedials.com/history Accessed 10 Jan. 2013.

63 Machell to Woodham-Smith, 5 Dec. 1961, Hamish Hamilton Archives.

64 Ibid., Woodham-Smith to Machell, 10 May, 17 Aug., 24 Oct. 1962.

65 Ibid.

66 Ibid., 8 Feb. 1962.

67 Ibid., 9 Aug. 1962.

68 McDowell to Woodham-Smith, 4 Feb. 1962, Box 5, File 3, Boston.

69 Paul Usherwood, "Lady Butler's Irish Pictures," *Irish Arts Review* (1984-1987), Vol. 4, No. 4 (Winter, 1987), p. 47.

70 Ibid., p. 49.

71 Woodham-Smith to Mrs Patterson, Cambridge, 17 March 1962, RSL Archive.

72 Ibid., Patterson to Woodham-Smith, 7 Aug. 1962.

73 Ibid., Woodham-Smith to Patterson, 12 Oct. 1962.

74 Ibid., 16 Feb. 1954, 9 March 1954. The topic of Woodham-Smith's lecture was, "The Quality of Contemporary Literature". Hugh Trevor-Roper was initially to be one of speakers, but was replaced by Cicely Wedgwood.

75 F.S.L. Lyons, in a mean-spirited review of *The Great Hunger* (see below), suggested, "If comparisons were not invidious, perhaps even odious, one might say that she was the C.V. Wedgwood of Irish history, with all that implies on both sides of the ledger," p. 78.

76 The *Economist*, 10 March 1997.

77 Obituary, *Independent* (London), 10 March 1997.

78 Ibid.

79 Ibid.

80 Mary O'Dowd, "From Morgan to MacCurtain: Women Historians in Ireland from the 1790s to the 1990s," in Maryann Gialanella Valiulis and Mary O'Dowd (eds), *Women and Irish History. Essays in Honour of Margaret MacCurtain* (Dublin; Wolfhound Press, 1997), p. 56; Nadia Clare Smith, *A "Manly Study?" Irish Women Historians, 1868-1949* (Hampshire: Palgrave Macmillan, 2006), pp 2-3.

81 Patterson to Woodham-Smith, 21 Aug. 1962, MSS Ad. 9437/10/1, RSL Archive.

82 Ibid., Elizabeth Bowen to Patterson, 17 Sept. 1962.

83 Ibid., Newspaper clipping, "Last night Cecil Woodham-Smith addressed the Royal Society of Literature," *Irish Times*, 17 Nov. 1962.

84 Ibid., Woodham-Smith to Patterson, Cambridge, 16 Nov. 1962.

[85] Machell to Woodham-Smith, 12 Nov. 1962, Hamish Hamilton Archive.

[86] DESTITUTE PERSONS (IRELAND) BILL, 15 Feb. 1847, *House of Lords Debates*, vol. 89 cc. 1324-53. It was Lord Brougham who attacked Lucan.

[87] Woodham-Smith, *The Reason Why,* pp 119-123.

[88] This was suggested by Deputy Andrews TD in a Dáil debate, *Dáil Éireann*, Vol. 456, 5 Oct. 1995. In her private correspondence and public interviews, Woodham-Smith refers to the tragedy as the Famine.

[89] A local history society in Rathmines in Dublin included "The Great Hunger" in its lecture programme in 1902, "Rathmines Branch" in *Northants Evening Telegraph*, 20 Dec. 1902. By the time of Woodham-Smith's publication, this epithet was in usage, but not as much as "The Famine", "Nuns," (an article about the Great Hunger in west Cork), *Irish Examiner*, 25 May, 1960. The BBC Home Service broadcast a series of radio programmes entitled, "The Great Hunger, 1845-48," in early 1848, see, for example, *Hartlepool Northern Daily Mail*, 24 March 1948 and *Hull Daily Mail*, 16 April 1948.

[90] Victoria Davis, *Restating a Colonial Vision: a reconsideration of Patrick Kavanagh, Flann O Brien and Brendan Behan* (University of Texas, 2005) p. 108. Davis also, incorrectly, claims that, based on her own research, neither phrase had been used before.

[91] *The Great Hunger* was the title of a 1918 novel by the Norwegian writer, Johan Bojer. It is about a spiritual hunger, and a yearning for knowledge of hard science and religion:
www.amazon.com/Great-Hunger-Johan-Bojer/dp/0884110648
Accessed 15 Jan. 2016.
It was also the title of a 1955 book by French ethnologist and explorer, Paul-Emile Victor, concerning the 1882-83 famine in Greenland:
http://www.amazon.com/The-Great-Hunger-Paul-Emile-Victor/dp/B0000CJ34A

[92] "Colourful historian of Ireland and stalwart of Trinity College Dublin:" R.B. McDowell Obituary, *Guardian*, 14 Sept. 2011.

[93] Woodham-Smith to Machell, 23 Oct. 1962, Hamish Hamilton Archive.

[94] *Irish Independent*, 2 Nov. 1962.

[95] Ibid., "Never Call me a Novelist," 23 Nov. 1962.

[96] Ibid.

[97] James S. Donnelly Jr, "The Great Famine and its interpreters, old and new," *History Ireland,* Issue 3 (Autumn, 1993), vol. 1, 27-33.

[98] Ó Gráda, *Making History,* p. 97.

[99] *Irish Independent*, 23 Nov. 1962.

[100] In comparison, *The Great Famine*, in its first two years of publication, had not sold its 2,000 print run, see Cormac Ó Gráda, "Introduction" (Lilliput Press, 1994).

[101] *Irish Independent*, 1 June 1963.

[102] Ibid.

[103] *Irish Times*, 4 Feb. 1963.

[104] *Irish Independent*, 23 Nov. 1962.

[105] *Sunday Independent,* 3 Feb. 1963.

[106] *Irish Independent*, 23 Nov. 1962.

[107] Ibid., 22 Nov. 1962.

[108] *Irish Times*, 4 Feb. 1963.

[109] *Irish Independent*, 1 June 1963.

[110] In 1963, the Irish government issued two postage stamps highlighting this international campaign, *cath ar ochras:*
www.stampboards.com/viewtopic.php?f=17&t=50321&start=50
Accessed 14 Nov. 2015.

[111] *Irish Independent*, 1 June 1963.

[112] "Famine Papers in Dublin: Mayo protests," *Irish Independent*, 17 Dec. 1962.

[113] Ibid., 28 Dec. 1962.

[114] Ibid.

[115] Jenifer Hart (1914-2005) authored "Sir Charles Trevelyan at the Treasury," *English Historical Review* (1960) LXXV, 92-110.

[116] Woodham-Smith to Machell, 30 Jan. 1964, Hamish Hamilton Archives.

117 *Western People*, 28 Dec. 1962; also see, *Irish Times*, 5 and 15 Jan. 1963.

118 Roger to Cecil, 13 Dec, 1962, Hamish Hamilton Archives.

119 Letter from Aidan Clarke to *Irish Times*, 15 Jan. 1963.

120 *The New York Times*, 26 May 1963.

121 Ibid.

122 Francis Finegan, *Studies. An Irish Quarterly Review,* vol. 52, No. 207 (Autumn, 1963), pp 329-30.

123 *Irish Times*, 9 Nov. 1963.

124 George Woodham-Smith to Machell, 12 Nov. 1963, Hamish Hamilton Archive.

125 Ibid., 9 Jan. 1964.

126 *Irish Independent*, 27 April 1964. Woodham-Smith reported to feel "extremely pleased and honoured."

127 Tierney, a Classics scholar, was President from 1947 to 1964. See:
www.ucd.ie/president/pastpresidents/michaeltierney/
Accessed 3 May 2015.

128 *Irish Independent*, 27 April 1964.

129 1964 Honorary degrees conferred at the National University of Ireland, see:
http://irishphotoarchive.photoshelter.com/image/I0000eiWFYIUMbEg
Accessed 4 Jan. 2016.

130 Ó Gráda, *Making History*, p. 130.

131 *Glasgow Herald,* 29 Dec. 1964.

132 St Hilda's Archive, Cecil Blanche Woodham-Smith (PR 003/18):
http://www.sthildas.ox.ac.uk/college/college-archive
Accessed 5 June 2014.

133 Quoted in DNB entry, p. 1. This quote also appeared on the dust cover of the 1991 paperback issue, published by Penguin.

134 Conor Cruise O'Brien to Woodham-Smith, 11 June 1963, Hamish Hamilton Archive.

135 In *States of Ireland* (1972), he explained his revised view of Irish nationalism. In 1996, O'Brien joined the United Kingdom Unionist Party and was elected to the Northern Ireland Forum.

136 In the 1969 general election in the Republic of Ireland, O'Brien had been returned as a Labour Party TD for Dublin.

137 Frank O'Connor, "Murder Unlimited," *Irish Times*, 10 Nov. 1962.

138 "This Most Distressful Country," *The New York Times*, 14 April 1963.

139 "Genocide," *New Statesman* (London) vol. 64, 23 Nov. 1962.

140 Leonard Woolf Archive. It contains nine letters not directed to the Editor of the *New Statesman*.
www.sussex.ac.uk/library/speccoll/collection_catalogues/woolf.html
Accessed 22 May 2015.

141 Brendan Behan to Woolf, December 1962, E.H. Mikhail (ed.), *The Letters of Brendan Behan* (Montreal: McGill-Queen's University Press, Nov. 1991), pp 215-16.

142 Ibid, John Freeman, ed. of *New Statesman* to Behan, 9 Jan. 1963, p.215.

143 John Michael Elliott Hinton (1923-2000), a British philosopher who lectured at the University of Oxford from 1958, was a fellow of Worcester College, Oxford from 1960.

144 Letter to the Editors, *New York Review of Books,* 6 May 1965.

145 *The Great Hunger*, p. 407.

146 Review by F.S.L. Lyons, *Irish Historical Studies* (1964-65) p. 77.

147 *Irish Times*, 21 Jan. 1957.

148 Lyons, *Review,* p. 78.

149 Ibid., p. 79.

150 Ó Gráda, "Making History," p. 98.

151 Machell to Woodham-Smith, 30 May 1973, Hamish Hamilton Archive.

152 *Independent*, 30 Jan. 1994.

153 Roy Foster's article appeared in the first issue of *The Irish Review*. It was entitled, "*We are all revisionists now,*" 1 (1986), 1-5.

154 Elizabeth Malcolm, "'On Fire': The Great Hunger: Ireland 1845-1849," *New Hibernian Review,* vol. 12, no. 4, Winter, 2008, 143-48.

155 Footnote in Peter Gray, Kendrick Oliver (eds.), *The Memory of Catastrophe* (Manchester University Press, 2004), p. 61.

156 John Crowley, William J. Smyth, Mike Murphy (eds), *Atlas of the Great Irish Famine* (Cork University Press, 2012), p. xii

157 Ibid., p. xiii.

158 *Irish Independent,* 27 April 1964.

159 Woodham-Smith to Sheila Wingfield, 11 April 1971, NLI, Sheila Wingfield Papers, MS 29,047 (44).

160 "A Painting of the Famine," *Irish Press*, 1 June, 1966**.**

161 Ibid., 19 Dec. 1973.

162 Obituary of Woodham-Smith by The Royal Society of Literature, RSL Archive. MS ad. 9437/10/1, March 1977.

163 *Times*, 17 March 1977.

164 For example, the Woodham-Smiths were mentioned in the article, "Party of London High Society," *Times,* 30 May 1963.

165 Cecil Woodham-Smith in *Dictionary of National Biography, 1971-80* (Oxford University Press, 1986) pp 244-46.

Works Cited

Archives consulted:

The Archive of the Royal Society of Literature, GBR/0012/MS RSL, Department of Manuscripts and University Archives, Cambridge University Library.

Sheila Wingfield Papers, MS 29,047 (44), National Library of Ireland.
Cecil Woodham-Smith Letters, Mayo County Library.
Cecil Woodham-Smith Papers, Howard Gotlieb Archive, Boston University.
Cecil Woodham-Smith File, Hamish Hamilton Archive: DM1352, University of Bristol.

Secondary Sources:

Crowley, John and William J. Smyth, Mike Murphy (eds.). *Atlas of the Great Irish Famine.* Cork University Press, 2012.

Dáil Éireann Debates.

Davis, Victoria. *Restating a Colonial Vision: a reconsideration of Patrick Kavanagh, Flann O Brien and Brendan Behan.* University of Texas, 2005.

Dictionary of National Biography, 1971-80. Oxford University Press, 1986.

Donnelly, James S., Jr "The Great Famine and its interpreters, old and new," *History Ireland,* Issue 3 (Autumn, 1993), vol. 1, 27-33.

The *Economist.*

Edwards, R. Dudley and T. Desmond Williams (eds.). *The Great Famine: Studies in Irish History, 1845-52.* Dublin: Browne and Nolan, 1956.

Finegan, Francis. *Studies. An Irish Quarterly Review,* vol. 52, No. 207 (Autumn, 1963), pp 329-30.

Foster, Roy. *"We are all revisionists now," The Irish Review, 1 (1986), 1-5.*

Glasgow Herald.

Gray, Peter, and Kendrick Oliver (eds). *The Memory of Catastrophe.* Manchester University Press, 2004.
Guardian (London).
    Hartlepool Northern Daily Mail.

Hart, Jenifer. "Sir Charles Trevelyan at the Treasury," *English Historical Review* (1960) LXXV, 92-110.

House of Lords Debates.

Hull Daily Mail.

Independent (London).

Irish Independent.

Irish Press.

Irish Times.

Kinealy, Christine. *A Death-Dealing Famine. The Great Hunger in Ireland* (London: Pluto Press, 1997).

Longford, Elizabeth. "Smith, Cecil Blanche Woodham (1896–1977)," in *Oxford Dictionary of National Biography*. Oxford UP, 2004.

New Statesman.

Northants Evening Telegraph.

Lyons, F.S.L. *Irish Historical Studies* (1964-65) 76-79.

Malcolm, Elizabeth. "'On Fire': The Great Hunger: Ireland 1845-1849," *New Hibernian Review,* vol. 12, no. 4, Winter 2008, 143-48.

Mikhail, E.H. (ed.). *The letters of Brendan Behan*. Montreal: McGill-Queen's University Press, Nov. 1991.

McDowell, R.B. *McDowell on McDowell: A Memoir.* Dublin: Lilliput Press, 2012.

New York Review of Books.

The New York Times.

Northampton Mercury.

Ó Gráda, Cormac. "Making History in the Ireland of the 1940s and 1950s: the Saga of the Great Famine." *The Irish Review* (1992), 87-107.

Royal Academy, *Catalogue of paintings and other works by Anthony Devas* (London: Royal Academy, 1959).

Smith, Nadia Clare. *A "Manly Study?" Irish Women Historians, 1868-1949*. Hampshire: Palgrave Macmillan, 2006.

Sunday Times.

The *Times* (London).

Usherwood, Paul. "Lady Butler's Irish Pictures," *Irish Arts Review* (1984-1987), Vol. 4, No. 4 (Winter, 1987), 47-49.

Valiulis, Maryann Gialanella and Mary O'Dowd (eds). *Women and Irish History. Essays in Honour of Margaret MacCurtain.* Dublin; Wolfhound Press, 1997.

Western People.

Whelan, Kevin. "The Revisionist Debate in Ireland." *Boundary* 2, 31, 1 (2004), 179-205.

Woodham-Smith, Cecil. *The Reason Why: the Story of the Fatal charge of the Light Brigade.* London: Constable, 1953. *The Great Hunger, 1845-49.* London: Hamish Hamilton, 1962.

Chapter Two

Asenath Nicholson and school children in Ireland

Maureen Murphy

Schools were the litmus test for Asenath Nicholson (1792-1855), the American schoolteacher, reformer and philanthropist who walked through Ireland in 1844 and 1845 and wrote *Ireland's Welcome to the Stranger* (1847), her account of rural Ireland on the eve of the Great Irish Famine. Nicholson was an experienced educator who was called a "famous teacher" in 1884, half a century after she had left Chelsea, Vermont, where she was born and where she had established her first school at the age of 16. She also had founded schools in Elizabethtown, New York, and in New York City where she worked to bring literacy to Irish immigrants. Nicholson's ideal school was based on a rigorous standard of basic literacy because an ability to read the Bible and to write about one's life and reflections were essential to her belief in personal salvation. While she was an ardent abolitionist and aware of the limitations of race on education, she had not experienced the limitations of class, gender and religion that she met in the Irish schools she visited. Later, when she returned to Ireland during the Great Irish Famine, she realized that school could and did provide the means to feed as well as to educate the children of the Irish poor. For Nicholson, during her time in Ireland, the local school was the standard by which she judged the condition of the Irish poor in the area. What did she look for in the schools she visited and what measures did she use to judge the education that they provided?

In her Irish travels, Nicholson visited all types of schools: hedge schools, national schools, Erasmus Smith schools, schools maintained by local landlords, schools organized by religious societies to proselytize poor, rural Catholics, schools organized by religious orders and industrial schools. It was significant that she had arrived in Ireland at a moment of transition in the country's education system. State-assisted primary education had been introduced by the British government when it established national schools in 1831. It was the government's intention that the schools would foster political and cultural bonds between Ireland and Britain after the 1800 Act of Union between Great Britain and Ireland, which had taken effect on 1 January 1801. National schools spelled the end of the hedge school in Ireland, but they still existed, particularly in remote parts of rural Ireland, when Nicholson arrived there in the early 1840s.[1]

The Irish-born travel writers Samuel and Anna Hall knew the hedge school system, but when they returned to Ireland in 1841 to write their three-volume *Ireland: Its Scenery, Character etc.* (1843), they remarked that there were far fewer in existence.[2] Two years later, Nicholson visited a hedge school in Oughterard, Co. Galway, where the schoolmaster quizzed students individually in Latin grammar as was the custom.[3] On this occasion, Nicholson described the schoolmaster, his presentation of one of his students to conjugate a Latin verb for her to admire and the extravagant speech she gave in return. They finished their *opera bouffe* with a flamboyant exchange between schoolmaster and visitor marked by a series of bows as Nicholson took her leave.

The Oughterard schoolmaster shared similarities with Matt Kavanagh, the hero of William Carleton's 1830 story "The Hedge School." Carleton based Kavanagh on Pat Frayne, the hedge schoolmaster at Findermore, Co. Tyrone, who was a feature of Carleton's own boyhood. Frayne inspired Carleton to become a hedge schoolmaster himself, but it was his Matt Kavanagh that became the most famous of hedge schoolmasters. His abilities were impressive: "Philomath and Professor of the Learned Languages, ready to teach book-keeping by single and double entry, geometry, stereometry, mensuration, navigation, gauging, surveying, dialing, astronomy, astrology, austerity and fluxions ...." While in the Classics, everything from Aesop's fables and the colloquies of Erasmus to Cornelius Agrippa and Cholera Morbus, and anything from Greek Grammar to Irish, and a small taste of Hebrew upon the Masoretic text, was taught.[4]

Nicholson would have recognized the benefits of Latin grammar and mathematics and her sense of humor would have allowed for the master's bombastic language, but she was not sentimental about the disappearance of the hedge schools; she thoroughly approved of the introduction of the national schools that would require that all children be taught through English. Like the schools of her native New England, the national schools focused on basic literacies, and she describes her visits to two schools: one in Urlingford, Co. Kilkenny, in 1844 and one in Oughterard in 1845. Noting that the two national schools in Urlingford were providing the younger generation in the village the education that their elders lacked, Nicholson described the pupils as demonstrating "...the best specimen of reading I ever heard in any country":

> A class of boys read a chapter on the nature of the atmosphere; the teacher then requested them to give a specimen of synonymous reading. This was readily done, by dropping every noun, in the course of the lesson and giving a corresponding one of the same import. It was so happily executed, the listener would not imagine but the work was read out of the book. I did so, and in no case, did a pupil hesitate to read fluently. Their specimens of writing were praiseworthy, and their knowledge of arithmetic in all the schools is beyond what I could expect.[5]

Nicholson's positive experience was replicated the next year in the west of Ireland when she visited the national school on her way to Oughterard, Co. Galway. She was again impressed by the quality of reading and grammar and she was particularly impressed with the children's mastery of basic arithmetic, a knowledge, she remarked, that was "...beyond the years of children in other countries."[6] Confident that this standard could be found elsewhere in Ireland, Nicholson wished continued success to the national schools in Ireland "for the more I see of them, the more do I expect that great good will be the result."[7]

While Nicholson was impressed with the national schools, she noted the difference when the system was not supported by the local clergy. In Clifden, Co. Galway, a decaying national school kept by a poor widow who was paid ten pounds, suffered from a lack of interest by locals who withdrew their boys and by the prohibitions of the Archbishop of Tuam, John McHale, "the Lion of the West." Nicholson was sympathetic to the Clifden widow and to another poor Protestant teacher in a distant glen near Glengarriff who taught upon a "desolate mountain" in order to "do what she could for the benefit of the wild mountaineers for such a scanty remuneration" (five pounds a year).[8]

In a country without an institutionalized separation of church and state and where the Church of Ireland was the Established Church until 1869, sectarianism was an issue; however, Nicholson reported in some places, a reputation for educational excellence trumped sectarianism. In Kilkenny, for example, a Catholic teacher was popular with the "higher class of Protestants" who were eager for their daughters to study with her. They worked out the matter of religious instruction.[9] Going on to Wexford, Nicholson stayed with a poor Catholic woman who decided to send her children to a Protestant school "...because it is the best one... my parents never larnt me to read, and my children shall not be bred in such ignorance."[10] In Clifden, Roman Catholic students left the national school to attend the Protestant school where they were "advanced to grammar and geography."[11]

A reformer whose causes included abolitionism and temperance, Nicholson's democratic principles informed her opinions about Irish schools. She believed that education could provide employment, self-sufficiency and even a degree of social mobility. Education was certainly part of her work with the poor Irish in New York; therefore, she was critical of any limitations to school children based on class. Indeed, Nicholson's position on education and mobility was validated by the success of immigrants who arrived in New York at the end of the 19th century with a knowledge of English and the literacies acquired in the country's national schools. While national schools were functioning when Nicholson arrived in Ireland in 1844, she visited other schools that were established by landlords for the tenants' children, schools that bore the marks of a landlord's religious or class prejudices.

When Nicholson visited the estate of the Earl of Wicklow, she briskly reported that boys attending the school could stay to the age of 14; however, she paused to consider the class-based education at the three schools run by the Countess of Wicklow, and she fumed that the class-based education of the tenant children was not only undemocratic, but un-Christian insofar as to limit a child's ability to use her/his talents in the service of God:

> I visited one of Lady Wicklow's schools and saw a group of cleanly, well managed children, who are instructed by a maiden lady of good capacity. The children are Roman Catholics and Protestants and on enquiring into their attainments, the answer was, 'they are educated according to their rank; they belong to the lower order, and reading, writing, arithmetic and a little knowledge of the maps is all the education they will ever need.' This was a dark spot in the picture, which emphatically said (contrary to the injunction occupy till I come [Luke 19:13), 'Hither shall thou go and no further.' What does this principle say to the wise plan of the Almighty in the distribution of his talents? If the Savior gave them to the poor, was he wise in doing so? Did he say, when he gave five talents, 'I give you these five; but as you belong to the poor of the world, you must hide all but one' (Matthew 25: 14-30). What steward over God's poor can give a good account of his stewardship, who has directly or indirectly checked the rising of an intellectual talent which would be used for the glory of God or the benefit of man?[12]

After visiting Wicklow, Nicholson returned to Dublin and visited a school, probably in Summerhill, founded by Lady Harberton "to educate not to convert."[13]

> Here was a school of little boys instructed in the scriptures and the first rudiments of geography; a privilege which, though they were the children of the poor, was not denied them, as in Lady Wicklow's school. The school of young girls was as good in arrangement as I had ever seen; order, cleanliness and attention were strikingly manifested. The superintendent was intelligent and thorough to the last degree in all her investigations. The reading examination in the scriptures, in ancient and modern geography, arithmetic and grammar, showed honorable faithfulness in both teacher and pupil. But I regretted sincerely the severity of the superintendent. A little more tenderness mixed with her rebukes, I could not but think would have accomplished as

much good, and left a more favorable impression on the hearts of the pupils.[14]

To depict the failing of "this otherwise excellent teacher," Nicholson chose the heroic couplets used to describe the schoolmaster of Sweet Auburn in Oliver Goldsmith's *The Deserted Village*:

> Full well the busy whisper circling round
> Conven'd the dismal tidings when she frown'd.[15]

Nicholson resorted to Goldsmith again when she met a schoolmaster on a road near Westport who told her about the district and warned her not to climb Croagh Patrick alone (she paid no attention, climbed the holy mountain, got lost and made a perilous descent). Nicholson used Goldsmith once more to describe a schoolmaster in Mayo whom she considered argumentative:

> In arguing too, the parson owned his skill,
> For even tho' vanquished, he could argue still;[16]

Nicholson never actually visited Goldsmith's country nor did her coach to Dublin take her to the home of a Goldsmith neighbor, novelist Maria Edgeworth of Edgeworthstown, Co. Longford. It is a mystery why Nicholson never mentions her. Sir Walter Scott, a favorite Nicholson novelist, attributed his *Waverly* novels to Edgeworth's influence; by 1839, Edgeworth was the astute and effective manager of her family's estate. She shared Nicholson's interest in education, an interest encouraged by her father Richard Lovell Edgeworth who was, in turn, influenced by Jean Jacques Rousseau's *Practical Education* (1798). Like Rousseau, and the modern developmental psychologist Jean Piaget, the Edgeworths believed that children's learning should be informed by their stages of development, hands-on learning and learning through recreation. Nicholson, on the other hand, favored a more didactic pedagogy; she looked for students to be busy at skill and drill. For Nicholson, literacy was not only important for practical reasons: literacy was valuable in an English language culture and of considerable advantage to one who might consider emigrating to the United States, and English was necessary for the Bible reading that was essential to the personal salvation of Congregationalists and Presbyterians.

Had Edgeworth and Nicholson met, they no doubt would have talked about education as well as their respective experiences in Connemara. Edgeworth's long letter to her family about her tour to the west was published later in *The Life and Letters of Maria Edgeworth* (1895). Moreover, had the two ladies met during the Great Famine, they would have had still more to talk about. Edgeworth applied for grants to provide relief work for her tenants; her application to the Central Relief Committee with its data about local conditions is an important Famine document that demonstrates the difference between money earned doing relief work and the cost of basic food in Edgeworthstown. While she admired the work of the Central Relief Committee, Nicholson devised her own program of Famine relief, but she too received support from the Central Relief Committee for her rural poor.[17]

Nicholson always made it a point to visit institutions that provided social welfare. Surprisingly, she found that before the Famine, schools in Irish poorhouses or workhouses and in prisons were providing opportunities for education and employment. During her first days in Dublin, in June 1844, she visited a poorhouse in the city, probably the North Dublin Union Workhouse on Brunswick Street, where she noted with approval that the inmates who were able "were at work or in school."[18] The following month, while visiting Tullamore, King's County (now Co. Offaly), she inspected the local jail and the Union workhouse, where funds allowed only 300 inmates to be accommodated in a facility designed for 700; however, Nicholson described conditions inside as satisfactory: "A flourishing school was in operation, the specimens of writing doing honors to the teachers. The children are fed three times a day; they get a noggin of milk at each meal, with porridge."[19] Even during the Famine, when she visited the prison at Spike Island, Co. Cork, Nicholson found that there was a school offering instruction on a two-hour rotation basis to teach the basic literacies. When the teacher was showing the school to Nicholson, he paused and remarked about his 300 pupils, "these persons are docile, and I believe honest; their only crime being taking food when starving."[20]

Nicholson expected more from the schools founded by the Protestant missionary societies at Achill and Ventry, communities she considered two "cities on a hill"; however, she found herself disappointed in the mission schools. Instead, she admired the Presentation Nuns' school in Ventry because they disregarded class when educating their pupils. When asked whether the girls in Miss Rae's class were using the maps in the classroom to study geography, Miss Rae told Nicholson, "the maps are for the boys; these are the daughters of the lower order, and we do not advance them."[21] The next day at the school for 300 children run by Presentation Nuns, a school where "lessons in grammar, geography and history would do honor to any school," Nicholson was told, "though they are the children of the poor, we do not know what station God may call them to fill. We advance them as far as possible while they are with us."[22]

When Nicholson moved on to Rev. Edward Nangle's mission colony at Dugort, on Achill Island, she visited the schools before she met Nangle himself. She was offended by the lack of civility on the part of the teacher of the infant school, a behavior that Nicholson believed was responsible for the children's inattention to their lesson.[23] She had a better experience at the female school and reported that the courteous teacher in the boy's school produced good results with his students. Nicholson examined them on a chapter from the Acts of the Apostles and pronounced their answers satisfactory and a measure of their good training. Her later meeting with the Nangles was unpleasant and Edward wrote of Nicholson in the *Achill Herald* that he suspected "she is the emissary of some democratic and revolutionary society." Nonetheless, Nicholson praised the literacy and civility of the colony's teachers.[24]

Her first tour of Ireland "to investigate the condition of the Irish poor" included her first impressions of Irish schools. She left Dublin in September 1845, just as the first potato blight was reported. No doubt Nicholson had kept in touch with Irish friends and read about a second potato failure in the autumn of 1846. Feeling a Divine calling to help, Nicholson returned to Ireland in December to work among the Irish poor. She described her visits to some two dozen schools and reported visiting others in Part III of *Lights and Shades of Ireland* (1850), her account of the Famine that was published separately as *Annals of the Famine in Ireland* (1851). During the spring of 1847, she lived in Dublin where she worked feeding and teaching poor families in the Liberties to prepare their own meals, a nutritious porridge made from Indian corn. This Indian meal, which arrived for her from America aboard the relief ship the *Macedonia,* she brought to the Presentation Nuns' school at George's Hill before she left for Belfast.

When Nicholson travelled to Belfast in July 1847, she met the women of the Belfast Ladies' Association for Irish Destitution who, among their projects, supported industrial schools. Nicholson visited some of the industrial schools along the coast of Antrim and reported observing young girls sitting outdoors in groups occupied in "fancy" knitting. She also praised the Belfast Ladies Association for the Relief of Irish Destitution in Connaught, who supported the work of Dr. John Edgar, the Presbyterian minister and the Honorable Secretary of the Home Mission of the Irish Presbyterians. By the end of 1846, with the help of the Belfast Ladies' Association, Edgar had established 144 schools, primarily in counties Mayo and Sligo.[25] The success of this scheme could be seen in the fact that by 1850, 32 Connaught schools earned £1,000 per year from these activities.[26] Moreover, these school mistresses employed more than 2,000 poor girls and women.[27]

Nicholson was impressed by the charitable women's educational projects. She described a school, possibly the Ladies' Industrial School founded in 1847, where "...the children of the most degraded class were taken and placed."[28] Nicholson regarded that school as a transforming experience for the impoverished children, a change brought about by basic education and by instruction in needlework and knitting that would give them the possibility of earning a living for themselves and their families. Nicholson would have been familiar with a similar combination of work and study that her abolitionist friends introduced to the Oneida Institute in Whitesboro, New York to make education more affordable to poor boys.

Nicholson mentioned that she visited another one of Dr. Edgar's schools on Samuel Bourne's estate in Rossport, Co. Mayo, in 1848, but she disapproved of a curriculum limited to knitting and sewing that did not provide instruction in the basic literacies.[29] She saved her sympathetic approval for the voluntary school started by a Miss Carey, daughter of the Mayo coast guardsman Frederick Carey, who worked for a year to teach poor children to read and to see that they were fed at least once a day. Later, in a letter to her friend William Goodell written from London in 1849, Nicholson reported that Miss Carey was evicted from her school and the children sent back to their mountain cabins to die. An agitated Nicholson anguished whether she should return to Ireland to do what she could for the children and perhaps to die with the poor.[30]

The food in Miss Carey's school had been provided by the British Relief Association founded on the first day of the year in 1847 to provide relief for the Irish poor. Their agent for Mayo and Sligo, the Polish explorer and geologist Count Pawel Strzelecki, devised what history would call "the first school lunch program," a scheme that Christine Kinealy has described as "spectacularly successful and unusually popular with both the poor and with relief officials."[31] The essential element of Strzelecki's efficient and economical school lunch program was a loaf of a dense rye bread, which the Count assured the British Relief Association was popular with the children. As he informed them, "the children like and delight in eating it."[32]

Nicholson admired the work of the British Relief Association; indeed, she supported any effort to bring relief to the hungry poor. She did not, however, approve of their black bread. She described a school in Partry, near Ballina, where the local curate gathered "a few half dead children" in a new chapel, perhaps at Kilkeeran, who used the stairs for desks and benches while they waited, famished, for their bread. There was another school in Ballycroy, Co. Mayo, where nearly 100 children, barefoot and shivering, huddled together while they waited for their ration of 10 ounces of bread.[33] Southwest in Louisburg, in April of 1848, when she visited the pauper school with a friend from Ballina, possibly the national school in Fallduff, Nicholson found the same sad sight of the 90 barefoot pupils of Anthony Egan squatting on the floor in their rags waiting for black bread.[34]

Nicholson was so obsessed with the black bread provided to schoolchildren that she interrupted her Famine narrative after the fifth chapter for one devoted to expostulating with the authorities about three matters: poorhouses, turnips and black bread. She described her first sight of the bread. Children in a poor village between Achill and Newport, perhaps Mulranny, showed her the bread they received at school. Nicholson began her tirade against the black bread by saying "my only regret is that my powers of description are so faint that I cannot describe one-half of what might be told of the novel article used for many a month in the county of Mayo."[35] What she did say is that the bread was "sour, black and the consistency of liver."[36] Nicholson visited a girls' school where the bread was distributed and secured a sample that she mailed to a friend in London to take to the committee there, presumably the British Association, to let people know what food was deemed appropriate to give to the Irish poor. According to Nicholson, the bread never reached its destination.

Nicholson objected that the black, rye flour was a cheap substitute for better flour. As the author of *Nature's Own Book* (1835) and the proprietor of vegetarian and temperance boarding houses in New York, her views about nutrition were uncompromising. She had firm opinions about bread and bread making which she regarded as "...*above* all and *over* all...the ultimatum of a housekeeper's ambition. If this be not *wholesome*-if she fails *here*, all else may go for nothing."[37] She believed that the best bread was made from coarsely ground, unbolted wheaten flour washed clean before grinding though she did allow that rye, barley or oatmeal bread was allowable if it were prepared according to Nicholson's rules. Her own regime for relieving the hunger of her families in the Liberties had been a porridge made of Indian corn that was thoroughly ground and cooked thereby sparing her people the digestion problems that Indian corn could bring if it were not prepared properly. After her terrible winter witnessing hunger and suffering in Erris in 1847-1848, Nicholson made her way to Cork via Tuam, Co. Galway, where she found for the first time since she went to the west of Ireland, children with a normal demeanour, "the ruddiness of look and buoyancy of manner" among the 400 pupils of the Presentation Sisters, the half dozen nuns "hiding from the world yet completely overwhelmed with it."[38] How did the sisters manage to see that the children thrived? They fed them on a diet of Indian meal.

While Nicholson's ideas about nutrition were sound and her regime probably offered a better diet for children, porridge made of Indian meal demanded equipment for preparing the corn and boilers to process the Indian corn into a digestible porridge. Given the primitive conditions of rural schools, the black bread, though it may have been less salubrious, did not require any special preparation. Strzelecki claimed that his daily meal of black bread reached "over 1,000 children of all persuasions" in western Mayo.[39] The black bread became a metaphor for the condition of Ireland's most vulnerable members: their young. While Nicholson was in Mayo during the winter of 1847-1848, she extended her relief efforts to the Achill colony. Some of the schools that she revisited during the Famine were those in the Dugort colony where she spent Christmas of 1847 and where she distributed clothes to children in some of Nangle's 11 schools. Nangle did not meet Nicholson; however, when the superintendent of his schools told him that she had visited schools with clothes for the poorest of the children, the former had the grace to praise, however grudgingly, her work among the poor: "If she can do any good I am glad of it."[40] Nicholson did the most good during the Famine not only by her ministering to the poor but also by bearing witness to their suffering. Her most poignant accounts of suffering were those of the children she met in schools.

For one who valued education, and argued for access to education, believing that children were kept from school because of poverty and hunger, or that they became weaker and died because of the meager rations that they were given at school, were conditions about which Nicholson raged. Having worked among the Irish in New York and having employed Irish young women in her Graham boarding houses, she realized that education was the best preparation for emigration, and those were the reasons why she visited Irish schools, celebrated the good that she found and criticized the limitations imposed by class, poverty and proselytism. Like the schoolmaster in *The Deserted Village*, the love Nicholson "bore to learning" informed her passion that Irish children, in the word of Henry Adams, "know enough to know how to learn."

Endnotes

[1] The late Brian Friel's play *Translations* (1980) describes the end of a hedge school in Donegal in 1833.

[2] Mr. and Mrs. S.C. Hall, *Ireland: Its Scenery, Character &* c. (London: How and Parsons, 3 vols, 1842, 1843), vol. III, p. 260.

[3] Asenath Nicholson, *Ireland's Welcome to the Stranger* (1847), ed. Maureen Murphy, Dublin: Lilliput Press, 2002, p. 287.

[4] William Carleton, "The Hedge School" in *Traits and Stories of the Irish Peasantry.* Carleton was a hedge schoolmaster in Newcastle, Co. Down before he made his way to Dublin. Thomas Flanagan compared Frayne/Kavanagh with the village schoolmaster in Oliver Goldsmith's *The Deserted Village*, his idyllic evocation of "Sweet Auburn" where heroic couplets memorably describe the village schoolmaster who, like Chaucer's Clerk of Oxford, "gladly wolde he lerne and gladly teche."

[5] Nicholson, *Ireland's Welcome to the Stranger*, p. 66. There were two national schools in Urlingford, Co. Kilkenny, in 1837: one supported by the earl of Kilkenny and one by a Mr. Fitzpatrick for 70 boys and 70 girls. See Samuel Lewis, *Topographical Survey of Ireland* (London, 1837), p.671.

[6] Nicholson, *Ireland's Welcome to the Stranger*, p. 286.

[7] Ibid. P.J. Dowling discusses the popularity of arithmetic as a school subject, a subject that pupils continued to study even after their school days were over, p. 60.

[8] Ibid., p. 211. See also Samuel Lewis who described five public schools and nine private schools in Glengarriff which were supported by Lord Bantry (*Topographical Dictionary*, vol. II, p. 165).

[9] Nicholson, *Welcome*, p.169.

[10] Ibid.

[11] Ibid., p. 293.

[12] Ibid., p. 35.

[13] Ibid., p. 186.

[14] Ibid., p. 53.

[15] Oliver Goldsmith, *The Deserted Village*, in *Selected Works*. Ed. Richard Garnett (Cambridge, MA, 1951), p. 612.

[16] Ibid.

[17] Margaret Kelleher contrasts Nicholson's and Edgeworth's response to the challenge of Famine relief in *The Feminization of Famine* (Cork, 1997), pp 94-5.

[18] Nicholson, *Welcome*, pp 29-30.

[19] Ibid., p. 25.

[20] Ibid., p. 153.

[21] Ibid., p. 274.

[22] Ibid., p. 275.

[23] Ibid., p. 323.

[24] Ibid., p. 337.

[25] Christine Kinealy, *The Kindness of Strangers: Charity and the Great Hunger in Ireland* (London: Bloomsbury, 2013), p. 191.

[26] Helen Hatton, *The largest amount of good: Quaker Relief in Ireland 1658-1921* (Montreal, 1993), p.186.

[27] Maria Luddy, *Women and philanthropy in nineteenth-century Ireland* (London, 1995), p. 187.

[28] Mary McNeill, *The life and times of Mary Ann McCracken 1770-1866: A Belfast Panorama* (Dublin, 1960), p. 265.

[29] Asenath Nicholson, *Annals of the Famine in Ireland* (1851), Maureen Murphy (ed.) (Dublin: Lilliput Press, 1998), p. 98.

[30] Maureen Murphy, *Compassionate Stranger: Asenath Nicholson and the Great Irish Famine* (Syracuse, 2015), p. 220.

[31] Kinealy, *The Kindness of Strangers,* p. 4.

[32] Ibid., p. 190.

[33] Nicholson, *Annals of the Famine in Ireland*, p. 121.

[34] Ibid., p. 136.

[35] Ibid., p. 112.

[36] Ibid., p. 113.

[37] *A Treatise on Vegetable Diet, with Practical Results; or, A Leaf from Nature's Own Book* (Glasgow, 1848), p. 16.

[38] Nicholson, *Annals of the Famine in Ireland,* p. 145.

[39] Kinealy, *The Kindness of Strangers,* p. 189.
[40] Nicholson, *Annals of the Famine in Ireland,* p. 105.

Works Cited

Carleton, William. "The Hedge School," *Traits and Stories of the Irish Peasantry*.

Coolahan, John. *Irish Education: Its History and Structure.* Dublin: Institute of Public Administration, 1981.

Dowling, P.J. *The Hedge Schools of Ireland.* Cork: Mercier Press, 1968.

Flanagan, Thomas. *The Irish Novelists. 1800-1850.* New York: Columbia University Press, 1958.

Goldsmith, Oliver. "The Deserted Village," *Selected Works.* Ed. Richard Garnett. Cambridge, MA: Harvard University Press, 1951. pp. 607-627.

Hall, Samuel C. and Anna Maria Hall. *Ireland: Its Scenery, Character* & c. London: How and Parsons, 3 vols, 1842, 1843.

Hatton, Helen. *The Largest Amount of Good. Quaker Relief in Ireland 1658-1921.* Montreal: McGill-Queen's University Press, 1993.

"The Irish Oyster Easter" (John Fisher Murray), "Some Account of Himself by the Irish Oyster-Eater," *Blackwood's Edinburgh Magazine,* 45 (1839), 186.

Kelleher, Margaret. *The Feminization of Famine.* Cork: Cork University Press, 1977.

Kinealy, Christine. *Charity and the Great Hunger in Ireland. The Kindness of Strangers.* London: Bloomsbury, 2013.

Lewis, Samuel. *A Topographical Dictionary of Ireland*, 2 vols. London: S. Lewis, 1837.

Luddy, Maria. *Women and Philanthropy in Nineteenth-Century Ireland.* London: Cambridge University Press, 1995.

McNeill, Mary. *The Life and Times of Mary Ann McCracken 1770-1866. A Belfast Panorama.* Dublin: Alan Figgis, 1960.

Murphy, Maureen. *Compassionate Stranger. Asenath Nicholson and the Great Irish Famine*. Syracuse: Syracuse University Press, 2015.

Nicholson, Asenath. *Annals of the Famine in Ireland*. Ed. Maureen Murphy. Dublin: Lilliput Press, 1998 (1851).

Ireland's Welcome to the Stranger. Ed. Maureen Murphy. Dublin: Lilliput Press, 2002 (1847).

Transactions of the Central Relief Committee of the Society of Friends During the Famine in Ireland in 1846 and 1847. Dublin: Hodges and Smith, 1852.

A Treatise on Vegetable Diet, with Practical Results; or, A Leaf from Nature's Own Book. Glasgow: John M'Combe, 1848.

Chapter Three

"Nearly starved to death": The female petition during the Great Hunger

Ciarán Reilly

The mid-1990s witnessed an explosion of interest in the Great Irish Famine, from the local to the international, evidenced not only in the scholarly publications which emerged, but also in the memorials and sites of commemoration developed across the world. This "re-awakening" of scholarship was broadly welcomed, as the "great silence" which had pervaded for decades was also reflected in the dearth of publication on the subject. The period since the sesquicentenary commemoration in 1995 has continued to be a fruitful one for Famine scholars, and, indeed, within the last five years a number of important publications have emerged.[1] However, within these "new" studies there still remain a number of subjects/topics to which little attention has been paid. For some of these topics it is argued that the sources do not allow for further study. In this respect, the cottier class, estimated to be more than three million people in 1841, left little by way of testimony of their plight, and so have been largely neglected by historians.[2] At the bottom of the social and economic pyramid, and entirely dependent on the potato, the cottier class were amongst the first to disappear with the onset of Famine in 1845. To date, their voices have remained hidden in the Famine narrative, mainly because of the supposed paucity of sources.[3] Indeed, since most were deemed to have been illiterate, they were unlikely in the first place to have left any written account of their lives behind. Consequently, the cottier class remains the largest body of people about whom we know the least. Moreover, largely because of the landholding system in 19th century Ireland, many cottiers do not appear in estate rentals, on eviction lists or, indeed, in other public documents. This chapter aims to address this lacuna in Famine studies by providing an insight into the lives of cottiers through the petitions written by women during the 1840s.[4]

The definition of cottier was at best "imprecise" and "often vague," which perhaps lends another reason for their underrepresentation in the historiography.[5] Moreover, the term landless labourer and cottier were interchangeable and often used as one and the same. Indeed, even the commissioners of the Poor Law Inquiry in the 1830s had difficulty in ascertaining who exactly cottiers were, noting that it was a term "variously employed and understood."[6] A cottier was generally a holder of a quarter acre of land or less, but in Co. Cavan and elsewhere, it could include a person holding up to three acres or more. Cottiers usually rented a small patch of ground from a farmer and in return paid their rent in labour. In that respect they were "bound" workers with little recourse to the law. This system was something which suited landlords and their agents for it removed the necessity of dealing with the lower orders. For more than a decade prior to the Famine, and in some instances for several generations before, cottiers lived in endemic poverty. When the potato blight struck in 1845 this was already a population on the brink of collapse, or as Gearóid O'Tuathaigh contends, "the most insecure class."[7] This insecurity was also compounded by the decline in cottage industries from the 1820s onwards. Overseen by women, income from these cottage industries (which included spinning, weaving, basket making and dressmaking) had long ensured the survival of cottier families.

Although largely absent from the historiography, women feature prominently in the imagery and iconography of the Famine, as they do in the folklore of the catastrophe. Indeed, as Lysaght argues, they are frequently represented in folklore for their benevolence and goodwill. Here, in particular, the horror stories of the Famine are always counter balanced with the generosity of women.[8] However, the plight of women during the Famine was far more complex than that portrayed in folklore. In his book, *The Last Conquest of Ireland (Perhaps)*, John Mitchel wrote that in "Black '47," the worst year of the Famine, so desperate were the starving poor that "insane mothers began to eat their children, who died of famine before them."[9] While such an example may have been apocryphal, the language and descriptions used in petitions allows for a more nuanced understanding of the role and fate of females during the Famine.[10]

Petitions offer a unique insight into life in Famine Ireland and, in particular, to the role, function and value which was placed on women. Located more than 64 miles away, there were a number of disparities between the fortunes of the female inhabitants of Strokestown, Co. Roscommon and Tullyvin, Co. Cavan. In Cavan, the petitions suggest that there was collective action taken to support women, particularly the young and unmarried, while, in stark contrast, the Famine appears to have furthered divisions and the breakdown of familial and community bonds in Strokestown. To a certain degree, this helps explains the sense of hopelessness which predominates in the text of the petitions. However, despite these differences, both sets of petitions provide a remarkable insight into how, for women, the Famine period was one of empowerment, enabling them to take on new roles within the family and community.

Located on the edge of Ulster, on the eve of the Famine the Tullyvin estate belonged to the Lucas Clements family, while on the edge of Connaught, Strokestown was long associated with the Mahon family. Significantly, the two estates were experiencing differing fortunes on the eve of the Famine, which would ultimately affect how their tenantry fared when the crisis commenced. Very much in the ascent, the Lucas Clements family built Rathkenny House, near Tullyvin, in 1829, which was described by a contemporary as being "lately erected…a beautiful modern mansion."[11] Importantly, Theophilus Lucas Clements, a prominent member of the Grand Orange Lodge, was resident on his Cavan estate, working closely throughout the 1830s and 1840s with resident gentry, clergy and others. Strokestown, on the other hand, had been left to drift into chaos, owing largely to demise of the third baron Hartland in 1836 and a number of uninterested and inactive land agents.[12] The Strokestown tenants had been frequently abandoned in the past and, when the Famine commenced, the memory of disaster brought a sense of foreboding. In 1832, for example, during the cholera epidemic, which claimed thousands of lives, those of means, it was claimed, had fled on the first report of disease and for several weeks the town was deserted, there were no fairs or markets and no business transacted. Such apathy apparently stemmed from the fact that "the town was owned by a nobleman absentee for ten months of the year and no information could be gathered from the agent."[13]Although the two estates differed in terms of active management, the twin evils of middlemen and subdivision had left a grossly overpopulated and overcrowded population. In particular, in the two decades before the Famine, subdivision allowed a huge population of cottiers to emerge. Ultimately, this population explosion created an impoverished tenantry, mainly belonging to the cottier class.

These were amongst the first to seek relief in Strokestown and Tullyvin in 1846. For example, in that year, Major Denis Mahon oversaw the relief scheme of over 4,000 people on a weekly basis at Strokestown, most of whom were not his direct tenants. It was a similar situation in Cavan where Lucas Clements and the Tullygarvey relief committee catered for almost 2,000 cottiers, three times a week, who were provided with a pint of "good soup."[14]

It was in the midst of such trying circumstances that the tenantry on both estates were compelled to petition their landlord for help. Here, amongst these two communities, women played an important role in doing so. Interestingly, the petitions reflect women's changing role during the Famine: from provider to aggressor to victim. The petitions reveal how women coped with the Famine crisis and how they strove to overcome it, showing remarkable restraint and resilience in the process. Take for example, the petition of the widow Ann Johnston of Arvagh, Co. Cavan, who in 1847 described herself as being "reduced to the last degree of poverty." Accepting her fate, Johnston concluded that her only consolation was the fact that "her distress cannot be of much longer duration," as she was 86 years old.[15] As the Famine depredations continued, tenants like Johnston naturally looked to their landlord for help, and many did so in the form of a written petition.

Of course, the widespread use of and the writing of petitions to landlords and their agents pre-dated the Famine. For example, the petition was a favoured method of those sentenced to imprisonment or transportation in the early part of the 19th century, while many estate archives contain tenants' petitions from the early 1700s.[16] However, in the late 1830s there was an upsurge in the writing of petitions, coinciding with events such as the "Night of the Big Wind" in 1839, which had a devastating impact on the cottier class. Indeed, as early as the 1820s tenants on the Lucas Clements estate were well versed in such matters, and in times of hardship or distress appealed to the benevolence of the landlord. The 1823 Clements petition, for example, referred to the "sacrifice of necessary comforts" that tenants were making. Deferential in tone, the petition was signed by 89 tenants, including a large proportion of women. This petition ultimately had the desired effect on the landlord who afforded relief during their temporary distress. However, group petitions like this, signed by family, friends and neighbours, were often devoid of personal circumstances or grievances. In that sense we are denied the individual "human experience" in a time of crisis.[17]

However, this "human experience" is aptly captured in the content of the female Famine petitions of the Mahon and Lucas-Clements estate. Written on scraps of paper, the petitions are varied in scope, size and content. While some were hastily written, others were carefully crafted, suggesting that a level of preparation went into writing them. Moreover, in the case of the Roscommon petitions, the language and style highlight a certain level of literacy, or at the very least some formal education on the part of the petitioner. It would also indicate that the people wrote petitions on their own, choosing not to consult with neighbors or friends, many of whom could not offer them any assistance anyways. Occasionally, petitions bore a familiar pattern and were perhaps the work of a local schoolteacher or someone well versed in such matters. According to Davis, where the petitioner was illiterate, a specialist writer was required, which in itself means that the petitions lend themselves to linguistic or rhetorical analysis as texts.[18] In the case of the Cavan and Roscommon petitions, it appears that the petitioners had knowledge of how other petitions and documents were framed. For example, some of the words used, such as "implore" and "perfidiousness," suggest a legal or learned knowledge or maybe that these were words used in newspaper reports and other publications. Certainly, the opening lines in most of the petitions began with the phrase, "The humble petition," something which was widely used in parliamentary petitions. In addition, some of the petitions resembled existing religious texts and he widow Killmartin of Strokestown whose petition mirrored the Catholic *orare*.[19]

petition also gave an air of authenticity to a particular claim. Here petitioners
or clerk who could vouch for their character, indicating that they knew or were
personally acquainted with such people. Petitions were also frequently accompanied by a letter
of reference, often from strong farmers and middlemen whom it was hoped could carry favour
with the landlord. This was not unusual given the willingness of farmers and middlemen to act as
guarantor for loan funds.[20] Markings on the letters and envelopes would indicate that the
majority of these petitions were posted, although some chose to deliver their plea in person
while they waited on an answer.[21] This was also necessary where the landlord or relief committee
member reneged on their earlier word.[22] Naturally, owing to extreme deprivation and want,
petitioners were assertive in tone, the widow Neary of Strokestown being a case in point. In 1847,
she indicated that she "never will be of any further trouble to your honour or any other
gentleman in the country" if given 10 shillings to help her go to England.[23]

For the most part, the petitions came from individual women, including those who had been
widowed or abandoned. In a number of instances (and in conjunction with other sources) the
petitions allow us to identify the age, denomination and occupation (where there was a cottage
industry in the house) of these cottiers and their families. Ascertaining the social and economic
circumstances of the petitioners allows us to interrogate further the true impact of Famine on
local communities. Significantly, the petitions also highlight the changing role and function of
the women during the Famine. Where formerly women had been in charge of provisions and
maintained the homestead, they now turned providers.[24] Indeed, women assumed the public
face of the family, communicated with the landlord and made representations to the local relief
committee for inclusion on public work schemes. Understandably, in the majority of cases the
immediate survival of the family was paramount and so the petition became a useful weapon in
their arsenal.[25]

This changing role of women is also aptly captured in the provision of relief, with women more
likely to queue for food than men. For example, an examination of the 1846 Strokestown relief
records indicates that almost 90 percent of applicants were women. Of these, a significant
number were listed as "widows," suggesting, perhaps, that men were more susceptible to death
in the early stages of the Famine or that they were too proud to look for relief.[26] Interestingly,
when the relief lists are compared with those of the Strokestown Loan Fund accounts, it
presents an entirely different picture. Established in 1839 in the wake of the "Night of the Big
Wind," which occurred in January of that year, this money was loaned to tenants with high rates
of interest. Men, it seems, were more likely to avail of the loan fund rather than seek Indian meal,
largely because money was given to those seeking assistance, which, in turn, could be spent in
public houses and *shebeens*. Indeed, the use of loan fund money to purchase alcohol was a
particular problem at Strokestown and, on the eve of the Famine, Major Denis Mahon exerted
every effort at preventing recipients from spending it in local public houses.[27]

In writing pleas for assistance, petitioners knew that they would have to describe why they
should be given relief over the multitude that applied, and so the documents appear carefully
thought out. For the same reason, however, petitioners may have been guilty of exaggeration
and so their claims may not always reflect reality. While we have no way of knowing the
authenticity of the claims made in these petitions, they do provide a great insight into the varied
circumstances of those most affected and how they chose to represent their plight. In the case
of those sent to Theophilus Lucas Clements in Cavan, the frequency with which he received

petitions meant that petitioners had to keep the message simple and straight to the point, although some were prone to repeating themselves.[28]

As already alluded to, there were different scenarios in Roscommon and Cavan in which women applied for assistance during the Famine. In Strokestown, it was predominantly petitions for food, shelter or to be retained on the land; whereas in Tullyvin, the main concern was employment on the public works schemes. For many of the petitioners who sought employment on the public works their circumstances were exacerbated by the fact that they had a number of daughters, who were in their eyes "of no use" in terms of labour. Indeed, this problem of having too many girls was exactly what perturbed Ann and Mary Shalvey in Co. Cavan in 1847. Seeking work on the public works, the Shalveys' noted that their circumstances were particularly acute because there was "five of them without a father."[29]

Often maligned as merely "roads going nowhere," the importance of the public work schemes to cottiers cannot be underestimated. In the case of Tullyvin, surely thousands more would have perished had they not been supplied with work. Be that as it may, the petitions also highlight that there were obvious flaws and abuses with the scheme, and naturally many sought to rectify these injustices. In many instances, petitioners saw this as the legitimate way in which to seek redress for the wrongdoing of the relief committee members. Of course, at times the female petitions poured scorn on the public work officials. Catherine Brady in Cootehill, for instance, claimed that it was due to the jealousy of the supervisor that she could not get work on the local scheme.[30]

Irrespective of the various types of petitions in Cavan and Roscommon, most had an obvious similarity which necessitated their writing the plea in the first place—hunger. Interestingly, hunger came in many guises and did not always signify a lack of food. As Peter McQuillan has argued, the word "gorta," or hunger, has different meanings in several European languages.[31] For example, the derivation of the word in some languages means "hot," "bitter" or "hurt." Certainly, the tone of several petitions from the Mahon and Lucas-Clements estates reflects these feelings of bitterness and hurt on the part of the petitioners. This was particularly true where women had experienced abandonment—husbands, family and friends—as evident in the numerous descriptions of women as "childless," "friendless" or "orphaned." Indeed, within the Strokestown petitions, the recurring theme is one of abandonment where petitioners highlight this sense of isolation and despair. For example, in 1849 the widow Mary Duignan pleaded for assistance as she was "aged, worn, childless and friendless."[32] It was desertion and abandonment which ultimately drove some women to resort to outrage and a host of criminal activity during the Famine, which, in turn, helps explain the "great silence" which pervaded in its aftermath. Of course such behaviour also lends itself to the question of culpability, a subject which has long been avoided by Famine scholars.

Women were also guilty themselves of abandonment and many chose the workhouse as a place of refuge for them and their children. An examination of the inmates in Roscommon workhouse in 1851 reveals that over 200 people were tenants of the Mahon estate at Strokestown. Of this number, some 66 percent were female and over 40 percent were listed as being abandoned or deserted. Amongst those resident in the house were Mary Farrell, aged 27; her son James, aged 4, and daughter Betty, aged just one and a half years. According to the register, her husband Pat was "gone to America." Likewise, Winifred Hannelly, who had four young children, was also abandoned by her husband.[33] Evidently, some women sought refuge in the workhouse until money or a passage to America was provided for, as the case of the Coggins family suggests, but the vast majority of these women would never be reconciled with their husbands or ewhere, for those who did seek sanctuary in the workhouse, they were left in the elderly. For example, Catherine Shevlin in Cootehill, Co. Cavan begged for assistance ndmother and I are nearly starved to death." Interestingly, the correspondence also that caution should be exercised where the word "orphan" or "orphaned" is used, as not a... ere left bereaved. In Cavan, for example, Mary Brady of Tullyvin described herself as both a "widowed mother" and a "poor orphan" following the death of her husband.[35]

The death of a husband was a particularly cruel blow to the family unit, reflected in the sentiments of one Strokestown native who lamented that her "mind has been impaired with grief after the death of her husband."[36] Of course, the demise of the head of household also created a scenario with which many women were not used to. They were now forced to initiate contact with the landlord and his agent seeking compassion and/or assistance. Moreover, for the first time they now assumed the public face of the family. Indeed, some such as Catherine Keary challenged decisions made by their husbands. In this instance Keary claimed that her late husband surrendered their land against her wishes as he was "senseless with the fever."[37] Remarkably, in many of the petitions penned by "widows," there is an air of restraint despite their difficult circumstances. Take, for example, the case of the widow Bourke of Strokestown who lamented the fact that she could not pay her rent since "god in his infinite mercies afflicted the people with the loss of their potatoes."[38] Bourke, who saw the Famine as act of providence, was typical in her refusal to blame the landlord class or those in authority for her woes. In this respect, most petitions usually ended with prayerful messages in the hope that the landlord would "hear their blessings."[39]

The female Famine petitions also tell us much about the mind-set of individuals and how people viewed their own personal poverty. Those, like Catherine Brady in Cootehill, were rather forthright in their assessment of their chances of surviving another winter, claiming that she would "inevitably starve."[40] The petitions also reveal attitudes towards the poor and the descriptions used to categorise poverty. One overseer of relief work in Cavan casually described people as either "destitute" or "quite destitute," apparently there being a difference in these people's circumstances. While some petitions might appear petty in nature, it was obvious that for some, they had been unjustly treated and so sought retribution. This was certainly true of Bridget Magee, who like so many others, suggested how neighbours were getting preferential treatment: "Mick Reilly had 2 in the work has 7 in family 7 acres. She has 9 acres 5 in family orphans & only one in work."[41]

This breakdown of communal and familial bonds was evident in other ways. At Strokestown, women actively strove to keep a firm grip on the land and many were not afraid to stake their claim. In some cases laying claim to land also involved intimidation, trespassing and committing crime. In this regard, petitions afford an insight into the division of land both during and after the Famine. Some petitions took the form of advising of the good character of an individual and indicated the newcomers who were taking up land from evicted tenants. The taking up of land was something which preoccupied many petitioners—anxious that "outsiders" would not be given their land. This was something which exercised a lot of worry in Strokestown, particularly in 1849 when plans were put in place to bring English and Scottish farmers to the Mahon estate.[42] Such a plan had been made possible by the mass clearances which had taken place at Strokestown over the previous two years. Despite the creation of this so-called "breathing space," there was still a clamor for access to land. Women also suffered in this intense drive to gain access to land. The fate of the widow Stuart of Tully, near Strokestown is a case in point. In 1849, she claimed that her neighbours threatened to burn her house if she paid the rent; something she had done regularly throughout her long life on the estate.[43] Mistreatment of

"NEARLY STARVED TO DEATH": THE FEMALE PETITION DURING THE GREAT HUNGER women also came at the hands of family members, further underlining this breakdown in family and community bonds during the Famine. This was best illustrated in the petition of the widow Kilmartin of Strokestown, who wrote in July 1848:

> Honoured Sir, I most humbly request you won't be displeased with me for this addressing you hoping the extinction of your mercy shall be fully shown forth to me in this my pitiful case by giving me time for this rent until harvest I have buried my husband and two children this month past and lost your rent by burying them. I beg liberty to state that my father in law wants to put me out of my place and also damages what was committed by means of public works. The morning after my husband was buried his father and sister came and should force the only beast I had and one goat for a long charge he said he paid for burying charges so much and did not I beg liberty to state that my husband paid him a fine of fifty shillings for it. And he wants to put me out for nothing he put me from getting the relief and the other children lying and has Not a bit nor sup to give them Thanks be to god for all his mercys. Your far fair character gives me to understand that you will not close up the bowels of compassion against me with regard to what I most humbly request and for so doing your supplement will as in duty bound ever pray.[44]

Female petitions written during the Famine allow an insight into the lives of those who endured the worst excesses of hunger. From the plea of the Cavan woman, Catherine Shevlin, who was "nearly starved to death," to that of her neighbour, Alice Donnocho [sic], who claimed to be 'almost starved to death', we see the last gasp efforts at survival by women. The petitions confirm the sense of isolation and despair which prevailed owing to abandonment or the death of a husband or family members. The plight of Catherine Maguire of Strokestown typified these awful circumstances. In this instance, Maguire's petition appealed for help as she was "deaf, dumb and orphaned and destitute of friends."[45] Likewise, Eleanor Smyth noted how she had no children or relatives and with disease in her eyes, causing her to be nearly blind, she had little hope of providing for herself.[46]

The voices of women, so often absent from the Famine narrative, are recorded in these petitions which outline the myriad of problems and circumstances they faced. These petitions offer descriptions of poor, deaf, orphaned, abandoned, destitute, and in many cases simply "broken" women, informing on the fractured nature of society during the Famine. More importantly, they introduce us to the world of the cottier, helping to retrieve the voices of those who were amongst the first to succumb to hunger when the Great Famine struck. The petitions are emotive and powerful, and also serve to illustrate wider problems regarding the impact of the calamity. These documents also highlight that at certain times and places, "hunger" meant something different to the affected population. For many, there was a "hunger" for food, shelter, accommodation or support. These documents, which contain the very "language of hunger," also tell us much about the pre-Famine literacy, and perhaps challenge the casual assumption that this was an island of illiterates. They also illustrate, how, during this brief window, that is, the Famine years, women were empowered, determined to overcome adversity, challenge authority and fight for the survival of their families. Naturally, the silence which pervaded in the aftermath of the Great Famine at local and community level had much to do with the lived experiences of those who had survived. For many, including women, their memories were often too painful to recount, while for more, guilt and shame were attached to their actions.

For the petitioner, there was an expectation that their pleas would be answered. The case of Alice Donnocho [sic] of Cootehill does, however, allow us to follow on from the initial petition and chart the family's progress through the Famine years, as a number of people wrote to support her claim. It remains unclear whether it was this communal support or her own petition, which enabled Donnocho [sic] to survive the Famine. Perhaps, it was the latter which read:

> Honoured chairman, you were so good as to allow my child Margaret Donocho to be in in the place of my deceased husband Henry Donnocho but this was not done neither she nor I got any employment we are in a state of starvation I and my four orphans got no work this three weeks I beg your honour will enter my name and my little daughters names. My name is Alice Donnocho and my daughter's name is Margaret Donnocho. We are not able to hold out any longer I and my children are almost starved to death so I beg your honour will take pity on us Your honour wrote with me on this day week to get my daughter's name in place of her poor father but nothing was done for me yet I implore your honour to grant me and my child work on the Cornakill line and the others on the Cornacarew line I am your honours miserable humble servant.

The severe want, as experienced by the Donnocho [sic] family, was representative of so many during these years. However, as already alluded to, it is important to bear in mind that not every petition was genuine and one has to guard against exaggeration and falsehood. Take, for instance, the case of Margaret Ingraham of Strokestown, who, in 1849, appealed to the landlord, Henry Sandford Pakenham Mahon, to have her case taken into consideration, which was duly obliged.[47] Unfortunately, this does not appear to have changed her circumstances and, throughout the early 1850s, she made several similar requests for food and relief and survived a number of eviction notices. Remarkably, when Ingraham died in 1863, she was found to have over £147 in her possession, despite having spent much of her life petitioning for help.[48]

Yet, for all we learn from these documents the question remains—did these petitions fall on deaf ears? The fate of entire families hung on petitions and in the words scribbled on scraps of paper, or in the recommendation of others. Two final examples are worth noting. The petition of Mary Lattimore of Cootehill in 1846 was particularly distressing. On this occasion, Lattimore applied for "a small compliment of flesh meat" to feed her starving children. It was a short, sincere plea for help, made all the more poignant for the fact that it was dated Christmas Eve.[49] Likewise, in July 1850 Catherine Larkin was brought before the Strokestown Petty Sessions; her only crime being that she had walked on the grass in Strokestown demesne. Petitioning that she would not be imprisoned, Larkin pleaded for leniency owing to the fact that she had an infant child "still on the breast."[50] Whether either request was granted or not remains unclear. One is left to wonder were the Lattimore and Larkin families' part of the Famine dead or were their petitions for assistance and mercy answered?

Endnotes

[1] See, for example, John Crowley, Mike Murphy and William Smyth, *Atlas of the Great Irish Famine* (Cork, 2012). In addition, a number of local studies have provided ground-breaking analysis of how the Famine played itself out at a local level, including Helen O'Brien's, *The Famine clearance in Toomevara, county Tipperary* (Dublin, 2010).

[2] To date, there has been little attention paid to cottiers. See Caoimhin O'Danachair, "Cottier and landlord in pre-Famine Ireland" in *Bealoideas*, 48/49 (1980-81), pp154-65; Theo McMahon and Maire O'Neill, "The cottiers of the Shirley estate in the civil parishes of Donaghmoyne, Killanny,Magheracloone and Magheross 1840-1847" in *Clogher Record*, vol. 20, no. 2 (2010), pp 243-86 & Patrick J. Duffy , "Irish landholding structures and population in the mid-nineteenth century" in *The Maynooth Review / Revieú Mhá Nuad* , vol. 3, no. 2 (Dec., 1977), pp 3-27.

[3] See Ciarán Reilly, *Strokestown and the Great Irish Famine* (Dublin, 2014), p. 8.

[4] The petitions examined here form part of the Strokestown Park House Archive (now located in Strokestown Park House) and the Lucas-Clements Archive (an uncatalogued collection in the possession of the CSHIHE, Maynooth University).

[5] See Ciarán Reilly, "The world of the cottier: Understanding the lower levels of society during Ireland's Great Famine" in *CollEgium*, vol. 20 (forthcoming, 2017).

[6] *Reports of the Commissioners for inquiring into the Condition of the Poorer Classes*, 1836, Appendix H., part II, p. 4.

[7] Gearóid O'Tuathaigh, *Ireland before the Famine 1798-1848* (Dublin, 1972), pp 133-4.

[8] Patricia Lysaght, "Perspectives on women during the Great Irish Famine from the oral tradition" in *Béaloideas*, 64/65 (1996-1997), p. 77.

[9] John Mitchel, *The Last Conquest of Ireland (Perhaps)* (1860), p. 212.

[10] It should be noted that I have used the term petition to describe these documents as the writer describes themselves as petitioner. In a number of instances, the "petition" might be more correctly referred to as a "proposal" given the nature of the content.

[11] Quoted in Angelique Day & Patrick McWilliams, *Ordnance Survey Memoirs of Ireland, Vol. 40: Counties of South Ulster 1834-8* (Belfast, 1998) p. 21.

[12] See Reilly, *Strokestown and the Great Irish Famine*, chapter one.

[13] Ibid., p. 15.

[14] "Minute book of the Rathkenny Relief Committee, 1846" (Lucas-Clements Archive).

[15] "Petition of the widow Ann Johnston of Arvagh, county Cavan, 1847" (Lucas-Clements Archive).

[16] See, for example, Bláthnaid Nolan, "The experience of Irish women transported to Van Diemen's Land (Tasmania) during the Famine" in Ciarán Reilly (ed.), *The Famine Irish: Emigration and the Great Hunger* (Dublin, 2016).

[17] See Lex Heerma van Voss, "Introduction" in *International Review of Social History*, vol. 46, supplement S9 (December, 2001), pp 1-10.

[18] Natalie Zemon Davis, *Fiction in the archives. Pardon tales and their tellers in sixteenth-century France* (Stanford, 1987) pp 10-15.

[19] For this, I am grateful to Dr. Mary Burke, University of Connecticut.

[20] See, for example, the records of the Irish Reproductive Loan Fund (National Archives, London), particularly for Co. Roscommon.

[21] See for example "Petition by Richard Jackson on behalf of Widow Murtagh," 23 March 1849 (Strokestown Park Archive).

[22] For example, the petitioners, Ann and Mary Sharkey were told to write the petition to the committee (Lucas-Clements Archive).

[23] See, for example, M. Kelly to J.R. Mahon, 17 Sept. 1847 (Strokestown Park Archive).

[24] Lysaght, "Perspectives on women during the Great Irish Famine," p. 73.

[25] Interestingly, petitioners at the Shirley estate in Co. Monaghan overwhelmingly sought assistance in emigration to America as opposed to any other form of relief. See Shirley estate papers (P.R.O.N.I., D3531).

[26] In the case of Strokestown, for example, of the assisted emigrants in 1847 (the so-called "1490") some 13% of the families were led by widowed women.

[27] "Rules of the Strokestown Loan Fund, 1839" (Strokestown Park Archive).

[28] See, for example, "Petition of Alice Donnocho, nd" (Lucas-Clements Archive).

[29] Ibid., "Petition of Ann & Mary Shalvey, nd." See also "Petition of William Moore, nd."

[30] Ibid., "Petition of Catherine Reilly, nd" (Lucas-Clements Archive).

[31] Paper delivered by Peter McQuillan, "Lexical expression of hunger and Famine in Irish" at '*An Droim Deileoir: The Great Famine and Language, Linguistics and Representation*' Conference, at University of Ulster, Belfast, 26-28 March 2015.

[32] "Petition of the widow Mary Duignan, 30 Nov. 1849" (Strokestown Park Archive).

[33] "A return of paupers who were and are in the [Roscommon] workhouse from 25 March to the present date, 17 Nov. 1851" (Strokestown Park Archive).

[34] For the story of the Coggins family see *Freemans Journal,* 9 Sept. 1852.

[35] "Petition of Mary Brady, nd" (Lucas-Clements Archive).

[36] H.A. Lavendar to Thomas Roberts, 19 Oct. 1849 (Strokestown Park Archive).

[37] Ibid., "Petition of Catherine Keary, 10 Dec. 1849."

[38] Ibid., "Petition of the Widow Bourke, 1849."

[39] See, for example, Ibid., "Petition of Widow Kennedy, 15 Jan. 1848".

[40] "Petition of Catherine Brady, nd" (Lucas-Clements Archive).

[41] Ibid., "Petition of Bridget Magee, nd." The same was true of the widow Malone who informed on her neighbour Luke Smyth of Nutfield.

[42] See John Ross Mahon to Henry Sanford Pakenham Mahon, 20 Jan 1848 (N.L.I., Pakenham Mahon papers, MS 10,103(3).

[43] Interestingly, a "widow Stuart" of Tully was listed as being among the 1847 emigrant scheme to Canada.

[44] "Petition of Widow Kilmartin, 14 July 1848" (Strokestown Park Archive).

[45] Ibid., "Petition of Catherine Maguire, 11 December 1849."

[46] Ibid., "Petition of Eleanor Smyth, 29 April 1848."

[47] "Petition of Margaret Ingraham, 29 Nov. 1850" (Strokestown Park Archive).

[48] *Connaught Telegraph*, 2 Sept. 1863.

[49] "Petition of Mary Lattimore, 24 Dec. 1846" (Lucas-Clements Archive).

[50] "Petition of Catherine Larkin, 26 July 1850" (Strokestown Park Archive).

Works Cited

Crowley, John, Mike Murphy Mike and William Smyth, *Atlas of the Great Irish Famine*. Cork: Cork University Press, 2012.

Day, Angelique and Patrick McWilliams. *Ordnance Survey Memoirs of Ireland, Vol. 40: Counties of South Ulster 1834-8*. Belfast: Institute of Irish Studies, 1998.

Duffy, Patrick J. "Irish landholding structures and population in the mid-nineteenth century" in *The Maynooth Review / Revieú Mhá Nuad*. Vol. 3, no. 2 (Dec., 1977), 3-27.

Lysaght, Patricia. "Perspectives on women during the Great Irish Famine from the oral tradition" in *Béaloideas*. 64/65 (1996-1997), 63-130.

Nolan, Bláthnaid. "The experience of Irish women transported to Van Diemen's Land (Tasmania) during the Famine" in Ciarán Reilly (ed.), *The Famine Irish: Emigration and the Great Hunger*. Dublin: The History Press, 2016.

O'Brien, Helen. *The Famine clearance in Toomevara, county Tipperary*. Dublin: Four Courts Press, 2010.

O'Danachair, Caoimhin. "Cottier and landlord in pre-Famine Ireland" in *Bealoideas*. 48/49 (1980-81), 154-65.

O'Tuathaigh, Gearóid. *Ireland before the Famine 1798-1848*. Dublin: Gill and Macmillan, 1972.

McMahon, Theo and Maire O'Neill. "The cottiers of the Shirley estate in the civil parishes of Donaghmoyne, Killanny, Magheracloone and Magheross 1840-1847" in *Clogher Record*. Vol. 20, no. 2 (2010), 243-86.

Mitchel, John. *The Last Conquest of Ireland (Perhaps)*. Irish National Publishing Association, 1860.

Reilly, Ciarán. *Strokestown and the Great Irish Famine*. Dublin: Four Courts Press, 2014.

van Voss, Lex Heerma. "Introduction" in *International Review of Social History*. Vol. 46, supplement S9 (December, 2001), 1-10.

Zemon Davis, Natalie. *Fiction in the archives. Pardon tales and their tellers in sixteenth-century France*. Stanford, 1987

Chapter Four

"A picture of Famine and wretchedness." The women of County Leitrim during the Great Hunger

Gerard MacAtasney

On 26 April 1847, Denis Booth and Rev. George Shaw informed the Irish Relief Association that:

> Ellen Beirne of Headford, in this part of the parish of Annaduff, died of starvation. She was not interred for fourteen days and on the fifteenth day part of the remains (the remainder having been torn and eaten by dogs) was buried and not in consecrated ground but in a hole in a bog.[1]

Some weeks earlier, the parish priest of Drumshanbo, Father Heslin, related how: "a poor woman (herself a picture of famine and wretchedness) has been at my home carrying her dead child in her arms—it was a skeleton and must have died of hunger." From the same source, related to him by John Gellmor, a laborer on the public works, came the following harrowing scene:

> A number of the men employed on a public road subscribed to get a coffin for a child which had died of starvation. But the mother of the child spent the money meant for the coffin on food. When the child was eventually buried by the same group of men they noticed that the eyes and parts of the legs and thighs had actually been eaten by rats.[2]

These accounts of female suffering during the Famine are often the only time they are referenced in accounts at a local level. Reliance by historians on the records of the British government-sponsored Relief Commission simply serves to reinforce this stereotype. It is rare to find the names of women among lists of contributors to relief committees. Instead, these are dominated by members of the clergy, minor gentry and tenant farmer class—overwhelmingly male in their composition. However, the files of such relief agencies as the Society of Friends (Quakers) reveal the extent to which local women played a significant part in relief throughout the county in the period 1846-49.

While correspondents to the Relief Commission often expressed their frustration at the inadequacy of the government's response, they were generally respectful due to the fact that they were appealing to a government department for aid. However, those who wrote to the Society of Friends did not feel the need to demonstrate such deference. Furthermore, because a significant number of them were female, it demonstrated that, although they were regarded as merely the wives and daughters of local landlords and clergy, they often represented the most radical section of Irish life. Indeed, this otherwise silent voice in the mid-19th century proved to be one of the most outspoken and critical on the causes of the catastrophe and the ineffectual response of the British government.

In Leitrim, one of the most prolific correspondents to the Society was Penelope Johnston of Kinlough, an area bordering southwest Co. Donegal. In January 1847, she claimed that three-fourths of the population of the district was in need of public relief and described her efforts to establish a soup shop by which she was able to distribute 10 gallons each day. Some of the food was given out freely and some at one penny per quart. While such gratuitous distribution was abhorred by the government, it was recognized by the Quakers as essential in such an unprecedented emergency. Hence, they assured her that if she was able to raise more subscriptions and increase the daily distribution to between 70 and 100 gallons per day, they would support her with a new boiler and £20 in cash. The problem for Johnston, as with others attempting to stem the tide, was the fact that, as she put it herself, "many persons of large property do not reside here."[3] Meanwhile, Mrs. J.M. Kirkwood lamented the fact that in her district on the outskirts of Carrick-on-Shannon "there is not a single person able to afford the least relief but Mr Kirkwood." She revealed there were only four families not in want and dismissed the utility of the public works where the average daily wage of eight to ten pence "will purchase a very scanty portion of food for six, eight and, in some cases, ten persons." As a consequence, since November 1846, the Kirkwoods had been making a daily distribution of soup to a dozen families while, at the same time, endeavoring to find as much work as possible for the laborers. However, as Kirkwood herself admitted, such schemes could not employ one in 10 of those seeking to avail of this assistance.[4]

In January 1847, in response to constant and urgent demands for direct food provision, the British government rushed through special legislation—the Temporary Relief Act (Soup Kitchen Act)—for the setting up of relief committees under the auspices of a new relief commission. Consequently, the public works were to be wound up as food was to be provided for those unable to enter workhouses. However, the sudden closure of such works and the inevitable bureaucratic and administrative delays in establishing a system of national soup kitchens resulted in a hiatus in relief provision.

The importance of public works to thousands of people was crystallized in the words of T. Curly, a conducting engineer for Co. Leitrim, who commented that one week's suspension of wages "would bring them to actual starvation."[5] Thus, while there had been universal criticism of the insufficient wages paid to laborers, there was incredulity at the news that those works were to be phased out. Hence, the problem for private funds was that they would inevitably face much greater demand in the period between the works being closed and the new relief mechanism coming into operation. In addition, there was increasing evidence of a reluctance by already diffident subscribers to give further support to soup kitchens. Thus, on 8 March, John Hudson informed the Quakers that a proposed private soup shop had not yet been established in Glencar as people were "waiting to see what the new Government measure will be."[6]

To compound problems, there was no uniform closure of the works and it appeared that the dismissals impacted to a greater degree on some areas than on others. For example, Letitia Veevers, who afforded relief to more than 100 laborers, explained that their "abrupt Dismissal" was particularly severe in the Mohill area due to the fact that in her locality spring work was always a few weeks later than in those parts of the country where the soil was of a better quality and less wet. Thus, the huge demand for work from labourers could not be met by local farmers "who continue as much as possible to perform their farming operations with the aid of their own families or servant boys." Despite her realism in acknowledging that "some time must elapse" before the new measure came into operation, she painted a stark picture of the impact the crisis had made on her community:

The people are daily dropping off all around us. In the barony of N 1847—there were 35,714 people and I have heard those who ought well informed on the subject state that (if deaths continue at the sai July next, including those who are flying to America and elsewhere (a carry them), there will not be 24,000 remaining. In the small townland containing only forty acres—and on which there were only thirty-six inha eighteen have died since the scarcity began to be felt. Everything was so, ...eath for sustenance and they did not leave as much as would procure coffins fo ...ir remains. It is remarkable that the great majority of those who have fallen were boys and men. There are instances not far from this where the survivors, not able to procure coffins, have buried their dead under the floor of their cabins in which the deceased had lived—others conveying them to bogs and gardens. Last week I heard of a young man having been met on the road carrying on his back the bodies of his little brother and sister who had died of fever. They were slung on by a hay rope and the bodies only covered with hay and the poor mother followed to the field holding up the limbs of the deceased to prevent them dragging on the ground.[7]

In an effort to both encourage local industry and foster an ethic of self-reliance, the Society of Friends was particularly keen to support those who endeavored to establish small-scale local efforts, usually in some branch of the weaving manufacture. Thus, they sent funds to William Noble who was employing 52 women at spinning and five men at weaving in Drumshanbo,[8] while in Derrycarne, Letitia Nisbett was aided in her employment of "a few Men" to weave linen, drugget and corduroy.[9] Elizabeth Peyton, who engaged some people in "fine knitting" and spinning wool and flax, hoped the Quakers would be able to initiate something on a larger scale:

Your benevolent society might perhaps be able to get something established in these backward parts of the North which might give permanent employment to many of our poor women and children. We have numbers who can spin and knit but no market to be had for either stockings or linen save the purchase of a few individuals of that class who make the best bargain they can and consequently as our poor people put it "they have only bought work, I might, Sir, as well have been idle."[10]

Her husband maintained that this initiative had been "the means of raising a spirit of industry in this neighbourhood hitherto unknown to them" with some children earning nearly £3 in six weeks. However, as his wife had alluded to, the problem was obtaining a market for the finished goods and he enquired if the Quakers could help in this. Yet, even the Quakers were not disposed to intervene in the sale of clothes.[11] In Kinlough, Penelope Johnston was managing a similar operation and, with a grant of £10 from the Quakers, she was able to employ spinners and weavers in making flannel and linen. This was then sold to the needy of the area who paid in weekly installments.[12]

Always keen to acknowledge the humanity of those they were supporting, the Quakers diversified their relief effort from the spring of 1847. Hence, in addition to continuing their food distribution, and aware of the needs of the increasing numbers of distressed, they also invited applications for clothing. By April, William Noble of Drumshanbo, who had received "the making of thirty petticoats," estimated there were at least 200 heads of families, both men and women, in want of various items such as coats, trousers, gowns and petticoats. In addition, "a great many children and young persons of both sexes are in these respects wretchedly off."[13] Similarly, in Fenagh it was reported that "a great proportion" were in a "miserable state for want of clothes" while George Mansfield noted that those in Keshcarrigan who would have previously been

...ed as "wanting" were now "nearly naked."[14] When J.M. Kirkwood of Woodbrook Lodge ...eived 100 articles of clothing from the Quakers, including calico and blankets, she assured them that there was no danger of such items being pawned by recipients due to their fear of subsequently "never receiving other relief." She emphasized the importance of such grants given that "there is scarcely a single person who does not want clothing" while, "even those who have not hitherto a need for food are nearly naked, having spent their all."[15]

It was a similar scenario elsewhere. Anne Devenish, writing from nearby Rush Hill, estimated there were not less than 200 families who were in a "wretched condition for every description of clothing." She had previously received some supplies from a ladies' society in London but, by the middle of April, this had all been distributed. She was sent two bundles of clothes—a total of 100 garments—by the Quakers.[16] While Mary Johnston of Aghacashill estimated the number in need of clothing in her area at around 250 people,[17] her neighbors, Elizabeth and Hannah Peyton of Driney House, were clothing 30 families, while Annadelia Slack was supporting 60 families (a combined total of around 400 individuals) in the adjacent townlands.[18] Similar clothing funds were also established in Mohill, Keadue, Carrigallen, Kinlough and Croghan.[19]

Many individuals either chose or were forced to labor in isolation but some were willing to combine their efforts. Thus, in an attempt to supply clothing in the Carrick-on-Shannon area, where there were "instances of widows with young children in a most destitute state," J.M. Kirkwood informed the Quakers she would work with Margaret Kirkwood of Lakeview and Mary Peyton of Springfield.[20] Although Matilda Shanly of Riversdale "would as soon act on my own responsibility," she stated her willingness to work with Rev. Clifford and Father Cassidy to clothe the poor in Riversdale and Aghoo West, where there were "at least 60 persons in the most wretched state for want of clothing and at least 20 men who cannot work in the cold for want of garments."[21]

On 1 May, the Temporary Relief Act officially came into operation in the county with the opening of soup kitchens in the Carrick-on-Shannon electoral division. Five days later, soup kitchens opened in Glenade and Kinlough in the Ballyshannon union and, by 17 May, all divisions in the Carrick union were in operation. However, in the parish of Kiltoghert, Father Peter Dawson stated that "not half" of those in need were included with only "the helpless"—a total of 1,280—eligible, out of a population of 13,000. He also asserted that "in most cases" people would surrender their land if allowed to remain in their houses, "which would not be permitted."[22]

Evidence of inertia in the Carrick area emerged with his claim that "those who should be most active seem paralysed by the extent of the calamity." It transpired that the town soup kitchen had closed on 21 April, yet, in spite of having a total balance of £207, which was transferred to the new finance committee, no relief had since been forthcoming.[23] On 18 May, over a fortnight after the act had been in operation in the electoral division, Jane Isabel Banks informed the Quakers that the clerk of the Carrick-on-Shannon relief committee had not received a sufficient number of official sheets from Dublin, thereby ensuring a delay of another fortnight. She was working in conjunction with Martha Brown in the only relief effort then in existence in the town. They had received food from the Society and distributed this as wages to 130 people whom they employed at knitting. To try to ensure the success of their enterprise they were seeking orders for clothes from friends "in England and elsewhere." In the preceding three months, Banks had sold more than £100 worth for the benefit of her school and this had placed those in receipt of aid "above want." She asked the Quakers to help her obtain orders for "plain and fancy knitting, shawls of the most beautiful finish, stockings, collars, [and] cuffs."[24]

Jane Corbett also painted a grim picture of the town, where there had been "᠁ these last few days" due to further increases in the price of provisions and "grea᠁ falling ill." She spoke of "children dying in the streets and older persons on the roa᠁ fields" and alluded to the fact that the new relief had proved disappointing in that or᠁ pounds of meal a day was allowed to families of five or six. She regarded this as "a mer᠁ and stated that people "appear exasperated." Previous days had seen a "significant ingre᠁ country people" who had warned the magistrates that, "they would not starve while they hᴗd cattle to stay ... or shops to rob." Consequently, there was "great excitement in the area." On 21 May 1847, Elizabeth Forster described the previous two days as being "so full of trouble and anxiety," but things appeared to have subsided in consequence of the rations of meal being increased and the fact that "Miss P[eyton]" had distributed food. She added, with some relief, that Peyton's initiative had moved people away from her locality, noting how "they flock where there is a morsel to eat."[25]

A couple of weeks after soup kitchens had opened in Keshcarrigan and Drumshanbo, the ineffective nature of the relief operation there had become apparent to Mary Johnston and Annadelia Slack. After witnessing the distribution of official rations, they were adamant that alternative measures would have to be pursued in order to feed those not placed on the relief lists, due to their being in possession of a couple of acres of land. For example, in the "very mountainous district" of Aghacashill the people were in the "greatest possible distress," particularly the "poor females who are most anxious to get employment of any kind." To aid them in their endeavors, Johnston received half a ton of rice and a similar quantity of Indian meal, which could be utilized as payment to females, while Slack obtained a half ton of meal.[26]

By this stage, complaints about various aspects of the system were commonplace. Certainly the evidence from those who had been previously running their own private relief schemes was that the government initiative was extremely limited. Rev. Hamilton, the vicar of Eastersnow, expressed disappointment that the measure "does not afford that full measure that has been supposed it would or that is required." Further, he maintained that:

> It makes no provision that is practically of any use for insufficient employment and wages as may be seen by looking at the fourth class of persons to be relieved. The lowest food of a cheap description it is intended to be sold to such persons and yet in another part of the act nothing can be sold under market price. But the truth is no measure can at all meet all want in a calamity like the present.[27]

However, Hamilton's next comments articulated what many people had been thinking:

> The impression on all persons is that the destitution is rather greater under the new measure than under the works. If there were works along with the measure there would be something like adequate provision then.[28]

Hence, in light of the fact that people holding land or in employment were officially excluded, Jane Ellis of Brooklawn, Ballinamore, who had been distributing meal and cooked rice for months, announced her intention to continue her efforts. She noted that although almost all the able-bodied men were still employed in early June on public works many were in a "most destitute state." Her efforts were boosted by a grant of a half a ton of Indian meal.[29] Similarly, Alicia Crofton of Lakefield, Mohill was determined to feed all those excluded from public relief by means of her private fund which she intended to operate with her children, Duke and Alicia

Maria. The effects of fever and dysentery in the area were evident in that people were "afflicted with swollen limbs" and were unable to move about "except with difficulty." The Quakers sent her one ton of Indian meal and five hundredweight of biscuit.[30]

A familial approach was also evident in Drumshanbo where the Nobles, Rev. William and his sister Mary Ann, were engaged both in feeding those in need and continuing, and, indeed, expanding, their employment scheme with 170 women at spinning and 28 men weaving. Their food supply was largely dependent on the Quaker fund and on 7 June they received a further half ton of Indian meal and rice. With the aid of the relief committee's boilers, they were thus able to feed those in need three days a week.[31] Ellen Lawder, who was supplying 120 people independently of the relief committee, was in no doubt that had it not been for the Quaker charity those in receipt would "inevitably follow hundreds of their poor countrymen to the grave."[32] In Newtowngore, Rev. O'Brien maintained a soup kitchen distributing rice and oatmeal; but Catherine Godley of nearby Killegar sought to establish her own relief effort to feed those holding land and hence barred from receiving government support. She wished to support them until the next harvest because if they were "forced to sell their last cow or give up their land now to enable them to apply for relief they will be kept in perpetual poverty." Indeed, she believed that many who were unable to support themselves until that time "still have good prospects ... if we are to be blessed with a plentiful harvest."[33]

As the government's new relief mechanism stuttered into action, the situation faced by those attempting to do the best they could in increasingly difficult circumstances was encapsulated in the following comments from Anne Percy of Garadice in Ballinamore:

> In the district of Lower Drumreilly, which contains thirty-eight townlands, there is much poverty and destitution, especially amongst small farmers holding from one to five acres of ground. The public works were a great source of relief and means of subsistence but for some time back an entire stop having been put to them the poor have been entirely thrown on the relief committee which for some unaccountable circumstance are now without funds or in a position to afford relief. Hence, there is the greatest possible distress in the locality.[34]

To aid her in her relief efforts with the vicar of Drumreilly, Rev. Thomas Pentland, she received a grant of one ton of Indian meal from the Quakers.[35] Matilda Shanly of Riversdale was scathing in her criticism of the relief effort in the Ballinamore area. In accordance with the government guidelines, no share of the "scanty allowance" was given to those with land or in employment. Nevertheless, she alleged that "no attempt" had been made to obtain aid under the Temporary Relief Act "due to the want of exertion on the part of the landed proprietors." She had been feeding between a dozen and 14 families (about 100 individuals) in the townlands of Riversdale and Aghoo and noted that, "between this house and the town, a distance of one mile, at least thirty persons are lying in fever at the back of ditches and at the roadside." She also remarked that on the land of her neighbor, Dr. Collins of Murrin: "I have known many of his tenantry to die from want and he sent, I believe, nearly 100 of them free to America."[36]

The importance of privately-run initiatives was highlighted by the fact that Emily Auchmuty had, by the end of August, distributed 10 cwt of rice to 250 families "of the most destitute," encompassing more than 700 people. Crucially, this number represented more than the official total maximum in receipt of rations recorded for the electoral division under the government measure. Without the efforts of those such as Auchmuty, the existence of many depended on either the unlikely possibility of work or on public charity due to the fact that the destitution suffered by them some months earlier had precluded cultivation of their land. In order to . her cope with the fever which was "now raging very much in the locality," the Society of Fr. sent her a half ton of rice.[37]

In the autumn of 1847, the British government introduced the Poor Law Extension Act by which all further relief was to be received under the auspices of the poor law. For the first time, outdoor relief was to be allowed under very restrictive guidelines while the able-bodied poor were to be offered the workhouse test as the primary source of relief. In such circumstances, those private efforts which had been operating since late 1846 continued throughout the county, aided once again by the Society of Friends. In late 1847, the Quakers, aware of the chronic condition of the people after almost three years of distress, attempted to clothe as many as possible. Once again, concerned individuals—the majority of whom were females—sought to obtain as much of this relief as they could. Two of the most important questions on the Society's clothing application forms concerned the cost of clothing as the Society dispatched the materials, which were then made into trousers, shirts, coats, etc., by those in receipt. However, the Quakers hoped that people would be encouraged to purchase these rather than receive them free. In addition, they were concerned to ensure that clothes received would not be pawned for money, food or alcohol.

Certainly, with regard to Co. Leitrim, they were left in no doubt that the clothes could be either purchased or pawned. For example, Emily Lawder, writing from Fenagh, informed them that while at least 100 people were without clothing, it would prove very difficult to sell any amount received. She emphasized there was "no danger" of clothes being pawned as "such a thing as a pawn office is not more than ten miles."[38] Clara Dickson, writing from Woodville, Bundoran, sought clothing for the people of the townland of Tawly in the parish of Rossinver. She claimed that two-thirds of them were now in a "suffering condition" through want of clothing as, "everything has been expended on provisions since the potato blight."[39] On 1 May 1848, she began distributing clothing to people from a number of townlands, and the following list offers an illustration of those in receipt of such:

Date	Name	Residence	Number in Family
1 May	John Conolly	Tawley	2
8 May	Biddy Gilmartin	Gortawly	8
" "	Neddy Gallagher	" "	9
10 May	Mary O'Beirne	Tawley	9
15 May	Mary Murray	" "	6
18 May	Pat Sheils	" "	14
20 May	J. Conolly	Cloonty	9
29 May	Biddy McGowan	Tawly	4
" "	Mary Reilly	" "	14
8 June	Mary Sweeney	Tullaghan	6

Figure 1: Clothes Distributed by Clara Dickson in the Parish of Rossinver, May–June 1848.

William Noble of Drumshanbo stated that his wife and sisters would help in the distribution of clothes to "at least 700 in need." He asked for shirts, coats and trousers for men and shifts, petticoats and gowns for women. As in Fenagh, nobody could afford to purchase these necessities and hence he also requested a supply of second-hand clothes if they were available.[40] A similar family effort was evident in Drumsna where Jane King proposed to work in conjunction with her husband, the Rev. Robert King. She estimated that out of a population of 5,000 at least two-thirds "are in a state of the utmost destitution and have not means to procure food, much less clothing." Her demands centred around the provision of blankets, "warm clothes," and shoes.[41] Two days later, two requests from the same area indicated a desire to focus on small groups in need. Rev. Francis Kane had decided, "for many reasons," to restrict his effort to 60 children aged 6 to 14 years, and one of the reasons appears to have been his experience that "the system of selling clothes made up by benevolent persons has been tried and failed signally."[42] Meanwhile, another small-scale effort was evident in a scheme managed by Emily Auchmuty of Kilmore House in Drumsna, who wished to clothe 180 women and children in Kilmore and Skea.[43] The preponderance of females in this particular aid effort was emphasised by the application of Elizabeth Peyton of Driney House, Keshcarrigan, who, in attempting to clothe 29 families (110 individuals) in Gubnaveigh and Derigvon [sic], revealed "there is no one to join in the management, it being a large mountainous district."[44]

Meanwhile, Letitia Veevers of Mohill argued that the situation in Mohill in January 1848 was worse than it had been 12 months previously: "the want of clothing is much more apparent this year than it was last as destitution has increased ... and all want clothing—they are in wretched tatters." In an attempt to alleviate the situation, she had tried to encourage others to manage and distribute clothing, "but did not succeed in getting any to join her." Thus, she had spent much time working single-handedly on "teaching and taking in and giving out needle-work."[45] Remarking how "nakedness abounds to such an extent that I could not possibly get money here for any article," she pleaded for supplies of leather and flannel clothes of all kinds "as poor men are out in the wet lands here draining." She also stated that bed coverings such as sheets and blankets would be "most valuable and wanted" as "fever, dysentery, influenza and smallpox are raging here at present." Although the Quakers had officially ended food grants she also asked for a supply of rice, as "dysentery prevails so much and the poor are constantly coming to me for it but I have to give them a denial, which goes to my heart." She received a grant of five cwt of rice and a supply of clothing with the Society "leaving it to her own discretion whether to sell it at a reduced price or [have it] given gratuitously."[46]

Another long-term strategy implemented by the Society of Friends was to seek to reduce dependency on the potato. To this end, they made available grants of seeds of alternative foods such as cabbage, turnip, peas, etc. These grants were taken up with alacrity by individuals throughout the county who continued, in the face of huge destitution, to do all they could to aid their local populations. In Kinlough, there was significant demand for pea seeds, given that they required little manure. The importance of such was reflected in the following comments of Penelope Johnston:

> I never saw such excitement as the peas have caused. I have already been obliged from the demand to reduce the quantity. I intended giving four stones but now only two to each person unless extreme cases. I really think if I had 500 stone I could dispose of them at one shilling a stone. In Ballyshannon where peas are sold they pay two shillings a stone and even at that price quantities sold. I am getting lists for turnip seed made by persons I can rely on being exact.[47]

As far as Mary Johnston of Aghacashill, Keshcarrigan was concerned, the d. the people "habits of industry and honesty" and, at the same time, "prevent shopkeepers from charging so exorbitantly as they do." Such a supply would, the means of keeping many in their houses which will otherwise be obliged to Workhouse."[48]

While the distribution of seeds helped to alleviate the situation to some degree, much a tiny percentage of what was required. There were a number of circumsta... which ensured that destitution continued. Firstly, sickness prevailed in all localities, necessitating further aid from the Society of Friends. For example, Emma Lawder of Lowfield, Drumsna, requested a grant of rice, Indian meal, biscuit, sugar, soup and pea meal due to the fact that "all the poor Irish that were in England and elsewhere having been sent home naked." She described how:

> they were beyond lament all that called yesterday for relief who were sent away in a most distressing state when they found they had none to get as my distributions were on Mondays and Thursdays.[49]

As in other areas, dysentery and fever were rife in Drumsna and, according to Lawder, "a great number" of those given aid were supplied in their own homes, "being sick and weak and unable to come for food."[50] Meanwhile, Mary Johnston of Aghacashill reported that six families in one townland were ill with fever and described how she was attempting to aid them by supplying rice-water seasoned with sugar.[51]

Given this continued pressure on resources, various individuals were forced to exercise great prudence in the allocation of food. Hence, Emily Auchmuty of Kilmore House, Drumsna selected 11 families "of the poorest and most distressed" and gave them food twice weekly. She also supplied 60 "diseased and sickly persons" on a daily basis.[52] In the same way, the aforementioned J.M. Kirkwood cooked two stones each of meal and rice daily and she distributed a quart of the resultant stirabout to a variety of individuals. Those with fever were given a further two pounds of rice each day as a drink. She complained that "even those receiving the outdoor relief [from the Poor Law] are dying of starvation" in part due to the fact that "the bread is so bad invalids cannot eat it."[53] Perhaps, of even greater significance, was the fact that those who had been previously just able to survive were now coming into the circle of desperation. At the beginning of April 1848, Letitia Veevers noted how:

> The small landholders are heavily pressed with the rents, county cess and poor rates and with the support necessary for their families and renders it almost certain the bringing them on the list of paupers in the course of a very short time.[54]

Veevers' observations were corroborated by a series of letters from Penelope St. George during late 1848 and early 1849. In December, she had received a bale of clothing from the Society of Friends and by January was endeavoring to sell various items, but she informed the central committee that such sales would "take some time" as "the distress has lately increased."[55] By March 1849, she was enquiring as to the possibility of receiving food for "some very poor families whose wages are not sufficient to support their families" around Kinlough. Assuring the Friends that she had, "assisted all classes and denominations," she lamented that she was unable to do more as "clergymen now are not only badly paid but highly taxed."[56] In a further letter, she

...ed some cabbage and parsnip seeds to assist "the small struggling industrious farmers" ... would be unable to crop their land without it. Although acknowledging that there was "less sickness and distress than in the two former Years," she added that, "still, there is a great deal."[57] Having failed to secure a favorable reply, she revealed that the poor were now suffering and "vast struggles" had been made by them to get a crop down, despite being "half-starved and getting worse every day."[58] Her persistence saw her receive a grant of £7 from the Society and she utilized it in the employment of a dozen women each week working at flax, the latter supplied free by her brother. In this way, she was able to produce cheap clothing which she then sold to the poor. The women, being "industrious heads of families," received one stone of meal per week along with a dinner provided by herself. In addition, St. George supplied seven sick people with barley sugar and cocoa.[59]

In February 1847, Lionel Gisborne, one of the government's conducting engineers for Leitrim, had remarked that, due to increased levels of destitution, "the calls on private Charity" were "very great." In his opinion:

> The establishment of a few soup kitchens, by private individuals, tends greatly to support the portion of the population unable to work, and having no means of support; but it is a system which cannot be made pay on a small scale, and must consequently be to a limited extent.[60]

While Gisborne acknowledged the role of private relief, he certainly underestimated its extent. The fact that women were still actively engaged in relief efforts throughout the county well into 1849 illustrated both the extent of distress and the devotion of a few to the many. Unlike the British government, which sought to restrict relief as much as possible—highlighted by its introduction of the punitive Gregory Clause in August 1847 (which prohibited relief to anyone in possession of more than one-quarter acre of land)—the wives and daughters of the minor gentry and clergy of the county were activated by a desire to save the starving thousands in their midst.

While the debate rages as to responsibility for the Famine, it is interesting to note the perspective of Emma Lawder. Her family, beneficiaries of the huge land confiscations of the 17th century, were members of the Protestant Ascendancy, a social and political elite which, although a tiny minority of the population in Co. Leitrim, dominated all aspects of life. From late 1846, she immersed herself in efforts to relieve her starving neighbors and castigated the policy of the British government as resulting in "the general extermination of the people."[61] This opinion was not that of a social radical or proto Irish nationalist but stemmed from her frustration at the unwillingness of the government to make a concerted effort to aid those suffering as a consequence of the Famine. Between 1841 and 1851, the population of Leitrim declined from 155,000 to 112,000. Without the efforts of Lawder and many other women throughout the county, there is little doubt that many thousands more would have perished.

This short investigation demonstrates that even a subject like the Great Famine/*An Gorta Mór*, which has been covered in great detail, particularly since the 1990s, can benefit from the use of new sources. The under-used archive of the Society of Friends opens up many opportunities for the study of the subject. On the one hand, the huge number of letters and application forms allows for in-depth study at the local level, while the fact that correspondence is maintained until the early 1850s demonstrates both the longevity of the calamity and the ongoing efforts by the Quakers to alleviate suffering.

From the historiographical perspective the papers allow for the expression of voices all but lost in other major collections. As has already been noted, the Relief Commission records are almost totally dominated by male voices and opinions. This is reinforced in local studies by the use of newspapers in which women of rank were always referred to as the wife of the man concerned. Further, British parliamentary papers are similarly limited due to the fact that women could neither vote nor be elected as M.P.s.

The Society of Friends proved themselves to be compassionate and caring during the Great Famine but their archive for this period allows a previously unheard voice to become audible. Yes, these were indeed the wives and daughters of gentry and clergy but, through this source, they emerge as individuals in their own right prepared to say what they thought and to be fearless in a time of unprecedented disease and destitution in Ireland.

Endnotes

[1] Denis Booth and George Shaw, Drumsna, 26 April 1847 (Royal Irish Academy - hereafter RIA), Irish Relief Association application forms, vol. 24 Q 30, form 1020).

[2] Ibid., H. Heslin, W.C. Peyton and B. McKeon, Drumshanbo, 9 Feb. 1847. (vol. 24 Q 28, form 486, 3). See also Society of Friends Relief of Distress Papers (hereafter SOF), 2/506/37, form 71, Penelope Johnston, 12 Jan. 1847 (NAI).

[3] Ibid.

[4] J.M. Kirkwood, Woodbrook Lodge, Tumna, Carrick-on-Shannon, 24 Feb. 1847 (Irish Relief Association application forms, vol. 24 Q 29, form 838). An interesting perspective on mid-19th Irish society was offered by Kirkwood's comment that she did not wish to have her application made known because, "as a female, I should rather not have my name made public."

[5] Reprinted British Parliamentary Papers (hereafter BPP), vol. 7, Correspondence from January to March 1847 relating to the measures adopted for the relief of the distress in Ireland, Board of Works series [second part], p. 211.

[6] John Hudson, Glenlough, Sligo, 8 March 1847 (SOF, 2/506/37, form 561).

[7] Ibid., Letitia Veevers, Mohill, 23 April 1847 (SOF, 2/506/19, no number).

[8] Ibid., William Noble, Drumshanbo, 5 April 1847 (SOF [no number]).

[9] Ibid., Letitia F. Nisbett, Dromod, 21 June 1847 (SOF, no. 2201).

[10] Ibid., Elizabeth Peyton, Driney House, Keshcarrigan, 23 June 1847 (SOF 2/506/36, no. 2309).

[11] Ibid., G.H. Peyton, Driney House, Keshcarrigan, to committee, 3 July 1847 (SOF 2/506/20).

[12] Ibid., Penelope Johnston, Kinlough House, Bundoran, 30 June 1847 (box 2/506/37, form 122, 28 Dec. 1847).

[13] Ibid., William Noble, Drumshanbo, 5 April 1847 (SOF, 2/506/36).

[14] Ibid., George De La Poer Beresford, Fenagh, 17 April 1847 & George D. Mansfield, Keshcarrigan, 27 April 1847 (SOF [no number]).

[15] Ibid., no number, J.M. Kirkwood, Woodbrook Lodge, Carrick-on-Shannon, no date.

[16] Ibid., no number, Anne Devenish, Rush Hill, Carrick-on-Shannon, 22 April 1847.

[17] Ibid., no. 2269, Mary Johnston, Aghacashill, Keshcarrigan, 24 June 1847; box 2/506/37, form 127, 27 Dec. 1847.

[18] Ibid., 2/506/36, no 1556, Annadelia Slack, Annadale, Drumshanbo, 20 May 1847; no number, Hannah M. Peyton, Driney House, Keshcarrigan, 29 April 1847; box 2/506/37, form 108, Annadelia Slack, Annadale, Keshcarrigan, 30 Dec. 1847; additional letter (no. 505), 13 April 1848.

[19] Ibid., box 2/506/20, Penelope Johnston, Kinlough House, Bundoran, 30 June 1847; box 2/506/36, no. 379, T. K. Little, Castle, Mohill, no date; 2/506/37, form B 515 Alicia Crofton, Lakefield, Mohill, 4 June 1847; box 2/506/36, no number, Thomasine Sophia Saunderson, Keadue, 19 May 1847; no. 2439, John Fisher, Carrigallen, 29 June 1847; no. 1849, M.J. Peyton, Springfield, Carrick-on-Shannon, 18 May 1847.

[20] Ibid., box 2/506/37, form 7, J.M. Kirkwood, Woodbrook Lodge, Carrick-on-Shannon, 23 Dec. 1847.

[21] Ibid., form 151, Matilda Shanly, Riversdale, Ballinamore, 27 Dec. 1847.

[22] Ibid., form B252, Peter Dawson, PP Kiltoghert, Carrick-on-Shannon, 5 May 1847.

[23] Ibid.

[24] Ibid., form B409, Jane Isabel Banks, Carrick-on-Shannon, 18 May 1847.

25 Ibid., box 2/506/20, no number, Jane Corbett, Carrick-on-Shannon, 19 May 1847 and Elizabeth Forster to Dear Friend, Earlham Road, Norwich, 21 May 1847.

26 Ibid., form B460, Mary Johnston, Aghacashill, Keshcarrigan, 24 May 1847; form B461, Annadelia Slack, Annadale, 24 May 1847.

27 Ibid., no number, F. Hamilton, Eastersnow, Boyle, 26 May 1847.

28 Ibid.

29 Ibid., box 2/506/36, form B537, Jane Ellis, Brooklawn, Ballinamore, 4 June 1847.

30 Ibid., form B515, Alicia Crofton, Lakefield, Mohill, 4 June 1847.

31 Ibid., Box 2/506/20, form B561, Mary Ann Noble, Prospect, Drumshanbo, 7 June 1847 and reply from committee, 21 June 1847.

32 Ibid., no number, Ellen Lawder, Fenagh, to committee, 14 June 1847.

33 Ibid., box 2/506/36, form B685, Catherine Godley, Killigar, 25 June 1847.

34 Ibid., form B560, Anne Percy, Garadice, Ballimamore, June 1847 (no precise date).

35 Ibid.

36 Ibid., form B881, Matilda Shanly, Riversdale, Ballinamore, 31 Aug. 1847.

37 Ibid., box 2/506/7, no number, Emily Auchmuty, Kilmore House, Drumsna, to committee, 30 Aug. 1847.

38 Ibid., Clothing form 148, 1 Jan. 1848.

39 Ibid., Clothing form 485, Clara Dickson, Woodville, Bundoran, 10 April 1848.

40 Ibid., Clothing form 110, 4 Jan. 1848.

41 Ibid., Clothing form 86, 4 Jan. 1848.

42 Ibid., Clothing form 250, 6 Jan. 1848.

43 Ibid., Clothing form 150, 6 Jan. 1848.

44 Ibid., Clothing form 109, 8 Jan. 1848.

45 Ibid., Clothing form 285, 25 Jan. 1848.

46 Ibid., box 2/506/22, Letitia Veevers, Mohill, to committee, 19 Jan. 1848.

47 Ibid., box 2/506/7, Penelope Johnston, Kinlough House, Bundoran, to committee, 24 April 1848 and 27 April 1848.

48 Ibid., Mary Johnston, Aghacashill, Keshcarrigan, to committee, 7 April 1848.

49 Ibid., box 2/506/22, Emma Lawder, Lowfield, Drumsna, 25 April 1848.

50 Ibid.

51 Ibid., box 2/506/23, Mary Johnston, Aghacashill, Keshcarrigan, 17 June 1848.

52 Ibid., box 2/506/22, Emily Auchmuty, Kilmore House, Drumsna, 10 May 1848.

53 Ibid., box 2/506/23, J.M. Kirkwood, Woodbrook Lodge, 6 June 1848.

54 Ibid., box 2/506/7, Letitia Veevers, Mohill, 3 April 1848.

55 Ibid., box 2/506/9, Penelope St. George, Mount Prospect, to committee, 23 Jan. 1849.

56 Ibid., Penelope St. George to committee, 7 March 1849.

57 Ibid., 2/506/38, Penelope St. George to committee, 2 April 1849.

58 Ibid., 2/506/9, Penelope St. George to committee, 3 May 1849.

59 Ibid., 2/506/10, Penelope St. George to committee, 7 Sept. 1849.

60 BPP, vol. 7, Correspondence from January to March 1847 relating to the measures adopted for the relief of the distress in Ireland, Board of Works series [second part], p.211.

61 NAI, SOF, box, 2/506/10, no number, Emma Lawder, Longfield, Drumsna, to committee, 1 Dec. 1847.

Works Cited

Primary Sources

Society of Friends Relief of Distress Papers, National Archives, Dublin.

Irish Relief Association Application Forms, Royal Irish Academy, Dublin.

Secondary Sources

Reprinted British Parliamentary Papers, volume 7, *Correspondence from January to March 1847 relating to the measures adopted for the relief of the distress in Ireland*, Board of Works series [second part] (London: HMSO, 1847).

Chapter Five

"Meddlers amongst us": women, priests, and authority in Famine-era Ireland

Cara Delay

The image of the poor, suffering woman in Famine-era Ireland is only too familiar.[1] Both contemporary accounts and more recent historiography have consistently highlighted the plight of Irish women in the mid-19th century. During the Famine crisis, images such as that of Bridget O'Donnell, alongside written descriptions, represented suffering womanhood, particularly motherhood and, on the larger level, the suffering Irish nation.[2] When a member of a Cork Ladies' Association reported on conditions in her area in 1847, she wrote that "the young mothers and their famished infants…present scenes of distraction…far beyond my powers of description."[3] Moreover, as Margaret Kelleher and Stuart McLean have argued, during the Great Hunger, images of Irish women came to "personify the worst depredations of famine."[4]

According to most scholars, Irish women's status did not improve much in the years following the Famine. Historian Dympna McLoughlin writes that, "Labouring women and their children were particularly hard hit by the Famine and those that [sic] survived it faced extreme prejudice that militated against them."[5] Economic distress, meanwhile, was matched by an increasingly restrictive patriarchy. A newly disciplined Catholic clergy and an organized and powerful church bureaucracy systematically disempowered women in the post-Famine decades; women, historians have asserted, lost status at the hands of a newly repressive Catholic rural society.[6]

Women's suffering has been well documented; in recent years, however, new research has established that some Irish women were far from passive during and after the Great Hunger. From lamenting the dead to engaging in philanthropy to saving family members, women acted throughout the crisis. Christine Kinealy's work demonstrates the creativity and "alacrity" that philanthropic women brought to Famine relief efforts.[7] As Patricia Lysaght points out, depictions of women in folklore and popular culture feature the presence of the heroic female who, although a victim, also "confronts the Famine conditions in order to support her family and, when necessary, to bury the family dead, and the compassionate generous woman who recognizes the situation and supports her."[8] These accounts highlight the Irish woman as selfless and sacrificing, as one who embraced a culture of suffering, caring nothing for her own fate while focusing exclusively on the welfare of her children.[9] In some folklore narratives, women, usually categorized as mothers or grandmothers, also appear as "generous and compassionate to a less fortunate woman."[10]

Still another representation of Irish women in the Famine era has gained currency recently: that of the unruly, disorderly woman, most commonly found in studies of the workhouse. Anna Clark, Dympna McLoughlin and Gerard Moran have detailed documented cases of women, and in some cases teenage girls, vandalizing workhouses and attacking fellow inmates and workhouse officials.[11] Authorities at the time categorized these actions as disruptive and problematic. As Virginia Crossman posits:

Young women who had been brought up in the workhouse, or had spent long periods within it, were seen as a particularly problematic group, being described by one official as seeming to be "amenable to no persuasion, advice or punishment."[12]

The *Nenagh Guardian* in 1849 summarized a court case in which a female workhouse resident was charged with assaulting the workhouse master. The woman, Mary Costello, was described as "the amazon with the black patch on her eye." Upon being presented with their breakfast soup, Costello and several other women began to fight with each other and, in the process, throw the food on the ground. Costello then allegedly struck the master in the head. In this case, Costello was sentenced to three months' hard labor in prison.[13]

While 19th-century officials viewed such workhouse women as "…a potentially disruptive force in need of supervision, management, and regulation,"[14] Anna Clark argues that these women's acts of violence and resistance provide clear evidence of their agency and determination.[15] Clark demonstrates that female workhouse inmates manipulated and even undermined the authority of the state through their disorderly behavior, becoming, in the process, "active agents trying to exert some control over their own lives."[16] Indeed, even some contemporary accounts that purport to highlight female suffering and victimhood reveal glimpses of agency. A *Freeman's Journal* account of life in the Dingle workhouse is representative:

> The appearance of one woman among the lot, all being nearly the same, will serve as a sample of the entire. She seemed to be about fifty years of age, though certainly not thirty-two. Her figure was attenuated, and her countenance wan, the skin yellow and flabby; she seemed to have gradually, but within a short time, wasted away from the condition of a healthful, vigorous woman to that of a hopeless, famine-stricken old creature; the miserable rags in which she was clothed I couldn't venture to describe—it was almost painful to look at them; her hair lay as wild on her head as the seaweed on the shore—and her implorations in Irish to be 'taken out of that' were of the most vehement character, and of which no adequate idea could be conveyed to those not conversant with that language.[17]

Although the account describes this woman as "hopeless, famine-stricken," "old," "wan," and "wasted away," it also creates an image of wildness, disorderliness and vocal prowess. Mirroring the depiction of vocally subversive women in traditional Irish folklore narratives, the portrayal of this old woman's verbal outbursts suggest that she may have been desperate but certainly was not silent.[18]

These glimpses of women's resistance and agency require more investigation and analysis. Whereas most studies of women and conflict during the Famine have highlighted women's roles in state institutions (particularly workhouses) and their interactions with landlords or state officials, the focus of this chapter is on women's relationships with religious authorities, and in particular the Catholic clergy, during, and in the several decades or so after, the Great Hunger. Through an analysis of newspaper accounts, letters, court cases and understudied Catholic diocesan records, I posit that Catholic women were able to exercise significant influence and authority in the 1840s and 1850s through their role in the Catholic Church and their relationship with priests, and that this continued well into the post-Famine decades.

How did this work? Firstly, lay Catholic women and Irish clergy members often formed close alliances during and after the Famine. Designed often to preserve tradition, defend the faith, and/or combat proselytism, these relationships afforded women access to prestige and, in some cases, the protection of their priests.[19] Secondly, and perhaps more significantly, Irish-Catholic women overtly challenged their priests in the mid-to-late 19th century, calling them to task on Famine relief, clerical behavior and parish customs. As they did so, lay Catholic women also demanded an active voice in their religious and social lives. This analysis of both alliances and disputes between women and the Catholic clergy thus sheds new light on female agency and power in Ireland from the 1840s to the 1870s.

Even during the desperate years of the Great Hunger, lay Irish women retained their commitment to their Catholic faith. Descriptions of female distress and poverty during the Famine underscored women's devotion to Catholicism. In Sligo, in 1846 for example, a town "crowded with destitute creatures," according to the *Belfast Newsletter*, Sunday Mass was disrupted by "an awful occurrence, well calculated, indeed, to strike terror into the hearts of those present." A local poor woman, although ill, refused to miss Mass. Once she entered the chapel, however, she was overcome and "sank down, powerless and exhausted from hunger, in the pew set apart for the pauper worshippers." The woman, whose "haggard face" and "wretched appearance" demonstrated the "ravages of want and hunger" suffered by the local population, later died.[20] Other examples of women's commitment to faith and family include the accounts which featured Irish women moving heaven and earth, and sometimes the bodies of family members, to see their loved ones buried in consecrated graves. In Co. Tipperary in 1847, an old woman who had lost most of her family to disease and hunger dragged the corpse of her youngest daughter to the chapel yard and buried her, surreptitiously and alone, on the edge of consecrated ground. After carrying the coffin of her child, this woman "fell to the ground...and expired a victim to her fondness for her family, and reverential respect for their remains."[21] Here, newspaper summaries of women's devotion and determination also mirror depictions in folklore accounts. Patricia Lysaght analyzes many "accounts of mothers carrying their dead children to the graveyard in baskets on their backs, or simply tied to their backs with hay or straw rope."[22] In a Co. Kerry narrative, for example, a woman "brought her dead husband, wrapped in a sheet, on her back, to Kilsarcon churchyard to be buried.'[23]

Women's apparently unfailing commitment to their faith and families was matched only by priests' devotion to their parishioners. During the Great Hunger many Catholic priests and curates faithfully attended to their parishioners, risking illness and death to do so.[24] An account in the *Tralee Chronicle and Killarney Echo* from February 1847 reported that priests "almost live in their saddles, and even so, I am sure they cannot administer the rites of their Church to all who die within its pale."[25] When a woman crawled into an alleyway with her child in her arms in Kerry in 1847 to die, the local curate, Father Enright, crawled in with her to give her last rites.[26] One of the most striking realities that emerged during the Famine, then, was the close connection that developed between some priests and their female parishioners.

Even within Famine-era institutions such as the workhouse, the connections between women and priests were evident. An 1844 Roscrea workhouse dispute featured scuffling religious authorities and violent women. When a Protestant clergyman, the Rev. Edwards, called on a local man to offer him last rites, the sick man's wife, a Roman Catholic, protested. She rushed into her husband's room, "pulled the chair from under" Edwards and "threw him on the ground." Notably, this woman was closely followed by the local Catholic priest, who also nearly knocked down Edwards.[27] Here, the Catholic parishioner and her priest teamed up to prevent the Protestant minister from triumphing at a man's deathbed.

Likewise, an 1852 workhouse disagreement in Oughterard, Co. Galway was similarly telling: in this instance, again, a Protestant clergyman and a Catholic priest fought over who should attend to a dying woman in the workhouse.[28] Apparently registered as a Protestant, the woman allegedly wished to become a Catholic on her deathbed. When both the minister and the priest showed up at her deathbed, a skirmish broke out, with the two men battling physically. The women of the workhouse did not avoid the conflict, however. According to Rev. O'Callaghan, the Protestant clergyman, once the female workhouse inmates perceived that he had attacked their Catholic priest, they struck back. O'Callaghan later testified that they "surrounded" him and "rushed on" him to defend their priest.[29] The workhouse master also highlighted disorderly women in his description of the event: he claimed that as he witnessed the fight, he "heard the women screeching behind me" and "making most noise."[30] In this particular altercation, the priest's mission also was assisted by the workhouse matron and nurses, who told him that he had been sent for and ushered him to the side of the dying woman.[31] Here, then, women acted to champion Catholicism and their priest in a myriad of ways, including verbal aggression. As they supported their clergy and defended their faith, these women also laid claim to authority and influence, even as famine ravaged their communities.

Diocesan archival materials suggest that these close links between women and priests persisted well into the late 19th century. In the post-Famine era of the "devotional revolution" Irish Catholic priests were central figures in their parishes.[32] They not only managed religious life but also mediated conflicts and served as liaisons between lay Catholics and the outside world.[33] Within this environment, priests and women sometimes became allies, and many women viewed their priests as sources of information or even as confidantes.

Currently housed in the archives of the Cloyne Diocese, letters written to Bishop William Keane during the 1850s affirm that women sought help and support from their clergy, and particularly when there was trouble with their husbands at home. Indeed, lay women sometimes viewed their priests as substitute patriarchs, and priests stepped forward to assume such roles by helping or defending wives; together, then, lay women and their clergy could and did challenge the patriarchal consensus within the home. In January 1859, Ellen Walden of Queenstown composed a letter directly to Keane, asking him for help with her marital troubles.[34] One year earlier, a man named Philip O'Neill wrote to Keane to complain that his parish priest and curate were interfering in his marriage. One of the priests also wrote to Keane, however, claiming that O'Neill was "very harsh to [his] good wife" and that that was the cause of the dispute.[35] In this instance, the priests supported a woman against her abusive husband, and the husband resented their interference enough to contact his bishop.

The thousands of Irish women who were widows in the late 19th and early 20th centuries may have had uniquely supportive relationships with their clerics, with priests frequently intervening to give them particular assistance. In 1883, two Co. Clare clerics took it upon themselves to write to the local newspaper asking for public assistance in the troubling case of a destitute widow. The parish priest wrote that the woman was:

> ... in a most distressed condition; she has five young helpless children, the eldest only seven years old, and has hardly anything to give them to eat. Her husband died in America two years ago.

The curate also petitioned for help, explaining "I am perfectly aware of her very pitiable condition, and I believe those who would wish to give in *real* charity could not easily find a more deserving object."[36] Depicting this widow as a woman alone whose husband had died tragically, these priests came forward to aid her. In doing so, they also helped construct—or reinforce, as this concept already underpinned Poor Law relief—the idea of the deserving poor and affirmed the helplessness of widows with children, a theme that appears repeatedly in the correspondence held in Catholic diocesan archives.[37]

At times, the close relationships between priests and lay women garnered unwanted attention and even suspicion. Fellow clerics and their Catholic parishioners noticed what they perceived to be any inappropriate or potentially sexual contact between a priest and a lay woman. In the 1850s, a curate wrote to the new Bishop of Cloyne, warning of rumors that the parish priest was having an affair with the local teacher. The parishioners, according to the curate, now referred to the "School of Scandal." "It is useless for my fellow curate and me to endeavour to inculcate virtue', the frustrated cleric wrote, "for the people will say as they have before, "the priests themselves are worse.'"[38] The frequency of sexual relationships between priests and lay women remains unknown to us, but bishops' diaries and clerical correspondence reveal that such cases were not unheard of. Sexual scandals often appear in diocesan correspondence in veiled and coded language. When Cloyne's Bishop Murphy wrote to Rector Tobias Kirby at the Irish College Rome in 1856 with the claim that a parish priest in Kanturk had been denounced four times for soliciting in the tribunal and violating two penitents, he framed the missive as a general "scandal" but appeared to be describing sexual abuse and coercion.[39]

Rumors of closeness and confidence between women and priests caused concerns that they were conspiring to challenge the authority of husbands. Most of the cases outlined above occurred shortly after the publication of historian Jules Michelet's anticlerical *Priests, Women, and Families* (1845). Focusing on the French case, Michelet denounced the close relationship between women and Catholic priests, arguing that when the former confided in their clergy while in the confessional they undermined the authority of their husbands. In Michelet's view, the connections between women and priests threatened patriarchy and thus the natural order of the family. He feared that women would use their bonds with their clergy to their own advantage, usurping their husbands' power in the home.[40] Such fears were perhaps not unfounded, as the previous examples of priests supporting women who charged their husbands with abuse suggest.

For some women, in an age of church revival and renewal, the priest came to represent a caring and trustworthy authority figure, even a confidante. The relationship between women and priests, however, was sometimes more difficult.[41] In the close-knit world of the Irish-Catholic parish, and particularly during and after the Famine, conflicts and tensions between priests and women were as common as examples of trust and support. Some women demonstrated their disdain for the church and their priests; others put aside their commitment to their faith when faced with unprecedented want. A Limerick woman, Bridget Carroll, for example, broke into her own local Catholic chapel in 1849, stole some candlesticks, and attempted to pawn them.[42] In 1850, a Nenagh woman, Mary Burns, was accused of trespass and robbery when she allegedly stole potatoes from her neighbor. In court, Burns's neighbors called her "a great nuisance to the neighbourhood" and claimed that "her character is so obnoxious that the Priest at one time caused a number of persons to assemble to tumble her house."[43] Clearly, in this case, Burns and her priest had a history of discord.

Priests and lay women battled over much, including priests' duties, their management of parishes, and women's reputations in the parish. These conflicts involved tense verbal exchanges. As James C. Scott's work has demonstrated, even those who seem most powerless have powerful verbal weapons at their disposal, including "slander, gossip, [and] character assassination." These are weapons that even the rich or authoritative, in some cases, "cannot escape."[44] For Catholic women, gossip and slander remained potent tools from the 1840s right through the 1950s.[45] In one folklore narrative, a man's 90-year-old mother denounced a local priest for his corruption during the Famine. This priest, who managed food relief in Knocknagree, Co. Cork, allegedly failed to distribute Indian meal equitably; instead favoring his friends and relatives with more generous portions.[46] When the older woman verbally abused him, she called on a tradition of women's powerful words. As Eileen Moore Quinn demonstrates, the long history of the widow's curse in Ireland allowed seemingly outcast women to use their words to "question the establishment."[47] Similarly, Brophy argues that keening traditions, although under siege by the Famine, point to "the imaginative resistance of rural labouring women."[48]

The example of keening reminds us both that Irish women traditionally had recourse to speaking power and that such power was coming under attack in the 19th century. Although keening did decline in the 19th and 20th centuries, Irish women would continue to use their words, including gossip, rumor, oral traditions, and storytelling, to qualify their priests' power. Women's unruly words and actions were analyzed by John O'Sullivan, parish priest of Kenmare in Co. Kerry during the 1840s and 1850s. His unpublished diaries and writings, including a training manual for novice priests, relate numerous troubling instances of female gossip and disorderliness. For example, O'Sullivan asserted that station-masses became sites of unruly crowds because of women's disorderly tendencies and their determination to instigate local conflicts.[49]

A survey of Irish court cases provides further evidence of disputes between women and priests that made their way into the secular realm. Often, women took the initiative in these cases. In Templenoe, also in Kerry, in 1847, Julia Mara, described as a "decrepit, withered poor old woman" accused a priest of assault. She told the local court that the cleric, Rev. O'Sullivan, came into her house and "struck me three blows of a whip or a switch, or whatever he had in his hand and he hurted me." Mara's assertiveness is further confirmed by the fact that she initially refused to be sworn into the court unless she could give her testimony in Irish rather than English. Furthermore, she admitted that she "never went to church and never will with the help of God."[50] Unlike those women who staunchly supported their church and clergy during the Great Hunger, Mara overtly challenged both.

Others too came under the watchful eye of the cleric. In September 1855, the *Limerick Chronicle* reported that prostitutes had been "publicly warned from the chapel altar" by a local parish priest.[51] At the Kilkee Petty Sessions in 1855, the courts prosecuted a local curate, Father McMahon, for assaulting two notorious "young *ladies* from Kilrush." The priest apparently tore at their clothes and repeatedly beat them, even after receiving a previous warning from the court. McMahon's defense, according to *The Clare Freeman*, was that "he had a spiritual and temporal jurisdiction, which he may exercise at [his] discretion." The court punished him with a small fine. Several days later, one of the women involved, Bridget Cavanagh, was back in court; she claimed that she had been thrown down the stairs by an acquaintance because she had sworn against Father McMahon.[52]

Female activism and agency were evident not only through women's often-violent conflicts with priests, but also in the letters that they wrote to religious superiors. In 1850, in the Cloyne Diocese, an unnamed female parishioner wrote to Bishop Keane to alert him to a possible scandal. The parishioner's letter reads:

> There is a young woman staying in Mr. Davis' [the priest] house who is the greatest annoyance to the parishioners. He is under such subjection to her that he does anything she wishes him to do. We have nothing to say to himself if this woman were removed it would better his condition a great deal as she has always been a meddler since she came amongst us.[53]

The writer of this letter suggests that it was scandalous for a young woman, rather than the more typical older woman, to live with a priest, presumably as his housekeeper. The fact that the young woman appeared to control the priest made the situation particularly untenable. Additionally, the young woman was presumably not of the parish since she recently "came amongst us," and thus was an outsider who roused even more suspicion. When this other parishioner wrote to the bishop to report the allegedly suspicious relationship, she testified to the prevalence of gossip in the local area. She also, however, demonstrated her belief that she had a right to challenge priestly authority by reporting her cleric to his bishop, and she also used her literacy and access to the written word to do so.

Female literacy increased in importance throughout the 19th century as Ireland's educational system evolved. Contained primarily in Catholic diocesan archives, the numerous letters, written by Irish women to bishops in the 1840s and 1850s, commonly included complaints that their clerics were neglecting their duties or treating their parishioners unjustly. In March 1852, Mrs. G. Ryan, from Co. Tipperary, wrote a particularly scathing letter to Archbishop Michael Slattery of Cashel and Emly. In it, she informed Slattery of troubles in the parish of Inch where, she asserted, the local priests did not administer the sacrament of penance regularly. Meanwhile, Ryan wrote, the number of parishioners receiving communion had declined sharply in recent years. "I shall humbly state," Ryan wrote, "that I conceive it my duty as the mistress of a large family to make known to your Grace the neglected state of the parish."[54] She complained in particular that the current clergy was not performing its duties as those in the past would have; here, Ryan defended tradition and custom even as she reprimanded the newly trained professional priesthood. And Mrs. Ryan was not an insignificant parishioner: as mistress of Inch House, she oversaw one of the most wealthy and long-established Catholic estates in Ireland. Throughout the late 19th and early 20th centuries, as the work of Lindsey Earner-Byrne has demonstrated, Catholic women continued to write to their religious superiors to complain about clergy, report on local scandals, or beg for financial assistance.[55] The female assertiveness that may have begun before or during the Famine era, then, continued throughout the post-Famine era, despite the continued economic crisis and supposed decline in Irish women's social and religious status.[56] In 1882, a Dublin woman, Mary Power Laher, described her contentious relationship with her local priest in a letter to Archbishop McCabe. "I determined while you were in your retreat to leave nothing undone on my side to bring about a good feeling here & to save you any further trouble so I wrote myself to the P.P. a very nice letter...". Laher had apparently tried to make peace; as she described to McCabe, she appealed to the priest:

> Under the circumstances did he not think peace & a return to the old relations between us would be well. I was ready on my side & I wrote to him as an old friend of my boy's father and grandfather—I should be glad to see him at dinner the day of our arrival.

The response from the priest, however, was "curt." He declined the dinner invitation and rebuffed Laher's attempts to make peace. Next, Laher informed McCabe that this same priest was equally unpopular in a neighboring town and that the parishioners there were organizing to boycott him.[57]

An analysis of the interactions between female parishioners and priests prompts a reexamination of women's status in the Famine and post-Famine worlds. Most historians have argued that, during Ireland's "devotional revolution," a newly powerful Catholic patriarchy increasingly restricted Irish women's autonomy.[58] Others have described a post-Famine decline in Irish women's social and economic status alongside their enclosure in the private sphere.[59] Some women, however, retained more of a prominent public voice than previously thought. As scholars continue to complicate the picture of female passivity and martyrdom that have dominated Famine-era representations and even commemorations since, it is hoped that they will look to underutilized sources such as Catholic diocesan archives to find evidence of the meddlers whose actions testified to female agency and encourage us to rethink our analysis of Irish women's roles during and after the Great Hunger.

Endnotes

[1] I thank Mara Sholette at the College of Charleston for her help with the research for this chapter as well as Christine Kinealy, Ciarán Reilly, Jason King and the participants in the *Women and the Great Hunger in Ireland* conference at Quinnipiac University, June 2014, for the opportunity to present a version of this chapter as well as for helpful comments. Assistance from archivists and librarians at the Galway, Cloyne and Kerry Catholic Diocesan archives; the Dublin Diocesan Archives, and the National Library, Dublin, was also essential to the completion of this piece.

[2] Stuart McLean, *The event and its terrors: Ireland, Famine, modernity* (Stanford, 2004), p. 130, and Margaret Kelleher, *The Feminization of Famine: Expressions of the inexpressible?* (Durham, 1997), p. 2. Mid-19th-century Irish poetry, literature and imagery solidified the woman- (and often mother-) as-victim trope. For example, see McLean, *The event and its terrors*, p. 134. It is noteworthy that the cover of Kelleher's monograph features John Behan's sculpture "Famine Mother and Children."

[3] Quoted in, Patrick Hickey, "Famine, mortality, and emigration: A profile of six parishes in the Poor Law Union of Skibbereen, 1846-7" in Patrick O'Flanagan and Cornelius G. Buttimer (eds.), *Cork: History and Society: Interdisciplinary essays on the history of an Irish county* (Dublin, 1993), p. 880.

[4] McLean, *The event and its terrors* p. 137. Kelleher traces the centuries-long history of this phenomenon, which she calls the "feminization of famine." See Kelleher, *The Feminization of Famine*, pp 1-2. Still, as David Fitzpatrick notes, the mortality rates of women during the Irish Famine were lower than those of men, suggesting that "women were less likely to succumb than men" during the crisis. See David Fitzpatrick, "Women and the Great Famine" in Margaret Keller and James H. Murphy (eds) *Gender Perspectives in nineteenth-century Ireland: Public and private spheres* (Dublin, 1997), p. 52.

[5] Dympna McLoughlin, "The impact of the Great Famine on subsistent women" in John Crowley, William J. Smyth and Mike Murphy (eds) *Atlas of the Great Irish Famine, 1845-52* (Cork, 2012), p. 255.

[6] J.J. Lee, "Women and the Church since the Famine" in Margaret MacCurtain & Donncha Ó'Corráin (eds) *Women in Irish Society: The historical dimension* (London, 1979), pp 37-45 and Christine Kinealy, *A death-dealing Famine: The Great Hunger in Ireland* (London & New York, 1997), p. 153. For some recent challenges to this view, see the essays in Christina S. Brophy and Cara Delay (eds) *Women, reform, and resistance in Ireland, 1850-1950* (New York, 2015).

[7] Christine Kinealy, *Charity and the Great Hunger in Ireland: The kindness of strangers* (London, 2013), p. 145.

[8] Patricia Lysaght, "Women and the Great Famine: Vignettes from the Irish oral tradition" in Arthur Gribben (ed.) *The Great Famine and the Irish Diaspora in America* (Amherst, 1999), p. 23.

[9] Patricia Lysaght, "Perspectives on women during the Great Irish Famine from the oral tradition" in *Béaloideas*, 64/65 (1996-1997), p. 95.

[10] Ibid., p. 77. As Lysaght points out, depictions in the oral tradition of powerful Famine-era women tend to highlight women who were implicated in land-grabbing or evictions, as well as women who cursed others. Ibid., p. 122.

[11] Anna Clark, "Wild workhouse girls and the liberal imperial state in mid-nineteenth-century Ireland" in *Journal of Social History*, 39, 2 (Winter 2005), pp 389-409 and Dympna McLoughlin, "Workhouses and female paupers" in Maria Luddy & Cliona Murphy (eds) *Women surviving: Studies in Irish women's history in the 19th and 20th Centuries* (Dublin, 1990), pp 117-47. See also Ciara Breathnach, "Even 'wilder workhouse girls': The problem of institutionalisation among Irish immigrants to New Zealand 1874," in *The Journal of Imperial and Commonwealth History* 39, 5, Dec. 2011, pp 771-94 and Gerard Moran, *Sending out Ireland's poor: Assisted emigration to North America in the nineteenth century* (Dublin, 2013). The overwhelming majority of workhouse inmates during the Famine were women and children. See Fitzpatrick, Women and the Great Famine', pp 62-3, and Mary E. Daly, *The Famine in Ireland* (Dundalk, 1986).

[12] Virginia Crossman, "Viewing women, family, and sexuality through the prism of the Irish Poor Laws" in *Women's History Review*, 15, 4 (Sept. 2006), p. 545.

[13] *Nenagh Guardian*, 27 Jan. 1849.

[14] McLean, *The event and its terrors*, p. 136.

[15] Clark, "Wild workhouse girls," p. 392.

[16] Ibid.

[17] *Freeman's Journal*, 11 July 1851.

[18] For more discussion of the power of women's words in 19th century Ireland, see E. Moore Quinn, "'All I had left were my

words': The widow's curse in nineteenth and twentieth-century Ireland" in Brophy and Delay (eds) *Women, reform, and resistance,* pp 211-34, and Christina Brophy, "'What nobody does now': Imaginative resistance of rural labouring women" in *Women, Reform, and Resistance*, pp 185-210.

[19] Cara Delay, "Confidantes or competitors? Women, priests, and conflict in post-Famine Ireland" in *Éire-Ireland*, 40, 1 & 2 (spring/summer 2002), pp 107-25.

[20] *Belfast Newsletter*, 12 Nov. 1846.

[21] *Tralee Chronicle and Killarney Echo*, 20 Feb. 1847.

[22] Lysaght, "Perspectives on women," p. 116.

[23] Ibid.

[24] For the roles played by the Catholic clergy during the Famine years, see Donal A. Kerr, *A 'Nation of Beggars'? Priests, people and politics in Famine Ireland, 1846-1852* (Oxford, 1994) as well as his *The Catholic Church and the Famine* (Blackrock, 1996).

[25] *Tralee Chronicle and Killarney Echo*, 13 Feb. 1847.

[26] *Kerry Examiner*, 22 March 1847.

[27] *Nenagh Guardian*, 12 Nov. 1844.

[28] *Irish Examiner,* 8 Sept. 1852. For descriptions of a similar case, see *Freeman's Journal*, 4 March 1846.

[29] *Irish Examiner,* 8 Sept. 1852. See also *Connaught Telegraph*, 11 Aug. 1852.

[30] *Freeman's Journal,* 8 June 1852.

[31] *Connaught Telegraph*, 11 Aug. 1852.

[32] Joseph O'Cassidy, Rosmuck, to Bishop McCormack, 19 Oct. 1899 (Galway Diocesan Archive, Bishop Francis McCormack papers, File P/15/1 Rosmuck). On the "devotional revolution" see Emmet Larkin, "The Devotional Revolution in Ireland, 1850-75" in *American Historical Review*, 77, no. 3 (1972) pp 625-52.

[33] Tom Inglis, *Moral monopoly: The Catholic Church in modern Irish society* (Dublin, 1987), pp 46-50, 128. See also Cara Delay, "Language which will move their hearts: Speaking power, performance, and the lay-clerical relationship in modern Catholic Ireland" in *Journal of British Studies*, 53, 2 (April, 2014) pp 426-52.

[34] Ellen Walden, Queenstown, to Bishop Keane, 31 Jan. 1859 (Cloyne Diocesan Archive, Keane Papers, 1796.07/11/1859).

[35] Philip O'Neill, Ballymacoda, to Bishop Keane, 24 Feb. 1858 (Cloyne Diocesan Archive, Keane Papers, 1796.07/7/1858) and Rev. Thomas Murray to Bishop Keane, 3 Feb. 1858 (Cloyne Diocesan Archive, Keane Papers, 1796.07/8/1858).

[36] P. Nagle, Ennis, to Archbishop McCabe, 18 Mar. 1883 (Dublin Diocesan Archive, Drumcondra, Archbishiop Edward McCabe Papers, 1883 360/2).

[37] See, for example, letters written by widows to Archbishop Edward McCabe in the Dublin Diocesan Archives for the year 1880. For an analysis of letters from the early 20th century, see Lindsey Earner-Byrne, "'Should I take myself and my family to another religion[?]': Irish Catholic women, protest, and conformity, 1920-1940" in *Women, reform, and resistance in Ireland*, pp 77-100.

[38] W. McCarthy, Curate of Newmarket to Bishop Keane, 5 Dec. 1853 (Cloyne Diocesan Archive, Cobh, Bishop William Keane Papers, 1795.05/66/1853).

[39] Ibid., Bishop Murphy to Tobias Kirby, Irish College Rome, 31 July 1856.

[40] Jules Michelet, *Priests, women and families*, 3rd ed., translated by C. Cocks (London, 1846), p. 116.

[41] See Delay, "Confidantes or competitors?" *passim*.

[42] *Nenagh Guardian*, 21 Feb. 1849.

[43] Ibid., 29 May 1850.

[44] James C. Scott, *Weapons of the weak: Everyday forms of peasant resistance* (New Haven, 1985), p. 25.

[45] Rosaleen Fallon, *A county Roscommon wedding, 1892: The marriage of John Hughes and Mary Gavin* (Dublin, 2004), p. 21.

[46] Ned Buckley, Knocknagree, Co. Cork, repeating a narrative told to him by his mother, who was 90 years old at her 1934 death. Cited in Cathal Póirtéir, *Famine Echoes* (Dublin, 1995), p. 144.

[47] Quinn, "'All I had left were my words'", p. 213.

[48] Brophy, "'What nobody does now'", p. 185.

[49] John O'Sullivan, *Praxis Parochi in Hibernia* (Unpub. manuscript, Kerry Diocesan Archive, Killarney, draft and two volumes, 1850-52, vol. 1, p. 108).

[50] *Tralee Chronicle and Killarney Echo*, 14 Aug. 1847.

[51] Ignatius Murphy, *The diocese of Killaloe, 1850-1904* (Dublin, 1995), p. 260.

[52] *Clare Freeman*, 15 Sept. 1855. See also "Lord Dunboyne newspaper cuttings, Co. Clare civil and criminal trials" (NLI, Ms. 3456).

[53] "A Parishioner of Mr. Davis'" to Bishop Keane, 9 May 1850 (Cloyne Diocesan Archive, Cobh, Bishop William Keane Papers, 1795.07/16/1850).

[54] Mrs. G. Ryan to Archbishop Slattery, 4 Mar. 1852 (NLI, Archbishop Michael Slattery Papers, 1852/6, microfilm reel p. 6004).

[55] Earner-Byrne, "'Should I take myself and my family to another religion[?]'"

[56] See Brophy and Delay, eds., *Women, reform, and resistance.*

[57] Mary Power Laher to Archbishop McCabe, 17 July 1882 (Dublin Diocesan Archives, Archbishop Edward McCabe papers, 353/6).

[58] Lee, "Women and the Church since the Famine" and K.H. Connell, "Catholicism and marriage in the century after the Famine" in *Irish peasant society: Four historical essays* (Oxford, 1968), pp 113-61; Robert E. Kennedy, Jr., *The Irish: Emigration, marriage and fertility* (Berkeley, 1973) and Rita M. Rhodes, *Women and the family in Post-Famine Ireland: Status and opportunity in a patriarchal society* (New York and London, 1992).

[59] On the increasing power of the Church, see Larkin, "The devotional revolution" and Patrick J. Corish, *The Irish Catholic experience: A historical survey* (Dublin, 1985), and Desmond Keenan, *The Catholic Church in nineteenth-century Ireland: A sociological study* (Dublin, 1983). On the role of the clergy, see Kerr, *A 'Nation of Beggars'?.*

Works Cited

Archival Sources

Archive of the Archdiocese of Cashel and Emly at the National Library Ireland (NLI), Dublin
    Archbishop Michael Slattery Papers

Cloyne Diocesan Archive, Cobh
    Bishop William Keane Papers
    Bishop Timothy Murphy Papers

Dublin Diocesan Archive, Drumcondra
    Archbishop Edward McCabe Papers

McCabe Papers, Dublin Diocesan Archive, Drumcondra
    Galway Diocesan Archive, Galway
    Bishop Francis McCormack Papers

Kerry Diocesan Archive, Killarney.

John O'Sullivan, *Praxis Parochi in Hibernia*. Unpublished manuscript, draft and two volumes, 1850-52.

Lord Dunboyne newspaper cuttings, Co. Clare civil and criminal trials, Ms. 3337 (NLI).

Newspapers

Belfast Newsletter

Clare Freeman

Connaught Telegraph

Freeman's Journal

Irish Examiner

Kerry Examiner

Nenagh Guardian

Tralee Chronicle and Killarney Echo

Waterford News

Published Primary Sources

Michelet, Jules. *Priests, Women and Families*, 3rd ed., translated by C. Cocks. London: Longman, Brown, Green, and Longmans, 1846.

Secondary Sources

Brophy, Christina S. "'What Nobody Does Now': Imaginative Resistance of Rural Laboring Women," in *Women, Reform, and Resistance in Ireland, 1850-1950*, eds. Christina S. Brophy and Cara Delay. New York: Palgrave Macmillan, 2015, 185-210.

Brophy, Christina S. and Cara Delay, eds. *Women, Reform, and Resistance in Ireland, 1850-1950*. New York: Palgrave Macmillan, 2015.

Burke, Helen. *The People and The Poor Law in Nineteenth-Century Ireland*. Littlehampton: Women's Education Bureau, 1997.

Clark, Anna. "Wild Workhouse Girls and the Liberal Imperial State in Mid-Nineteenth-Century Ireland." *Journal of Social History* 39, 2 (winter 2005): pp 389-409.

Connell, K.H. "Catholicism and Marriage in the Century After the Famine," in *Irish Peasant Society: Four Historical Essays*. Oxford: Clarendon Press, 1968, 113-61.

Corish, Patrick J. *The Irish Catholic Experience: A Historical Survey*. Dublin: Gill and Macmillan, 1985.

Crossman, Virginia. "Viewing Women, Family, and Sexuality Through the Prism of the Irish Poor Laws." *Women's History Review* 15, 4 (September 2006), 541-550.

Daly, Mary E. *The Famine in Ireland*. Dundalk: Dundalgan Press, 1986.

Delay, Cara. "Confidantes or Competitors? Women, Priests, and Conflict in Post-Famine Ireland." *Éire-Ireland* 40, 1 & 2 (spring/summer 2002), pp 107-125.

—— "'Language Which Will Move Their Hearts': Speaking Power, Performance, and the Lay-Clerical Relationship in Modern Catholic Ireland." *Journal of British Studies* 53, 2 (April 2014): pp 426-52.

Earner-Byrne, Lindsey. "'Should I take Myself and my Family to Another Religion[?]': Irish Catholic Women, Protest, and Conformity, 1920-1940," in *Women, Reform, and Resistance in Ireland*, eds. Christina Brophy and Cara Delay. New York: Palgrave Macmillan, 2015, 77-100.

Fallon, Rosaleen. *A County Roscommon Wedding, 1892: The Marriage of John Hughes and Mary Gavin*. Maynooth Studies in Local History, no. 53. Dublin: Four Courts Press, 2004.

Fitzpatrick, David. "Women and the Great Famine," in *Gender Perspectives in Nineteenth-Century Ireland: Public and Private Spheres,* eds. Margaret Keller and James H. Murphy. Dublin: Irish Academic Press, 1997, 50-69.

Hickey, Patrick. "Famine, Mortality, and Emigration: A Profile of Six Parishes in the Poor Law Union of Skibbereen, 1846-7," in *Cork: History and Society: Interdisciplinary Essays on the History of an Irish County*, eds. Patrick O'Flanagan and Cornelius G. Buttimer. Dublin: Geography Publications, 1993, 873-918.

Inglis, Tom. *Moral Monopoly: The Catholic Church in Modern Irish Society*. Dublin: Gill and Macmillan, 1987.

Keenan, Desmond. *The Catholic Church in Nineteenth-Century Ireland: A Sociological Study*. Dublin: Gill and Macmillan, 1983.

Kelleher, Margaret. *The Feminization of Famine: Expressions of the Inexpressible?* Durham, NC: Duke University Press, 1997.

Kennedy, Robert E Jr. *The Irish: Emigration, Marriage and Fertility*. Berkeley: The University of California Press, 1973.

Kerr, Donal A. *A 'Nation of Beggars'? Priests, People and Politics in Famine Ireland, 1846-1852*. Oxford: Clarendon Press, 1994.

Kinealy, Christine. *A Death-Dealing Famine: The Great Hunger in Ireland*. London and New York: Pluto Press, 1997.

Larkin, Emmet. "The Devotional Revolution in Ireland, 1850-75." *American Historical Review* 77, 3 (1972), pp 625-52.

Lee, J.J. "Women and the Church Since the Famine," in *Women in Irish Society: The Historical Dimension*, eds. Margaret MacCurtain and Donncha Ó Corráin. Greenwood Press, 1979, 37-45.

Lysaght, Patricia. "Perspectives on Women During the Great Irish Famine From the Oral Tradition." *Béaloideas* 64/65 (1996-1997), 63-130.

—— "Women and the Great Famine: Vignettes from the Irish Oral Tradition," in *The Great Famine and The Irish Diaspora in America*, ed. Arthur Gribben. Amherst: University of Massachusetts Press, 1999, 21-48.

McLean, Stuart. *The Event and Its Terrors: Ireland, Famine, Modernity*. Stanford: Stanford University Press, 2004.

McLoughlin, Dympna. "The Impact of the Great Famine on Subsistent Women," in *Atlas of the Great Irish Famine, 1845-52*, eds. John Crowley, William J. Smyth and Mike Murphy. Cork: Cork University Press, 2012.

—— "Workhouses and Female Paupers," in *Women Surviving: Studies in Irish Women's History in the 19th and 20th Centuries*, eds. Maria Luddy and Cliona Murphy. Swords, Co. Dublin: Poolbeg Press, 1990, 117-147.

Murphy, Ignatius. *The Diocese of Killaloe, 1850-1904*. Blackrock, Co. Dublin: Four Courts Press, 1995.

Póirtéir, Cathal, ed. *Famine Echoes*. Dublin: Gill and Macmillan, 1995.

Rhodes, Rita M. *Women and the Family in Post-Famine Ireland: Status and Opportunity in a Patriarchal Society*. New York and London: Garland Publishing, Inc., 1992.

Scott, James C. *Weapons of the Weak: Everyday Forms of Peasant Resistance*. New Haven: Yale University Press, 1985.

Whelan, Kevin. "The Catholic Parish, the Catholic Chapel and Village Development in Ireland," *Irish Geography*, xvi (1983), 1-15.

Chapter Six

"Nearly naked": clothing and the Great Hunger in Ireland

Daphne Wolf

In the third year of Ireland's Great Hunger, the Commissary-General of the Army, Sir Randolph Routh, wrote to the Treasury Secretary, Sir Charles Trevelyan, from Ireland:

> I have been considering your question about clothing, and the quantity that you think is now in preparation under the care of the ladies in England, and your opinion that the distribution should be made by the ladies in Ireland. I think it would be a very popular measure here, and encourage many contributions in this article, and these unfortunate Irish are nearly naked.[1]

In these few lines, two English gentlemen say a lot about the state of clothing during the crisis of 1845-52. First, that clothing was something women understood well, and that the collection and distribution of it to the needy was properly within a woman's capacity and station to manage. Then, by including the "ladies of Ireland" in the enterprise, they tacitly acknowledge that there was a class of women in both countries capable of this work, whose own state of dress was never going to be subject to public scrutiny. This appears to eliminate those Irish women who had traditionally been in charge of washing, mending and storing their families' clothes, but who had lost that function along with their potato crops. Routh goes on to suggest that the transfer of used clothing might be much more palatable to certain donor communities than other relief efforts had been, presumably those aimed at feeding people directly or giving them viable employment. Finally, with some feeling and obvious embarrassment, Routh lets us know that he finds the state of Irish "un-dress" painful to behold.

In the wide scholarship on the plagues of starvation, homelessness and disease that assailed the Irish people during the Famine of 1845-52, there is little research to be found on the specific impact of the lack of clothing during that time.[2] Yet, the loss of dignified apparel had a devastating effect on those suffering from the potato blight. This loss was perceived, addressed and represented by contemporary observers in ways that provide insight into their attitudes toward dress and the body, particularly in regards to women.[3] By examining official and private records that touch on the clothing of the poor, this study will reflect on the personal distress and psychological damage connected with being "nearly naked." The lack of clothing during the Famine will be interrogated as a distinct hardship separate from hunger, and one that provides a specific understanding of the resourcefulness of the Irish poor, the place of women in the politics of philanthropy, and the long term effects of deprivation.

Pre-famine dress in Ireland was at least "comfortable and diverse," as evidenced by the quality of garments provided in the workhouses, which were deliberately designed to be of a lesser value than those available outside.[4] However, even that level of wearing apparel in Irish rural communities had been deteriorating during the economic downturns of the 1820s and 1830s.[5] Donations of garments for the Irish poor had been collected long before the Famine by private organizations like the Penny-A-Week Clothing Society in Kildallen (Co. Cavan) that distributed 114 "flannel petticoats" and 47 "bibs and aprons" in 1841.[6] After the blight arrived in 1845, visitors' reports, along with parliamentary and private charity records, show that the further undressing of the Irish followed a trajectory different from that of the evaporating potato crop or the rush to eviction by landlords. Clothing had its own currency in Irish life that was not quite equivalent, in social or psychological terms, to the struggle for food and shelter.

We cannot assume that the Famine-era Irish did not have feelings about their clothes, or that there were no strategies or aspirations involved in getting dressed just because their options were so limited. Mairead Dunlevy, the former curator of the National Museum of Ireland, provides evidence that people in the early 1800s dreamed of abandoning their traditional dress (and their poverty) "in favour of fashionable clothing...[as] shown by the extravagant promises of silks, satins and 'cloth-enduring' made to loved ones in Irish poetry."[7] Post-Famine, an American journalist observed that Irish women added "tawdry lace" to their traditional cloaks in imitation of fashions from London and Paris,[8] and one could suppose that they did the same earlier. Those who study the psychology and sociology of fashion remind us that clothing has meaning far beyond the fundamental functions of providing warmth and protecting modesty. Status and sexual attractiveness are closely related to what we wear and, even in the poorest communities, choices are made about fabric, arrangement, and decoration, which all function as signs of identity, or even as the very substance of identity.

People's access to those markers of selfhood disappeared during the Famine when their normal garments were replaced with donated clothes or workhouse garb. Any personal damage that resulted from this loss and the re-clothing process was most likely under-acknowledged, obscured by the more immediately calamitous effects of starvation and homelessness. Yet, while starvation and eviction stripped people of health and comfort, the lack of clothing divested them of privacy, dignity and individuality. Reliance on soup kitchens and workhouses was humiliating, even when lifesaving, but being in society without one's own proper clothing would tend to unhinge any sense of self, even in rural areas where tattered clothing was commonplace. Secondhand clothing was not distasteful to the Irish lower classes (in fact, it was a vital part of their economy), but charitable donations of clothes from far away allowed strangers and institutions to assess and regulate the starving people in their most intimate bodily practices of fashion and hygiene.[9] This controlling mechanism would have operated even if the recipients were unaware of it or were grateful for the donations.

While there is no adequate name for the condition of not having enough to wear—"clothelessness" does not work—the crisis nevertheless achieved metaphorical potency when outsiders latched on to the lack of clothing in Ireland as a powerful literary and visual image. Newspapers and reports from the British government and from charitable organizations during the Famine used the words "naked" or "nearly naked" over and over again to refer to the Irish. These terms could actually signify anything from bare arms, to a short skirt, to no clothes at all. Even the writer and philosopher Thomas Carlyle, after a visit in 1849, was reduced to describing Ireland in strictly sartorial terms: "the whole country figures in my mind like a ragged coat; one huge beggar's gabardine, not patched, or patchable any longer."[10]

Visual depictions of the starving Irish in periodicals such as the *Illustrated London News* consistently used tattered and ill-fitting clothing to signify cataclysmic deprivation. Historian Margaret Crawford argues that images like James Mahony's, "*Boy and Girl at Cahera*" and

"NEARLY NAKED": CLOTHING AND THE GREAT HUNGER IN IRELAND

"*Bridget O'Donnell and Children*" depict people with relatively "strong and muscular" limbs, which are not anatomically emaciated. For Crawford, their suffering is conveyed primarily through their facial expressions, disheveled hair, and the shapeless, torn clothing that bares their arms and legs.[11] Niamh O'Sullivan, curator of Ireland's Great Hunger Museum in Hamden, Connecticut, states that Famine artists were often classically trained, but "had little or no experience of looking at unfiltered images of trauma, distress, or even poverty…[and] had to find new ways of visualizing what had not been imaginable before."[12] She sees the O'Donnell family as more "skeletal" than muscular, but says their rags intensify the sense of desperation because they reveal so much of their bodies.[13] O'Sullivan argues that Victorian readers found these "images of Irish Famine distress in the illustrated press as shocking as we find famine reportage today."[14] Information about clothing gleaned from these illustrations must be considered within the context described by Emily Mark-Fitzgerald, who calls Famine imagery a "mercurial, emotional and highly politicized endeavor"[15] and part of a "chaotic and culturally determined phenomenon constituted within Ireland's colonial relationship" and Victorian visual practices.[16]

Irish dress had been a target of British criticism for centuries before the Famine. In medieval times, native Irish fashion was described as "barbarous."[17] Both the Statutes of Kilkenny in 1367 and the Tudor governments in the 16th century forbid English people living in Ireland to dress in the Irish style.[18] In 1596, English poet Edmund Spenser criticized the Irish use of long, hooded mantles that covered the whole body, claiming they provided camouflage for thieves and rebels. An Irish woman, Spenser suggested, used the mantle as a disguise for "lewd exercises," and as swaddling clothes for her "bastard."[19]

Nineteenth-century visitors to Ireland before the Famine reacted to the clothing of the Irish poor in a manner remarkably similar to this historic discourse, with the words "naked" and "ragged" appearing frequently in travelers' accounts. The ubiquitous cloak worn by Galway women was labeled "the shroud of all untidiness," since it covered up "destitution beneath."[20] The cloak, which did double-duty as a blanket by night, was also called a "cover-slut" and a "woolen hide-all" that discouraged care for the apparel underneath.[21] George Nicholls, in his 1838 reports on the Poor Law in Ireland, was dispirited by the appearance of most of the Irish poor. He found a "depression of feeling" in the country people that showed in "their dress, in the dress of their children."[22]

Yet, there are other indications that Irish people were not always so badly clothed. In 1834, visitor Henry D. Inglis was impressed with the custom in Co. Kerry of washing clothes and stretching them to dry (without fear of theft) on the hedges overnight. He was equally delighted to see "red petticoats, and bright yellow shawls" on Sundays in Tarbert. There he observed that "so smart were the women's caps that every hood was thrown back to let them be seen."[23] Surveys conducted by the Royal Dublin Society from 1801-32, and reports by other visitors, show that, in the early years of the 19th century, most Irish people were fairly well dressed by wider European standards. In the western counties, people used the fleece of their own sheep to spin and weave woolen fabric at home; they also made linen clothing and knitted stockings.[24] Even though they were only able to replace their everyday vests, trousers and jackets every few years, and had to resole their shoes frequently, many laborers still had special clothes for Sunday. Pawnbrokers did a brisk business in these garments that were pledged on Monday and redeemed the next Saturday, while second-hand clothing vendors also prospered. When the potato crop failed in 1845, those who still had decent clothing would eventually turn to these already established practices by selling or pawning whatever they could spare, anticipating that the next harvest would be bountiful and they would then be able to buy their clothes back.[25] It was not, and they could not.

By giving up their clothes, the starving Irish reacted to this catastrophe with a familiar remedy, resulting in progressive levels of "clothesless-ness" according to what was already owned. The use of clothing as barter actually served to mask some effects of the Famine, and may thus have contributed to a delay in the government's response. As long as people had some clothing and household goods available to pawn or sell, "the extent of their distress remained unknown" to the outside world.[26] One bishop decided in 1848 to use donated funds to buy back 540 pawn tickets issued before Christmas, rather than use the money for direct relief.[27] Unfortunately, the reprieve from hunger achieved by selling clothes did not last long. Gradually it became apparent that:

> the great coat which the male peasantry used to wear is now very seldom to be seen. The female peasantry...struggle to keep their cloak; it is always the last article which they take to the pawnbroker.[28]

Wary observers predicted that "this visitation will probably spread through the higher grades of society if not speedily checked."[29] Soon, the number of people attending church on Sundays began to diminish "from their inability to appear decently clad."[30] Giving up their clothes forced people to give up their social and religious lives as well.

For the Quaker Jonathan Pim, the issue of clothing was a "question of great difficulty" and one that "was everywhere felt" in Ireland.[31] Like other observers, he believed the lack of warm, protective clothing fostered disease, a situation exacerbated by "the extreme difficulty of personal cleanliness when the same clothes are necessarily worn night and day." Pim also suggested that while the potato blight affected the supply of clothing in Ireland, the modernizing influence of the English economy also played a role. The home industries of rural families who had traditionally made their own clothes had for some time been disrupted by the popularity of "cheaper but less durable fabrics" and goods imported from England, which were bought in shops with cash earned from labor abroad.[32] During the Famine, with all available cash being used to procure food, the shops were not frequented. Tailors and shoemakers were out of work because no one could pay for their services, since pigs and poultry (which also provided the cash for purchases of clothing) had been sold as well. [33]

The outsiders who were put in charge of clothing the Irish, government officials and private philanthropists, negotiated the boundaries between charity and the invasion of privacy with varying degrees of understanding and respect. Any clothing provided by the government was technically bound by Poor Law regulations but, as suggested in the letter from Routh to Trevelyan, attitudes may have been more flexible when those regulations were applied to clothes as opposed to food. The British Ordnance office shipped thousands of bundles of rugs, blankets and jackets, shirts and trousers deemed "condemned" or "unserviceable" to Ireland at no cost to the Poor Law Unions.[34] These garments were specifically for men; it was much more difficult to find government surplus clothing for women.[35] When Routh told Trevelyan that "half the country is naked," the Treasury approved the general distribution of old "army and navy clothing," after workhouse inmates were supplied.[36] Yet, it was not until 1849 that a separate government inquiry into the state of clothing outside the workhouse was conducted.[37]

It was in the workhouse that the bulk of government spending on clothing occurred and where government control was most strongly felt. Even allowing for the necessity of maintaining sanitary conditions, official language brimmed with disgust at the clothing and habits of the destitute. On entering the workhouse, people had to surrender whatever they were wearing in exchange for workhouse clothing. Their old clothes were "cleansed and purified" and then stored, since the inmates would have to wear them again if they left the workhouse. Cleaning directions were explicit:

> The best way of cleansing will be to boil the clothing for a couple of hours, to destroy the Vermin...In some instances the old clothing will be so bad as to be totally unfit for the cleansing process. In such case it may be destroyed, and if the pauper to whom it belonged should quit the house, he may be furnished with the clothing left by some deceased inmate.

The old clothes were to be stored above the room in the workhouse designated for the Board of Guardians meetings (presumably to keep them safe), unless the Guardians objected to being so close to "infection, or annoyance by vermin," in which case other arrangements for storage could be made."[38]

Workhouse dress was designed to resemble that of household servants, with the use of broad stripes (later adapted into prison clothing) sometimes used as a kind of branding device.[39] The condition and distribution of these garments was supposed to be tightly regulated. Nicholls decreed that children's clothing must "be kept in perfect repair, not a stitch or button should be wanting." If closer inspection revealed imperfections, the proper authorities should be notified "as will prevent a Recurrence of the Neglect."[40] Use of workhouse clothing also was imagined as a way to control the inmates. In Co. Sligo, for example, wardsmen and women were appointed from the "well-conducted inmates of the house" to assist the master and matron in maintaining discipline and, in return, were given better rations and "a better description of clothing." Conversely, those who were guilty of "Misconduct" would have a special "mark on the jackets of the men and the caps and bed gowns of the women." Hospital patients also got a mark on their clothing, to prevent them from wandering into other parts of the workhouse undetected.[41]
In reality, control and relief were often nonexistent. Although the Poor Law required each workhouse to maintain sufficient supplies of clothing and bedding for inmates, reports from around the country indicated that compliance was very spotty and some unions were unable to provide any clothing at all.[42] In the Trim Union, the Board of Guardians was dissolved because, among other reasons, the state of clothing in the workhouse was "absolutely scandalous," with "boys in tatters."[43] In the Roscommon Union, more than 500 were reported "suffering from cough and chest affections (sic) for the want of sufficient clothing," and more than 100 recovered fever patients could not leave their beds because they had nothing to wear.[44] In Westport, Co. Mayo and Manorhamilton, Co. Leitrim, the probationary wards were dangerously overcrowded because there was not enough workhouse clothing to admit the people waiting there.[45] A workhouse doctor in Castlerea, Co. Roscommon wanted "warm clothing and shoes... for the children—the cold in the feet having a great effect in producing dysentery."[46] The Bantry Union in Co. Cork had room for an extra 200 people, but was prevented from admitting them because an order for clothing had not been filled.[47] Likewise, Scariff in Co. Clare could only clothe half the paupers in its care,[48] while in Clifden, Co. Galway, the Union could not pay a contractor £200 for the clothing it ordered.[49] Such was the appalling circumstances the Cavan vice-guardians told the Poor Law Commissioners in 1848 that some of the inmates under their care had gone for over a month without once changing their clothes.[50] The lack of clothing hampered relief efforts at every step.

It directly affected the efficacy of public works projects, as workers were often so badly dressed that they could not function in their jobs. In Co. Longford, novelist and educator Maria Edgeworth noted that "men and boys who can get employment in draining especially, cannot stand the work in the wet for want of strong shoes."[51] At Rossgarrow in Co. Donegal, a Mrs.

Hewitson asked the Belfast Ladies' Association for additional donations of clothes for workers because:

> some men are now working on the roads in thin linen jackets; and many starving beings, male and female, some of tender age, are now expecting employment on them, and anxiously imploring a covering from the exposure they are subject to at such work.[52]

Combined with punitively low wages and harsh weather conditions, the lack of warm clothing forced many willing laborers to avoid the public works altogether.[53] In 1847, William S. Crawford, M.P. told a House of Lords committee that if more people were allowed to receive clothing outside the workhouse, they would be more likely to find work and not be a burden on the Union. His unsympathetic questioner on the committee responded by suggesting that if clothes were distributed so freely, the result might be that "thousands of persons who had clothes would put them on one side, and come and apply for relief."[54]

Along with the British Relief Association, the Society of Friends was a leader among private relief organizations in spearheading efforts to supply clothes to the starving, and in helping to organize and distribute donations from England, America and elsewhere.[55] In addition, various private ladies' groups mobilized to help provide clothing, with the Ladies' Clothing Committee of London a prominent force.[56] In February 1847, the Quaker Ladies' Committee published a pamphlet, *An Appeal for clothing the Naked and Destitute Irish* that begged for "*useful, warm, necessary* clothing upon a large scale for the unclad (and unless something be done in a few weeks, nothing short of the naked) peasantry of Ireland." This job was to be given into the "hands of the women of England, old and young, rich and poor," with the implication that correct domesticity was still available on that side of the Irish Sea. "Stout flannel jackets for the men and boys," were recommended, with "flannel petticoats and stout calico under garments for the women and girls' made of 'the coarsest and warmest material, in order to prevent pawning."[57] Another appeal acknowledged that "no pen can adequately describe the afflictive, humiliating, and truly horrifying," state of those with nothing to wear. It asked manufacturers, warehousemen and shopkeepers for "pieces of goods, old and soiled, of little use to them" and invited the rich and middle class to open their wardrobes for "old garments never likely to be worn again."[58]

The Quaker ladies were so busy that a special sub-committee just for clothing was appointed in January 1847, and by April, they had hired three clerks and a packer, and arranged for a donated warehouse. The committee managed contributions of £2,464 to purchase clothing ("suitable for the poor, and chiefly of Irish manufacture") and distributed 210 bales of old and new clothes. However, by July, donations had dried up and when committee members found themselves doing all the work, they disbanded in August.[59] A second sub-committee was then formed with the mandate to purchase fabric to make new clothes, thus creating jobs for poor women. It also distributed new and used clothing, including a vast supply from America, and spent £6,333 to buy and distribute clothes throughout Ireland before it also ran out of funds in April of 1848.[60]

Historian Christine Kinealy has described how other private ladies' groups also took it on themselves to establish industrial schools "to provide longer-term benefits in the form of giving women employment skills, especially those of spinning, weaving and knitting."[61] A women's group in Brooklyn, New York, arranged for a local merchant to sell Irish-made goods sent through the Dublin Ladies' Committee for All Ireland.[62] Cultural studies scholar, Christian Huck, believes these ladies' groups "probably did what's worst: they meant well." He concludes that their actions only served to reinforce the impression that "the Irish stand closer to the naked and uncultivated beast than to a well-dressed and civilized human (i.e. English)."[63] Margaret Kelleher, in contrast, describes the activities of these women as "throwing an interesting light on the increasingly vexed question of the location of female activity in public or private spheres."[64] Despite the difficulty in finding markets for Irish goods, the economic potential of women's needle-work challenged the status quo. Consequently, the "repose of aristocratic society, and the leisure of the cloister were disturbed."[65]

A further insight into the clothing of the Famine Irish comes from Asenath Nicholson, an American who led her own private relief operation in Ireland from 1847-49, and who wrote about the ways that the lack of clothing affected the people she encountered on her journeys. According to Nicholson, the first starving person she met in Ireland was a man who had pawned or sold all of his family's garments "that would fetch any price."[66] She then met a Dublin couple who had pawned the woman's last dress and the man's last coat to pay their rent.[67] After leaving her trunks of dresses under the care of a woman with whom she had lodged, Nicholson was shocked to find on her return that the woman had pawned 14 of Nicholson's garments to feed her own family. The woman freely admitted her act, and said she was only following the precepts Nicholson had taught her, "that life was more valuable than property, and when that was in peril, property became the moral right of him who had tried every expedient to save life." Perplexed, Nicholson finally decided the woman "had flung me back on my own principles by acting up to hers, and what could be said?"[68]

Nicholson also discovered that offering clothing to those with little to wear involved complex negotiations. "People of a higher class in general showed a meanness bordering on dishonesty" when offered second-hand clothing to buy, which they then bargained to get as cheaply as possible, or for no cost at all. The truly destitute, who always expected to be oppressed, did not show much propensity for haggling, she observed, nor any sense of jealousy when donations were given to some and not to others. She also recorded how hard it was for her to distribute clothes in a schoolroom to certain children while other equally deserving students received nothing. One sympathetic teacher pointed out the neediest children to Nicholson privately, so she could approach them out of the classroom.[69]

New clothes were not always welcome. Buying a suit and hat for one orphan boy, Nicholson was astounded when he refused to part with his old rags. He wept loudly: "Now I shall surely die with the hunger; if they see me with nice clothes on, they will say I tell lies, that I have a mother that minds me; and lady, you won't burn them old clothes." Suspecting that a new suit of clothes might disqualify him for relief in official eyes, he clung to his "bundle of filthy, forbidding garments, as the only craft by which to save his life...The silk handkerchief almost seemed to frighten him."[70] The necessity to appear poorer than you actually might have been—in order to save yourself—could be a curious legacy of the strict Poor Law regulations. Circumstances made the outward appearance of destitution both regrettable *and* desirable at the same time. A modern observer might well wonder how pervasive such a complicated reflex was, and how long it took to dissipate.[71]

Many other questions emerge that cannot yet be answered. One obvious consideration would be the implications of being ill-clad on the self-images of Irish women as future sexual partners. Other questions might focus on regional or geographical differences in clothing deficiencies,[72] or on the complicity of pawnbrokers and merchants in the shortages. How did family members and neighbors deal with the appearance of those around them who were no longer properly dressed? Could they still converse, and look each other in the eye? After the Famine, were attitudes toward dress any different from what they had been before 1845? Clothing, and its absence, thus played a significant role in the complicated exchanges that took place during the Great Hunger within the Irish community, as well as between it and the outside world. Consideration needs to be given to the immediate and long-term effects of such a mass disrobing, and the inevitable shame that accompanied it.

Endnotes

[1] Sir R. Routh to Mr. Trevelyan, 13 Feb. 1847, *Correspondence from January to March, 1847, relating to the measures adopted for the relief of the distress in Ireland, Commissariat series. [Second part.]*, p. 142 [796] H.C. 1847, lii. 333.

[2] One exception is Hilary O'Kelly, "Famine and Workhouse Clothing," John Crowley, William J. Smyth, Mike Murphy (eds.) *Atlas of the Great Irish Famine* (New York, 2013), pp 145-149.

[3] See Margaret Kelleher, *The Feminization of Famine, Expressions of the Inexpressible?* (NC: Durham, 1997). Kelleher questions why women have been used so commonly to represent famine in visual and literary depictions, and why they are routinely seen in those works as being more resilient than men, pp 9-11.

[4] O'Kelly, p. 145.

[5] Mairead Dunlevy, *Dress in Ireland* (New York, 1989), p. 141.

[6] *Report of the Kildallen Penny-A-Week Clothing Society, for the Year 1841* (Cavan, 1841).

[7] Dunlevy, *Dress in Ireland*, p. 137.

[8] William Henry Hurlbert, *Ireland Under Coercion, The Diary of an American* (Edinburgh, 1888), pp 179-180.

[9] Dunlevy, *Dress in Ireland*, pp 135-42.

[10] Thomas Carlyle, *Reminiscences of my Irish journey in 1849* (New York, 1882), pp 3-4.

[11] Margaret Crawford, "The Great Irish Famine 1845-9: Image versus reality" in Raymond Gillespie and Brian P. Kennedy (eds.), *Ireland: Art into History* (Dublin, 1994), p. 81.

[12] Niamh O'Sullivan, *The tombs of a departed race: Illustrations of Ireland's Great Hunger* (CT: Quinnipiac University Press, 2014), p. 11.

[13] Ibid., p. 24.

[14] Ibid., p. 11.

[15] Emily Mark-Fitzgerald, *Commemorating the Irish Famine: Memory and the Monument* (Liverpool University Press, 2013), p. 1.

[16] Ibid., p. 3.

[17] Giraldus Cabrensis, quoted in Dunlevy, *Dress in Ireland*, p. 13.

[18] Ibid., p. 28, pp 43-4.

[19] Edmund Spenser, *A view of the present state of Ireland*, ed. W. L. Renwick (Oxford, 1970), pp 50-3.

[20] Samuel C. Hall and Anna Maria Hall, *Ireland: Its scenery, character, &c* (3 vols, London, 1843), iii, p. 473.

[21] Ibid., vol. ii, p. 272.

[22] George Nicholls, *Poor Laws–Ireland, Three Reports to Her Majesty's Principal Secretary of State for the Home Department* (London, 1838), p. 9.

[23] Henry D. Inglis, *Ireland in 1834, A journey throughout Ireland during the Spring, Summer and Autumn of 1834* (2 vols, 3rd ed., London, 1835), i, p. 269.

[24] Jonathan Pim, *The condition and prospects of Ireland and the evils arising from the present distribution of landed property: With suggestions for a remedy* (Dublin, 1848), p. 111.

[25] James H. Tuke, *A visit to Connaught in the Autumn of 1847: A letter addressed to the Central Committee of the Society of Friends, Dublin* (2nd ed., London and New York, 1848), p. 29.

[26] *Transactions of the Central Relief Committee of the Society of Friends during the Famine in Ireland, in 1846 and 1847* (Dublin and London, 1852), p. 190.

[27] Christine Kinealy, *The kindness of strangers: Charity and the Great Hunger in Ireland* (London and New York: Bloomsbury, 2013), p. 139.

[28] *Fourteenth report from the Select Committee on Poor Laws (Ireland); together with the proceedings of the committee, minutes of evidence, appendix, and index*, p. 272, H.C. 1849, (572), xv Pt. ii., p. 177.

[29] *Transactions of the Central Relief Committee*, p. 377.

30 *Fourteenth report from the Select Committee* (572), p. 253; O'Kelly, p. 146.

31 Pim, *The condition and prospects of Ireland*, p. 111, p. 113.

32 Ibid., p.111.

33 Ibid., p. 69.

34 *Correspondence from January to March, 1847,* BPP [796], p. 139.

35 Ibid., Mr. Erichsen to Mr. Trevelyan, 3 March 1847, p. 221.

36 Ibid., Sir R. Routh to Mr. Trevelyan, 3 March 1847, and Mr. Trevelyan to R. Routh, 6 March 1847, p. 212.

37 "Appendix No. 4," *Fourteenth report from the Select Committee* (572), pp 249-283 [919].

38 *Report from the Select Committee of the House of Lords on the laws relating to the relief of the destitute poor, and into the operation of the medical charities in Ireland; together with the minutes of evidence taken before the said committee,* p. 775, H.C. 1846 (694) (694-II) (694-III), xl Pt.I.1.

39 O'Kelly, pp 146-147.

40 *Report from the Select Committee...House of Lords* (694), p. 768.

41 Ibid., p. 63.

42 *First annual report of the Commissioners for Administering the Laws for Relief of the Poor in Ireland, with appendices,* p. 8, H.C. 1847-48 [963], xxxiii, p. 337.

43 *Papers relating to Proceedings for Relief of Distress, and State of Unions and Workhouses in Ireland, 1848, Fifth Series,* pp 128-131, H.C. 1847-48, [919] [955] [999], liv.313, lv.1, lvi.1

44 Ibid., p. 207.

45 Ibid., p. 247, p. 274.

46 Ibid., p. 303.

47 Ibid., p. 252.

48 Ibid., p. 493.

49 Ibid., p. 562.

50 Ibid., p. 414.

51 Quoted in Kinealy, *The Kindness of Strangers*, p. 156.

52 Ibid., p. 148.

53 Ibid., p. 26.

54 *Report from the Select Committee... House of Lords* (694), p. 396.

55 The British Relief Association spent £67,099 in one year for food and clothing for school children. See *First annual report... Laws for Relief of the Poor in Ireland* [963], p. 18.

56 Kinealy, *The Kindness of Strangers*, p. 163.

57 Lucy Bradshaw, 'An Appeal for Clothing the Naked and Destitute Irish, addressed to all classes, and especially to the Women of England' in William and Mary Howitt (eds.) *Howitt's Journal of Literature and Popular Progress* (3 vols, London, 1847), i, p. 58.

58 *Transactions of the Central Relief Committee,* p. 377.

59 Ibid., pp 379-81.

60 Donations were recorded from New York, Philadelphia, Boston, Charleston, S.C., Newark, N.J., Cincinnati, Ohio, etc. See *Transactions of the Central Relief Committee,* p. 72, pp 335-45, pp 383-84.

61 Kinealy, *The Kindness of Strangers*, p. 164.

62 Ibid., p. 230.

63 Christian Huck, "Clothes make the Irish: Irish dressing and the question of identity" in *Irish Studies Review,* xi, no. 3 (2003), p. 273.

64 Kelleher, p. 94.

65 Susan Meredith, quoted in Kelleher, p. 90.

66 Asenath Nicholson, *Annals of the Famine in Ireland,* ed. Maureen Murphy (Dublin, 1998), p. 38.

67 Ibid., p. 43.

68 Ibid., pp 171-2.

⁶⁹ Ibid., p.107.

⁷⁰ Ibid., pp 84-5.

⁷¹ A similar tactic has been identified in the home decoration of Irish tenant farmers as a way to avoid rent increases. See Claudia Kinmonth, *Irish Country Furniture* (New Haven & London, 1993), p. 177.

⁷² O'Kelly says there were differing levels of clothing deprivation reported at the county level, p. 146.

Works Cited

Primary Sources

Note: Parliamentary sources were viewed on *House of Commons Parliamentary Papers*, (www.ProQuest.com) (Last accessed 16 Oct. 2015). Pagination in notes refers to printed page.

Correspondence from January to March, 1847, relating to the measures adopted for the relief of the distress in Ireland, Commissariat series [Second part.]. H.C. 1847 [796] lii. 333.

First annual report of the Commissioners for Administering the Laws for Relief of the Poor in Ireland, with appendices. H.C. 1847-48 [963] xxxiii. 337.

Fourteenth report from the Select Committee on Poor Laws (Ireland); together with the proceedings of the committee, minutes of evidence, appendix, and index. H.C. 1849 (572) xv Pt.II. 177.

Papers relating to Proceedings for Relief of Distress, and State of Unions and Workhouses in Ireland, 1848. H.C. 1847-48 [919] [955] [999], liv.313, lv.1, lvi.1.

Report from the Select Committee of the House of Lords on the laws relating to the relief of the destitute poor, and into the operation of the medical charities in Ireland; together with the minutes of evidence taken before the said committee. H.C. 1846 (694) (694-II) (694-III) XI Pt.I.1, XI Pt.II.1, 697.

Nicholson, Asenath. *Annals of the Famine in Ireland,* Maureen Murphy (ed.). Dublin: Lilliput Press, 1998.

Report of the Kildallen Penny-A-Week Clothing Society, for the Year 1841. Cavan, 1841. Available at the National Library of Ireland. (www.//catalogue.nli.ie/Record/vtls000538723) (Accessed 7 Aug. 2015).

Note: The following sources were viewed on www.books.google.com (Accessed 15 Oct. 2015).

Bradshaw, Lucy. "An Appeal for Clothing the Naked and Destitute Irish, addressed to all classes, and especially to the Women of England," *Howitt's Journal of Literature and Popular Progress*, William and Mary Howitt (eds.) (2 vols.) London, 1847, ii.

Carlyle, Thomas. *Reminiscences of My Irish Journey in 1849*. New York: Harper and Bros., 1882.

Hall, Samuel C. and Anna Maria Hall. *Ireland: Its Scenery, Character, &c* (3 vols.) London: Low, Marston, Searle, 1842, ii and iii.

Inglis, Henry D. *Ireland in 1834. A Journey throughout Ireland during the Spring, Summer and Autumn of 1834* (2 vols. 3rd ed.) London: Whittaker and Co, 1835.

Nicholls, George, Esq. *Poor Laws – Ireland, Three Reports to Her Majesty's Principal Secretary of State for the Home Department*. London: Clowes and Sons for HMSO, 1838.

Pim, Jonathan. *The Condition and Prospects of Ireland and the Evils Arising from the Present Distribution of Landed Property: With Suggestions for a Remedy*. Dublin: Hodges and Smith, 1848.

Spenser, Edmund. *A View of the Present State of Ireland,* W.L. Renwick (ed.) Oxford University Press, 1970.

Transactions of the Central Relief Committee of the Society of Friends during The Famine in Ireland, in 1846 and 1847. Dublin: Hodges and Smith, 1852.

Tuke, James H. *A Visit to Connaught in the Autumn of 1847, A Letter Addressed to the Central Committee of the Society of Friends, Dublin* (2ⁿᵈ ed.) London and New York, 1848.

Secondary Sources

Crawford, Margaret. "The Great Irish Famine 1845-9: Image versus Reality," Raymond Gillespie and Brian P. Kennedy (eds), *Ireland, Art into History*. Dublin: Town House Pub., 1994, 75-88.

Dunlevy, Mairead. *Dress in Ireland*. New York: Collins Press, 1989.

Huck, Christian. "Clothes Make the Irish: Irish Dressing and the Question of Identity." *Irish Studies Review,* xi, no. 3 (2003), 274-284.

Kelleher, Margaret. *The Feminization of Famine, Expressions of the Inexpressible?* Durham: Duke University Press, N.C., 1997.

Johnson, Kim and Sharon Lennon. "The Social Psychology of Dress," *Berg Fashion Library* (www.bergfashionlibrary.com).

Kinealy, Christine. *Charity and the Great Hunger in Ireland, The Kindness of Strangers* London and New York: Bloomsbury Press, 2013.

Kinmonth, Claudia. *Irish Country Furniture*. New Haven and London: Yale University Press, 1993.

Mark-Fitzgerald, Emily. *Commemorating the Irish Famine: Memory and the Monument* Liverpool University Press, 2013.

O'Kelly, Hilary. "Famine and workhouse clothing," John Crowley, William J. Smith, Mike Murphy (eds.), *Atlas of the Great Irish Famine*. New York University Press, 2013, 145-149.

O'Sullivan, Niamh. *The Tombs of a Departed Race, Illustrations of Ireland's Great Hunger*. Hamden, CT: Quinnipiac University Press, 2014.

⌘

Chapter Seven

The Famine Irish, the Grey Nuns, and the fever sheds of Montreal: prostitution and female religious institution building

Jason King

On 9 June 1847, the Grey Nuns, or Sisters of Charity, entered the fever sheds in Montreal to care for typhus stricken Famine Irish emigrants. During that summer, an estimated 100,000 Irish people fled on "coffin ships' to Canada, 20 percent of whom perished at sea and in quarantine stations in New Brunswick, Grosse Île (5,400), Montreal (6,000) and further inland. The most detailed and evocative eyewitness accounts of their suffering can be found in the French language annals of the Grey Nuns of Montreal which are over five hundred pages in length; but they played little role in shaping historical accounts and the popular memory of the Irish Famine migration, largely because they were unpublished.[1] These records have now been digitized, transcribed, and translated in a Digital Irish Famine Archive that provides a major resource for the study of the Irish Famine migration. In 2015, I expanded this digital archive in partnership with Ireland's Great Hunger Institute at Quinnipiac University, and I also curated an exhibit with the Institute's Founding Director, Christine Kinealy, entitled 'Saving the Famine Irish: The Grey Nuns and the Great Hunger' that ran until March 2016, and then transferred to the Glasnevin Museum in Dublin, and the Centaur Theatre and the Grey Nuns' Hospital National Historic Site in Montreal.[2] Both the digital archive and the exhibit provide eyewitness observations from the vantage point of the nuns about the suffering of Famine Irish emigrants. This chapter seeks to further redress the historiographical record by examining how the Grey Nuns sought to shape and make sense of their story.

According to one of the Grey Nun testimonials:

> The names of the first Sisters who went to the SHEDS are barely mentioned in the convent annals; what a regrettable gap. However, do we ignore them? Is it not the entire community... that we see on its feet?[3]

These convent annals not only recall the experiences of the Grey Nuns, but they also recount them in the collective voice of the "entire community." Elsewhere, I have argued that the story of the Grey Nuns and their rescue of Irish Famine orphans did not become popularized until a generation after the event, especially as it was mediated and transmitted in John Francis Maguire's *The Irish in America* (1868), which brought together French-Canadian and Irish Catholic recollections of 1847 when relations between them appeared particularly fraught.[4] In providing homes for Famine orphans and widows, the Grey Nuns helped create distinct Irish-Catholic social institutions that later became a focal point for communal self-definition and charitable support.[5] Furthermore, French-Canadian female religious communities, including the Grey Nuns, were widely regarded as figures of infamy in the decade before the Famine migration because of the aspersions cast upon them in *The Awful Disclosures of Maria Monk or, The Hidden Secrets of a Nun's Life in a Convent Exposed* (1836).[6]

This chapter examines how the Grey Nuns themselves interpreted their story and ascribed meaning to their experiences of caring for Famine Irish emigrants in the fever sheds of Montreal. More specifically, I will argue that in providing homes for Irish widows and orphans, they helped create a set of women-led institutions as an autonomous, female religious community that was not subordinate to civil or ecclesiastical male authority. Particular emphasis is placed on the influence of both gender and genre in shaping their testimony under the auspices of a singular, collective voice that reinforced their sense of social cohesion and self-determination. Yet their testimonials also repressed acute feelings of anxiety about female sexual impropriety, based not only on the allegations of Maria Monk but also longstanding associations between vulnerable Irish women and prostitution in Montreal in the decades before the arrival of Famine emigrants in 1847. Their legacy of institution building was inspired by a sense of compassion, devotion and self-sacrifice as well as these anxieties about unregulated Irish female sexuality.

On the surface, the endeavours of the Grey Nuns to provide homes for Famine orphans and widows could be attributed to suppressive social mores that found expression in what James Smith has influentially described as "the architecture of containment." "In its concrete form," he avows:

> Ireland's architecture of containment encompassed an assortment of institutions, including mother and baby homes, industrial and reformatory schools, mental asylums, adoption agencies, and Magdalen laundries. These institutions concealed citizens already marginalized by a number of interrelated social phenomena: poverty, illegitimacy, sexual abuse, and infanticide.[7]

Although Smith's study focuses on 20th-century Ireland, the discourse of containment he explores has its origins partly in 19th-century North America, and especially in the controversy surrounding Maria Monk that erupted in 1836, precisely around accusations of the institutional concealment of female and child victims of illegitimacy, sexual abuse and infanticide. Indeed, at the heart of the Maria Monk controversy is a sense of public fascination and repulsion with the concealed women and children incarcerated in these institutions and their propensity to develop lurid fantasies about them. However, the annals of the Grey Nuns do not corroborate Maria Monk's disclosures nor do they have their origins in a discourse of containment. Rather, they express their compassion for Famine Irish emigrants and a spirit of female fellowship that is registered in the institutions they helped create. They also attest to the delicate negotiations between the Grey Nuns and civil and religious male authorities to gain access to the fever sheds. According to the annal:

> They were welcomed with great courtesy and deference by the government steward, who gave all authorization necessary to the Grey Nuns to visit and take care of the pestilent, authorizing them to engage faithful men and women. The venerated Mother Superior, almost surprised by this cordial welcome, is not surprised when she learned that she was preceded by the good M.J. Richard [Father John Jackson Richards]. Seeing the embarrassment of the steward in finding sufficient personnel to tend to the needs of the sick and dying, he suggested asking the Sisters of Charity if they would provide aid.

This steward was protestant; he knew little about Catholic institutions, and did not know who to address himself to; we understand his satisfaction in seeing the Grey Nuns offer themselves. He hastened to conduct them to a home almost in ruin by the river, under the name of the hospital.

What a spectacle unravelled in the eyes of this good mother and her company! Hundreds of people were laying there, most of them on bare planks, pell-mell, men, women and children. The moribund and cadavers are crowded in the same shelter, while there are those that lie on the quays or on pieces of wood thrown here and there along the river.[8]

The Grey Nuns' first impression is the harrowing spectacle of dead and dying Irish emigrants lying haphazardly and unattended in makeshift fever sheds at the water's edge, the "moribund and cadavers... crowded in the same shelter." They also note the cultural confusion surrounding the arrival of the Famine Irish, for whom the Protestant English authorities were not only unprepared but uncertain how even to approach the Grey Nuns, given their unfamiliarity with "Catholic institutions." Most important is their insistence that the Grey Nuns offered themselves of their own volition to care for the fever victims.

Since Marguerite d'Youville had founded the order in 1738, the Grey Nuns had been led by a succession of strong women, including their Mother Superior Elizabeth McMullen in 1847. The sight of numerous Irish cadavers "was a spectacle that should have discouraged Mother McMullen and her generous companions," records the annal. Yet, "on the contrary, they felt their souls lifted to the heights of the mission that the heavens were preparing for them."[9] Although "they were welcomed with great courtesy and deference by the government steward," the site of the fever sheds quickly became a contested cultural space and setting for intense ethno-religious rivalry.[10] Elsewhere I have noted that Father John Jackson Richards – "the good M.J. Richard" above – worked closely with the Grey Nuns to create a separate fever shed for Irish-Catholic orphans in fear that the "Protestants will seize them" shortly before he perished on 23 July 1847.[11] He had arrived in Montreal 40 years earlier as a Methodist preacher, only to become a Catholic convert himself. Indeed, in an affidavit dated 31 October 1807, he solemnly declared that:

after maturely examining the reasons of which the truth of the catholic apostolic roman church is established, I renounce the Methodist sect to which I formerly belonged & of which I was minister – That of my own will & accord I embrace the faith of the said Catholic apostolic Roman church, that I believe what she believes, & condemn what she condemns, & that in the bosom of this church, out of which there is no salvation, I wish to live.[12]

In 1817, Father Richards became the first priest to provide English language services for Montreal's Irish Catholics, and along with the Grey Nuns he tended to the needs of the poor. More to the point, the nuns had to negotiate not only gender hierarchies within the church but also the bitter ethno-religious rivalries that existed in 19th-century Montreal and especially in the compressed space of the fever sheds. Nevertheless, they were not subordinate to civil or ecclesiastical male authorities. After Father Richards's death, the Grey Sisters cooperated with his successor, Father Patrick Dowd, to establish and administer St. Patrick's Orphan Asylum which became a focal point of the city's Irish community.[13] And yet:

consistent with the internal regulations of the community, the Grey Nuns refused to acknowledge his authority in writing, but they tolerated his everyday involvement in the admission of children and management of their personnel.[14]

Thus, the Sisters wielded a high degree of autonomy that was unusual in female religious communities in mid 19th-century North America.

In her ground-breaking study entitled *Habits of Compassion: Irish Catholic Nuns and the Origins of New York's Welfare System, 1830-1920* (2006), Maureen Fitzgerald argues that New York Archbishop John Hughes exerted increasing control over the city's Sisters of Charity in requiring them to staff Catholic schools rather than provide charity for the poor. In her own words:

> The inability of an educational strategy to meet the needs of poor Catholic immigrants was glaring and became more so as famine immigration began. What had been a relatively poor immigrant population became a painfully destitute and miserable congregation of famine survivors, and Hughes's efforts to funnel Catholic funds and labor power into the Catholic educational system seemed to Protestants and many Catholic observers a heartless dismissal of the depth of misery around him. What Hughes failed to perceive or acknowledge was that the hundreds of thousands of destitute Irish who arrived at the New York port throughout the Famine decade held only the most tenuous ties to the formal Catholic Church, and his intransigence in ignoring their needs only distanced them further. Not least important, steering the community's labor power and funds toward education and away from charities left charities, particularly work with children, open to native-born, Protestant reformers.[15]

Indeed, a generation would pass before New York would develop an Irish-Catholic social infrastructure to care for abandoned and destitute children in the form of the Catholic Protectory (1863), an institution whose origins were documented by Mary Anne Sadlier in her novel *Aunt Honor's Keepsake* (1863).[16] By contrast, the Grey Nuns were able to steer their own efforts into charitable institution building for Famine Irish orphans and widows without coming under external control. Nevertheless, they did have to tread carefully to circumvent the authority of Montreal's Bishop Ignace Bourget who came increasingly into conflict with much of the city's clergy, and especially its Irish community leaders, in the decades following the Famine.[17] Two weeks after they entered the fever sheds, the Grey Nuns were forced to withdraw on 24 June 1847 because of illness and fatalities within their ranks. They were replaced by the Sisters of Providence, a female religious community founded only three years earlier by Émilie Tavernier Gamelin. Unlike their predecessors, the Providence Sisters worked under the watchful eye of Bishop Bourget. Before taking the veil, Émilie Tavernier Gamelin had cared for destitute, elderly women for over a decade since 1832, and she maintained close ties across the community with Catholic benefactors as well as members of the anti-clerical *Patriote* movement, who had instigated a rebellion in 1837.[18] As Mother Superior of the Providence Sisters, she had considerably less autonomy. After they were summoned to the fever sheds by Bishop Bourget, the Providence Sisters, like the Grey Nuns, were struck by the spectacle of Irish suffering in their midst:

> From hundreds of the sick, couched upon straw, in the wrestlings of their agony came forth dolorous cries; little children, who were still clasped in the arms of mothers who had died during the night, wept and cried; corpses lying here and there, already exhaled the odor of death; women who were scarcely able to drag themselves about, sought in that frightful chaos, for a husband or child of whose fate they were ignorant. Such was the dismal picture presented by that field of suffering.

> The Sisters set to work at once, causing the dead to be removed, and lavishing their care upon the sick.[19]

As the Grey Nuns had done, the Sisters of Providence provided homes for Irish orphans, and they accompanied Bishop Bourget when the children were evacuated from the fever sheds on 11 July 1847 at his behest to their shelter in the heart of the city.[20] Yet, even before the typhus epidemic was fully contained, Mother Gamelin was confronted with increasing clerical strictures. "Between September and October 1847," notes Bettina Bradbury, Bishop Bourget

> listed fifty-seven indictments: Émilie sought to keep too much control in her own hands; she desired the esteem of the world too much; there was so much work to do that religious observances were neglected; silences were not being observed; the novices were not being trained properly, nor kept sufficiently apart from the sisters; and so on.[21]

Indeed, Mother Gamelin had even been censured for wanting to keep "the locks of hair that she had saved from each of her three dead children" close to her heart.[22] In contrast, the Grey Nuns' Mother Superior, Elizabeth McMullen, kept her distance from Bishop Bourget and other clerical authorities to preserve the independence of her sisters. Consequently, the Grey Nuns enjoyed an extraordinary degree of autonomy in the fever sheds, which reinforced their sense of faith and fidelity to one another.

The Grey Nuns' spirit of female fellowship is repeatedly emphasized both in the content and especially the style of their annals. In his ground-breaking study *Imagined Communities: Reflections on the Origins and Spread of Nationalism* (1983), Benedict Anderson borrows from Walter Benjamin to distinguish between "what Benjamin calls Messianic time, a simultaneity of past and future in an instantaneous present," and an idea of "homogenous, empty time," in which simultaneity is, as it were, "transverse, cross-time, marked not by prefiguring and fulfilment, but by temporal coincidence, and measured by clock and calendar."[23] Anderson associates the latter with the rise of print-capitalism, the literary forms of the novel and the newspaper, and origins of national consciousness in the 18th century; he ascribes the former apprehensions of "messianic time" to religious communities and scribal culture that corresponds with the outlook of the Grey Nun annals. More specifically, the annals are written from the collective viewpoint of the entire community in which temporal distinctions between past and "instantaneous present" are frequently collapsed to suggest the immediacy of Irish suffering and religious sacrifice even years after their recollection. In inscribing and reciting the annals, the Grey Nuns do not merely summon to memory the deeds of their fellow sisters and predecessors, but they relive their experiences in an "instantaneous present." The names of individual sisters became subsumed within the entire community under the auspices of the pronoun "we." Thus, their collective recollection of their arrival in the fever sheds is recounted in the present tense to give the events of years ago a sense of imminence and urgency:

> Despite the mud and other inconveniences, the sisters made their journey within twenty minutes, already hearing the groans of the ill and the wails of the dying. . . We disperse ourselves in this unfamiliar maze. . . Could we imagine for a moment the spectacle this multitude of men and women piled pell-mell offered, up to three or four in the same bed, indifferent to everything, groaning, however, heartbreakingly? We were running here, running there . . . supporting a poor, dying woman, ripping away from her the poor infant she clung to so close to her heart. . . We point out the heavens to another while wiping away his agonizing sweat. We have the cadavers taken away from those still breathing, and we took a look around us . . . We step outside the shelter only to find more of the miserable poor, recumbent without salvation, we eagerly go to their aid, multiplying our steps without counting. What misery! Who could describe them? This is

not just a family, or one hundred that are ill, but almost an entire nation feeling the anxieties of this agony.[24]

In recounting their experiences, the Grey Nuns largely eschew individual deeds to emphasize the actions of the entire community. Their narrative is focalized from the perspective of a present tense, collective voice that conveys the nuns' sense of disorientation and the intensity of Irish suffering when they first arrived in the sheds. The sheer scale of Irish misery is also intimated in the figure of the "poor infant" ripped away from the "dying woman" who becomes a synecdoche for the family and the "entire nation feeling the anxieties of this agony."

Moreover, when the annal does focus on the deeds of individual sisters, it is in roving glimpses that appear almost cinematic in their juxtaposition of single figures standing in for them all. Impressions of individual nuns flash briefly into view and then quickly recede. This passage below is focalized from a collective vantage point that oscillates between the pronouns "we" and "I" in an "instantaneous present" tense that also collapses any distinction with the past:

> The odour that these cadavers produced and the horror they naturally caused add to the distressing picture of this situation. We, nevertheless, see the sisters calmly patrolling around the diverse enclosures; they take charge of the department Mother McMullen trusted them with. Sister BRAULT expends energy, as well as showing remarkable strength to gently care for her beloved sick...

> Sister Desjardins appears to us as an unchanged, flowering figure. Oh! If she had in this moment her brushes and a canvas, she would faithfully reproduce the gloomy scenes of our sad shelters. But it is to these poor sick individuals that she presently gives all her time.

> Over there, at the end of the dark corridor, I see the silhouette of Sister Marie [Barbeau]. She strives to find the most miserable.[25]

In fact, Sister Marie (Barbeau) perished on 21 July 1847 as a result of caring for Famine emigrants, but with each retelling of her story in the annal's "messianic time" she rejoins the community of her sisters to help alleviate the "most miserable" of the suffering Irish emigrants. Her silhouette evokes her liminal position between past and present, individual action and communal recollection, life and death.

More broadly, the act of writing and reading the annals in an "instantaneous present" reinforced the nuns' sense of communal identity and individual and collective sacrifice in carrying out their charitable activities and religious duties. They not only commemorated the deeds of their fallen sisters, but also recorded the founding of institutions that they helped to create. The annals also obliquely registered the nuns' anxieties about Irish female sexuality which had become synonymous with prostitution in Montreal in the decade before the Famine migration and the arrival of unprecedented numbers of destitute Irish women and children. In her recent study *Beyond Brutal Passions: Prostitution in Early Nineteenth-Century Montreal* (2015), Mary Anne Poutanen has noted that female Irish emigrants were especially vulnerable to becoming prostitutes and increasingly prominent in Montreal's sex trade in the late 1830s and early 1840s.[26] She explains:

> A penniless, young, single Irish woman disembarking after a long and treacherous voyage crossing the Atlantic did not have the same breadth of options as did a [French]

Canadian woman with access to an extended family and long-standing links to the community.[27]

She further expounds, "Newcomers, including those who were Irish and unmarried, turned to sex commerce to solve the more immediate need of securing food and shelter."[28] Indeed, Poutanen dwells on the propensity of vulnerable Irish women to enter Montreal's sex trade because of their precarious social position and absence of familial and cultural networks for their support. In her own words:

> Most (in terms of overall numbers) of the streetwalkers were Irish immigrants. As racialized subjects, being single, Irish and Catholic presented a host of problems for these newcomers, who found themselves near the bottom of a hierarchy of whiteness... That unmarried female Irish immigrants were considered outside the purview of appropriate male authority embodied in father and husbands – having migrated on their own – adds another complex layer. These women were targeted because of their ethnicity, marital status, social class, and, as recent immigrants to British North America, because their livelihoods were precarious and thus considered suspect.[29]

Clearly, by the early 1840s, Irish immigrant women were often being stigmatized as streetwalkers throughout the city of Montreal.

These problems were immeasurably compounded, however, by the arrivals of the Famine Irish in much greater numbers than past emigrants. Soon after the Famine influx, Father Patrick Dowd, who worked closely with the Grey Nuns, protested vehemently about female emigrant neglect in a letter to his father back in Ireland: "I have had a very large number of emigrants this year," he claimed, adding:

> Whole cargos of widows with small children and young females emptied out from poor houses in the south and west land here not knowing where to turn to – their young exposed to the worst of dangers from their exposed condition. The widows unable to work from the burden of their children. This is one of our greatest embarrassments in Montreal. Why send out a poor woman with three or four helpless children to lose herself and them in a strange land where she will have no neighbour or relative to pity or assist her? Hundreds of children are yearly in this country [sent out] by the cruel – I would say barbarous – policy of your landlords and Poor Law Guardians.[30]

It was the anxiety that these vulnerable young Irish women and children would follow in the footsteps of their emigrant predecessors because of "their exposed condition" that motivated the Grey Nuns to create institutions for their support.

The Sisters' apprehensions about unregulated female sexuality were also compounded by the legacy of Maria Monk. In her *Awful Disclosures* (1836), which became the second best-selling book in the Ante-Bellum United States (after *Uncle Tom's Cabin*), Maria Monk directly implicated the same priests and nuns who cared for Famine Irish emigrants in Montreal's fever sheds in 1847 in her lurid tale of their illicit sexual relations and strangulation of their unbaptized infants.[31] More specifically, Maria Monk alleged that she had to flee the Hôtel Dieu convent in Montreal after she was impregnated by the Irish community parish priest, Father Patrick Phelan, who sought to murder their child to dispose of the evidence of their unholy coupling.[32] By definition, their illegitimate child was proscribed from birth in wedlock, the sacrilegious progeny of Catholic clergy and female religious who were betrothed to the Lord but had broken their sacred vows in acts of "criminal intercourse."[33] The sacrilegious image of the uncloistered nun with the Irish child in Maria Monk's *Awful Disclosures* became inverted and transfigured into the sacred memory of the nuns who broke their cloister to care for Irish infants in Montreal's fever sheds in 1847.

In fact, Maria Monk had masqueraded as an uncloistered nun who had escaped from her convent, yet was in reality a former inmate of Montreal's Magdalen Asylum. According to an affidavit from the Matron of the Asylum in 1836, "Maria has for many years led the life of a stroller and prostitute... [and] she found her to be very uncertain and grossly deceitful."[34] The question of whether she had fled from a respectable convent or a disreputable Magdalen Asylum was at the heart of the controversy and veracity of her tale. In spite of the aspersions she cast, the same affidavit affirmed that Monk's "description given of the Hôtel Dieu Convent is alone applicable to the Magdalen Asylum."[35] As Poutanen notes: "the institution was fenced, as was typical of Magdalen asylums elsewhere. A magdalene had to give up contact with the outside world since her reform necessitated isolation, confinement, and enclosure."[36]

Montreal's Magdalen Asylum was also quite a short-lived institution, which operated only from 1829 to 1836.[37] Nevertheless, Maria Monk's sensational account of a nun who breaks her cloister to save her illegitimate child stirred public fascination and seemed to corroborate the most sinister impressions of the convent as an architectural site of containment for the concealment of ostensibly wayward women. Her *Awful Disclosures* cast a long shadow over the city's convents and female religious communities.

Inevitably, the legacy of Maria Monk had intensified the Grey Nuns' anxieties about Irish female sexuality when faced with the arrivals of destitute emigrant women in Montreal with few options other than to follow in her footsteps as strollers and prostitutes. Ironically, the very same Father Patrick Phelan whom Monk had accused of impregnating her played a significant role in helping the Grey Nuns create institutions to care for vulnerable Irish women, widows and orphans. In his papers can be found notice of a hastily convened meeting of charitable women and female religious on 28 August 1847 to protect the "young and destitute female emigrants" in their midst. The notice reads:

> It has occurred to several benevolent friends of religious that the young and destitute female emigrants from whom their parents and natural protectors have been prostrated by the unsparing ravages of the scourge with which it has pleased Divine Providence to visit those landing on our shores, should have some shield interposed between them and the pernicious wishes of temptation to which through their forlorn and helpless condition they must inevitably be exposed. With this charitable and praiseworthy object in view, it has been thought desirable to secure charitable premises for their reception and accommodation. Of the zealous and benevolent cooperation of the ladies of this congregation is earnestly requested in order to the carrying out of the great + charitable object of affording refuge + protection to these poor destitute females...
>
> A meeting will be held at [?] o'clock today or tomorrow afternoon at [blank space] where measures will be adopted for... the preservation of the purity of these helpless beings of their own sex, to render their valuable assistance and cooperation in this most praiseworthy endeavour.[38]

As a result of the meeting, the Grey Nuns helped to establish and administer St. Ann's Asylum, from which their handwritten "Rules to be observed by the Emigrant widows and young women received in the St Ann's Asylum" survives.[39]

This "Asylum for the adult female orphans at the Sheds" opened at the end of September, 1847.[40] According to the *Montreal Pilot*, its object was "to prepare these females, by moral and industrious training, for the duties of servants or assistant housekeepers in the various departments of domestic economy."[41] Even in the midst of a typhus epidemic, the author expressed anxiety that unprepared and unscrupulous servants could

> bring no warrant for industry, and no certificate of moral character or worth. Hence disease, intemperance and dishonesty often find their way into the nursery, and even to a larger circle of domestic labours, and afford a spectacle which parents and children are often painfully constrained to witness.[42]

Thus, adult female orphans and widows were offered the prospect of not just physical but also moral rehabilitation in moving from the fever sheds to train as domestic servants in St. Ann's Asylum.

Nevertheless, the Grey Nuns endeavoured to create a compassionate and mutually supportive environment as recorded in the "Rules to be observed by the Emigrant widows and young women." The document provides an overview of Famine Irish women's daily existence in a hastily improvised shelter that appears austere and mundane, but the complete obverse of the lurid descriptions of Maria Monk. The rules stipulate that these recently bereaved emigrant widows should lead a contemplative lifestyle quite similar to being in a convent, in which their appearance, daily periods of silence and frequent prayer, domestic chores, departures from the asylum, exchange of goods, meal times, hours for receiving visitors, and for sleep are all meticulously prescribed. On the surface, their routine might not seem all that different from the Magdalen Asylum in which "all aspects of community life were regulated."[43] Whether the young women in St. Ann were consoled or disconcerted by their highly regimented existence after their ordeal in the fever sheds, there can little doubt about what transpired behind the asylum walls. The observance of their rules could hardly fuel lurid fantasies about the concealment of vulnerable young women that Maria Monk had purported to expose. There could be no "awful disclosures" of such a meticulously documented daily regimen. More importantly, the emigrant widows and young women were not incarcerated in the asylum but rather encouraged to be mutually supportive and "endeavour to heal each other" in a spirit of female fellowship. Indeed, the Grey Nuns sought to transmit their own spirit of female fellowship to the widows and orphans in their care.

Their archival records also reveal the Sisters' vigilance in preserving their independence in the process of institution building. Although St. Ann's asylum was a temporary facility that closed soon after the Famine influx in April 1848,[44] the Grey Nuns also collaborated with Father Patrick Dowd to establish and administer St. Patrick's Orphan Asylum, which became the cornerstone of Montreal's Irish Catholic social infrastructure from 1851 until the early 1970s.[45] In the Grey Nuns' annal entitled "Foundation of St. Patrick's Asylum," Father Dowd is recalled as "the young Sulpician… who arrived from France on the 21st June 1848, and was almost immediately appointed chaplain for the poor Irish." He is also described as "a zealous young priest who was willing to work" tirelessly with the Grey Nuns to care for Irish emigrants.[46] One of the most poignant sections of the annal recounts how Father Dowd was cast in a King Solomon-like role to reunite the lost Irish child, Rose Brown, with her mother, Suzanne, after they became separated and Rose was adopted, only for them to be miraculously reunited.[47] When the Famine orphans in the nuns' care were stigmatized for walking to church with "no shoes" and "barely clothed" in a paupers' procession, Father Dowd promised and delivered clothing and "footware for the following Sunday."[48] The annal repeatedly pays tribute to him and his "incredible sacrifice to build this house."[49]

Nevertheless, the Grey Nuns refused to acknowledge Father Dowd's authority in writing. Moreover, they received written assurances from him that their independence would not be compromised when the orphanage was incorporated in 1855. On 19 February 1855, Father Dowd wrote to the Grey Nuns' Mother Superior:

> In order to determine finally the Direction of the St. Patrick's orphan asylum, and thereby prevent any misunderstanding or difficulty arising on the subject in future, I respectfully submit to the Community, through you, the following arrangements...In the first place, the Sisters placed in the Asylum by their Superior shall not be interfered with, in any respect, in the observances of the Rules of the Community; and shall not be required to change those Rules, or to depart from them, in any particulars, by the Director of the Asylum, unless with the consent, and under the authority of their Superiors...You will perceive that this arrangement requires no new concession on part of the community.[50]

Thus, the Grey Nuns, unlike the Providence Sisters or Sisters of Charity in New York, maintained a high degree of autonomy in their charitable activities and received a written guarantee that their authority "shall not be interfered with" nor undermined without their consent. At a time when other female religious communities were coming increasingly under the control of their male superiors, the Grey Nuns made "no new concessions" nor compromised their independence. Indeed, when a bitter war of words broke out between Montreal's Bishop Bourget and Father Dowd about who had done more to care for Famine orphans a generation after their arrival in 1866, the sisters remained above the fray and continued to operate the asylum they had helped create unhindered by either of them.[51] They vigilantly preserved their institutional prerogatives which other female religious communities struggled to maintain.

In conclusion, the Grey Nuns' annals recount their legacy of institution building in response to the Famine influx which engendered anxieties about unregulated female sexuality based on the increasing association of vulnerable Irish women with prostitution in Montreal, particularly in the wake of the allegations of Maria Monk. Unlike other female religious communities, they did not relinquish their autonomy in creating homes for Irish orphans and widows. They entered the fever sheds of their own volition and negotiated with English civil and French-Canadian ecclesiastical authorities to preserve their independence in caring for Famine emigrants and creating institutions for their support. The Grey Nuns' annals do not recount their experiences as past events but in an "instantaneous present" tense that foregrounds communal over individual endeavour with a sense of immediacy and self-sufficiency that reinforces their collective identity. In this instantaneous present, the silhouette of Sister Marie (Barbeau) is summoned to memory to rejoin her female religious community from whose ranks she had fallen in caring for Irish emigrants, an ephemeral shadow that flickers to life with each retelling of the story. It is a story of institution building that in no way conforms to *The Awful Disclosures of Maria Monk*. Nor does it corroborate suspicions that they helped to create an "architecture of containment" for the concealment of the Irish widows and orphans, such as the Magdalen Asylum from which Maria Monk's accusations had originated. This is not to deny that the Grey Nuns sought to profess their faith rather than empower women, nor that they internalized the prejudices of their age, especially towards prostitutes who received little charitable aid from Montreal's female religious orders.[52] Nevertheless, they encouraged the Famine Irish widows and children in their care to be mutually supportive and to "endeavour to heal one another" in the same spirit of female fellowship that is registered in the annals. Ultimately, that spirit found lasting expression in the Grey Nuns' legacy of establishing autonomous female-led institutions to care for Famine Irish orphans and widows who had nowhere else to turn. As Christine Kinealy contends, "their story is one of kindness, compassion, and true charity... a remarkable story that deserves to be better known."[53]

Endnotes

[1] See Jason King, "The Remembrance of Irish Famine Migrants in the fever sheds of Montreal" in Marguérite Corporaal, Christopher Cusack, Lindsay Janssen (eds.) *Global Legacies of the Great Irish Famine: Transnational and Interdisciplinary Perspectives* (New York, 2014), pp 245-66.

[2] See http://faminearchive.nuigalway.ie [accessed 6 Dec. 2015]. Also see, http://www.quinnipiac.edu/institutes-and-centers/irelands-great-hunger-institute/saving-the-famine-irish-the-grey-nuns-and-the-great-hunger/ [accessed 6 Dec. 2015].

[3] Grey Nuns Famine Annal, 'The Typhus of 1847', *Ancien Journal*, Volume II (1847), 33-49; See http://faminearchive.nuigalway.ie/docs/grey-nuns/TheTyphusof1847.pdf; [accessed 6 Dec. 2015].

[4] John Francis Maguire, *The Irish in America* (London: Longmans, Green and Company, 1868), quoted in Jason King, "Remembering Famine orphans: The transmission of Famine memory between Ireland and Quebec" in Christian Noack, Lindsay Jannsen, and Vincent Comerford (eds.) *Holodomor in Ukraine and Great Famine in Ireland: Histories, Representations and Memories* (London, 2012), 115-144; Jason King, "French-Canadian and Irish Memories of Montreal's Famine Migration in 1847" in Patrick Fitzgerald, Christine Kinealy, and Gerard Moran (eds.) *Irish Hunger and Migration: Myth, Memory and Memorialization* (Connecticut, 2015).

[5] Marguérite Corporaal and Jason King, 'Irish global migration and memory: Transnational perspectives of Ireland's Famine exodus" in *Atlantic Studies: Global Currents*, 11, no. 3 (2014), pp 306-7; Jason King, 'L'Historiographie irlando-québécoise: conflits et conciliations entre Canadiens français et Irlandais', *Bulletin D'Histoire Politique*, 18, no. 3 (2010), pp 22-27.

[6] Jason King, "Remembering and Forgetting the Famine Irish in Quebec: Genuine and false memoirs, communal memory, and migration," *Irish Review*, 44 (2012), pp 20-41.

[7] James Smith, *Ireland's Magdalen Laundries: and the Nation's Architecture of Containment* (Notre Dame, Indiana, 2007), p. xiii.

[8] Grey Nuns, *Ancien Journal* II, 16.

[9] Ibid.

[10] See Jason King, "The Remembrance of Irish Famine Migrants in the Fever sheds of Montreal," pp 245-66.

[11] Grey Nuns Famine Annal, *Ancien Journal*, Volume I (1847), 18. See http://faminearchive.nuigalway.ie/docs/grey-nuns/GreyNunsFamineAnnalAncienJournalVolumeI.1847.pdf [accessed 6 Dec. 2015]. See also King, "French-Canadian and Irish Memories of Montreal's Famine Migration in 1847," p. 97.

[12] Unpublished affidavit. Department of Archives. Society of the Priests of Saint-Sulpice, Montreal. P1:21.30. 11.

[13] Grey Nuns Famine Annal, *Foundation of St. Patrick's Asylum* (1849). See http://faminearchive.nuigalway.ie/docs/grey-nuns/GreyNunsFamineAnnalFoundationofStPatricksOrphanAsylum.pdf [accessed 6 Dec. 2015]. See also King, "Remembering Famine Orphans," pp 115-44.

[14] Sherry Olson, "St Patricks' and the Irish Catholics" in Dominique Delandres, John A. Dickson, Oliver Hubert (eds.) *The Sulpicians of Montreal: A History of Power and Discretion, 1657-2007* (Montreal, 2013), pp 303-18.

[15] Maureen Fitzgerald, *Habits of Compassion: Irish Catholic Nuns and the Origins of New York's Welfare System, 1830-1920* (Urbana and Chicago, 2006), pp 49-50.

[16] Mary Anne Sadlier, *Aunt Honor's Keepsake* (Montreal and New York, 1863).

[17] See King, "Remembering Famine Orphans," pp 115-44.

[18] Bettina Bradbury, *Wife to Widow: Lives, Laws, and Politics in Nineteenth-Century Montreal* (Vancouver, 2011), pp 298-300.

[19] Anna T. Sadlier, *Life of Mother Gamelin: Foundress and First Superior of the Sisters of Charity of Providence* (Montreal, 1912), pp 191-92.

[20] Ibid., p.193.

[21] Bradbury, *Wife to Widow*, pp 317-18.

[22] Ibid., p. 317.

[23] Benedict Anderson, *Imagined Communities: Reflections on the Origins and Spread of Nationalism* (London, 1983), p. 24.

[24] Grey Nuns, *Ancien Journal* II, pp 18-19.

[25] Ibid., p. 22.

[26] Mary Anne Poutanen, *Beyond Brutal Passions: Prostitution in Early Nineteenth-Century Montreal* (Montreal and Kingston, 2015), p. 172.

[27] Ibid., p. 143.

[28] Ibid., p. 315.

[29] Ibid., pp 137-38.

[30] Unpublished letter from Father Patrick Dowd, Montreal Seminary, 25 Oct. 1850, to his father, Patrick Dowd, Listulk, Dunleer, Co. Louth. I am grateful to Gabriel Mathews for making this letter available to me.

[31] Maria Monk, *Awful Disclosures of Maria Monk as exhibited in a narrative of her sufferings* (New-York, Howe and Bates, 1836); King, "Remembering and Forgetting the Famine Irish in Quebec," pp 20-41.

[32] J.J. Slocum, *Confirmations of Maria Monk's Disclosures concerning the Hôtel Dieu nunnery of Montreal; preceded by a reply to the priest's book* (London, 1837), p. 292.

[33] Ibid., p. 47.

[34] Maria Monk, affidavit of Madame D.C. McDonnell [sic], matron of the Montreal Magdalen Asylum, Ste. Genevieve Street (Montreal, 1836), p. 1.

[35] Ibid.

[36] Poutanen, *Beyond Brutal Passions*, p. 155.

[37] Ibid., pp 151-7.

[38] Unpublished notice. Department of Archives. Society of the Priests of Saint-Sulpice. Montreal. 03/34. #13, 14, 15 Phelan.

[39] Unpublished 'Rules to be observed by the Emigrant widows and young women received in the St Ann's Asylum'. Archival Services and Collections, Sisters of Charity of Montreal [Grey Nuns]. L008/C,7.8.

[40] *Montreal Pilot*, 30 September 1847.

[41] Ibid.

[42] Ibid.

[43] Poutanen, *Beyond Brutal Passions*, p. 155.

[44] Grey Nuns, "The Typhus of 1847," p. 75.

[45] Ruth Rost Levy's *Bittersweet Reflections* (Ottawa, 2007) provides a largely positive mid-20th -century account of the Grey Nuns and St. Patrick's Orphanage from the perspective of a child who was raised there.

[46] Grey Nuns, *Foundation of St. Patrick's Asylum*, p. 11.

[47] Ibid., pp 9-11. Rose Brown is listed as one of the orphans under the care of the Grey Nuns who was placed "with her mother" in their unpublished "Orphans of Point St. Charles" document dated 19 March 1848. Archival Services and Collections, Sisters of Charity of Montreal [Grey Nuns]. SGM 89.

[48] Grey Nuns, *Foundation of St. Patrick's Asylum*, p. 13.

[49] Ibid., p. 17.

[50] Unpublished letter. Department of Archives. Society of the Priests of Saint-Sulpice. Montreal. P1-35-111.

[51] King, "Remembering Famine Orphans," pp 130-3.

[52] Poutanen, *Beyond Brutal Passions*, p. 95.

[53] Quoted in Matthew Skwiat, "The Grey Nuns at Quinnipiac" in *Irish America*, see http://irishamerica.com/2015/05/the-grey-nuns-at-quinnipiac/ [accessed 6 Dec. 2015]. Christine Kinealy and Jason King brought that story to a larger audience in the "Saving the Famine Irish: The Grey Nuns and the Great Hunger" exhibit that they curated at Quinnipiac University, 1 April 2015 – 18 March 2016. http://www.quinnipiac.edu/institutes-and-centers/irelands-great-hunger-institute/saving-the-famine-irish-the-grey-nuns-and-the-great-hunger/; accessed 6 Dec. 2015.

Works Cited

Anderson, Benedict. *Imagined Communities: Reflections on the Origins and Spread of Nationalism.* London: Verso, 1983.

Bradbury, Bettina. *Wife to Widow: Lives, Laws, and Politics in Nineteenth-Century Montreal.* Vancouver: University of British Columbia Press, 2011.

Corporaal, Marguérite and Jason King. "Irish Global Migration and Memory: Transnational Perspectives of Ireland's Famine Exodus." *Atlantic Studies: Global Currents* 11, no. 3 (2014), 301-320.

Fitzgerald, Maureen. *Habits of Compassion: Irish Catholic Nuns and the Origins of New York's Welfare System, 1830-1920.* Urbana and Chicago: University of Illinois Press, 2006.

King, Jason. "French-Canadian and Irish Memories of Montreal's Famine Migration in 1847," in Patrick Fitzgerald, Christine Kinealy and Gerard Moran (eds.), *Irish Hunger and Migration: Myth, Memory and Memorialization*, 95-106. Hamden, Connecticut: Quinnipiac University Press, 2015.

—— "L'Historiographie irlando-québécoise: conflits et conciliations entre Canadiens français et Irlandais." *Bulletin D'Histoire Politique* 18, no. 3 (2010), 13-36.

—— Irish Famine Archive (2015). Available from http://faminearchive.nuigalway.ie; accessed 6 Dec. 2015.

—— Irish Famine Archive (2015). Grey Nuns Famine Annal, *Ancien Journal*, Volume I (1847); available from http://faminearchive.nuigalway.ie/docs/grey-nuns/GreyNunsFamineAnnalAncienJournalVolumeI.1847.pdf; accessed 6 Dec. 2015.

—— Irish Famine Archive (2015). Grey Nuns Famine Annal, "The Typhus of 1847," *Ancien Journal*, Volume II (1847), available from http://faminearchive.nuigalway.ie/docs/grey-nuns/TheTyphusof1847.pdf; accessed 6 Dec. 2015.

—— "Remembering and Forgetting the Famine Irish in Quebec: Genuine and False Memoirs, Communal Memory, and Migration." *Irish Review* 44 (2012), 20-41.

—— "Remembering Famine Orphans: The Transmission of Famine Memory Between Ireland and Quebec," in *Holodomor in Ukraine and Great Famine in Ireland: Histories, Representations and Memories,* ed. by Christian Noack, Lindsay Jannsen, and Vincent Comerford, 115-144. London: Anthem Press, 2012.

—— "The Remembrance of Irish Famine Migrants in the Fever Sheds of Montreal," in *Global Legacies of the Great Irish Famine: Transnational and Interdisciplinary Perspectives* ed. by Marguérite Corporaal, Christopher Cusack, Lindsay Janssen, 245-266. New York: Peter Lang, 2014.

Monk, Maria. *Awful Disclosures of Maria Monk as exhibited in a narrative of her sufferings.* New York: Howe & Bates, 1836.

Olson, Sherry. "St Patricks and the Irish Catholics," in *The Sulpicians of Montreal: A History of Power and Discretion, 1657-2007*, ed. by Dominique Delandres, John A. Dickson, Oliver Hubert, 303 -318. Montreal: Librairie Wilson & Lafleur, 2013.

Poutanen, Mary Anne. *Beyond Brutal Passions: Prostitution in Early Nineteenth-Century Montreal.* Montreal and Kingston: McGill-Queens University Press, 2015.

Sadlier, Anna T. *Life of Mother Gamelin: Foundress and First Superior of the Sisters of Charity of Providence.* Montreal, 1912.

Sadlier, Mary Anne. *Aunt Honor's Keepsake.* Montreal and New York, 1863.

Skwiat, Matthew. "The Grey Nuns at Quinnipiac," *Irish America*: http://irishamerica.com/2015/05/the-grey-nuns-at-quinnipiac/; accessed 6 Dec. 2015.

Smith, James. *Ireland Magdalen Laundries: and the Nation's Architecture of Containment*. Notre Dame, Indiana: Notre Dame University Press, 2007.

Slocum, J.J. *Confirmations of Maria Monk's Disclosures concerning the Hôtel Dieu nunnery of Montreal; preceded by a reply to the priest's book.* London: James S. Hodson, 1837.

—— *Awful Disclosures by Maria Monk of the Hôtel Dieu Nunnery of Montreal*, 3rd edition. London: James S. Hodson, 1851 [1836]).

Chapter Eight

"Permanent deadweight": female pauper emigration from Mountbellew workhouse to Canada

Gerard Moran

On 16 July 1853, the *Primrose* left Limerick port with emigrants bound for Quebec. Among the passengers were 50 girls from the Mountbellew workhouse in Co. Galway whose passage was paid by the local board of guardians, and who were being sent to Canada to start a new life. The national and local newspapers barely mentioned that the girls were leaving, which was not surprising given the massive exodus taking place from Ireland in the immediate years after the Great Famine. The Mountbellew girls were part of an emigration process put in place over the previous five years by which young workhouse females had their passage paid to the colonies. While the press had little comment on these paupers that were leaving, equally the story of those sent to Canada from the workhouses has received little attention from historians. This chapter builds on earlier research that explores the sending out of Ireland's poorest emigrants, who had their fares paid by the British government, landlords, poor law unions, and philanthropists and who have been largely overlooked in the history of Irish emigration.[1]

Throughout the 19th century, Ireland's greatest export was her people, with an estimated eight million leaving between 1815 and 1914, mainly for English-speaking destinations. The exodus was not uniform and major differences and contrasts are evident in relation to patterns, trends and experiences. Regardless of this diversity, until recently Irish emigration was treated as a homogenous activity, with interest concentrating on the second half of the 19th century because of the Great Famine exodus and the legacy that followed. The diversity and range of the emigration was ignored and overlooked, with no attempt to examine the various sub groupings who left. While emigration in the post-Famine period was increasingly paid through remittances from friends and relations who had already settled in North America, the poorest sections of Irish society were unable to avail themselves of this source. What is sometimes airbrushed out of the emigration debate is the role that the assisted passage schemes played in the emigration experience and the fact that many factions of the poor would have been unable to leave without the financial support of landlords, the government, philanthropists and agencies such as the Poor Law. Between 1848 and 1889, the Poor Law assisted more than 67,000 people to emigrate, nearly two percent of the total who left.[2] Almost 20,000 were sent between 1848 and 1859, the "invisible emigrants" of whom, with the exception of those assisted under the Female Orphan Scheme to Australia, little is known.

The problem with the Poor Law Union records for the study of emigration for the 1850s is that, when they exist, some of the minute books are less detailed than others. Some provide information on the names, ages, the length of time the emigrants spent in the workhouses, the electoral divisions they came from, the clothing they received for traveling and the date they left the workhouse; while for others the data is terse, just giving the numbers that were sent. As a result, it is difficult to provide the complete picture of the emigrants sent out from the workhouses during the Great Famine, but this can be compensated for in a small number of unions, such as the 50 female paupers assisted to Quebec by the Mountbellew union on the *Primrose*.

When the Poor Law was established in Ireland in 1838, its function was to provide relief for the destitute poor through the workhouse system. One hundred and thirty workhouses were built in the country and while the majority were functioning when the potato crop failed in 1845, most had been operational for less than three years and were not in a position to deal with the catastrophe with which they had to contend. By late 1846, most of the workhouses were filled to capacity, such as in Gort, Co. Galway, where the funds were totally exhausted by November. Twelve months later, their position had deteriorated as a result of the government's decision to wind down the public works schemes, while the subsequent introduction of the Gregory Quarter Acre clause led to large-scale evictions.[3] Landlords cleared their estates of tenants with small holdings who were in arrears with their rents for a number of years, aware that these people would receive relief in the workhouses. While the figure for the clearances between 1847 and 1848 are entirely inaccurate, large-scale evictions that took place between 1848 and 1854 resulted in 48,740 families—or one-quarter of a million people people—being evicted although, as James Donnelly points out, this figure does not include families who "voluntarily" gave up their holdings to the landowners, such as on the Shirley estate in Co. Monaghan.[4] The dispossessed turned to the workhouses for sanctuary in numbers that the system was unable to handle. The Poor Law was never designed to cope with a famine situation, and its architect, Sir George Nicholls, had made this clear to the government in 1838. Within 10 years of its establishment, the Poor Law had to deal with such a national crisis with the situation being even worse along the western seaboard where large-scale evictions had taken place as in the Kilrush, Clifden, Westport and Castlebar unions. Between July and December 1848, 6,098 people were evicted in the Kilrush union and George Poulett Scrope, a sympathetic English politician, estimated that 20,000 were evicted between 1847 and 1848, while in east Galway, a series of evictions had been carried out on the Gerrard estate at Ballinlass near Mountbellew between 1846 and 1848.[5] By June 1849, as a result of eviction, 30,000 people in the Kilrush union, more than half the population, depended on the Poor Law for survival.[6]

There was extreme pressure on the Poor Law between 1848-52 because of the increasing demands being placed on its services. In many areas, it was unable to cope with the rising pauper population who sought admission into the workhouses. This crisis was exacerbated by the failure to collect the rates needed for the upkeep of the system. By June 1850, the combined inmate population in the workhouses was more than 260,000 representing nearly four percent of the entire population. Some unions were unable to cope with the demands on their limited resources. In January 1850, the Scariff workhouse in Co. Clare could not take in any further inmates. The Naas union, in Co. Kildare, in February 1851, had 1,443 inmates, although its capacity was only 1,386, while there were 4,556 paupers in Limerick workhouse by December 1849.[7] In January 1848, the vice-guardians in the Galway union had to restrict admissions to the aged, the infirm and widows with children under 15 years after it reached full capacity when those evicted from the Blake estate at Tully arrived in a poor and wretched condition.[8] In Galway, by March 1849 the paupers were sleeping four and, in some cases, five to a bed, leading to demands that the number of inmates be reduced by 425 because of severe overcrowding. Similar conditions existed in the Kilrush workhouse in the early 1850s.[9]

A number of measures were introduced in an attempt to deal with a system unable to cope with the crisis. These included the provision of outdoor relief, the creation of auxiliary workhouses and, in 1850, the number of Poor Law unions was increased from 130 to 163. In some unions the auxiliary workhouses accommodated more paupers than the main union building. Carrickmacross union in Co. Monaghan had 17 auxiliary workhouses, while Ballinasloe, which included the Mountbellew area up to 1850, had 16 auxiliary buildings, many unsuitable for human habitation as they included former grain stores, stables and a brewery. As a result of these pressures, it had been decided to increase the number of Poor Law unions in 1850 and among the new unions established were Portumna and Mountbellew. For this reason, they did not become operational until 1852; the Mountbellew paupers continued to be accommodated in the Ballinasloe workhouse, but were under the control of the newly elected board of guardians. At the end of June 1850, there were 999 inmates in the new Mountbellew workhouse.[10]

When the Mountbellew union was established, plans were already in place to reduce the number of paupers through assisted emigration to British colonies. While provision had been made under the 1838 Poor Law legislation permitting unions to provide the funding for emigration to the colonies, the take up was low because of opposition from ratepayers and guardians who refused to sanction the additional spending. It was not until 1848 that most unions saw the advantages of assisted emigration as a way of reducing the long-term inmate population and, in particular, clearing the workhouses of young female orphans. Three-quarters of the workhouse adult population were women, and while some were deserted, the majority used the Poor Law as a safety net when their husbands left for North America or Britain in search of work and with the intention of sending back the passage fares so that the rest of the family could join them. Some women attempted to enter the workhouses stating they were widows, but it was found their husbands had left to seek work abroad.[11] This did not always happen as large numbers of emigrants died on the Atlantic crossing or at the quarantine stations at Grosse Île in Quebec or Partridge Island in New Brunswick. Sometimes, the emigrant decided to start a new life forgetting about the family they had left in Ireland. This problem was highlighted by Col. W.A. Clark, the Poor Law inspector for the Kenmare and Killarney unions, in Co. Kerry, in April 1849 when he stated:

> ...they are not heard of for months, and a great many when they get there marry again; they forget they have wives and families at home, and their wives and families remain as permanent paupers in the workhouse.[12]

Even before the failure of the potato in 1845, widowed and deserted wives formed a large section of the inmate population, accounting for 39 percent of the occupants of Nenagh workhouse in the early months of 1843. With the onset of the Great Famine, the number of females entering the workhouses increased significantly and by March 1847, 75 percent of the adults in both Nenagh and Cork were women.[13] Not only did females outnumber males, but their stay in the workhouse tended to be longer. Sometimes they became long-term inmates, regarded by Poor Law officials as "permanent deadweight"—that is, a continuous burden on the union's rates. It led to the Poor Law commissioners constantly seeking ways of reducing the number of females so that the unions' financial burden could be lowered. Attempts also were made to locate husbands who had deserted their wives and families, and when located they were prosecuted, but this was not always successful. The authorities also tried to send inmates to Britain to reside with friends or relations who were employed, but these paupers usually returned and re-entered the workhouse. Paupers also were sent to other institutions such as prisons for breaking the workhouse rules and to workhouse hospitals to reduce the number of female inmates.

One group in particular caused the authorities great concern: those women born or reared in the workhouses and those who had been admitted at a young age. They tended to be the most troublesome, involved in fighting and, on occasions, rioting.[14] It was feared they would become institutionalized and unable to adjust to life outside the workhouses. There were other problems with the large number of females: the difficulty of finding enough work to keep them occupied and out of trouble. While males could be employed at breaking stones or farm work, there were not enough jobs for the females. Even Mountbellew had a large female inmate population in June 1850: 382 were adults and 199 were children aged between 9 and 15 years, representing nearly 60 percent of the total number of paupers.[15]

The number of children entering the workhouse also alarmed the authorities during the Great Famine and in the following decades the workhouses became a dumping ground for deserted children. Often they were abandoned by their parents or by a single mother as no other institution would accommodate them. While many had been orphaned during the Famine, there was a sizeable group who were deserted by their parents or deposited there until such time as they were in a position to send for them. Between March 1848 and August 1850, nearly one-third of children aged 15 and younger who had been admitted to the Cork workhouse had been abandoned by their parents. Tullamore workhouse in King's County (now Offaly) had 1,157 children aged 15 and younger by July 1848, and by the middle of 1849, nationally there were more than 90,000 children in the workhouses.[16] The methods of desertion of children were many and varied, from leaving infants at the door of the workhouse to their abandonment in fields and towns. The most common approach was for the family to enter the workhouse and for the father or mother to abscond leaving the children in the care of the Poor Law authorities. As the family was segregated on entering the workhouse, for a long time the children were not aware they had been abandoned and their long-term fate was likely to be within the workhouse. These children were a cause of concern to the authorities because, in the short- to medium-term, there was little chance of them leaving the institution. The authorities were most anxious to send these inmates to the colonies.

The year 1848 saw the initiation of the assisted emigration schemes, which were primarily used to send large numbers of young female orphans to the colonies. Australia and Canada desperately needed female domestic servants, and, as a large redundant female population resided in the workhouses, it was only natural that the colonial authorities turned to them to overcome their labor shortages. The Female Orphan Scheme thus came into being in 1848 and, over the following two years, 4,114 workhouse girls from 118 Poor Law unions were sent to Australia. The boards of guardians' participation was largely influenced by the decision of the Australian authorities to pay the transport costs to the colony so the unions' only expenditure was the travel arrangements to Plymouth and the provision of new clothing for the emigrants.[17] While the numbers from each workhouse was small, the largest groups coming from Skibbereen (110), Enniskillen (107) and Roscrea (90), they were quickly replaced in the workhouses by other destitute paupers. The unions, nevertheless, were able to rid themselves of those who otherwise would have been a permanent burden on the Poor Law's resources.[18] Those assisted were mainly in the 14 to 18 year age cohort and the Australian authorities' representative selected the girls from lists of applications drawn up by each board of guardians. The success of the Australian schemes led to a demand for changes in the existing funding arrangements for assisted emigration from the workhouses. While it was argued that sending the paupers would benefit the colonies and provide the inmates with a fresh start in life, the real motive was that it was an economic remedy to the unions' deteriorating financial problems. Denis O'Connor, the clerk of Limerick Poor Law Union, argued that there was no other way of dealing with the large number of servant boys, and in particular servant girls, in the workhouses except by emigration, otherwise they would remain a continuous constraint on the rates.[19] The Earl of Clancarty, the chairman of the Ballinasloe board of guardians and one of the principal landowners in east Galway, also urged that greater powers be given to local guardians to enable the poor to emigrate and he called for greater flexibility in the amounts of money the guardians could give toward emigration.[20]

The success of the Female Orphan Scheme to Australia, and the increasing demands that the emigration schemes be extended, resulted in new legislation being enacted in 1849, largely due to the urgings of William Monsell, the MP for Limerick, which allowed the boards of guardians to apply to the Poor Law commissioners for loans for emigration purposes.[21] In 1853, the remaining funds in the Rate-in-Aid Grant, amounting to nearly £10,000, were made available to the poorer unions along the western seaboard for emigration purposes. These changes resulted in a greater take-up for emigration, with Canada as the main destination, because costs were lower.

By the early 1850s, Canada was experiencing a period of major economic prosperity, which led to high wages and an increased demand for all types of labor. In late 1853, for example, laborers were earning up to 4/- (shillings) a day and the demand for female domestic labor greatly exceeded the supply. The emigration authorities in Canada looked to the Irish workhouses to meet this need. Agents such A.C. Buchanan in Quebec and A.B. Hawke in Toronto constantly wrote to the newspapers and the Poor Law unions stressing the high demand for emigrants. At this time, the United States was the destination of choice for the vast majority of Irish emigrants; this led the Canadian authorities to adopt a more concerted approach to entice emigrants from Britain and Ireland to the colony. Unlike the Poor Law schemes to Australia, the Canadian officials had no input into the type of workhouse emigrant who came to the colony, as they had no direct involvement in the selection process, this being left to the Poor Law union officials. The Canadians contributed no financial assistance toward the transport costs of the emigrants and there were occasions where unsuitable workhouse paupers arrived in the colony as with the 80 inmates sent from the Cork workhouse to New Brunswick on the *Susan* in 1850, or the group of widows and their children assisted from the New Ross and Gorey workhouses in 1858 and 1859.[22] While the Canadians recommended the type of emigrant that should be sent, when they should arrive in the colony, and the amount of "landing money" that should be forwarded to the emigration agents in Canada, they did not know the caliber of the person travelling until the boats arrived in British North America. Those selected tended to be in the 14 to 30 age cohort and had spent long periods as workhouse residents. The 65 girls sent by the South Dublin Union in 1856 ranged in age from 15 to 23.[23] They had spent between three and 14 years living in the workhouses, indicating that many knew little of life outside of the institution and were totally dependent on it for survival.[24]

The reports from the Canadian emigration agents to the Poor Law unions in Ireland, however, encouraged them to send further groups of females. In 1851, Buchanan told the Kilrush guardians that the girls from the union had been provided for, had secured comfortable employment, and the following year he reported that all of the paupers sent out in 1851 had been employed within two weeks, "owing to the difficulty in obtaining female domestic servants throughout the country."[25] In February 1852, Hawke, the chief emigrant agent for Upper Canada, stated he would take 1,500 workhouse girls and provide them with immediate employment as domestic servants.[26] Such correspondence undoubtedly persuaded many unions to send their young female paupers. During 1851-52, 470 paupers, or more than nine percent of the population of Kilrush workhouse, were assisted to leave, facilitated by a £2,000 Treasury grant. All were unmarried adult females and they were sent to Quebec because of Buchanan's exhortations. Also, it was cheaper than providing assistance to transport them to Australia or the United States.[27] In 1852, 3,825 people received assistance from the Poor Law to emigrate at a cost of

£14,041, including 567 from Newcastle, 432 from Nenagh and 147 from Killydysert (Co. Clare).[28] Inevitably, the newly established unions such as Mountbellew would also engage in the emigration programme.

With the formation of the new unions in the early 1850s, there were teething problems and friction between the new and old boards of guardian. The source of this tension was primarily over the money that was owed to the old unions from the new unions for upkeep of the paupers until the new workhouses opened. By the time the workhouse opened in Mountbellew on 17 May 1852, when 26 male and 30 female paupers were transferred from Ballinasloe, inmate numbers were on the decline and ratepayers argued that the new unions were no longer needed. By July 1852, the Ballinasloe guardians complained that money was outstanding from both the Portumna and Mountbellew unions with the latter owing £4,000. The existing Poor Law unions also faced major financial difficulties with Tuam being more than £9,000 in debt and, in January 1850, the union had to borrow £1,500 to pay its bills.[29] Issues also arose in relation to the transfer of paupers to the new workhouses. When the workhouses opened in 1852, many paupers refused to leave the Ballinasloe workhouse, and even when the transfers had been completed, they wanted to be sent back from Portumna and Mountbellew. Many inmates had been in the Ballinasloe workhouse close to eight years, and were institutionalized within its buildings and did not want to embrace a new regime, new buildings and personnel they did not know. Consequently, assisted emigration was seen as the panacea to the financial and disciplinary problems of the new unions.

The structures of the workhouse emigration varied considerably, each union adopting different criteria and approaches as to who should receive assistance. A feature of the Poor Law emigration schemes of the early 1850s was that many of the newly formed unions embraced the sending of paupers even before their workhouses had opened, Corofin in Co. Galway being an obvious example.[30] There are a number of possible explanations. The guardians realized it would be best if the long-term female paupers were not transferred to the newly opened workhouses as they had a poor work ethic and a disorderly approach to the institution's rules, which could impact negatively on other inmates. It was easier to send them to the colonies and thus reduce a recurring expenditure. The new unions saw how successful the previous emigration schemes had been; the Ballinasloe Poor Law Union had been among the first to engage with the Female Orphan Scheme when 57 girls were sent to Australia in 1848. In May 1852, an unsuccessful attempt was made to secure money from the Colonial Land Emigration Office to assist some of the workhouse's able-bodied paupers to travel to Australia.[31]

By the early 1850s, the Mountbellew guardians were providing assistance to help individuals leave. In February 1852, they gave £7 toward the emigration costs of Mary Mannion, a widow from Killeen and her five children, aged between 3 and 12 years, to travel to North America. Her landlord, Lord Clonbrock, provided the rest of the passage costs. Joseph Kelly, another Galway landowner, was prepared to give assistance and in December 1851 he paid part of the passage fare for the Forde and Tyrell families from Caltra to emigrate, with the Poor Law providing the rest.[32] In February 1853, the guardians received sanction from the Poor Law commissioners to provide £2/10s from the rates to enable a female pauper to emigrate to North America.[33]

Prior to the opening of the workhouse, the Mountbellew guardians sought permission from the Colonial Land and Emigration commissioners to send a number of females to Australia, and in November 1852, 30 girls sailed from Plymouth on the *Travencore* for western Australia. The total cost to the union was £105, two-thirds of their annual upkeep in the workhouse. Of the original list, four girls were replaced because they were in an unfit medical state, and the workhouse master, Mr. Joyce, accompanied the girls to Plymouth. Among those assisted were Catherine Tully and Mary Anne Taylor from Castleblackeney, Mary Dooley from Clonbrock and Mary Mannion from Ballinakill.[34]

The Mountbellew guardians wanted to clear the workhouse of their "permanent deadweight" and wished to do so quickly, for within weeks of the departure of the girls to Australia, preparations were being made to offload another group of young females. There were, at that time, 440 inmates under the care of the union, 125 classified as able-bodied females. In February 1853, the workhouse master, Mr. Joyce, was directed to prepare and submit the names of 50 young women who had been resident in the workhouse for more than two years, so they could be sent to North America.[35] While the preparations for those sent to Australia were conducted by the colonial authorities, the Mountbellew guardians had to make the arrangements themselves. The emigration schemes were well planned and organized because of consultations between the Canadian authorities and individual Poor Law unions, such as Newcastle, Rathkeale and Listowel. In 1852, a directive was sent to all boards of guardians by the Poor Law commissioners as to procedures, when the emigrants should travel, the recommended landing money that should be sent to the emigrant agents in Canada etc. In March 1853, the Mountbellew guardians sought tenders for outfitting the emigrants for items such as shoes, towels, cotton stockings, pocket handkerchiefs, combs and marine soaps, etc.[36]

The Mountbellew guardians advertised for tenders to convey the girls to North America. The shipping agents John Miley of Eden Quay, Dublin, and Francis Spraight of Limerick were among those who carried the workhouse emigrants to America. The agents were responsible for the girls until they disembarked at Quebec and New Brunswick, although most unions employed chaperones to accompany the emigrants on the voyage. Many shipping agents gave the unions extended credit terms, loans or provided additional food on the Atlantic crossing to secure the tender. The Mountbellew guardians encountered difficulties when they sought a tender to convey the girls to Canada, largely because of the mass exodus that was taking place from the country to North America. Eventually, Mr. Gibson's tender, a shipping agent from Kilrush, was paid £3/16s/6d to transfer each pauper to Quebec and he agreed to provide additional rations on the journey.[37] However, complications developed as Gibson was unable to secure a ship at a time that the guardians wanted and, in late June, they were unhappy because the girls still had not departed. It was feared their late arrival in the colony would result in them being unable to secure employment. Gibson was threatened that, unless he took immediate action, the union solicitor would take proceedings against him.[38] Eventually, on 16 July 1853, the Mountbellew girls left Limerick on the *Primrose* and arrived in Quebec on 6 September.

The 50 girls selected provide an indication of the type of inmate that the unions sent to Canada. They ranged in age from 15 to 40 years, the eldest being Jane Kelly from Mountbellew and Biddy Ruane, who was under the protection of the union at large.[39] While nearly all the girls met the age criteria, the sending of Jane Kelly and Biddy Ruane suggests officials availed themselves of an opportunity to transfer—and thereby rid themselves of—a small group of paupers who were unlikely to secure positions in the colony. The girls had spent between two and eight years as workhouse paupers, with Mary Clark from Annagh, who was 19, and Mary Killarney aged 21 from Derryglassan, having spent the least time in the institution. Four had spent over seven years in the workhouse: Catherine Connolly, aged 20, and Biddy Barrett aged 16, both from Ballinakill, and Jane Murray from Derryglassan and Kitty Rabbitt, aged 18, from Castleffrench.[40] However, as Chris O'Mahony points out in his study of emigration from the Co. Clare workhouses, there are discrepancies with the official records.[41] An examination of individual unions and the minute books that exist show that the figures do not always tally with the official Canadian returns in the parliamentary papers. In some cases, the figures are lower for specific years; for others, they are higher. While the Mountbellew records give the names of 50 girls, the Quebec records state that 55 arrived on the *Primrose* from the workhouse.[42] The length of time that the girls spent in the workhouses is important as it highlights their ages when admitted and suggests how, in the long term, they could become institutionalized and a permanent burden on the rates. Nine of the Mountbellew girls were under 10 years when they first entered: Jane Murray from Derryglassan was the youngest at 8, while Fanny Geraghty from Tameboy, Anne McGrath from Cooloo and Ellen Egan from Castleffrench were all 9.[43] While there is no concrete evidence, the indications are that the majority of the girls were orphans. It is unlikely the girls would have wanted to go to Canada if they still had family members living in the Mountbellew-Ballinasloe area. The fact that they were mainly orphans is suggested by the number of sisters who received assistance: Margaret Coffey was 19 years and her sister, Mary, from Cooloo had been in the workhouse for more than three years. Mary Dowd from Cloonkeen was 20 years and her sister, Winny, 17, when admitted to the Ballinasloe workhouse in 1849.

The marketability of these inmates outside of the workhouse was a problem as paupers did not receive sufficient training for the outside world. The situation was not as bad for males as they could be employed as agricultural laborers or in unskilled positions. Females were different because of the vast numbers in the workhouses, thus their employment prospects were bleak. There were constant complaints that the girls were not suitable for domestic work, as a result of the lack of training within the workhouses. In 1861, Nicholas Mahony, a Poor Law guardian in Cork, stated that little was being done to provide the females with work experience and apprenticeships for life in the outside world. Criticizing the way that the girls were kept in the workhouses, he said:

> They acquire no knowledge of any kind of household work; they have nothing to do but attend to meals or their schools; they take what is given them, and do not know where it comes from, how it is cooked, or its cost. A great many of them have never had a knife, or a fork or a plate in their hands, and, as servants they are perfectly useless.[44]

The longer the girls remained in the workhouse, the less likely they would be suitable as domestic servants. Female workhouse paupers were seldom sought after as domestic servants in Ireland. As there was an adequate supply of female labor outside of the workhouses, employers were not prepared to take on paupers. If workhouse females wanted such positions they had to travel outside of Ireland, and in particular to North America, where there was a major demand for their services. However, even there the suitability of such women for these positions was often questioned. As many of the Mountbellew girls sent to Canada had entered the workhouse at such a young age, they had acquired few of the fundamental skills to be domestic servants when they left in 1853. One of the great concerns in the workhouses in the late 1840s and early 1850s was that there was not enough work to occupy the female inmates, resulting in them being bored and refractory. While they did not have the necessary skills for domestic service, the guardians were still availing themselves of the opportunity to be rid of them.

Unions adopted different approaches as to whom they would send to Canada. In Claremorris and Ballina, the guardians sent girls from the poorest electoral divisions as it would reduce the rates paid, while Ballinrobe only assisted those who had been resident in the workhouse for the longest time.[45] Mountbellew union adopted a procedure which incorporated both approaches. The girls came from 13 electoral divisions in addition to three, who were looked after by the union at large. Nine came from Derryglassan, six from both Castleblakeney and Cooloo, and five from Mounthazel.

While the Poor Law unions were responsible for the emigrants until they arrived in North America, once they disembarked at Quebec they were taken in charge by the Canadian authorities. Landing money forwarded to A.C. Buchanan was used to send those emigrants to destinations where there was a demand for labor. Buchanan's correspondence to the guardians in Ireland indicated the destinations that the girls were forwarded to. For example, the 96 girls from the Macroom workhouse who arrived in Quebec in 1851 on the *Hope* were sent to the Bay of Quinte and Belleville where they were immediately employed. Ninety-two girls sent from Newcastle union around the same period on the *Georgina* were forwarded to Toronto, and Buchanan reported all secured positions.[46] Although Buchanan indicated that the girls were employed as soon as they arrived at their destinations, he was not telling the full story. Their unsuitability as domestic servants was already evident by their failure to secure positions in Ireland. It was generally agreed that the training the young girls received in the workhouses was inadequate. Mr. Woodlock, who had tried to train the females in Dublin and Cork workhouses in the 1850s, found it difficult to get suitable girls to undertake industrial training such as laundry work or sewing. They were unsuitable for training as servants as they were incapable of being useful in any house; ignorant of the ordinary things of life; not even knowing the names of common objects and household utensils.[47] One critic said the girls were as suitable to domestic service "as a bear is to dance the polka on his tail."[48]

While Buchanan and Hawke gave favorable descriptions of the women when they arrived in Canada, it was only when they reached their final destinations that the true opinions of Canadian employers became obvious. The girls were sent to the rural parts of Ontario where demand for female labor was high and where they would not be together. However, it soon became apparent that they were unsuited to the type of work needed, an obvious reference to their workhouse training. They were unable to milk cows or carry out the chores they were assigned. Most women quickly became disillusioned with their situation and left the rural areas for the bright lights of the larger towns and cities.[49]

As the girls' limited capabilities was realized by Buchanan, some groups were sent to Bytown on their arrival, where the Sisters of Charity had opened an institution and took charge to train them for domestic service work.[50] However, Buchanan never conveyed this information to the guardians in Ireland. Among the groups sent to Bytown for retraining were 21 girls from the Oughterard workhouse and a group from Kilrush union.[51] Why did Buchanan and others continue to encourage the guardians to send female paupers when they were clearly unsuited for the positions available? One possible explanation was the pressing need for female labor in the colony in the early 1850s and so the paupers' limitations were accepted to avoid pressure being put on the Canadian economy. It was easier to encourage the paupers to come to the colony and retrain them as domestic servants than to jeopardize economic progress. Also, as they were young, there was a better possibility of them adapting to a new life. The absence of names and other information in the Poor Law minute books or in the Canadian sources means that it is difficult to trace the lives of most of these emigrant girls. In many cases, they do not have an identity and can be compared to those who died in the workhouses during the Great Famine and were buried in unmarked graves. As orphans, they ended up in unknown destinations in North America, often untraceable by family and friends.

What became of the Mountbellew girls after they arrived in Quebec on the *Primrose* on 6 September? According to Buchanan, along with a group from the Parsonstown union, they were sent to Toronto and Hamilton, where there were immediate employment positions.[52] The Mountbellew guardians had forwarded £50 landing money to Buchanan to pay for their travel to these destinations. What is unclear is whether they were sent immediately or stayed for a period with the Sisters of Charity in Bytown to be retrained. The information from the Mountbellew Poor Law Minute Books allows us to follow the trail of the emigrants in Canada over a period of time. Some did become domestic servants, as was the case with Anne McGrath who, in 1861, was a servant in the home of Joseph Parker in Montreal, but Catherine Kilgannon and Jane Kelly did not fare so well. Catherine Kilgannon from Derryglassan was 15 years old when she left on the *Primrose*, having spent six years in the workhouse. In the 1861 Canadian census, she was listed as living at Pembroke, Renfrew County, Ontario, married with three children, although her husband was classified as absent. She could not read or write and her occupation was listed as a washer woman. There is no trace of her in the 1871 census in Ontario and, like others, she may have left for the United States. Jane Kelly was 40 years old and had spent five years in the workhouse when she departed for Quebec, leaving one institution in Ireland for incarceration in another in Canada. In the 1861 census, her occupation was listed as a tailoress, but she was resident in a lunatic and idiot asylum and described as being of unsound mind, having been committed to the institution in 1857. In 1881, she was still a resident of the asylum.[53] In 1861, Ellen Egan was living in Toronto and working as a bread-maker, but the following year she moved to the township of Alice and Fraser in eastern Ontario after marrying William Parker. She died in Guelph in February 1915.[54]

Compared to the Female Orphan Scheme to Australia, little information is available on those workhouse inmates sent to Canada. While Buchanan informed the unions that the emigrants had arrived and where they had been sent to, the Poor Law Minute Books do not mention any correspondence between the former paupers and union officials. As far as the guardians were concerned, they had dispensed with a long-term problem and had other issues to contend with rather than inquire as to how their former inmates were faring. In 1861, Nicholas Mahony told the Select Committee on the Poor Law that the Cork guardians had made no attempt to ascertain the fate of any of the 1,200 girls assisted from the workhouse between 1848 and 1860.[55] The absence of correspondence from former inmates would suggest that the girls saw no reason to keep in touch or, as the example above illustrates, they were illiterate. As orphans and former long-term inmates they wanted to forget their association with the institution.

The story of the Mountbellew girls sent to Canada provides an insight into the emigration schemes undertaken by the Poor Law unions. Nearly 15,000 inmates, the vast majority of whom were young females, left the workhouses. A number of conclusions can be reached from the evidence from the Mountbellew sources. All unions that engaged in the assisted emigration schemes to North America saw it as an opportunity to get rid of their long-term pauper inmates in an attempt to reduce expenditure and lower operating costs. The primary motive of the vast majority of guardians was economic and not philanthropic in that their responsibility for the girls ended when they disembarked at the Canadian ports. The new unions, as with Mountbellew, wanted to transport their paupers before they settled in the workhouse. The unions adhered to the general rules for conveying the emigrants and they were better cared for than those who paid their own passage fare. The evidence suggests the workhouse paupers were happy to leave and start a new life in Canada as they had seen other inmates depart for a fresh start in the colonies since 1848. Demand for places on these schemes was greater than the number of places available and, in unions such as Ennis and Kilrush, women left their employment and entered the workhouses hoping that they could be sent to Canada when the next group was being sent out.[56] Tragedy and demographic circumstances determined the extent of the success of the schemes. The potato crop failure of the 1840s had resulted in the workhouse system being unable to cope with the large numbers admitted as paupers. Demand for female labor in Canada provided them with the opportunity of a better life. The workhouse paupers who left in the immediate years after the Great Famine were part of "the invisible emigrant army." The Mountbellew paupers who came to Canada in 1853 allow us to unravel part of this story.

Endnotes

[1] Gerard Moran, *Sending Out Ireland's Poor: Assisted Emigration to North America in the Nineteenth Century* (Dublin, 2004 and 2013), p. 137.

[2] *Report from the Select Committee on Colonization, together with the Minutes of Evidence*, HC 1890 (354), xli, p. 352, q. 5680.

[3] Christine Kinealy, "The response of the Poor Law to the Great Famine in county Galway" in Gerard Moran and Raymond Gillespie (eds.), *Galway: History and Society* (Dublin, 1994), p. 380.

[4] James S. Donnelly Jr., *The Great Irish Potato Famine* (Stroud, 1991), pp 139-40.

[5] Ignatius Murphy, *A people starved: Life and death in West Clare, 1845-51* (Dublin, 1996) and Tom Crehan, *Marcella Gerrard's Galway estate, 1820-70* (Dublin, 2013).

[6] *Galway Mercury*, 16 June 1849.

[7] *Nation*, 12 Jan. 1850; Eva Ó Cathaoir, "The Poor Law in County Wicklow" in Ken Hannigan and William Nolan (eds.), *Wicklow: History and Society* (Dublin, 1994), p. 537; *Limerick Reporter*, 14 Dec. 1849. By the end of August 1850, there were 3,172 inmates in Ennistymon workhouse. See North Clare Historical Society/Fas Community Response Project, *Ennistymon Union Minutes of Board Meetings, 1839-1850*, meeting dated 6 Sept. 1850, book 9 (Ennistymon, 1992), p. 18.

[8] *Galway Vindicator*, 22 and 29 Jan. 1849.

[9] Minutes of Galway Poor Law guardians, dated 31 March 1849 (Galway Co. Library, minute book, Nov. 1848-Aug. 1840); Murphy, *A People Starved*, pp 76-7.

[10] Minutes of Mountbellew Poor Law guardians, dated 29 June 1850 (GCL, Mountbellew Poor Law minute book, May 1850-Jan. 1850).

[11] *Fourth Report from the Select Committee of the House of Lords appointed to inquire into the Operation of the Irish Poor Law, and the expediency of making any amendment to its enactment, together with the minutes of Evidence*, HC 1849 (365), xvi, p. 765, q. 7870.

[12] Ibid., pp 754-5, q. 7793.

[13] Daniel Grace, *The Great Famine in Nenagh Poor Law Union, Co. Tipperary* (Nenagh, 2000), p. 27, 125 & Michelle O'Mahony, *Famine in Cork City: Famine Life at Cork Union Workhouse* (Cork, 2005), pp 46-7.

[14] For riots and insubordination in the workhouses in this period see Gerard Moran, "Disorderly conduct: Riots and insubordination in the workhouses during the Great Famine" in John Cunningham and Niall Ó Ciosáin (eds.), *Society and Culture in Ireland since 1750: Essays in Honour of Gearoid Ó Tuathaigh* (Dublin, 2015) pp 160-80: Virginia Crossman, "The New Ross workhouse riot of 1887: Nationalism, class and the Irish Poor Law" in *Past and Present*, 179 (May, 2003), pp 135-8.

[15] Minutes of Mountbellew Poor Law guardians, dated 29 June 1850 (GCL, Mountbellew Poor Law minute book, May 1850-Jan. 1850).

[16] O'Mahony, *Famine in Cork City*, p. 105; Joseph Robbins, "The emigration of Irish workhouse children to Australia in the nineteenth century" in John O'Brien and Pauric Travers (eds.), *The Irish Emigrant Experience to Australia* (Dublin, 1991), p. 34.

[17] See Richard Reid, *Farewell My Children: Irish Assisted Emigration to Australia, 1848-1870* (Spit Junction, NSW, 2011), pp 141-53.

[18] Trevor McClaughlin, "Lost children? Irish famine orphans in Australia" in *History Ireland*, vol. 8, no. 4 (Winter, 2000), p. 31.

[19] *Eighth Report from the Select Committee on the Poor Laws (Ireland)*, HC 1849 (237), xv, pp 73-4, qs 6979-80.

[20] *Ninth report from the Select Committee on the Poor Laws (Ireland)*, HC 1849 (259), xv, p. 87, qs 8381-4.

[21] Sir George Nicholls, *A History of the Irish Poor Law* (1856, rep. New York, 1967), p. 369; see also *Third Report from the Select Committee on the Poor Law (Ireland)*, HC 1849 (93), p. 80, q. 1793, 1796.

[22] See Gerard Moran, "Shovelling out Ireland's deadweight during the Great Famine: The Cork workhouse paupers sent to New Brunswick in 1850" (forthcoming).

[23] Six were 15 years old; 37 were 16 years old, seven were 17; six were 18 and nine were from 20 to 23 years old.

[24] *Report from the Select Committee on the Poor Law (Ireland), together with the Proceedings of the Committee, Minutes of Evidence and Appendices*, HC 1861 (408), x, p. 501. Twenty-four of the girls had spent more than 18 months in the workhouse.

[25] *Limerick Reporter and Tipperary Vindicator*, 24 Feb. 1852; *Galway Vindicator*, 9 June 1852; *Papers Relative to Emigration to the North American Colonies*, HC 1852-3 (1650), lxviii, p. 9.

[26] *Nation*, 6 March 1852; *Galway Vindicator*, 13 March 1852.

[27] Chris O'Mahony, "Emigration from the workhouses of County Clare, 1848-59" in Matthew Lynch and Patrick Nugent (eds.), *Clare: History and Society* (Dublin, 2008), pp 272-4. When the emigration schemes were initiated, there were 5,000 inmates in the Kilrush workhouse and seven auxiliary workhouses that had to be rented to accommodate the pauper population.

[28] *Seventh Annual Report of the Commissioners for Ministering the Laws for the Relief of the Poor in Ireland with Appendices*, HC 1852-3 (1645), lxviii, p. 8, 146-9.

[29] *Tuam Herald*, 2 Jan. and 2 Feb. 1850. In the early 1850s, Tuam was one of the unions which discussed sending its long-term pauper inmates to North America and 40 girls, who were long-term residents in the workhouse, indicated they were prepared to go abroad if their passage was paid, idem, 5 March 1853.

[30] In early 1852, the Corofin guardians applied to the Poor Law commissioners for funds to send 200 of the young inmates to the colonies arguing "they are wasting their youth and strength, which in any of the British colonies would be valuable to themselves and others," see Michael McMahon, "The first ten years of Corofin Poor Law Union, 1850-60" in Ciarán Ó Murchadha, *County Clare studies: Essays in memory of Gerald O'Connell, Sean Ó Murchadha, Thomas Coffey and Pat Flynn* (Ennis, 2001), p. 161.

[31] *Western News*, 29 May, 19 June 1852. While emigration was seen as one way of reducing the pauper population, the guardians also availed themselves of other opportunities such as sending young male paupers to join the army and the navy, see *Ninth report of the Select Committee on the Poor Law* (Ireland), HC 1849 (301), xv, p. 91, q. 8425; *Galway Vindicator*, 27 May 1854.

[32] Moran, *Sending Out Ireland's Poor,* p. 137.

[33] *Tuam Herald*, 19 Feb. 1853.

[34] Minutes of Mountbellew Poor Law guardians, dated 7 July 28 Aug.; 23 Oct. 1852 (GCL, Mountbellew Poor Law minute book, March 1852-Oct. 1852); *Western News*, 20 Nov. 1852.

[35] *Tuam Herald*, 26 Feb. 1853.

[36] Ibid., 26 March 1853.

[37] Minutes of Mountbellew Poor Law guardians, dated 26 March 9 Apr. 1853 (GCL, Mountbellew Poor Law minute book, Nov 1852-May 1853).

[38] Ibid., week ending 25 June 1853.

[39] Forty-four were under 20 years, while four were between 21 and 26 years.

[40] Minutes of Mountbellew Poor Law guardians, week ending 5 March 1853 (GCL, Mountbellew Poor Law minute book, Nov 1852-May 1853).

[41] Chris O'Mahony, "Emigration from the workhouses of county Clare," p. 274.

[42] *Papers relative to Emigration to the North American Colonies,* HC 1854 (1763), xlvi, p. 31.

[43] Minutes of Mountbellew Poor Law guardians, dated 5 March 1853 (GCL, Mountbellew Poor Law minute book, May 1850-Jan. 1850).

[44] *Report from the Select Committee on the Poor Law (Ireland); together with the Proceedings of the Committee, Minutes of Evidence and Appendices*, HC 1861 (408), x, pp 89-91, qs 1706-78.

[45] Moran, *Sending Out Ireland's Poor*, p. 147.

[46] A.C. Buchanan to R.A. Doran, dated 11 Nov. 1852 in *Papers relative to Emigration to the North American Colonies*, HC 1852-3 (1650), lxviii, p. 28.

[47] Helen Burke, *The People and the Poor Law in nineteenth-century Ireland* (Sussex, 1987), p. 223.

[48] *Limerick and Clare Examiner*, 16 Dec. 1848.

[49] Dympna McLoughlin, "Superfluous and unwanted deadweight: the emigration of nineteenth-century pauper women" in Patrick O'Sullivan (ed.), *The Irish World Wide,* vol. iv: *Irish Women and Irish Migration* (Leicester, 1995), pp 83-4.

[50] From September 1847, the Sisters of Charity, or Grey Nuns, were taking in Irish widows and orphans from Grosse Île and Montreal, and made arrangements that the orphans be adopted by families in Quebec. The centres included a house for female orphans at Murray St. and for boys at St Alphonse's Hall. See Annals of the Grey Nuns, *Ancien Journal*, vol. ix, 1847 at www.faminearchive.nuigalway.ie, p. 75, 84, 102-3, 105-8; also Sisters of Charity of Montreal, "Grey Nuns" Archives and Collections: Fonds L007, Orphelin at St. Patrick, Montreal, Foundation of St Patrick's Asylum, www.faminearchieve.nuigalway.ie.

[51] Ibid.

[52] *Papers relative to Emigration to the North American Colonies*, HC 1854 (1763), xlvi, p. 39.

[53] I wish to acknowledge this information from Linda Fitzgibbon of the Dept. of Irish Studies, Concordia University, Montreal.

[54] I wish to acknowledge this information from Dr. Regina Donlan, Moore Institute, NUI Galway.

[55] *Report from the Select Committee on the Poor Law (Ireland), together with the Proceedings*, HC 1861 (408), x, p. 101, qs 2085-9.

[56] See Moran, *Sending Out Ireland's Poor*, p. 138; Ciarán Ó Murchadha, *Sable wings over the land: Ennis, County Clare and its wider community during the Great Famine* (Ennis, 1998), p. 224.

Works Cited

Burke, Helen. *The People and the Poor Law in Nineteenth-Century Ireland*. Sussex: Philip, 1987.

Crehan, Tom. *Marcella Gerrard's Galway Estate, 1820-70*. Dublin: Four Courts Press, 2013.

Crossman, Virginia. "The New Ross workhouse riot of 1887: Nationalism, class and the Irish Poor Law." *Past and Present*, 179 (May 2003) 135-58.

Donnelly, James S. Jr. *The Great Irish Potato Famine*. Stroud: Sutton Publishing, 1991.

Grace, Daniel. *The Great Famine in Nenagh Poor Law Union, Co. Tipperary*. Nenagh: Relay Books, 2000.

Kinealy, Christine. "The response of the Poor Law to the Great Famine in county Galway" in Gerard Moran and Raymond Gillespie (eds). *Galway: History and Society*. Dublin: Four Courts Press, 1994.

McClaughlin, Trevor. "Lost children? Irish famine orphans in Australia." *History Ireland*, vol. 8, no. 4 (Winter, 2000), 30-34.

McLoughlin, Dympna. "Superflous and unwanted deadweight: the emigration of nineteenth-century pauper women" in Patrick O'Sullivan (ed.). *The Irish World Wide, vol iv: Irish Women and Irish Migration*. Leicester: Leicester University Press, 1995.

McMahon, Michael. "The first ten years of Corofin Poor Law Union, 1850-60" in Ciarán Ó Murchadha. *County Clare Studies: Essays in Memory of Gerald O'Connell, Sean Ó Murchadha, Thomas Coffey and Pat Flynn*. Ennis: CLASP, 2001.

Moran, Gerard. *Sending Out Ireland's Poor: Assisted Emigration to North America in the Nineteenth Century*. Dublin: Four Courts Press, 2004 and 2013.

—— "Disorderly conduct: Riots and insubordination in the worhouses during the Great Famine" in John Cunningham and Niall Ó Ciosáin (eds.). *Society and Culture in Ireland since 1750: Essays in Honour of Gearoid Ó Tuathaigh*. Dublin: Lilliput Press, 2015.

—— "Shovelling out Ireland's deadweight during the Great Famine": The Cork workhouse paupers sent to New Brunswick in 1850" (forthcoming).

Ó Murchadha, Ciarán. *Sable Wings over the Land: Ennis, County Clare and its Wider Community during the Great Famine*. Ennis: CLASP Press, 1998.

Murphy, Ignatius. *A People Starved: Life and Death in West Clare, 1845-51*. Dublin: Irish Academic Press, 1996.

Nicholls, Sir George. *A History of the Irish Poor Law*. 1856, rep. New York: Augustus M. Kelley, 1967.

Ó Cathaoir, Eva. "The Poor Law in County Wicklow" in Ken Hannigan and William Nolan (eds.). *Wicklow: History and Society*. Dublin: Four Courts Press, 1994.

O'Mahony, Chris. "Emigration from the workhouses of County Clare, 1848-59" in Matthew Lynch and Patrick Nugent (eds.). *Clare: History and Society*. Dublin: Four Courts Press, 2008.

O'Mahony, Michelle. *Famine in Cork City: Famine Life at Cork Union Workhouse*. Cork: Mercier Press, 2005.

Reid, Richard. *Farewell My Children: Irish Assisted Emigration to Australia, 1848-1870*. NSW: Anchor Books, 2011.

Robbins, Joseph. "The emigration of Irish workhouse children to Australia in the nineteenth century" in John O'Brien and Pauric Travers (eds). *The Irish Emigrant Experience to Australia*. Dublin: Poolbeg Press, 1991.

Chapter Nine

The lore of Women:
Irish expressive culture in New England
after the Great Hunger[1]

Eileen Moore Quinn

Lawrence McCaffrey describes women who emigrated from Ireland to the United States after the Great Hunger as "strong and sovereign . . . and the most important civilizing element in Irish America."[2] As we seek to understand the impact of how such earth-shattering events of hunger, famine, death and loss altered patterns, practices and behaviours both in Ireland and abroad in Irish America, it behooves us to ask how Irish women immigrants exercised the characteristics that McCaffrey describes. We also might attempt to answer questions posed by Hasia Diner:

> What effect did the predominance of women as migrants have on the economic, social and cultural patterns of Irish America? The kinds of family the Irish carved out in America as well as the work patterns, educational achievements and sense of self of Irish women need to be examined in light of female-dominated migration.[3]

This chapter takes as its starting point a review of the traditional oral practices said to have held sway in Ireland "for centuries." Although such practices were, especially before the Great Hunger, defined as particularly male in character, they did provide room for the insertion—as well as the *assertion*—of Irish women. Their folkloric repertoire, comprised of the local, the familial, the musical and the prayerful, could be deployed and delivered *ad hoc*, unfettered by more normalized structures of utterance. The chapter then proceeds by examining the fact that disruption affected the most highly ritualized male practices and behaviours, causing them to deteriorate to the point of nonexistence. Yet, because some aspects of Irish oral tradition, although flawed and fractured, did survive abroad, what ensues is an exploration as to the reasons and forces behind the "staying power" of some genres and the roles played by Irish women in oral preservation processes. Unfortunately, apart from a few sources,[4] there is a dearth of information about the role that women played in the transmission of Irish folklore. Admitting as much, Guy Beiner regrets that, in Ireland, "women were often overlooked in favor of the more collective and public forms of history-telling."[5]

During the final decades of the 20th century, I collected Irish-American verbal art from Irish American residents in New England—a region specifically comprised of six northeastern states: Rhode Island, Maine, Massachusetts, New Hampshire, Connecticut, and Vermont—who were born in the United States and whose ancestors had migrated from Ireland. Located via such media outlets as radio stations and Irish American newspapers, my consultants contributed *smideríní*— bits and pieces—of memory about the oral practices of their forebears.[6] My collecting efforts were an attempt to shed light on the collective as well as the unique aspects of Irish-American memory.[7] In doing so, I sought to match my data, filtered as it was through the lens of immigrants' descendants, to Irish and Irish American historical and folkloric records, a method considered vital for presenting a balanced view of "attitudes, prejudices and stereotypes [and] for supplying information about national myths, images, and symbols."[8]

In my gathering of oral traditional lore from children and grandchildren of Great Hunger immigrants, I gleaned no detailed, long or involved narrative of the blight, the evictions or the "passage over." Rather, when stories were told, it was the stark definition or label that rose to the fore, searing in one's consciousness images of upheaval (coffin ship)[9] and heartbreak (No Irish Need Apply). Such mnemonic smidgens of life are what Cathal Póirtéir calls "shattered pieces of memory."[10] They were not unlike those uttered by some survivors of the Holocaust whose reminiscences emerged as "a staccato of snapshot images . . . in a state of rising extremity, without plot development."[11]

Moreover, post-Famine trauma resulted in what Seán de Fréine calls the "Great Silence," the reluctance on the part of those who survived the Hunger to speak about what had occurred.[12] In the old country, "many coped with what they had witnessed by simply pushing the traumatic experience to the back of their minds, never to be resurrected in their lifetime."[13] Kathleen Villiers-Tuthill recognized that the same practices ensued among those who immigrated to the New World—*an oileán úr*—the United States:

> [The Famine] was a memory left behind in the old country. Those who [survived] rarely talked of those years to family or friends, and if they did they failed to pass on the true horror of that experience; it was something they survived, but [it was] not to be dwelt on.[14]

These insights are confirmed by my findings. For instance, one consultant, in discussing her Co. Kildare paternal grandfather, revealed, "he came to this country at the age of twelve but never talked about Ireland, nor did his father." Another, in discussing her grandmother's lack of willingness to discuss her past, stated, "she hated the boat. She must have come steerage." Yet a third commented on her mother's refusal to eat potatoes.

It is interesting to point out that these three interviewees were women; it was they who held the knowledge of their forebears' values, feelings, beliefs, practices, and cultural eschewals. As shall be elaborated further, a perusal of the types of oral lore collected in New England reveals that women, especially mothers and grandmothers, were reported to have operated as vehicles for narrativization, that is to say, for the *process* of telling one's cultural story and preserving group memory; to a large extent, it was their daughters who were listening.

I found that most verbal items were jumbled in recall or remembered only partially. Frequently, my consultants acknowledged that their memories were desperate attempts to construct a narrative without knowing how the original began or ended. Many wondered about their forbears' origins, grappling with the question as to whether certain events had actually occurred. In addition, they asked me to explain the meaning of historically mnemonic expressions like "[He was] as bad as Barrington's bloodhounds,"[15] and "[The] curse of Cromwell [on you]."[16] If consultants were able to reproduce a word in the Irish language—for instance, a toast like the single word *Sláinte*! (Health!)[17] –it was uttered frequently in garbled form: "Slahnke!" In addition, many contributors confessed that they knew little about their ancestors' lives in Ireland, who they were, where they came from, or when they emigrated. This lack of personal ancestry aligns with Peter Quinn's assertion that the pattern of Irish-American recall seems to be "a reconstruction of mute and fragmentary remains that will always be incomplete."[18] In effect, although descendants may have preserved some memories of their parents' and grandparents' words or expressions, oftentimes they lacked the knowledge of what those words or expressions actually meant.

Notwithstanding this fragmented nature of folk memory, it is worth emphasizing that there exists a form of retention known as "archival memory," a process that might best be understood by recognising that, although oral tradition may confuse places and details, "it seldom varies concerning the actual event and chief actors."[19] Episodes of strong emotion stand the greatest chance of being recalled with a high degree of veracity; so too, do those events that are unique and peculiar. Since people do not consciously falsify information when discussing particular historical events, their firsthand oral accounts are able to provide "complementary, not incompatible information" that can be trusted with some degree of reliability. In this manner, archival memory ensures transmission and accurate reporting years later.

Aligned with archival memory is collective memory, "knowledge of the past based on a shared cultural stock of knowledge socially transmitted in lessons, rituals, traditions, proverbs, and other forms."[20] Fluctuating in order to survive, it must adapt to align with the group's *modus operandi*.[21] Should it fail to do so, group knowledge will be forgotten.[22] It is in this regard that Irish women's aforementioned penchant for speaking their minds must be understood, for, as Margaret Lynch-Brennan notes, despite the heavy-handed nature of Irish patriarchal culture, a long-standing and enduring cultural tolerance for the verbally defiant behavior of Irish women and girls prevailed beyond the years of famine and emigration. Although misunderstood and maligned by commentators abroad, and despite the power of the "devotional revolution"[23] that prescribed certain behaviours for Irish women, that long-standing latitude enabled Irish women to continue to "use their keen verbal skills to assert themselves."[24] As shall be made clear, these and other aspects of Irish women's folkways and verbal art were to serve them in good stead as they settled into their new lives across the Atlantic. However, before we can understand how such oral traditional license occurred, it is incumbent upon us to understand the nature of oral traditional practices in pre-Great Hunger Ireland. Characterized as an "intimate face-to-face world," the period was dominated by music, song and story."[25] Particularly in the Irish language speaking regions of Ireland, "scenes of gaiety and joy"[26] occurred on evenings between Halloween [*Oíche Shamhna*, 31 October], and St. Patrick's Day [*Lá le Pádraig*, 17 March]. During that time, "welcoming houses"[27] —those known for offering hospitality—opened their doors night after night to the so-called "Gaelic storyteller" [*sgéalaí; sgéaltóir*] who spun, among other tales, those of the heroes of Ulster[28] and *An Fhiannaíocht*.[29] The latter concerned the legendary seer Finn Mac Cool [*Fionn Mac Cumhaill*] and his mythical troupe of warriors.[30]

In light of this kind of repertoire, perhaps it goes without saying that this was a particularly masculine world where a male storyteller took his seat of honour at the hearth, the "soul . . . of the people of the house" and ironically the quotidian domain of its *bean a tighe* [woman of the house].[31] In this ritual of inversion,[32] seated beside a roaring fire that turned to embers as the evening progressed, he spun his tales, providing community members with "the oral literature of escape" from penurious living conditions[33] and entertaining them for *airneán* [a storytelling session], *oíche áirnéail* [a night of storytelling] or *céilidh* [a singing gathering].[34]

However, although the storytelling tradition served as the edifice of the culture and functioned to mitigate pre-Great Hunger travail,[35] the nature of its rigid dimensions contributed to its eventual collapse during the post-Hunger period. Specifically, its highly ritualized "pillars of support"[36] were constructed in terms of space (the aforementioned privileged seats by the fire); time (the previously discussed "winter months" from November to March); repertory (hero tales, the *sine qua non* of the Irish narrative)[37]; and, perhaps most important, the storytellers themselves, men who directed their cache of tales to predominantly male listeners).[38] The salience of this unidirectional focus cannot be underestimated, for it enables us to examine each structural pillar of support in order to gain a perspective as to how the storytelling tradition suffered abroad. We also come to understand how and in what ways other types of lore emerged as agents for social change in Irish oral tradition.

In terms of space, after Irish immigration to America, the storyteller's honored seat by the fire became a thing of the past; some immigrants may have been fortunate enough to have roofs over their heads, but fireplaces were items of luxury. One consultant revealed that her father, a civil service employee, would walk her through Irish neighborhoods in winter, pointing out chimneys from which no smoke emanated. As for the pillar of time, the aforementioned calendrical custom of night visiting between Halloween and St Patrick's Day lost its meaning. Although those with Irish ancestry reported celebrating St Patrick's Day, the celebration of Halloween—notwithstanding the fact that consultants recollected episodes of mischief and fun—was not recollected as a particularly Irish event. Moreover, although the twin pillars of "the hero" and the storyteller who could recount his feats had been held in profound regard before the Great Hunger, they were muted abroad. Especially in New England—an area known for maintaining prejudicial attitudes which can be traced to the bombastic rhetoric of Cotton Mather, who as early as 1700 had called Irish immigrants "Sons" of Satan[39] —folk expressions of an Irish hero in the classic sense of the term became ludicrous. Kerby Miller, noting that those with "intense devotion to the verbal arts" preserved "motif of exile" in addition to "tales of ancient gods and warriors," suggests that the latter retention endured even among emigrants who had embraced a mythic view of America before leaving Ireland. However, once there, they became physically and psychically debilitated by an experience for which they been improperly unprepared.[40]

Certainly, when compared with the exuberance of tales of heroic taunts, jaunts and feasts, the terms "exile" and "emigrant" connote enervation, displacement and loss. Kenneth Nilsen recalled collecting a tale of a "Phil McGown," but whether the story was a bastardization of *the* Fionn Mac Cumhaill could not be ascertained from the thinness of the data.[41] Moreover, although a semblance of a "hero-like" character appeared in later Tin Pan Alley songs and Vaudeville skits, by then the figure had become a laughingstock.[42]

All of these examples indicate that the weight of hunger, starvation, death and immigration seriously compromised key elements of Irish verbal art. Devoid of its former pillars of space, time, tradition bearer and repertoire, it could no longer resonate within the parameters of New England Irish life. Finally came the loss of audience.[43] In a Boston tavern, a man attempting to recite a tale of *Cú Chulainn*—thought to be "the greatest Irish hero"[44] —was overruled with the words, "Ah, sit down and shut your trap; we don't want to listen to ye!"

The naysayer's dissuasion brings us to another salient conjecture as to why the particularly male Irish storytelling tradition deteriorated after hunger-induced immigration. In New England, living the *truth* of circumstances had inured audiences against hearing "the tale," which Vladimir Propp defines as synonymous with the "lie" or the "falsehood."[45] "There is a [Irish] proverb that says, 'Tell a story, compose a lie, or get out' [*Inis scéal, cum bréag, no bí amuigh*], and it was taken seriously, especially in Irish-speaking districts."[46] Heeding the proverbial dictum, classic storytellers often ended their narratives by confronting truth and falsehood:

> That's my story, and if there's a lie in it, so be it [*Sin é mo scéal agus má atá bréag ann, bíodh*].[47]
> *Bhal, bhí sin fíor nó bhí seandaoine i Leitir Choilleadh á inse domhsa, go raibh sé fíor.*

[Well, that was true, for the old people in Letterkillew told it to me, that it was true].[48]
That's my story, and if there's a lie in it, let there be.
Tis long ago I heard it from my father.[49]

In retrospect, it seems to be the case that, although such denouements aligned well with the ritualized rubric of the tradition before the Great Hunger and were accepted as part of the storyteller's formulaic, their ambivalent stance regarding the truthfulness of the storyteller's repertoire could only be tolerated within a certain kind of undergirded world in which fantasy and myth were permitted. Once the willing suspension of disbelief had been repudiated and it had become clear to listeners that formulaic utterances were incapable of providing opportunities to "share a sense of *lived* experience,"[50] storytelling as it had functioned in Ireland met its demise.

However, as adumbrated above, there were other genres of the Irish oral tradition less shackled by the ritualized practices and behaviors demanded of the storytelling tradition; they ensured that some semblance of Irish oral lore would survive. It is to that repertoire, mainly the preserve of women, which this essay now turns.

Séamus Delargy, former Director of the Folklore Commission in Dublin, in what Alan Dundes describes as a "pivotal essay,"[51] provided an in-depth look at the story-tellers' world, his audience, and his craft. Before the Great Hunger, Delargy reveals, another type of deliverer of oral tradition, the *seanchaí* (or *seanchasaí*) commanded a broader range of lore called *seanchas*. By and large "associated with women," *seanchas* included "local tales, family-sagas, or genealogies, social-historical tradition, and the like."[52] Although these branches of oral tradition were "frowned upon by the men,"[53] it was women who excelled in them.[54] It was they who "could recount many tales of a short *realistic* type about fairies, ghosts, and other supernatural beings" and it was they who could include in the mix "music and folk-prayers."[55] Interestingly, a proclivity for realism and authenticity on the part of Irish women may have endured into more recent times, for Seán Mone notes that the great ballad singer Sarah Makem was uncomfortable with lying games, saying, "no use in telling a lie and the truth beside it."[56]

Delargy also provides further insight into women's role in the transmission of Irish folklore before the Great Hunger:

> While women do not take part in the storytelling, not a word of the tale escapes them, or if their relatives or close friends make any slip or hesitate in their recital, it is no uncommon experience . . . to hear the listening woman interrupt and correct the speaker.[57]

Albeit brief, these revelations regarding women in the storytelling tradition provide insight as to how the linguistic division of labor operated. Delargy's personal observations that *not a word of the tale escapes them*, and that women *interrupted and corrected* those who hesitated or slipped in their recitals, prompt us to realize how they inserted themselves into the narrative process in ways that were both accepted and customary. What is more, Irish women's penchant to claim their knowledge at *ad hoc* moments, to insist upon what they believed to be the *more accurate* or *truthful* transmission of oral tradition, and to countermand the misrepresentation of any aspect of the storyteller's repertoire deemed to have been delivered incorrectly, offer a glimpse into how, even after the main traditional pillars structured by the storytelling tradition had given way, a *habitus*—an inclination, proclivity or, in Bourdieu's parlance, an "unconscious principle of the ethos"[58]—endured such that Irish women would continue to engage in hortatory rhetoric, defined as "direct speech between speaker and hearers . . . in a style congruent with the ordinary speech of those engaged."[59] Women deployed the language of exhortation to maintain and preserve certain aspects of Irish traditional culture.

It is important to note that such rhetoric did not exist in a vacuum; rather, in Ireland it took its place alongside that of the widow who cursed against perceived injustice;[60] that of resourceful women who "challenged the [workhouse] system" to their own advantage;[61] and that of independence-seeking women who tested the boundaries of women's roles to the edge of life itself.[62] Such forms conveyed, not the *lies* or fiction of folk tales and hero tales, but the vivid and all-too-truthful circumstances of their quotidian lives. Women were described as collaborating with one another in simplifying and re-contextualizing their verbal repertoires under rapidly changing circumstances, running the gamut of emotion and conveying the all too truthful and bitter realities that Angela Carter describes as "...the poverty, hunger, shaky family relationships, all-pervasive cruelty, and also, sometimes, the good humour, the vigour [and] the straightforward consolations of a warm fire and a full belly."[63] Likewise, Angela Bourke notes that the task of the *mná caointe*—the Irish women lament poets who grieved the dead—was to confront "... all of the stages of what modern psychology recognizes as the *process* of grieving: denial, anger, bargaining, sadness and acceptance."[64]

This course of action is important in attempting to come to grips with the trauma that persisted after the Great Hunger, for what is especially striking about women's lore in New England is the very thing that the storytelling tradition lacked: flexibility. Women's lore needed no ritual of hearth or home to be deployed; rather, its *ad hoc* nature meant that it emerged in situations both timely and apt. Quick with a retort to the question, "how are the children?" a woman was said to have answered, "they are good in patches," a riposte that tacitly acknowledged her own efforts to improve her families' lives and to having achieved some modicum of success in doing so. On other occasions, consultants revealed their mothers' overt acknowledgement of the dire circumstances in which they found themselves. One recalled her mother's expression, "Oh Maurice, so many of us here and nothing for us," words which can be understood as both plaintive and hortatory, for they speak to a simultaneous sense of victim and urgent agent. "Maurice," real or imaginary, was being subtly and poetically goaded to alter familial circumstances by finding employment and caring for his family.[65]

Such inducement was part and parcel of cultural values instilled in Irish women. The rhetoric on the role of Irish mothers in the preservation of Ireland's language and culture can be dated at least to the middle of the 19th century and continued well into the 20th century. "The nation is the result of motherhood," decreed a *Dublin University Magazine* article in 1859;[66] nearly half a century later, Butler prognosticated that the future of Ireland's nationhood rested upon the shoulders of Irish women at home:

> . . . becoming imbued themselves with true nationality, they [Irish women] will, one and all, make their homes centres of Irish life. They will have the proud consciousness of knowing that in making the homes of Ireland Irish they will be doing the best day's work that has ever been done to make Ireland a nation in the fullest, truest, sense of the word.[67]

Then, too, "on the other side of the pond," the influence of Catholicism on the creation and maintenance of the ideals to which women should aspire was evident; Irish Americans were willing to pay homage to a religious hierarchy preaching the "twin gospels of respectability and resignation..."[68] Pulpit decrees trickled down to localities: "It was the parish priests of the ghettos who led their flock on the great march towards respectability, responsibility and patriotism."[69]

When it came to the role of women in the home, similar sets of values were "expressed by clerics who sermonized on the duties of women to their families."[70] Timothy Meagher notes that the Church dictated that the daughter's role was to work but, "The wife's role was to be a mother."[71] Such rhetoric resulted in Irish mothers in America becoming "Catholic superwomen" entrusted with the task of transmitting religious values, ideas, and affective ways of thinking.[72] Religious paraphernalia like rosary beads and holy pictures proliferated in Irish American religious life. New styles of private and public observances, such as praying the rosary and attending devotions, were promulgated with renewed vigor,[73] as was, in Angela Martin's apt phrase, "Heteropatriarchal Law" that reconstructed women's bodies in public and private space.[74]

On the other hand, even as the Church's power attempted to dominate, it is important to stress that the lives of the Irish continued to be ordered by numerous spiritual aphorisms delivered via a variety of formulaic expressions for "invoking powers not generally deemed part of ordinary human potential."[75] In Irish America, mothers delivered directly petitionary invocations like "Please God," "God willing," and, as one interviewee testified regarding a favorite utterance of her mother, "God increase your store, and put it in your heart to give me more." Uttered in social interactions with friends, neighbors and relatives, folk-prayers (*paidreacha dúchais*) seeking protection and prosperity could hardly be distinguished from greetings and blessings; they ensured smooth societal functioning and reflected "not so much a devout Christianity as a sense that the social encounters of everyday life represent[ed] something important in the wider scheme of things, and [were] worthy of divine or supernatural expression."[76]

Then, too, in keeping with their penchant for verbal remonstrations, Irish women in America drew upon their talent for uttering inflammatory "prayer curses" when the situation called for it. Consultants recalled their mothers' diatribes commencing with the words "God give me strength," "The Saints preserve us," "Oh, for the love of God," "Oh for the love of Mike," "Mother of God," and "Holy Jesus." They remembered what might be called "The Jesus, Mary, and Joseph formula," which invoked the Holy Family in a variety of ways which indexed, according to context, maternal anxiety, fear, animosity, or exasperated curiosity:

> Jesus, Mary, and Joseph!
> Jesus, Mary, and Joseph, pray for us.
> Jesus, Mary, and Joseph, what are ye up to now?

One consultant recalled a mother's prayer that both pleaded for patience and delivered a warning: "Mother used to say, 'Jesus, Mary, and Joseph, give me patience. The tears are very close to your eyes.'" Such expressions are not dissimilar from those collected by Éilis Brady among Dublin street mothers: "Although the words used [were] at times excessive, the tone of their delivery [was] usually of mock exaggeration, intended to impress the neighbors as much as to chastise the child."[77] Yet it was equally the case that Irish women faced a dual socialization dilemma: how to insure that their offspring survived in a new culture and simultaneously vouchsafe that they become imbued with the culture of their native homeland. To face the challenge, some Irish women in New England were said to have been as forthright and assertive as any man. Speaking of his grandmother, one consultant recalled: "I remember her telling me, 'It isn't because I hate you that I beat you; 'tis because I have the authority.'"

Many pithy expressions and sayings were remembered verbatim – or nearly so. Consultants described mothers and grandmothers as being inclined to ridicule any person not striving to be the best as well as anyone pretending to be.[78] One informant recalled that she was taught the names of her forebears—her *ginealas*, genealogy—and to never forget that she was "as good as the best of them."[79] Linking her own greatness to a member of her family tree, she revealed:

> My mother was an O'Toole who had relatives named O'Malley, Burke, [and] McGrail. Granuaile [Grace] O'Malley was claimed as an ancestor. She refused honours from Queen Elizabeth I by remarking, 'Make me a duchess, who was born a Queen?'[80]

Likewise, some Irish mothers transmitted Irish language expressions to their children. One consultant revealed:

> She taught me, or I picked up, simple phrases in Gaelic such as 'It's hot/cold;' 'Open/shut the door;' 'How are you?;' 'Where are you going?;' 'Sit down.' She and my grandmother (born in Holyoke of Irish parents) often spoke Irish together, usually when they didn't want me to know what they were saying.

Quoted speech is defined as "a frame in which the speaker is temporarily standing in for someone else and thus suppressing certain aspects of herself in favor of expressing aspects of the quoted one."[81] From the examples presented here, we learn how an Irish mother may have vicariously instilled aspects of the Irish language in her child.

Despite this kind of intentional transmission, it is equally important to mention reports of Irish women strategizing, negotiating, and finessing their way beyond the negative attitudes and biases foisted upon them. In doing so, some genealogical traditions were rejected outright. As Maureen Murphy insightfully argues, despite the fact that they were "only jokes," stereotypes of "Bridget" and "Biddy" infiltrated Irish American consciousness, stimulating those who had served as domestics to maintain vigilance in their awareness of the political and economic parameters of gender oppression and to reject their culture's former naming practices.[82] "Never name any one of your daughters 'Bridget,'" young women were told. When asked why, mothers' answers were nearly identical: "We were all 'Bridgets' back then." "Back then" continued into the early 1950s in some places, for as one of my consultants recalled, "in New York, most families brought Irish girls over as indentured servants in the 1920s through the early 1950s."[83]

Just as genealogical examples form part of the collection, so, too do the aforementioned "frowned upon [by men]" proverbs (seanfhocail). Many of the latter were recalled with a high degree of accuracy, some heard in New England for the first time as they fell from the lips of Irish immigrants. The more trenchant take their place along the side of the wry and humorous: "If you want to be praised, die; if you want to be blamed, marry"; "You can't make a silk purse out of a sow's ear"; "Health is the poor man's doctor"; "It's only a bargain if you need it"; "When all else fails, welcome haws"; "Man makes plans and God laughs"; and "You'd think she never stepped over a cowflop." By being delivered in crucial and contextual moments of truth and accuracy, each proverb, idiom or saying in its own right had the effect of accomplishing its purpose: to utter the voice of authority without having a specific voice at all, and thus to transmit the values of Irish culture to the next generation.

In addition, Irish women in America utilized short narratives (seanchas) to, as discussed above in terms of collective and archival memory, transmit and preserve an awareness of their former traditional practices. Unlike the folktale or hero tale [German Märchen], the legend [German Sage] is a narration reported to be "true." Of key importance is the fact that the telling of legends can be more "easily accommodated to women's routine[s] of constant domestic activity."[84] Robertson notes that "Irish women on the whole do not wish to act in witty dramas: they prefer emotional domestic scenes. Some, especially the old ones, live in drama, a [favorite] theme often being a maternal one."[85] Wit is inevitable in such circumstances; however, it emerges within the larger awareness of the need to convey a moral.

In Irish America, similar patterns ensued. Consultants discussed their mothers' folk beliefs in terms of superstitions (*piseógaí*) and prophylactic and propitiatory behaviors. In Irish America, the reproductive nature of anecdotes contributed to their survival; some interviewees noted that their Irish grandmothers had heard the legends from their own grandmothers:

> She said her grandmother told her this story. There was a boy who always slapped his mother. When he died and was buried, a hand appeared in the center of the grave. The mother was told she would have to go to the graveyard and slap the hand before it would go back into the grave. She did, and it disappeared.[86]

Another difference between *Märchen* and *Sage* concerns the latter's pragmatic aspects:

> Instead of the far away and long ago of folktale, they [legends] deal with a more-or-less recent past; instead of princesses, widows' daughters and giants, they deal with 'real' people, often very similar to the members of their audience, and [people who are] often named. Legends of the supernatural appeal to the credulity of listeners with detailed descriptions of familiar environments, life and work; they are valuable repositories of practical information therefore, but their central 'plot' is usually an extraordinary encounter of some kind. Most legends are short, and easily remembered.[87]

"At our probing," revealed one, "she would tell tales of the will-o'-the-wisp or the black dog, the pooka.[88] These would make us shiver, especially if a stair creaked when going to bed, as well as a dog that barked at night, or a rooster that didn't wait for morning to crow." As they had in Ireland, such legends functioned abroad as dramas in miniature; it was as if scenes within the household could be imagined and elaborated through sayings, superstitions, moral diatribes and highly-powered outbursts.

Coupled with such unwritten codes of cultural transmission were consultants' memories of their mothers' and grandmothers' belief in and hope for beneficence. Biddie Early, one of Ireland's mythical legendary healers—also referred to as "Shaking Biddy Early" by some—was identified as a wise woman [*bean feasa*]. One woman, noting that her "mother often talked about Biddy," insisting: "[I] must tell you about Biddy Early . . . (she) was very much alive." By the deployment of predominantly symbolic means, Biddy Early embodied the attributes of the quintessential powerful woman who healed what we might reference today as "crisis trauma."[89] Her solutions for societal afflictions usually involved repairing breaches—otherworldly as well as communal— that may have been overlooked or ignored by those who had flaunted societal norms. In New England, especially in the epochal years after the Great Hunger, the well-being of the community revolved around the restoration of balance and harmony, and often it was the wise-woman's task, if and when social dynamics ruptured, to undertake appropriate means to restore them. The fictional resort to the wise woman is a narrative in which the community tells itself the truth about its relationships, albeit in coded and condensed form.[90]

Biddy Early's viability as a credible figure within New England Irish American communities was confirmed by many strong recollections of her *name*. Her appearance in times of social crisis may indicate that she was, if not "everywoman," at least *many* women who served as guardians of the social order whenever it encountered threat or needed bolstering. Likewise, it is highly probable that New England women caregivers, faced with the tasks of rearing children in the paths of societal righteousness, utilized the legend of Biddy Early as one of their many verbal strategies and as part of a larger repertoire of oral tradition and verbal art.

An awareness of how this kind of lore enabled Irish women abroad helps to answer the question posed by Hasia Diner at the outset regarding the predominance of women migrants and their effect on the economic, social and cultural patterns of Irish America. If, as McCaffrey argues, women were the most civilizing element in Irish America, arguably it was their collective lore that came to their aid in the process. This chapter has argued that, although a literal as well as figurative folkloric division of labour prevailed within the storytelling tradition before the Great Hunger, yet the ritual pillars of support that undergirded the *sgéaltoir*'s narrations—spaces, times, repertoires, and the storytellers themselves—along with what they entailed, embodied, and privileged, collapsed under the weight of hunger, starvation, immigration, and loss.[91] In essence, the storytelling tradition's demise was the result of the inability of those pillars to withstand massive psychic trauma. Rituals of storytelling were so intimately linked to rigid patterns and formulae that when one fell, the others were destined to collapse along with it.[92] Their inability to adapt is noteworthy, for, as mentioned above, flexibility—the hallmark of the lore commanded by Irish women—is key to the preservation of collective memory.

Although Delargy asserts that storytellers and their repertoires were privileged and that all other material was valued on a lower scale, this chapter has suggested that the unrestricted nature of women's lore enabled its continuance. In fact, it was that their repertoire—short narratives [*seanchas*], proverbs [*seanfhocail*], folk-prayers (*paidreacha dúchais*), genealogical lore (*ginealas*), and *bon mots* in Irish—that enabled Irish women abroad to make decisions about their roles and the actions they would engage in while activating them. Needing no structures of utterance or pillars of support by way of time, place, person or repertoire, women's lore could be—and was—deployed anywhere. Irish women used it to maneuver and negotiate their lives and circumstances within the six New England states: – Rhode Island, Maine, Massachusetts, New Hampshire, Connecticut, and Vermont – articulating cultural values and verbal art for themselves, their husbands, their children, and their communities. In possessing such ubiquitous qualities, Irish women's lore had a staying power preserved in Irish New England late into the 20th century, if not longer, and assured in folk memory as a result.

Endnotes

[1] Many people contributed to the creation as well as the improvement of this chapter; they include Christina Brophy, Mary Burke, Cara Delay, Séamus Pender, and the New England consultants who gave so much of their time in revealing memories of what their ancestors had told them. I wish to thank them all, as well as this work's editors who offered thoughtful and provocative suggestions. *Go raibh mile maith agaibh go léir.*

[2] Lawrence J. McCaffrey, "Diaspora Comparisons and Irish-American Uniqueness" in *New Perspectives on the Irish Diaspora*, ed. Charles Fanning (Carbondale IL, 2000), pp 15-27.

[3] Hasia Diner, "The Search for Bread: Patterns of Female Emigration" in *The Irish Women's History Reader*, ed. Alan Hayes and Diane Urquhart (London 2001), pp 178-179.

[4] See, for instance, Patricia Lysaght's references to Peig Sayers in "Traditional Storytelling in Ireland in the Twentieth Century" in *Traditional Storytelling Today: An International Sourcebook*, ed. Margaret Reid MacDonald (London: 1999), pp 264-272, and Seán Ó hEochaidh's references to Anna Nic an Luain in "*Tomhasannái ó Thír Chonaill* (Riddles from Donegal)," *Béaloideas* 19 (1949-1950), pp 3-28.

[5] Guy Beiner, *Remembering the Year of the French* (Madison WI, 2007), p. 187; see also J. H. Delargy, "The Gaelic Story-teller, with some Notes on Gaelic Folk-Tales," The Sir John Rhys Memorial Lecture (London, 1945), pp 1-47.

[6] For more on the methodology and the nature of the collection, see E. Moore Quinn, *Irish American Folklore in New England* (Dublin, 2009), pp 209-224, and E. Moore Quinn, "'She must have come steerage': The Great Famine in New England Folk Memory" in *Ireland's Great Hunger: Relief, Representation, and Remembrance*, vol. 2, ed. David A. Valone (Lanham MD, 2010), pp 163-164.

[7] Janet Nolan, "Silent Generations: New Voices of Irish America," *American Literary History* 17, no 3 (2005), pp 595-603.

8 Richard Dorson, *American Folklore and the Historian* (Chicago, 1971), 144. In my collecting efforts, I took into consideration the fact that my interviewees were literate and that some of what they contributed may have been gleaned from published sources. To control this, I eliminated published materials provided by consultants, including only personal correspondences and/or oral testimonials provided in interviews.

9 This was the designation given to the oftentimes small and poorly constructed ships upon which Irish emigrants sailed. Daniel O'Connell referred to them as "ocean hearses", cited in Potter, *To the Golden Door* (Boston, 1960), p. 155. A slogan of sailors, "Emigrants out and timber back," aptly described the practice of using Irish women, men, and children for human ballast in the crossings. See Edward Laxton, *The Famine Ships: The Irish Exodus to America, 1846-1851* (London, 1996), pp 233-4.

10 Cathal Póirtéir, "Introduction" in *The Great Irish Famine*, ed. Cathal Póirtéir (Dublin, 1995), p. 11.

11 Henry Greenspan, "Lives as Texts: Symptoms in the Modes of Recounting in the Life Histories of Holocaust Survivors" in *Storied Lives: The Cultural Politics of Self-Understanding*, ed. George C. Rosenwald and Richard L. Ochberg (New Haven, l992), pp 145-164.

12 Seán De Fréine, *The Great Silence* (Dublin, 1978).

13 Kathleen Villiers-Tuthill, *Patient Endurance: The Great Famine in Connemara* (Dublin, 1997), p. 148.

14 Ibid.

15 For more on this localized Co. Kerry expression, which survived from Penal Times, see Seán Gaffney and Séamus Cashman, eds., *Proverbs and Sayings of Ireland* (Dublin, 1979), p.17.

16 For more on the curse of Cromwell, see Patrick C. Power, *The Book of Irish Curses* (Dublin, 1974), p. 25.

17 Tómás De Bhaldraithe (ed), *English-Irish Dictionary* (Dublin, 1959), p. 331.

18 Peter Quinn, "Introduction: An Interpretation of Silences," *Éire/Ireland* XXXII, no. 1 (1997), pp 7-19.

19 Cited in Robert A. Georges and Michael Owen Jones, *Folkloristics: An Introduction* (Bloomington IN, 1995), p. 85.

20 Michael Schudson, "Preservation of the Past in Mental Life," *The Quarterly Newsletter of the Laboratory of Comparative Human Cognition* 9, no 1 (1987), pp 5-11.

21 Schudson, "Preservation of the Past," p. 5.

22 James Fentress and Chris Wickham, *Social Memory: New Perspectives on the Past* (Oxford, 1992), pp 58-59.

23 See Emmet Larkin, "The Devotional Revolution in Ireland, 1850-1875, *American Historical Review* 77 (1972), pp 625-652.

24 Margaret Lynch-Brennan, *The Irish Bridget: Irish Immigrant Women in Domestic Service in America, 1840-1930* (Syracuse, 2009), 36; see also pp 39; 71- 72; 80-81; and 114-117.

25 Kevin Whelan, "Clachans: Landscape and Life in Ireland before and after the Famine" in *At the anvil: essays in honour of William J. Smyth*, ed. Patrick J. Duffy and William Nolan (Dublin: 2012), pp 453-475.

26 Timothy P. O'Neill, "Rural Life," in *Social Life in Ireland, 1800-45*, ed. R. B. McDowell (Dublin, 1957), pp 43-56.

27 Such houses were known by different names in various parts of Ireland. For instance, Jenny McGlynn, one of Patricia Lysaght's consultants, refers to a dwelling that welcomed people in as a "rambling house," noting that "everyone rambled in." See Patricia Lysaght, "Traditional Storytelling in Ireland," p. 269.

28 Based on 5th century C.E. battles between the warring factions of Ulster and Connacht, the hero tales of the Ulster Cycle emerged in the Middle Ages on the lips of bards eager to entertain patrons who displayed a penchant for the lore of adventure. The Cattle Raid of Cooley [*Táin Bó Cuailnge*] features the exploits of a main protagonist, *Cú Chulainn*, who defeats Queen Maeve [*Medhbh*] to retain "possession of the great brown bull of Cooley." For more, see Ciaran Brady, ed., *The Encyclopedia of Ireland: an A-Z guide to its People, Places, History, and Culture* (New York, 2000), p. 170.

29 Niall Ó Dónaill, ed. *Foclóir Gaeilge-Béarla* (Dublin, 1977), p. 540.

30 The Fianna Cycle is an admixture of druidic lore and warrior-like feats of derring-do. It gained immense popularity in medieval times, and the tales were disseminated throughout the Celtic world. For more, see Patricia Lysaght, "Traditional Storytelling in Ireland," p. 265.

31 Lynch-Brennan, *The Irish Bridget*, pp 5-6.

32 For more on rituals of reversal, see John W. Morehead, "Rituals of Inversion" in *Encyclopedia of Humor Studies*, vol. 2, Salvatore Attardo, ed. (Thousand Oaks, CA, 2014), p. 648. Morehead notes that such rites take place at special events that provide "a frame that gives license for people to violate everyday cultural norms and social codes." The contravention of the norm is often "considered temporary, playful, or restricted to a special *time* and/or *place* [emphases added]."

33 Delargy, "The Gaelic Story-teller," p. 24.

34 Diarmuid Ó Muirithe, *A Dictionary of Anglo-Irish* (Dublin 1996), p. 25. The practice is described in the following manner: "All the neighbours gathered into one of the houses each night for the *airneál*, old men and women, young boys and girls.

After the youngsters would have dancing the storytelling would commence" (See this same source for alternative spellings of *airneál*. Note that the event took place *each night*.

35 Delargy, "The Gaelic Story-teller," p. 6.

36 Robert Helvey, *On Strategic Nonviolent Conflict: Thinking about the Fundamentals* (Boston, 2004). I borrow Helvey's metaphor of "pillars" loosely in order to examine how social change – in this case, in Irish verbal art – can occur.

37 The hero tale is equated with the German *Märchen*, a "folktale characterized by elements of magic or the supernatural": *Encyclopedia Britannica* (http://www.britannica.com/art/Marchen) (Accessed, 8 Feb. 2016).

38 Delargy notes that primarily the tales were told to and intended for an audience of men.

39 Michael P. Quinlan, *Irish Boston: A Colorful Look at Boston's Irish Past* (Guilford, CT, 2004), 7; see also Carlton Jackson, *A Social History of the Scotch-Irish* (Lanham, MD, 1993), p. 58.

40 Kerby Miller, *Emigrants and Exiles: Ireland and the Irish Exodus to North America* (New York, 1988 [1985]), pp 71; 104; 134-5.

41 Kenneth Nilsen, personal communication, no date.

42 For more on the emergence of a kind of "pseudo-hero" in Irish American life in nineteenth and early twentieth century Irish America, see E. Moore Quinn, "The Irish Rent . . . and Mended: Transitional Textual Communities in Nineteenth Century America" in *Irish Studies Review* 23.2 (2015), 209-224.

43 Rodgers, "Introduction," p. viii.

44 Daragh Smyth, *Cú Chulainn: An Irish Age Hero* (Dublin, 2005), 1. Smyth cites Declan Kiberd's assertion that the Cú Chulainn story falls into the category of "super myth" in that it generates a force "so powerful as to obscure the individual writer and to unleash an almost superhuman force."

45 Cited in Angela Carter, *Book of Fairy Tales* (London 2005), p. xiii.

46 Liam Mac Con Iomaire, *Ireland of the Proverb* (Dublin, 1994), p. 124.

47 Kenneth Nilsen, personal communication, no date.

48 Pádraig Eoghain Phádraig Mac An Luain, in Séamus Ó Catháin (trans.) *An Hour by the Fire* (Dublin, 1985), pp 21-22.

49 Seán Ó Súilleabháin, *Folktales of Ireland* (Chicago, 1966), p. 204. In Ireland, often it was necessary to validate a tale's accuracy by appealing literally to the "voices of the ancestors" – members of an older generation – for proof that the tales were true.

50 Carter, *Book of Fairy Tales*, xiii; italics added.

51 Alan Dundes, ed., *International Folkloristics: Classic Contributions by the Founders of Folklore* (Oxford, 1999), p. 157.

52 Delargy, The Gaelic Story-teller," p. 6.

53 Ibid., p. 7.

54 Ibid.

55 Ibid., pp 6-7; emphasis added.

56 Quoted by Seán Mone, "Sarah Makem – As I Roved Out" (Glos, UK: Musical Traditions Records, 2011): (http://www.mustrad.org.uk/articles/makem.htm) (Accessed 7 June 2015).

57 Delargy, "The Gaelic Story-teller," p. 7.

58 Pierre Bourdieu, *Outline of a Theory of Practice* (Cambridge, 1977), p. 77.

59 Thomas O. Sloan, *Encyclopedia of Rhetoric*, vol. 1 (Oxford, 2001), p. 280.

60 E. Moore Quinn, "'All I Had Left Were My Words'; The Widow's Curse in 19th and 20th Century Ireland" in Christina Brophy and Cara Delay (eds) *Women, Reform and Resistance in Ireland, 1850-1950* (New York, 2015), pp 211-233.

61 Cara Delay, "Deposited Elsewhere: The Sexualized Female Body and the Modern Irish Landscape," *Etudes irlandaises* 37, no. 1 (2012), p. 78.

62 Angela Bourke, *The Burning of Bridget Cleary* (New York, 1999).

63 Carter, *Book of Fairy Tales*, p. xiii.

64 Angela Bourke, "Lamenting the Dead" in Angela Bourke *et alia*, ed, *The Field Day Anthology of Irish Writing*, vol. 4 (New York, 2002b), 1365-1367; italics added.

65 Perhaps the name "Maurice" referenced the name of the woman's husband; if so, the rhyme would serve as an exemplar of family folklore; on the other hand, the expression may also have been used locally to index a general recognition of hard times for the Irish in a region of New England.

66 Quoted in Maria Luddy, "Women and Politics in Nineteenth Century Ireland" in *Women & Irish History*, ed. Maryann Gialenella Valiulis & Mary O'Dowd (Dublin, 1997), p. 101.

67 Quoted in Luddy, "Women and Politics," pp 101-102.

68 Bruce Nelson, "Irish Americans, Irish Nationalism, and the 'Social' Question 1916-1923," *Boundary 2*, 32.1 (2004), p. 149.

69 Patrick Bishop, *The Irish Empire* (New York, 1999), p. 107.

70 Luddy, "Women and Politics," p. 101.

71 Meagher, "Sweet Good Mothers," p. 342.

72 Dolan notes that, as early as the 1820s and 1830s, the Irish in America were aligning themselves with priests, playing central roles in the establishment of parishes, and taking part in the governance and control of the flock. For more, see Jay P. Dolan, *The American Catholic Experience: A History from Colonial Times to the Present* (New York, 1985), pp 165-168; 252.

73 Kevin Kenny, *The American Irish: A History* (Essex, 2000), p. 164.

74 Angela K. Martin, "The Practice of Identity and an Irish Sense of Place," *Gender, Place & Culture: A Journal of Feminist Geography* 4, no. 1 (1997): pp 89-114, passim.

75 Power, *Book of Irish Curses*, p. 91.

76 Carmel Fitzgerald, *Céad Míle Fáilte*: A Collection of Irish Greetings, Blessings and Photographs (Dublin, 2006), pp 5-6.

77 Éilis Brady, *All In! All In! A Selection of Dublin Children's Street-Games with Rhymes and Music* (Dublin 1975), p. 2.

78 Edward C. McManus, *The Nana in the Chair, and the Tales She Told: An Anecdotal Biography of Mary Dunne Ware (1860-1956)* (Bloomingon, IN, 2004), 212. This point is made vividly clear in McManus's discussion of his grandmother's use of "The Hero" (pronounced "Hair-O"), an expression deployed "to question the credibility" of someone offering unsolicited and unwelcome advice.

79 Cited in Mary McCaffery and Michael P. Quinlan, *Irish Trivia* (Boston, 1986), p. i.

80 Mary O'Dowd, "Grace O'Malley" in Brian Lalor, ed., *The Encyclopedia of Ireland* (Dublin, 2003), 827-828. Granuaile's [*Gráinne Mhaol*] name survives strongly in Irish folklore. Her official name was *Gráinne Ní Mháille*, or Grace O'Malley. She was acknowledged as a formidable force along the western coast of Ireland in the late 16th century. In 1593, she is reputed to have met Queen Elizabeth I in London to seek a widow's compensation after the death of her second husband, Viscount Mayo. Although no official record of Granuaile's meeting with Queen Elizabeth survives, it is believed that her demands were met.

81 Eileen Moore Quinn, "Entextualizing Famine, Reconstituting Self: Testimonial Narratives from Ireland" in *Anthropological Quarterly* 74, no. 3 (2001), pp 72-88.

82 Maureen Murphy, "Bridget and Biddy: Images of the Irish Servant Girl in Puck Cartoons (1880-1890)" in Charles Fanning, ed., *New Perspectives on the Irish Diaspora* (Carbondale IL, 2000), pp 152-175.

83 See Sharon Lambert, "Irish Women's emigration to England 1922-1960: The Lengthening of Family Ties," in *The Irish Women's History Reader*, Alan Hayes and Diane Urquhart, eds. (London, 2001), p. 181. Lambert notes that, between 1926 and 1951, approximately 52,000 women left Southern Ireland for the United States. Name change was imposed upon Bridget McGeoghegan who came to Boston from Donegal in 1923; her aunts insisted that she be called Bertha "because of the American Biddy jokes about Irish servant girls." See Lynch-Brennan, *The Irish Bridget*, p. xviii.

84 Angela Bourke, "Legends and the Supernatural" in *The Field Day Anthology of Irish Writing*, vol. 4, ed. Angela Bourke, et alia (New York, 2002a), p. 1284.

85 Olivia Robertson, *It's an Old Irish Custom* (New York, 1953), p. 95.

86 For a variant of this tale, collected from Co. Antrim in Ireland, see Séamus Ó Catháin, *Irish Life and Lore* (Dublin, 1982), pp 66-67.

87 Bourke, "Legends and the Supernatural," p. 1284.

88 "Pooka" is the Anglicized word for Irish *púca*, thought to be a solitary fairy disguised as a horse who wooed victims to the Otherworld on its back. See Kevin Danaher, *Irish Customs and Beliefs* (Cork, 2004), p. 95.

89 Géaróid Ó Crualaoich, *The Book of the Cailleach: Stories of the Wise Woman Healer* (Cork, 2003), p. 72.

90 Ó Crualaoich, *Book of the Cailleach*, p. 73.

91 "Sacred" rituals like patterns (devotions to local saints) were equally unsustainable in Irish America and underwent collapse. See Timothy Meagher, *Inventing Irish America: Generation, Class and Ethnic Identity in an American City 1880-1928* (Notre Dame, IN, 2001), p. 29.

92 Also collapsing under the weight of immigration were the "big" Gaelic songs, "what one might describe as the highest aspects of [the storyteller's] singing tradition." For more, see Bill Meek, *Songs of the Irish in America* (Dublin, 1978), p. 8.

Works Cited

Beiner, Guy. *Remembering the Year of the French*. Madison WI: University of Wisconsin Press, 2007.

Bishop, Patrick. *The Irish Empire*. New York: St. Martin's Press, 1999.

Bourdieu, Pierre. *Outline of a Theory of Practice*. Cambridge: University Press, 1977.

Bourke, Angela. "Legends and the Supernatural." In *The Field Day Anthology of Irish Writing*, vol. 4, edited by Angela Bourke et alia, 1284-1286. New York: University Press, 2002a.

Bourke, Angela. "Lamenting the Dead." In *The Field Day Anthology of Irish Writing*, vol. 4, edited by Angela Bourke et alia, 1365-1367. New York: University Press, 2002b.

Brady, Ciarán, ed. *The Encyclopedia of Ireland*. New York: Oxford University Press, 2000.

Brady, Éilis. *All In! All In! A Selection of Dublin Children's Street-Games with Rhymes and Music*. Dublin: Four Courts Press, 1975.

Carter, Angela. *Book of Fairy Tales*. Cork: Mercier Press, 2004.

Danaher, Kevin. *Irish Customs and Beliefs*. Cork: Mercier Press, 2004.

De Bhaldraithe, Tómás (ed), *English-Irish Dictionary*. Dublin, 1959.

De Fréine, Seán. *The Great Silence*. Dublin: An Gúm, 1978.

Delargy, J. H. "The Gaelic Story-teller, with some Notes on Gaelic Folk-Tales." The Sir John Rh s Memorial Lecture, 1-47. London, 1945.

Diner, Hasia. "The Search for Bread: Patterns of Female Emigration." In *The Irish Women's History Reader*, edited by Alan Hayes and Diane Urquhart, 178-179. London: Routledge, 2001.

Dolan, Jay P. *The American Catholic Experience: A History from Colonial Times to the Present*. New York: Garden City, 1985.

Dorson, Richard. *American Folklore and the Historian*. Chicago: University Press, 1971.

Dundes, Alan, ed. *International Folkloristics: Classic Contributions by the Founders of Folklore*. Oxford: Rowman and Littlefield, 1999.

Fentress, James, and Chris Wickham. *Social Memory: New Perspectives on the Past*. Oxford: Blackwell, 1992.

Fitzgerald, Carmel. *Céad Míle Fáilte*: *A Collection of Irish Greetings, Blessings and Photographs*. Dublin: Ashfield Press, 2006.

Gaffney, Seán, and Séamus Cashman, eds. *Proverbs and Sayings of Ireland*. Dublin: Wolfhound Press, 1979.

Georges, Robert A., and Michael Owen Jones. *Folkloristics: An Introduction*. Bloomington: Indiana University Press, 1995.

Greenspan, Henry. "Lives as Texts: Symptoms in the Modes of Recounting in the Life Histories of Holocaust Survivors." In *Storied Lives: The Cultural Politics of Self-Understanding*, ed. by George C. Rosenwald and Richard L. Ochberg. New Haven: Yale University Press, l992.

Helvey, Robert. *On Strategic Nonviolent Conflict: Thinking about the Fundamentals*. Boston: Albert Einstein Institution, 2004.

Holloway, Diane E. *American History in Song: Lyrics from 1900 to 1945*. San Jose: IUniverse. 2001.

Jackson, Carlton. *A Social History of the Scotch-Irish*. Lanham, MD: Madison Books, 1993.

Kenny, Kevin. *The American Irish: A History*. Essex: Longman, 2000.

Lambert, Sharon. "Irish Women's Emigration to England 1922-1960: The Lenthening of Family Ties." In *The Irish Women's History Reader*, ed. by Alan Hayes and Diane Urquhart, 179-187. London: Routledge, 2001.

Larkin, Emmet. "The Devotional Revolution in Ireland, 1850-1875. *American Historical Review* 77 (1972), 625-652.

Laxton, Edward. *The Famine Ships: The Irish Exodus to America, 1846-1851*. London: Holt, 1996.

Luddy, Maria. "Women and Politics in Nineteenth Century Ireland" in *Women & Irish History*, edited by Maryann Gialenella Valiulis & Mary O'Dowd, 889-108. Dublin: Wolfhound Press, 1997.

Lynch-Brennan, Margaret. *The Irish Bridget: Irish Immigrant Women in Domestic Service in America, 1840-1930*. Syracuse: University Press, 2009.

Lysaght, Patricia. "Traditional Storytelling in Ireland in the Twentieth Century" in *Traditional Storytelling Today: An International Sourcebook*, edited by Margaret Reid MacDonald, 264-272. London: Routledge, 1999.

Mac An Luain, Pádraig Eoghain Phádraig. *An Hour by the Fire*. Translated by Séamus Ó Catháin. Dublin: Comhairle Bhéaloideas Éireann, 1985.

Mac Con Iomaire, Liam. *Ireland of the Proverb*. Dublin: Town House, 1994.

Martin, Angela K. "The Practice of Identity and an Irish Sense of Place. *Gender, Place & Culture: A Journal of Feminist Geography* 4, no. 1 (1997), 89-114.

McCaffery, Mary, and Michael P. Quinlan. *Irish Trivia*. Boston: Quinlan Press, 1986.

McCaffrey, Lawrence J. "Diaspora Comparisons and Irish-American Uniqueness." In *New Perspectives on the Irish Diaspora*, edited by Charles Fanning, 15-27. Carbondale: Southern Illinois University Press, 2000.

McManus, Edward C. *The Nana in the Chair, and the Tales She Told: An Anecdotal Biography of Mary Dunne Ware (1860-1956)*. Bloomington, IN: Authorhouse, 2004.

Meagher, Timothy. "Sweet Good Mothers and Women out in the World: the Roles of Irish American Women in Late Nineteenth and Early Twentieth Century Worcester, Massachusetts." *US Catholic Historian* 5 (1986), 325-344.

Meagher, Timothy. *Inventing Irish America: Generation, Class and Ethnic Identity in an American City 1880-1928*. Notre Dame, IN: University Press, 2001.

Meek, Bill. *Songs of the Irish in America*. Dublin: Gilbert Dalton, 1978.

Miller, Kerby. *Emigrants and Exiles: Ireland and the Irish Exodus to North America*. Oxford: University Press, 1988.

Mone, Seán. "Sarah Makem – As I Roved Out." Glos, UK: Musical Traditions Records, 2011.

Morehead, John W. "Rituals of Inversion" in *Encyclopedia of Humor Studies*, Volume 2, edited by Salvatore Attardo, 648-649. Thousand Oaks, CA: Sage, 2014.

Murphy, Maureen. "Bridget and Biddy: Images of the Irish Servant Girl in Puck Cartoons (1880-1890)" in *New Perspectives on the Irish Diaspora*, edited by Charles Fanning, 152-175. Carbondale: Southern Illinois University Press, 2000.

Nelson, Bruce. "Irish Americans, Irish Nationalism, and the 'Social' Question 1916-1923." *Boundary 2* 32, no. 1 (2004), 147-178.

Nolan, Janet. "Silent Generations: New Voices of Irish America." *American Literary History* 17, no 3 (2005), 595-603.

Ó Catháin, Séamus. *Irish Life and Lore*. Dublin: Mercier Press, 1982.

Ó Crualaoich, Géaróid. *Book of the Cailleach: Stories of the Wise Woman Healer*. Cork: University Press, 2003.

Ó Dónaill, Niall, ed. *Foclóir Gaeilge-Béarla*. Dublin: Folens, 1977.

O'Dowd, Mary. "Grace O'Malley." In *The Encyclopedia of Ireland*, edited by Brian Lalor, 827-828. Dublin: Gill and Macmillan, 2003.

Ó hEochaidh, Seán. "*Tomhasannái ó Thír Chonaill* (Riddles from Donegal." *Béaloideas*, 19 (1949-1950), 3-28.

Ó Muirithe, Diarmuid. *A Dictionary of Anglo-Irish*. Dublin: Four Courts Press, 1996.

Ó Súilleabháin, Seán. *Folktales of Ireland*. Chicago: University Press, 1966.

Póirtéir, Cathal. "Introduction." In *The Great Irish Famine*, edited by Cathal Póirtéir, 9-17. Dublin: Mercier Press, 1995.

Potter, George. *To the Golden Door: The Story of the Irish in Ireland and America*. Boston: Little, Brown, 1960.

Power, Patrick C. *The Book of Irish Curses*. Dublin: Templegate, 1974.

Quinlan, Michael P. *Irish Boston: A Colorful Look at Boston's Irish Past.* Guilford, CT: Globe Pequot, 2004.

Quinn, E. Moore. *Irish American Folklore in New England*. Dublin: Bethesda, 2009.

Quinn, E. Moore. "'She must have come steerage': The Great Famine in New England Folk Memory." In *Ireland's Great Hunger: Relief, Representation, and Remembrance*, vol. 2, edited by David A. Valone, 161-180. Lanham MD: University Press of America, 2010.

Quinn, E. Moore. "The Irish Rent . . . and Mended: Transitional Textual Communities in Nineteenth Century America." *Irish Studies Review* 23, no. 2 (2015), 209-224.

Quinn, E. Moore. "'All I Had Left Were My Words': The Widow's Curse in 19th and 20th Century Ireland." *Women, Reform and Resistance in Ireland, 1850-1950*, edited by Christina Brophy and Cara Delay, 211-233. New York: Palgrave MacMillan, 2015.

Quinn, Eileen Moore. "Entextualizing Famine, Reconstituting Self: Testimonial Narratives from Ireland." *Anthropological Quarterly* 74, no. 3 (2001), 72-88.

Quinn, Peter. "Introduction: An Interpretation of Silences." *Éire/Ireland* XXXII, no. 1 (1997), 7-19.

Robertson, Olivia. *It's an Old Irish Custom*. New York: Vanguard Press, 1953.

Rodgers, W. R. "Introduction." In *An Old Woman's Reflections: The Life and Times of Peig Sayers*. Translated by Séamus Ennis, Oxford: University Press, 1962.

Schudson, Michael. "Preservation of the Past in Mental Life." *The Quarterly Newsletter of the Laboratory of Comparative Human Cognition* 9, no. 1 (1987), 5-11.

Sloan, Thomas O. *Encyclopedia of Rhetoric*, vol. 1. Oxford: University Press, 2001.

Smyth, Daragh. *Cú Chulainn: An Irish Age Hero*. Dublin: Irish Academic Press, 2005.

Villiers-Tuthill, Kathleen. *Patient Endurance: The Great Famine in Connemara*. Dublin: Connemara Girl Publications, 1997.

Wright, Robert L. ed. *Irish Emigrant Ballads and Songs*. Bowling Green: University Press, 1975.

Chapter Ten

Keeping hope alive:
Jane Elgee and Irish literature

Matthew Skwiat

Jane Francesca Elgee was a poet, translator, folklorist and nationalist in Ireland during the 19th century. Her work, particularly her poetry during the Great Famine in the 1840s, made her a national icon of Ireland and an influence on the next generation of Irish writers, including her son, Oscar Wilde, William Butler Yeats, George Bernard Shaw, Lady Gregory and Maud Gonne. The *Kerry Sentinel* proclaimed at her death in 1896 that she was the "National Poetess of the century,"[1] an evaluation that was reiterated by many 19th century critics and artists, but most importantly, by the Irish people themselves. She lived her life as a hero of the Irish public, but her reputation has since been trampled by the controversial legacy of her son and the perceived stain of inferiority that many critics have heaped on her work. Although writing during the age of Queen Victoria, "Speranza" (her chosen pen-name) drew inspiration from and reworked the conventions of the Romantic Movement, creating at once an emotionally resonant portrait of the Famine and a damning polemic of governmental incompetence. Percy Shelley and Lord Byron were her influences, but Speranza's poetry stands on its own and would continue to be a source of inspiration for the next generation of Irish writers. This chapter seeks to refocus the critical lens by releasing Speranza from the shadow of her son and placing her within the frameworks of Romanticism, Famine narratives and Irish literature itself.

So how did Speranza go from "National Poetess" to forgotten artist? The sources of this fall from grace are varied and are embedded in the cultural memory of Ireland, the overriding patriarchal influence of nationalist literature, as well as the character assassination by critics and some former friends made on her after her death. William Butler Yeats, a friend not only of Oscar but Speranza herself, recreated in his *Autobiography* a version of the older Wilde steeped in tragedy and elephantine in feature. He wrote:

> Lady Wilde when I knew her received her friends with blinds drawn and shutters closed that none might see her withered face, longed always perhaps, though certainly amid much self mockery, for some impossible splendor of character and circumstance.[2]

Yeats' Speranza seems a precursor to Tennessee Williams' Blanche Dubois in *A Streetcar Named Desire* and a far cry from the Speranza he drew inspiration from. Moreover, one of Yeats' early plays *The Hour Glass* (1903) had been inspired by Speranza's "A Priests Tale" from her *Ancient Legends of Ireland*.[3]

Equally damning was George Bernard Shaw, who possessed an acidic wit both on and off the stage, and who, like Yeats, had been a guest at Speranza's literary salons. In the early 1880s, Shaw was an up and comer in London who was without social or literary footing, but as he explains in "My Memories of Oscar Wilde," Speranza provided entrée into her bohemian circle of artists and intellectuals in London. Shaw notes she was "nice to me in London during my desperate days."[4] This provides just a glimpse into Speranza's generosity and social prestige later in life, but Shaw's recollections are, like Yeats', peppered with vindictive asides. He later mocked Speranza's supposed "gigantism," describing her "enormous" hands and "the gigantic splaying of her palm."[5] Shaw's comments once again illustrate that Speranza's memory, a mere 20 years after her death, was overtaken by caricature and was increasingly overshadowed by the notoriety (both good and bad) of her son.

By the early 20th century, the work of Speranza was being undergirded by the tragedy of her son's life and the titillating gossip that others were spreading of the Wilde family. Ironically, as the Irish Literary Revival was in full swing, a movement largely inspired by the Young Ireland Movement of the 1840s, Speranza herself was slowly being pushed to the margins. Newspapers and Irish statesmen sang the praises of the men of 1848 like John Mitchel and Thomas Francis Meagher, but for the women of that movement like Jane Elgee, Ellen Dempsey and Mary Kelly, there was nothing. Antoinette Quinn notes in "Ireland/Herland: Women and Literary Nationalism" that "nationalist women writers have been effectively erased from the Irish literary canon, and even Lady Gregory is better known on academic curricula as an adjunct to W.B. Yeats' Abbey Theatre career than a successful dramatist in her own right."[6] Irish female poets, including Speranza, were increasingly looked at as incompatible with a nationalist literature that was overwhelmingly male, even though the images and symbols of Ireland during this time were increasingly female: "queen," "mother" and "daughter." Yeats, along with Lady Gregory, repurposed the mythical Cathleen Ni Houlihan into a rousing symbol of Irish nationalism while Patrick Pearse's poetry repeatedly drew inspiration from the mother figure. Pearse's *Mise Éire* ("I am Ireland") reimagines the country as mother of Cúchulainn and "lonelier than the Old Woman of Beare,"[7] relying on past nationalist folklore steeped in feminine symbolism.

Maud Gonne in many ways exemplified Ireland with her larger-than-life personality, towering frame, and nationalist zest. Yeats, a lover of reinvention, even referred to Gonne as "The New Speranza" in an 1892 edition of the *United Irishman*.[8] It is unclear what Gonne's response was to this charming praise from Yeats, but it highlights the fleeting memory of Speranza's presence in the Celtic revival. Curiously, Speranza does not feature in any of the letters or written works of Lady Gregory, Maud Gonne or Countess Markievicz, which further reveals her diminished presence. The young Jane Elgee, however, had viewed herself as a prophetic voice of Ireland, seeing herself as a poet-priestess. For her, the poet was both mystical and eternal. She wrote in an 1845 poem, "Remonstrance," "the poet's place is by the Tree of Life,/ Whose fruit turn men into Gods."[9] She also told a fledgling young poet in 1881, "You and other poets are content to express only your little soul in poetry. I express the soul of a great nation."[10]

Speranza placed great faith in the poet and the symbolic imagery both mystical and revolutionary. She in many ways embodied the legendary warrior poet Oisín, whom she referenced in her poetry and wrote about in her works on Irish folklore. Oisín, coincidentally, also had a son, Oscar. Speranza was keen enough to note this, telling a friend at the birth of her second son, "he is to be called Oscar Fingal Wilde. Is not that grand, misty, and Ossianic?"[11] The legends and folklore of Ireland would continue to be an inspiration for Speranza years after the Young Ireland movement. She pieced together fragments of her husband William Wilde's folklore, and contributed her own articles. Yeats' review of Lady Wilde's *Ancient Cures, Charms, and Usages of Ireland* for the *Scots Observer* in 1890 serves as a reminder of Speranza's influence on the young Yeats, who was himself heavily involved in Irish folklore at this time. He wrote of the book that it is "the fullest and most beautiful gathering of Irish folklore in existence."[12] Speranza's connection to the Irish past was an extension of her own artistic creation and a reminder of both her literary influences and popularity during her lifetime.

It was, however, Speranza's poetry that made her both a literary success and an icon of the Irish people. Jane Elgee was born into a conservative Protestant household in 1822 or 1826 (sources differ). Outwardly, the family was propriety itself with some suggestion that her family name Elgee dated back to Italy with the Algati's of Florence.[13] Speranza herself relished this shaky bit of information telling friends and colleagues that she was a descendent of Dante. This comparison is of interest as it both highlights the flamboyant personality of Speranza while also drawing a connection to one of her biggest influences, Dante Alighieri. Dante's poetic flourish has been highly imitated, but for Speranza it was the combination of poet and nation that was inspiring. For example, Dante was one of the first poets in Italy to write in the Italian dialect and his poetry, especially during the nationalistic excitement of the 1848 revolutions, was influential in unifying Italy in the late 19th century. Speranza tapped into this spirit in her fiery poem "Sign of the Times," where she writes, "bravely done ye Roman Eagles, ye are fluttering at last;/ Spread your broad wings bravely and proud."[14] She was able to utilize the unifying and powerful spirit of poetry by imbuing it with passion and a dramatic oratorical flourish. Moreover, she would also take her pen name "Speranza" from the Italian for "hope"—Italian being one of the many European languages in which she was fluent. Years later, her son Oscar would parallel the fight of Irish independence and artistry with that of Rome, stealing a line from Byron's *Childe Harold's Pilgrimage,* Wilde said Ireland was the "Niobe of nations."[15]

Speranza's early attachment to poetry and her support of the Young Ireland movement has been much debated since the early 20th century. Patrick Byrne in *The Wildes of Merrion Square* (1953) noted her "excursion into patriotism was not a formative influence on her own life or that of her family."[16] Odd as this pronouncement is, the sources on Speranza's life point to a much different conclusion. Speranza grew up in a conservative household devoted to reading, but she herself had little artistic output. She claimed, "until my eighteenth year I never wrote anything."[17] Opinion is divided as to what propelled Speranza into a life of political activism. As she pointed out, "my family was Protestant and Conservative and there was no social intercourse between them and the Catholics and Nationalists."[18] Her son, Oscar, noted in a speech given in San Francisco that it was during the funeral of Thomas Davis where:

> she was wondering much what man had died who the people so loved, she asked who it was they were burying and learned it was the funeral of one Thomas Davis. That evening she bought and read his poems and knew for the first time the meaning of the word country.[19]

The tale itself appears apocryphal. Speranza wrote that she had received a volume of "Ireland's Library" which contained an issue of *The Nation* written by Charles Gavin Duffy. She notes, "I read it eagerly, and my patriotism was enkindled."[20] Somewhere amongst these two stories the truth lies, but what is most important is not so much how she became a Young Irelander, but what her poetry did for the struggling and famine-stricken land.

The backdrop for many of Speranza's most famous and best poems are clearly linked with the widespread poverty and death ravaging Ireland. Before Elgee became "Speranza," her famous pseudonym, she was John Fanshawe Ellis. Once Gavin Duffy learned of her gender, she adopted Speranza and her renown spread. Using both names, she would publish incendiary works in favor of a more culturally aware and revolutionary Ireland. At this time, the nationalistic movement in Ireland that had been begun by Daniel O'Connell was having its own identity crisis with new, younger members adopting a more democratic and militaristic rhetoric. Speranza sided with the new generation as can be seen in her vitriolic prose piece "*Iacta Alea Est*" (The Die is Cast). Written by Speranza but published anonymously in July 1848, it was an overwhelming castigation of the British government and their policies in Ireland. The authorities incorrectly attributed the treasonous article to Gavin Duffy. Speranza admitted she was the author, but Duffy was still put on trial for its alleged authorship.[21]

One of the paradoxes of Speranza's poetry is that its author was an anomaly, writing nationalist verse by day while attending regal galas at night. This, in some ways, has further complicated her legacy as many view her actions and ideas as contradictory. Robert Sherard, a biographer of Oscar Wilde, gives more attention to Speranza than most, but not all of it is kind. In his *Life of Oscar Wilde*, he dismissively notes:

> Her Nationalism was, of course, not sincere. It could not be. She had been trained as a Protestant and a Conservative. Her relations, those of whom she was most proud, were beneficed dignitaries under the British Crown, just as later her husband was to become by appointment, warrant, and viceregal favour, a dependent of royal favour … Lady Wilde's crassa Minerva did not allow her to cling to a cause of which she was so soon to discover was a hopeless one.[22]

Sherard's work appeared in 1906 and besides being the first biographer of Oscar Wilde, he reveals the diminished influence Speranza's name had in nationalist literature. Not only does Sherard dismiss her as "not sincere," his flagrant sexism and penchant for aligning Speranza directly with her husband and conservative family is deeply troubling and destructive to her image.

When taking into account Speranza's legacy, we must not only look at her nationalism, but the constructs of the poet. The poet, to Speranza, was not just an artist, but was a symbol of cultural and political change. Throughout all of her poetry, she correlates the poet with the immortal gods and the heroes of long ago. In "Man's Mission", Speranza juxtaposes the role of the poet with that of hero writing: "each must work as God has given/ Hero hand or poet soul."[23] She saw her own poetic voice as both a tool for combating social wrong and as a branch of hope under which the people of a nation could find safety.

Until the end of the 20th century, very little critical attention was paid to Speranza's poetry, and the commentary that was available was derisive and cruel. In *Oscar Wilde, an Illustrated Biography,* Martin Fido labels Speranza's poetry as "consistently dreadful,"[24] a view many literary critics are quick to rally behind. In the last 15 years there has been a historical resurgence in Speranza scholarship thanks in part to works by Christine Kinealy, Chris Morash and Marjorie Howes whose "Blood and Tears" in *Colonial Crossings* uncovers the importance of sentimentality in Speranza's works.[25] These revaluations (as well as the chapters contained in this book) are slowly challenging the accepted view of Speranza's works as being egregiously bombastic and laden with provocative propaganda.

What Speranza had done in some of her most popular poems like "The Famine Year" was to connect through rhyme the unraveling chaos of the Famine. Her many verses reflect with fractured beauty the devastation plaguing Ireland. For example, she writes in verse five, "one by one they're falling round us, their pale faces to/ the sky;/ We've no strength left to dig them graves—there let them lie."[26] Beneath the anger and vitriol in "A Famine Year" are passages filled with suffering and an articulate and heartbreaking reminder of the loss of life. In "The Voice of the Poor" she continues to give voice to the voiceless, writing:

Before us die our brothers of starvation:
Around are cries of famine and despair
Where is hope for us, or comfort, or salvation—
Where-oh! Where?
If the angels ever hearken, downward bending,
They are weeping, we are sure,
At the litanies of human groans ascending
From the crushed hearts of the poor.[27]

The vivid recreation of hunger and despair are readily apparent here as is the poignant recreation of grief and anger. To say that this is mere propaganda is obtuse, and what is sorely lacking is an understanding of the cultural and political time-frame these poems grew out of and the many layered roles played by Speranza as poet and bard.

The literary climate of the 1840s was reflective of a lingering Romantic Era in which the poet and writer tapped into the folkloric and nationalistic underbelly of the cultural psyche. Lord Byron and Percy Shelley are considered lasting influences on the work of Oscar Wilde, but it is important to note that they too married verses of poesy with political and social commentary that both inspired writers after them and stunned the audiences of their day. Shelley, it must be remembered, while admired by Victorian audiences for his lyrical brilliance in poems like "To A Skylark" and "To Jane" (not Jane Elgee) was by the end of the 19th century known more for his lyrics than his politics. Oscar Wilde, who preferred Byron, labeled Shelley as "merely a boy's poet,"[28] but that did not stop him from getting a line from "Hymn to Intellectual Beauty" painted on his dining room wall.[29] Shelley throughout his lifetime was very much the counter culture figure that later Modernist and Beat writers would gravitate toward. His provocative and atheistic poetry such as "Queen Mab," and political polemics like "England in 1819," were popular in the bohemian and counter-culture underworld. Biographer Richard Holmes in *Shelley the Pursuit* reminds us of the true grandeur of Shelley and his importance as a poet saying he was:

> ... a writer who moved everywhere with a sense of ulterior motive, a sense of greater design, an acute feeling for the historical moment and an overwhelming consciousness of his duty as an artist in the immense and fiery process of social change of which he knew himself to be a part.[30]

Speranza's admiration for Shelley is quite clear. Shelley saw the poet as "something divine,"[31] which he states in his *A Defense of Poetry,* a categorization Speranza herself used throughout her many works of poetry. He also viewed poetry as a branch that encompasses not only love, but virtue, friendship and interestingly patriotism. He asked:

> What were the scenery of this beautiful universe which we inhabit, what were our consolations on this side of the grave, and what were our aspirations beyond it, if Poetry did not ascend to bring light and fire from those internal regions where the owl winged faculty of calculation dare not ever soar?[32]

To this we may add beside light and fire, also hope, which is what Speranza herself brought to thousands of Irish. In "A Poet at Court," she ascribes to the poet a Shelleyian recreation of the prestige and majesty of the poet, noting his "anointed" bearing, "conscious majesty," while capping off her religious metaphors with his "reign as god o'er creation."[33] Here, Speranza combines the Celtic mythos of the poet as divine with a Romantic recreation of the poet as supreme creator.

The extent of Shelley's impact on Speranza is without question as her construction of the poet and her poetry make clear. Speranza was a voluminous reader and a lover of languages, purportedly knowing 10 (although, not Irish). Her greatest nod to the Romantics and Shelley in particular was in her poem "Le Reveille" (The Signal). Her opening line reads, "it was the lark-not the nightingale-/ Poured forth her notes of warning."[34] Here Speranza is cleverly juxtaposing the two Romantic muses found in John Keats's "Ode to a Nightingale" and Shelley's "To a Skylark." While both poems are reflections on nature and death, "Nightingale" is haunted by darkness whereas "Skylark" can be seen as a deliverance of death and melancholy and a symbol of revelation and a call to action. Shelley writes, "teach me half the gladness/ that thy brain must know/ Such harmonious madness/ From my lips would flow,/ The world would listen then—as I am listening now."[35] Shelley's skylark is used as a wakeup call, and while for Shelley it was arguably used as a muse for his art, Speranza cleverly mixes its artistic underpinnings with a political message. Her skylark has the piercing sound of rebellion and the "chant of a Nation's rise" which is "borne on the wings of the morning gale,/ It peals through the azure skies,/ Liberty's torch is bright!"[36] While Speranza's skylark lacks the ambiguity of Shelley's, his influence on her poetry is keenly felt as is the poetical and political rhetoric that made her poetry so popular.

Perhaps the greatest artistic and political inspiration for Speranza came from Lord Byron whose own poetry and life inspired generations of followers after his death. In her biography, *Byron: Life and Legend* (2002), Fiona MacCarthy notes that:

> Byron's importance is perhaps above all that of a survivor, the man of experience who has seen the world at its worst, lived a life of strange if often terrible excesses at a time of extreme revolutionary violence, but refused to be defeated.[37]

MacCarthy's biographical sketch of Byron serves as an enlarged metaphor for the writings of Young Ireland and Speranza in particular. In recent years, historians have correctly attributed the growing nationalism of the German Romantics like Schiller and Goethe to the budding Young Irelanders as well as the bombastic flourishes of Victorian historians like Thomas Carlyle and Thomas Babington Macaulay (see, for example, James Quinn's recent work, *Young Ireland and the Writing of Irish History*),[38] but the slowly eroding memory of Byron often gets forgotten. While today the poetry of Keats and Shelley may have eclipsed him, Byron in the 1840s and 1850s was the most popular poet of the Victorian world.[39] The possibility that Speranza read Byron is almost without question as much of her style, both artistic and personal, exemplified the Byronic hero. Her later salons were highlights of the Dublin bohemian social scene and her son Oscar was an aesthetic devotee of all things Byron.

It was, however, Byron's ability to both flaunt convention and inspire political action that had the greatest effect on Speranza's poetry. Eric Hobsbawm notes in *The Age of Revolution 1789-1848* that Byron, along with Keats and Shelley were the first writers "to combine romanticism and active revolutionism."[40] Byron embraced the Greek fight for independence; little known, however, was his relationship with Ireland. His social and political acumen was awakened by the 1798 Rebellion when he was just a small boy. One of his earliest heroes was Lord Edward Fitzgerald, one of the leaders of the Society of United Irishman who had died in prison. Byron confided in his journal: "If I had been a man, I would have made an English Lord Edward Fitzgerald."[41] Not only this, but Byron continued to voice his support for Irish causes and even satirically poked fun at King George IV's 1821 visit to Ireland in his fiery *The Irish Avatar or Messiah*.

The clearest impact Byron had on Speranza can be found in her poetry. In poems like

"Discipline" she marries art with humanitarian pathos of the downtrodden and forgotten, imploring her readers to "wait, like the Stoic,/ Brave, enduring, and strong/ Till the soul's strength heroic/ Bends the fetters of wrong." The poem ends with a very Byronic symbol of the Romantic power of the soul, "for the strong soul grows stronger/ By the combat and strife."[42] This same symbolism and imagery can be found in Byron's own political poems, whether he be drawing attention to the plight of Jews in "Oh Weep for Those," or musing on humanity and the soul in "On the Castle of Chillon."

Byron, known for his flowery verse, was also adept, like Speranza, at commenting on the social conditions plaguing his country. In "Song for the Luddites" symbolic gestures of liberty, war, and courage are expressed in the same moments of bombast found in Speranza's more polemical poems like "The Old Man's Blessing" or "Signs of the Times." Byron writes, "So we boys, we/ Will die fighting or live free,/ And down with all kings but King Ludd!"[43] Similarly, in Speranza's more socially aware poems, she places herself amongst the Irish people voicing their cries, like in "The Voice of the Poor" where she laments the poverty and death all around her. She is able to capture, unlike Byron, the intimate pathos of devastation plaguing her country. Byron had invested money and arms for the Greek cause, but died before he saw any action. His poetry like Speranza's in Ireland, symbolically rather than physically, united him with Greece and the Luddites. Speranza, in a particularly poignant passage, captured the physical and emotional turmoil wreaking havoc in Ireland, "day-by-day we lower sink and lower,/ Till the Godlike soul within,/ Falls crushed, beneath the fearful demon power/ Of poverty and sin."[44] Here, her poetry captures in vivid detail the plight of her fellow Irish men and women, taking Byron's symbolic political agitation and adding a visceral and human twist. Speranza's poetry went further than Byron's since it was dangerous to publish. The Treason Felony Act of 1848 made it possible for the British government to prosecute any person who promoted rebellion against the monarch: the penalty was death or transportation. The definition of Treason was also extended to include any person who "shall express, utter, or declare, by publishing any printing or writing ..."[45] Speranza avoided prosecution, but many of her fellow Young Irelanders did not. Her Romantic blend of politics and poetry made her an icon of the Irish people and a respected literary celebrity.

It is this Romantic spirit that Speranza was inspired by and of which her poetry is so very much a part. Speranza and the Young Ireland Movement did for Ireland what Byron, Keats and Shelley did for England. Her work was an inspiration to her son and to future generations of Irish poets and writers, decades before the Decadent Movement and the dandy as artist. She successfully married the political, cultural and artistic frameworks of poetry, making it both culturally rich and artistically accomplished. Speranza's contribution to nationalist politics and to an Irish literary revival calls for a reevaluation not only of her life, but the impressive collection of work she left behind. And significantly, she remains an important eye-witness to, and champion of, the Irish poor during the Great Famine. Like her more famous son, Jane Elgee—Speranza—crossed social, political, economic, cultural and gender divisions.

Endnotes

[1] *The Kerry Sentinel,* 8 Feb. 1896.

[2] W.B. Yeats, *Autobiographies.* Ed., Douglas Archibald and William O'Donnell (New York, 1999), p. 129.

[3] W.B. Yeats, *Selected Plays*, ed. Richard Allen Cave (New York, 1997), p. 58.

[4] G.B. Shaw, *Memories of Oscar Wilde* in Frank Harris's *Oscar Wilde* (New York, 1997), p. 330.

[5] Ibid.

[6] Antoinette Quinn, "Ireland/ Herland: Women and Literary Nationalism, 1845-1916" in Angela Bourke, Siobhan Kilfeather,

Maria Luddy, et. al (eds.) *The Field Day Anthology of Irish Writing Vol. 5: Irish Women's Writing and Tradition* (New York, 2002), p. 900.

[7] Patrick Pearse, *The Collected Works* (Dublin, 1917), p. 323.

[8] *The United Irishman,* 19 Jan. 1892.

[9] Lady Wilde, *Poems by Speranza* (Dublin, 1864), p. 73.

[10] Anna de Bremont, *Oscar Wilde and His Mother* (London, 1911), p. 77.

[11] H. Montgomery Hyde, *Oscar Wilde: A Biography* (New York, 1975), p. 6.

[12] W. B. Yeats. *Early Articles and Reviews: Uncollected Articles and Reviews Written Between 1886 and 1900.* Ed. John Frayne and Madeleine Marchaterre (New York, 2004), p. 114.

[13] *Kerry Sentinel,* 8 Feb. 1896.

[14] Lady Wilde, *Poems,* p. 22.

[15] Richard Ellmann, *Oscar Wilde* (New York, 1987), p. 196.

[16] Patrick Byrne, *The Wildes of Merrion Square* (London, 1953), p. 25.

[17] Robert Harborough Sherard, *The Life of Oscar Wilde* (New York, 1906), p. 46.

[18] Ibid.

[19] Michael O'Neill, "Irish poets of the nineteenth century. Unpublished Lecture Notes of Oscar Wilde" in *University Review*, 1, no. 4 (1955), p. 31.

[20] Sherard, *The Life of Oscar Wilde*, p. 24.

[21] See, Christine Kinealy, *Repeal and Revolution.1848 in Ireland* (Manchester, 2009).

[22] Sherard, *The Life of Oscar Wilde,* pp 64-5.

[23] Lady Wilde, *Poems*, p. 25.

[24] Martin Fido, *Oscar Wilde: An Illustrated Biography* (New York, 1973), p. 15.

[25] See Christine Kinealy. "The Stranger's Scoffing. Speranza, The Hope of the Irish Nation." The Oscholars, September 2008. Marjorie Howes. "Blood and Tears: Lady Wilde" in *Colonial Crossings Figures in Irish Literary History* (Dublin, Field Day Publications, 2006). Chris Morash, *Writing the Irish Famine* (New York: Oxford University Press, 1995).

[26] Lady Wilde, *Poems,* p. 11.

[27] Ibid., p. 14.

[28] Ellmann, *Oscar Wilde* p. 268.

[29] Ibid., p. 257.

[30] Richard Holmes, *Shelley: The Pursuit* (New York, 1974), p. xiv.

[31] Percy Bysshe Shelley "A Defense of Poetry" in Zachary Leader and Michael O'Neill (eds), *The Major Works* (New York, 2009), p. 675.

[32] Ibid., p. 696.

[33] Lady Wilde, *Poems*, p. 111.

[34] Ibid., p. 120.

[35] Ibid., p. 466.

[36] Ibid., p. 121.

[37] Fiona MacCarthy, *Byron Life and Legend* (New York, 2002), p. xiv.

[38] James Quinn, *Young Ireland and the Writing of Irish History* (Dublin, 2015).

[39] MacCarthy, *Byron Life and Legend,* p. 545.

[40] Eric Hobsbawm, *The Age of Revolution 1789-1848* (New York, 1996), p. 268.

[41] Ibid., p. 28.

[42] Lady Wilde, *Poems,* p. 52.

[43] Lord George Gordon Byron, *The Poetical Works of Lord Byron* (New York, 1860), p. 579.

[44] Lady Wilde, *Poems,* p. 15.

[45] 1848 c. 12 (Regnal. 11 and 12 Vict.); see also, Kinealy, *Repeal and Revolution.*

Works Cited

Belford, Barbara. *Oscar Wilde: A Certain Genius.* New York: Random House, 2000.

Byrne, Patrick. *The Wildes of Merrion Square.* London: Staples Press, 1953.

Byron, Lord George Gordon. *The Poetical Works of Lord Byron.* New York: D Appleton & Company, 1860.

De Bremont, Anna. *Oscar Wilde and His Mother.* London: Everett and Co., 1911.

Ellmann, Richard. *Oscar Wilde.* New York: Vintage Books, 1988.

Fido, Martin. *Oscar Wilde: An Illustrated Biography.* New York: Hamlyn, 1973.

Hobsbawm, Eric. *The Age of Revolution 1789-1848.* New York: Vintage Books, 1996.

Harris, Frank. *Oscar Wilde including Memories of Oscar Wilde by George Bernard Shaw.* New York: Carroll & Graff Publishers, 1997.

Holmes, Richard. *Shelley: The Pursuit.* New York: New York Review of Books, 1974.

Horan, Patrick. *The Importance of Being Paradoxical: Maternal Presence in the Works of Oscar Wilde.* London: Associated University Press, 1997.

Hyde, H. Montgomery. *Oscar Wilde: A Biography.* New York: Farrar, Straus and Giroux, 1975.

Kinealy, Christine. *Repeal and Revolution. 1848 in Ireland.* Manchester: Manchester University Press, 2009.
    "The Stranger's Scoffing. Speranza, The Hope of the Irish Nation." The Oscholars, September 2008.

MacCarthy, Fiona. *Byron Life and Legend.* New York: Farrar, Straus and Giroux, 2002.

O'Neill, Michael. "Irish Poets of the Nineteenth Century: Unpublished Lecture Notes of

Oscar Wilde." *University Review*, I, no. 4 (1955) 29-32.

Pearse, Patrick. *The Collected Works.* Dublin: Maunsel and Roberts, 1917.

Quinn, Antoinette. "Ireland/ Herland: Women and Literary Nationalism, 1845-1916" in *The Field Day Anthology of Irish Writing Vol. 5 Irish Women's Writing and Tradition,* Ed. Angela Bourke, Siobhan Kilfeather, Maria Luddy, et. al. New York: New York University Press, 2002.

Quinn, James. *Young Ireland and the Writing of Irish History.* Dublin: University College Dublin Press, 2015.

Shelley, Percy Bysshe Shelley. "A Defense of Poetry" in *The Major Works* ed. Zachary

Leader and Michael O'Neill. New York: Oxford University Press, 2009.

Sherard, Robert Harborough. *The Life of Oscar Wilde.* New York, Mitchell Kennerley, 1906.

Wilde, Lady (Jane). *Poems by Speranza.* Dublin: Y.M. O'Toole and Son, 1864.

Essays and Stories. New York: A.R. Keller and Co., 1907.

Yeats, W.B. *The Collected Letters of W.B. Yeats Volume 1865-1895.* Ed. John Kelly and

Eric Domville. Oxford: Clarendon Press, 1986.

Early Articles and Reviews: Uncollected Articles and Reviews Written Between 1886 and 1900. Ed. John Frayne and Madeleine Marchaterre. New York: Scribner, 2004.

Autobiographies. Ed., Douglas Archibald and William O'Donnell. New York: Simon and Schuster, 1999.

Selected Plays. Ed. Richard Allen Cave. New York: Penguin, 1997.

Chapter Eleven

"The skeleton at the feast": Lady Wilde's famine poetry and Irish internationalist critiques of food scarcity

Amy Martin

In January 1847, in the midst of the Great Hunger in Ireland, Jane Francesca Elgee, using the pen-name, "Speranza," published in the *Nation* newspaper what is arguably her most famous poem, "The Famine Year," originally called "The Stricken Land." Only 26 years old at the time of its publication, Elgee was already part of a group of poets central to the circle that produced most of the literary work of the Young Ireland movement that had founded the weekly paper. As a young female poet, she published her work alongside poets (the late) Thomas Davis and James Clarence Mangan, as well as writers such as John Mitchel and William Carleton. While she was one of several women to publish regularly in the *Nation* — including Mary Eva Kelly ("Eva"), Olivia Knight ("Thomasine") and Ellen Mary Downing — Speranza became the most well known. This was not only because of the enduring nature of her Famine poetry and her scholarship on Irish folklore, but because she would eventually become, after marrying William Wilde in 1851, the mother of Oscar Wilde. However, in 1847, she had only been writing poetry for the *Nation* for less than two years. While her rousing nationalist ballads gained her a literary reputation, her moving poetic representations of Famine victims in Ireland established her fame.

Historians have demonstrated convincingly that the Great Famine in Ireland was a historical watershed, a catastrophe that transformed many aspects of Irish life irrevocably. While the immediate cause was a fungus that attacked the subsistence crop of potatoes on which the Irish peasantry depended, the form of agrarian capital colonialism long established in Ireland had created a population vulnerable to famine.[1] Moreover, the continued exportation of food crops out of Ireland during famine conditions, as well as the relative lack of relief from Britain, contributed to the scale of the disaster. More than 25 percent of the nation's population perished.[2] One Irish historian describes it as one of the "most lethal famines in modern history in terms of excess mortality and population loss."[3] The deaths of between one and one and a half million people from 1846 to 1855 and the emigration of over two million changed the nation in ways that persist into the present.[4] As Melissa Fegan argues, the Great Famine was also "a major literary event, crushing the literary revival [of the 1840s]... and decimating the Irish publishing industry."[5] However, in the wake of a destroyed nationalist revival a substantial archive of Famine writings emerged. Scholars such as Margaret Kelleher, Chris Morash and Fegan have explored this rich archive of Famine literature. We could claim that an entire poetic tradition in Ireland emerges between 1845 and 1852[6] as well as important fiction such as Carleton's *The Black Prophet* that inaugurated the central place of Famine novels in Irish literature from the 19th century to the present. Into this historical and literary context stepped the young Jane Francesca Elgee. The daughter of Charles Elgee and member of an upper class, Anglican family with Unionist politics, she had a conversion experience to nationalism in 1845 upon witnessing the funeral of Thomas Davis, a founder of the Young Ireland movement. She began submitting poems to the *Nation* just a few months later, at first using a male pen name.[7] Charles Gavan Duffy, editor of the *Nation* at this time, described her as "a substantial force in Irish politics... a woman of genius."[8] She soon took the female pseudonym of Speranza, one that she would continue to use throughout her life as the stamp on her correspondence. All of this occurred on the eve of the Great Famine, and Elgee quickly began to publish poems that documented the unfolding events in Ireland.

"The Famine Year," her first famine poem appearing in January 1847, is notable for several reasons. By the winter of 1847, famine had already begun to ravage Ireland, and this poem ascribes particular causes to these conditions. Well before John Mitchel's famous contention in *The Last Conquest of Ireland (Perhaps)* that the Great Famine was a form of extermination, this poem disseminated a narrative of British responsibility for starvation in Ireland. "The Famine Year" also demonstrates that innovation of literary form was required to represent the catastrophe in Ireland. As Chris Morash contends, "famine does not sit comfortably in any of the established poetic idioms of the English tradition."[9] This intersection of catastrophic historical event and literary form accounts for Elgee's poetic experimentation. In "The Famine Year," she reworks the genre of the dramatic monologue that the Brownings used to such effect in the previous decade. Cornelia Pearsall argues persuasively that, connected intimately to psychological concerns, the dramatic monologue is inherently linked to trauma, not just in a descriptive sense, but as a performance of the traumatic experience itself.[10] Pearsall renames the form—the traumatic monologue. Elgee's traumatic monologue attempts to find a form that can represent collective rather than individual trauma.[11] Other famine poets wrote dramatic monologues of a sort about the catastrophe or used a call and response or query and answer structure. But they do not do so in as experimental a fashion, and the sheer proliferation of voices and experiences in "The Famine Year" distinguishes it. Elgee uses this same experimental form in other famine poems, such as "The Enigma" and "The Voice of the Poor."

The first stanza of the "The Famine Year" introduces us to this radical formal innovation. The reader does not encounter the single occasion or unitary voice of the dramatic monologue. Instead, he or she is unmoored into the events of a year's time, a temporal disorientation that is matched by frequent shifts of a question and response pattern:

> WEARY men, what reap ye?—Golden corn for the stranger.
> What sow ye?—Human corses[12] that wait for the avenger.
> Fainting forms, hunger-stricken, what see you in the offing?
> Stately ships to bear our food away, amid the stranger's scoffing.
> There's a proud array of soldiers—what do they round your door?
> They guard our masters' granaries from the thin hands of the poor.
> Pale mothers, wherefore weeping?—Would to God that we were dead—
> Our children swoon before us, and we cannot give them bread.

From the start, the reader encounters multiplicity: while grounded by the ignorant voice of a questioner who is clearly an outsider to famine conditions, the poem moves into a dizzying series of suffering voices who answer. Thus, the reader encounters distinct collectivities who experience the Famine differently. This dialogic structure continues throughout the poem, suggesting that the experiences of famine are multiple, shaped by gender and class. These voices destabilize the reader in an almost proto-modernist form and produce a disorientation that conjures the chaos of this year in Irish history.

From the first stanza of "The Famine Year," Elgee establishes certain central concerns for poets writing about the Famine. This essay will focus on one of these—an imperative to produce what I describe as a poetics of dehumanization and an iconography of the nonhuman. Not surprisingly, her poetic attention to the human and nonhuman emerges as she establishes the narrative of culpability to which I alluded earlier. References to "the stranger" and the "alien" suggest the history and persistence of settler colonialism and its attendant economy that have led to these events. We might expect that Elgee would describe those who are not strangers using a language of belonging and humanity, but instead they are "fainting forms." The word "forms" implies the shell of the body that has been emptied of human content, the dehumanization and defamiliarization of those who starve; this representation of famine victims is echoed in the image of corpses that are sown into the ground instead of seeds.

While this dehumanization is certainly a consequence of starvation, it begins in the relation between "the stranger" and "the poor" whose outstretched hands are ignored, in economic and social relations that predate and determine the faminogenic conditions[13] that lead directly to mass starvation. This dehumanization is then fully manifested in the effects of the famine which Elgee represents in later stanzas: the collapse of kinship and family structures, the disappearance of burial and mourning rituals, and the transformation of people into "forms," "tools" and "bones." The motif of humans who descend into nonhuman categories appears repeatedly in her famine poems. In "The Exodus," those who starve and die become "human wrecks," statistical "units" and "a drift of the dead where men should be." In "A Supplication" (1847), famine victims are stripped of the senses until they are "miserable outcasts" and "pariahs of humanity." There are immoveable "frozen barriers that divide us from other men" in "The Voice of the Poor" (1848). At stake then, in her famine poems is the question of who counts as human: who is worth saving and who is reduced to an object even before starvation takes hold. Elgee argues that distinctions between the human and the nonhuman stand at the center of understanding why the Great Famine occurred. Elgee identifies the ways in which defining who counts as human has urgent material consequences, particularly in the context of colonialism. She accomplishes this through a series of tropes — in particular the living skeleton, "human tools," and those buried "uncoffin'd." To illuminate the iconography of the nonhuman in "The Famine Year," I will explore two examples from the poem—the representation of gender and the family and Elgee's apocalyptic vision of reanimated skeletons.

Elgee uses a sophisticated exploration of gender and family to represent dehumanization. In the second stanza, the questioner addresses the children of the Famine, creating tragic pathos through an imaginative exploration of how small children experience starvation and death:

> Little children, tears are strange upon your infant faces,
> God meant you but to smile within your mother's soft embraces.
> Oh! we know not what is smiling, and we know not what is dying;
> But we're hungry, very hungry, and we cannot stop our crying.
> And some of us grow cold and white—we know not what it means;
> But, as they lie beside us, we tremble in our dreams.
> There's a gaunt crowd on the highway—are ye come to pray to man,
> With hollow eyes that cannot weep, and for words your faces wan?

Focusing on the suffering of children was a common representational strategy in famine writing in the late 1840s and early 1850s.[14] Here, while the child remains human, he or she is stripped of the fundamental markers of childhood. Elgee signifies this through the "strange" tears marking the unnatural condition of the grieving, despairing, perhaps dying child. Tears appear elsewhere in Elgee's poetic corpus to signify both colonial abjection and a mode of a transformation of affect in the reader that might lead to nationalist action.[15] In this stanza, the presence of children's tears marks an overturning of natural and divine order: "God meant you but to smile within your mother's soft embraces." At the same time, the poet invokes a Madonna and child tableau, only to reveal then its absence. The mother-child dyad suggests normative family and figures a naturalized and even holy relationship that has been destroyed. The destruction of this fundamental maternal relation—here presented as a reasonable, even unquestionable, expectation of the human—casts the Famine as an unnaturally destructive force. The power of this use of the maternal also derives from its challenge to contemporaneous writings in Britain that described the Great Famine in Ireland, following Malthusian logic, as a natural force that addressed overpopulation or, in some Evangelical discourse, as the divine will of God that required no intervention. The gendered pathos evoked by the absent mother rejects both of these understandings of famine at once.

The use of the maternal body makes clear the rehumanizing aspect of Elgee's poem. Margaret Kelleher has demonstrated powerfully that the spectacle of the starving mother and child was iconic in famine literature.[16] She argues: "the maternal image develops a much more unsettling and threatening quality, and becomes an expression of 'the unthinkable.'"[17] Elgee participates in this representation of women, yet at the same time she produces an absence, resisting the use of the maternal body as spectacle. If "the spectacle of famine... is thus frequently constructed through female figures," Elgee paradoxically reinforces and complicates this iconography. The mother's body still serves as a lynchpin in representing famine, but she is not subject to the scrutiny of the reader's gaze. Instead, we are faced with her eradication. This spectral mother provides the poet a release from the choice between the antithetical stock female characters of famine fiction and first-hand accounts: "the self-sacrificing mother and her 'monstrous' opposite."[18]

Elgee highlights the children's inability to understand what they witness with the line "we know not what it means" and with the repetition of "know not." The children's naiveté rejects once again any idea that these deaths are "natural." Instead, they face an unnatural disaster; the "cold and white" bodies of other children are, for them and for us, incomprehensible. Margot Backus has made the compelling argument that in Irish literary tradition, the Anglo-Irish Gothic centers on the sacrifice of children of this settler colonial class; the violence and trauma of the Ascendancy's origins is thus enacted on the bodies of children through various forms of pedophagy, which serve to legitimate the perpetuation of their domination.[19] In "The Famine Year," Elgee reworks this Anglo-Irish literary topos radically. As the starving children, clearly Irish-Catholic peasants, are consumed by famine, their destruction becomes a form of pedophagy that does not legitimate a colonial order but rather reveals the inhumanity at its foundation. This gruesome scene of children who sleep with corpses evokes the family scene that it replaces. The Irish children, and by extension the poem's readers—for the repetition of first-person plural implicates us—are haunted by a ghostly family scene that is rendered impossible in light of catastrophe.

The end of the stanza returns us to the voice of the questioner: "There's a gaunt crowd on the highway—are ye come to pray to man,/With hollow eyes that cannot weep, and for words your faces wan?" However, the speaker has been transformed by the voices of the children who starve. The "gaunt crowd" makes sense in a way that it has not before. Thus, the poem stages for the reader how its own pedagogic and political functions have begun to be fulfilled. The begging crowd resonates with historical realities of the Famine—the desperate need for charity and the regular use of petitions that peasants delivered to landlords to ask for relief. They appear both tearless and wordless at first, and this description moves the poem into a further exploration of dehumanization, as human speech and tears are stripped from those who starve and die. This crowd then speaks in a distinctly male voice:

> No; the blood is dead within our veins—we care not now for life;
> Let us die hid in the ditches, far from children and from wife;
> We cannot stay and listen to their raving, famished cries—
> Bread! Bread! Bread! and none to still their agonies.
> We left our infants playing with their dead mother's hand:
> We left our maidens maddened by the fever's scorching brand:
> Better, maiden, thou were strangled in thy own dark-twisted tresses—
> Better, infant, thou wert smothered in thy mother's first caresses.

This group of men exists at the paradoxical intersection between the dead and the living—"the blood is dead within our veins" –and they hide rather than seeking sustenance. As the stanza progresses, a narrative of male abandonment emerges. It was unusual for famine literature to explore the phenomenon of men who left wives and children, even though the occurrence is documented in petitions for charity during the Famine. With this choice, Elgee genders the domestic catastrophe of famine differently. The reader now encounters a normative masculinity compromised by the desperate hunger of those who, in the context of bourgeois norms of family, the men have been charged to protect. Accordingly, during famine, men are dehumanized through a collapse of masculinity.

At the same time, Elgee resists narratives of blame or lapsing into stereotypes of Irish men as feminized, violent or culturally deviant. Instead, the normative roles of husband and father are destroyed by the conditions of famine, and this drives the male speakers to a kind of madness. What might have been understood as an immoral or criminal act instead calls attention to those larger structural inequalities that produce famine. To highlight this, the male voices turn to the Gothic and the sensational, exploring the way that the crimes of murder and infanticide, crimes often figured as existing outside the bounds of the human, are preferable to witnessing the starvation of loved ones. The effects and experiences of famine are cast as more violent than crimes such as murder, as a kind of violence beyond murder in its scale and impact.

Throughout the remaining stanzas, Elgee continues to explore dehumanization by comparing humans to animals, figuring them as less than animal in fact, and through references to unburied corpses, which suggests the breakdown of funerary rituals. This leads us to a conclusion that relies on prosopopoeia[20] to represent the most profound scene of dehumanization in "The Famine Year." At some point, the reader begins to question whether we are listening to the voices of the living or the dead. In a complex reworking of the gothic, the poem's use of prosopopoeia dismantles the boundary between the human and the non-human. The voices of those who starve and have starved are not simply a haunting, ghostly presence. Their spectrality becomes the only presence in the poem, as the voice of the questioner drops away. Therefore, the dead here do not inhabit the realm of the supernatural or nonhuman, nor are they simply reinstated to the living and the natural. Rather the entire poem moves us into a space where life is saturated by death and the dead replace the living and the human as organizing consciousness. In this way, those rendered silent can speak; those written out of history are allowed to shape it and can tell the reader of their experiences in 1847.

Because the boundary between living and dead is unclear and unstable, the speakers' state reveals that they were consigned to a kind of deadness even before their actual demise. This dehumanization results not from a natural catastrophe but from the Irish people's eviction from their land and from the fold of humanity by those in power. Their destruction is caused by colonial domination and the exploitative presence of the British and Anglo-Irish landlords. As David Lloyd has suggested of famine writing, "the specter that returns is not simply that of the myriad unburied dead of the Famine, but the haunting resonance of the victim's dehumanization this side of death, the dehumanization that made their extrication thinkable and admissible."[21] Capitalist structures of expropriation and ideas about Irish racial inferiority lay the foundation for the rationalization and justification of famine mortality. Hence, the starvation of the Irish poor is manufactured by those who lay claim to the category of the human.

By the poem's final stanza, the multiple voices of the dead unite into a chorus, a powerful "we" who address those responsible for Irish starvation:

> We are wretches, famished, scorned, human tools to build your pride,
> But God will yet take vengeance for the souls for whom Christ died.
> Now is your hour of pleasure—bask ye in the world's caress;
> But our whitening bones against ye will rise as witnesses,
> From the cabins and the ditches, in their charred, uncoffin'd masses,
> For the Angel of the Trumpet will know them as he passes.
> A ghastly, spectral army, before the great God we'll stand,
> And arraign ye as our murderers, the spoilers of our land.

Critics have explored the ways in which this final vision of the "ghastly, spectral army" draws on a millenarian tradition concerning the apocalypse.[22] Sean Ryder describes how Elgee uses affectivity to pull the Irish reader into seeing the suffering and dying as fellow national subjects and to urge for anticolonial insurgency in the present. But, before these transformations can occur, the speakers first identify themselves as "human tools to build your pride." Here Elgee's oxymoronic phrase "human tools" allows the dead to lay claim to their humanity through the adjective "human." At the same time, the phrase calls attention to the ways in which they are made "tools," those whose only value lies in their dispossession and death. The word "tools" invokes the structures of colonial capitalism, suggesting their relationship to labor, to profit and to objectification. Like contemporaneous British factory workers called "hands," the hungry are reduced to their use-value. Of course they cannot labor as they starve, which asks the reader to consider what tool-like function they actually serve. The invocation of "pride" suggests that they serve an ideological function, standing as the necessary obverse of British and Anglo-Irish wealth and culture.

As these tools are transformed into an army of undead corpses, Elgee creates an apocalyptic, Gothic vision of terror, one that allows the "uncoffin'd masses" to gain a kind of political agency. While she describes the "army" as composed of "whitening bone" and as "ghastly" and "spectral," the explicit image of the skeleton is only implied. Famine poetry is saturated with skeletons both living and dead—the starving who have become skeletal, reduced to bones and thus unrecognizable, as well as the bones of the dead left unburied in cabins or roadsides. The implicit skeletons of "The Famine Year," however, are neither of these familiar figures. A millenarian vision with the reanimated skeleton at its center allows Elgee to imagine apocalyptic rebellion and vengeance. The legal language of the final line—"arraign ye as our murderers, the spoilers of our land"—imagines justice for the dead. When disease and death made resistance seem impossible, Elgee restores a complex humanity to the dead and poses their deaths as the condition of possibility for insurgency. Therefore, the skeleton signifies death and dehumanization, but also becomes the ground for political action.

While the apocalyptic frame for the poem's conclusion might seem to separate it from the present and from reality,[23] these resurrected skeletons that testify to their own destruction hold other potentials. The rise of the skeletal army, like the phrase "human tools," allows Elgee to create a scene of supernatural horror that insists on the ultimate, unassailable dehumanization of the victims of famine. However, as they are resurrected into an army, they are restored to humanity through a Christian tradition about the end of days; they reenter the world of the human to seek vengeance. At the same time, the monstrous—a discourse used so often to describe the Irish—is recuperated and transformed into a means of attaining justice. This paradox of the human and the nonhuman is central to the understanding of colonial famine that Elgee's poem produces. Unlike many other famine poems from the period, it makes the reader think differently about the structures and processes that lead to the deaths of the starving and recasts processes of dehumanization as the cause, as well as the effect, of famine.

While Elgee's poems are historically specific, her choice to represent the Great Famine in relation to the human and the nonhuman gives it an elasticity that she herself might not have imagined. These tropes have the capacity to serve as a site of possibility for thinking about food scarcity and famine internationally. Indeed, this is what anonymous Irish writers did in the 1860s and 1870s. In the *Nation* and *Irishman*, nationalist newspaper columnists write about repeated famines in India between 1865 and 1878 in relation to the experience of famine in Ireland in the 1840s. They draw on the iconography in the famine literature of the 1840s but in particular that which Elgee developed and disseminated. They press these representations of the nonhuman into the service of an internationalist understanding of famine, one in which food scarcity and starvation are understood as tools of colonial domination that travel across the globe over time. This internationalist critique argues, in almost prophetic terms, that famine moves systematically as a primary structure of empire and modernity.

If "The Famine Year" explores the ways that the Famine's dead haunt the living, Elgee's famine poems had their own afterlives. In 1864, by which time Jane Elgee had married Sir William Wilde and had become Lady Wilde, the first edition of Speranza's collected verse was published by James Duffy in Dublin, with a second edition appearing in 1867. This collection of her work was also published in Glasgow and London. The collection begins with a sequence of her famine poems, and "The Famine Year" is the first anthologized. Another edition appeared in 1871. The first edition was reviewed positively in various Irish newspapers including the *Nation* and the *Irishman* as well as publications such as the *Dublin Review*. Both editions were advertised regularly between 1864 and 1875, and Wilde's work was included in other collections of nationalist writing and poetry. Overall interest in her poetry was revived by the publication of her major works.[24] During this process, her famine poems served as what Pierre Nora calls a *lieux de memoire*, or site of memory,[25] for understanding the devastation that had occurred only 20 years earlier. In the *Nation* newspaper in 1875, a review of Rev. O'Rourke's book, *The Great Famine*, quotes the entire first stanza of "The Famine Year" as a way to illustrate the causes of the Great Famine in Ireland, and the reviewer explains:

> So wrote the gifted poetess, Lady Wilde, in the columns of the NATION in those terrible days; and many eloquent protestations, in prose and verse, then rang out against the system which left people to die of starvation in the midst of the plenty their hands had raised.[26]

The republication of her famine poems could not be more appropriately timed because they reappeared during a period when repeated famines took place in another region of the British Empire—India. Like the reanimated skeletons in "The Famine Year," food scarcity and starvation appeared over and over in various regions of South Asia—the Orissa famine from 1865-67, the Rajputana famine in the late 1860s, and then the catastrophic "Great Famine" in Southern India, specifically Bombay and Madras, from 1876-78, in which at the very least five and a half million people are estimated to have died. Mike Davis suggests that it is more likely that more than eight million perished in this last famine.[27]

The nationalist press in Ireland turned its attention to these repeated calamities in India and declared them unnatural disasters. A series of anonymous columns published in the *Nation* and the *Irishman* between 1865 and 1878 engage in a method that at first appears comparativist. Famine in India is compared to the Great Famine in Ireland as a method of generating sympathy for those suffering the conditions of starvation elsewhere. However, if contemporary critics have revealed sympathetic identification to be a "minefield" in the colonial context,[28] it is not surprising that these anonymous writers turn from it quickly. Instead, they argue that the historical and geographic movement of famine throughout the British Empire reveals a systematic use of food scarcity and starvation as methods of domination and exploitation. Over 100 years before work by Amartya Sen and others, these nationalist writers insist that famine is not about food shortage, but rather about global economic and social structures that ensure the impoverishment of many to preserve the wealth of a much smaller elite. As David Nally writes, "modern scholars tend to agree that famines do not necessarily *begin* with crop failures, droughts, or equivalent climatic hazards; rather, their violence is coordinated much earlier, when a population is made progressively vulnerable or slowly brought to the point of collapse."[29] These writers recognize that the persistence of famine is written into the very logic and structures of global modernity well before the modern scholars to whom Nally refers.

Between the years 1865 and 1878, more than 40 columns appeared in the *Nation* and the *Irishman* on famines in India. Looking at just one of these articles reveals this archive's typical arguments and its use of the iconography of the nonhuman. The anonymous article, "The Skeleton at the Feast," appeared in the *Irishman* on 20 January 1877 in the midst of the Great Famine of Southern India, also called the Madras famine. The article's title signals the degree to which the writer's analysis of famine in India mobilizes the tropes and discourse of famine literature in Ireland. The contrast between imperial wealth and colonial starvation that the article examines culminates in the powerful gothic tableau of "the skeleton at the feast." Here, colonial subjects sit at the abundant table of empire, haunting British wealth with their ghastly, emaciated presence. The skeleton who joins the feast is living — the hungry presence of those who are excluded from the imperial "meal," even as they witness it in the pageantry of Victoria, for example. Simultaneously, the skeleton is dead, representing the deaths of those who make the feast possible, the long history of famine in regions such as India and Ireland. Therefore, it is ultimately both living and dead, like the reanimated corpses of Elgee's poem, who refuse to die unacknowledged, unmarked, in the historical record, who proclaim their lost humanity rather than being represented as "surplus population" or as "encumbrances." Again, in almost the exact logic found in "The Famine Year," the skeleton proclaims its humanity and its profound dehumanization, condemning those who feast before it and threatening vengeance.

Early on, the writer establishes food scarcity and starvation as an historical pattern in India and throughout the empire:

> Wherever the British flag is advanced, treachery goes before and famine follows it. The creation of a famine has, at times, been the expressly avowed object of English statesmanship. The awful experiment has been tried more than once in this country— openly and avowedly in former times...It is but two years ago since we had news of a

famine in India — now again comes intelligence that that marvellously [sic] wealthy land is about to be ravaged — throughout Bombay and Madras— by another and a great famine.... This is a terrible commentary on the gilded pageantry of the proclamation of VICTORIA Imperatrix at Delhi![30]

The analysis that emerges over the course of the column has several claims at its center. First, famine is intimately related to empire and, the writer contends, is produced by the colonial state as a kind of experiment in domination and population management. As Gauri Viswanathan's groundbreaking work on colonial education has established, colonial space served as a "laboratory" for apparatuses of power that secured rule through both coercion and consent.[31] Indeed, Nally has argued that Ireland during the Famine served as a "utilitarian laboratory."[32] The writer here identifies famine as a series of open and avowed "experiments." This analysis reappears in a 15 December 1877 article on famine in Madras:

> Famine is a potent instrument—as we know in Ireland—in the hands of English rulers of subject peoples. It answers admirably as a means of weeding out and lessening the number of the disaffected, and is, in fact, an indispensable auxiliary to the military force which she has available to sustain her rule.[33]

Second, like Elgee and other famine writers, the columnist emphasizes the artificial nature of famine, that it is produced by imposed forces, presumably economic, agrarian and political. The juxtaposition of starvation with the "marvellously [sic] wealthy land" suggests profound pauperization and the extraction of crops that paved the way for colonial famines. In fact, this insight anticipates the "secret history" of Victorian famines provided by Mike Davis who explains: "Millions died, not outside the world system, but in the very process of being forcibly incorporated into its economic and political structures."[34] This is reinforced by the contrast between the display of wealth and opulence that came with declaring Victoria the Empress of India and "the phantasmagoria at Delhi and the skeleton at Deccan." Here the "phantasmagoria" and the skeleton" echo the logic and iconography of Wilde's poems while doing so in service of a nearly identical analysis of the causes of colonial famine.

Therefore, while the writer makes claims of sympathy for and solidarity with Indian people who suffer through famine, in earlier columns these gestures are grounded in a materialist analysis of how and why famine recurs:

> Well can we sympathise with the sufferings of the distant people who, in the fullness of the realization of that great fact that the scepter of the British Constitution rules them and protects them in the midst of that tropic land whose fertility has won for it the title of the 'granary of the world', starve like wild beasts, whose lives are an incumbrance (sic) and an inconvenience.[35]

This passage resonates with other newspaper columns from this year as well as Elgee's poems, which represent the starving as akin to animals and as reduced to a statistical or economical unit, two crucial forms of dehumanization. The assertion of sympathy here quickly shifts to a materialist analysis of Britain's global colonial economy and its reliance on famine:

> England has been enriched by their treasure, she has been enriched by their magnificent territories ... and this people by which she has gained so much are the periodical victims of the most shocking calamities that can befall a nation or a race.

The writer identifies the causes of famine in India as taxation, ruthless extraction and export of crops and raw materials even during scarcity of subsistence crops, and an exploitative rentier system.[36] Thus, he draws a clear connection between the forms of agrarian colonialism found in both Ireland and India.

Throughout these writings in the *Irishman*, there is a fundamental recognition that dehumanization is central to the experience of famine—that the dehumanization of certain populations allows the creation of policies and structures that produce starvation and death; that famine itself is dehumanizing; that the nonhuman as a category, for example the concepts of "encumbrance" and "redundancy" and "surplus population," is applied to those who starve even before the conditions of famine descend upon them. In this way, there is both a political and aesthetic continuity, and arguably a material relationship, between the projects of Elgee's famine poetry and this later archive. Indeed, the aspects of her famine poetry examined in this chapter make possible an internationalist critique of famine and empire that emerges fully in Ireland in the mid-19th century. With that in mind, I would like to provide a definitive literary history, one that demonstrates irrefutably the influence of Elgee's famine poetry on the writers of the *Irishman*. But the nature of the archive—for example, the anonymity of the staff writers meant to protect them from prosecution for treason felony—makes this a challenging goal. However, the *Irishman* issues that contain these writings on famine in India and Ireland simultaneously advertise Speranza's collected works as well as literary anthologies containing her famine poems. They publish reviews of her work during these years and cite her poems in articles on nationalist ballads and literature, and on histories of the Great Famine in Ireland. She is certainly not the only possible influence on this archive, but her poems about the experience of Irish famine and her analysis of its causes were in far-reaching circulation at the very same time. When writers in the *Irishman* invoke the living memories of the Great Famine in Ireland as a way to make sense of repeated famine in India, surely Jane Elgee's influential famine poems are a vital part of that memory that is activated in 1877, and in the years preceding.

In a review of the third volume of *Memory Ireland* in the *Dublin Review of Books*, Guy Beiner identifies what he sees as an absence in Memory Studies concerning the Famine in Ireland.[37] He suggests that many studies of famine memories focus on the 20th century and therefore omit forms of memory that appeared in the immediate generations after the Great Famine. Here, I also offer just one contribution to the project of excavating forms of remembering that appeared shortly after its conclusion in the mid-1850s. We see one instance in which memory of the Famine was recalled and transmitted just two or three decades later. The writers in the *Irishman* conjure memories of the Famine years and claim that "Ireland has not yet forgotten the terrible years of the famine when hundreds of thousands were left to die."[38] Through both the use of the first person plural and the invocation of the unitary subject of "Ireland" in these statements, these writers draw on readers' individual and family memories in the service of a vital political critique, one in which the example of Ireland's past could illuminate a global system of Empire and famine that had emerged over the course of the 19th century. Thus, collective memory serves as a political resource beyond the bounds of the national. Elgee's poems and their iconography are a clear part of those memories that are mobilized. These writings about India reach back to famine literature, such as Speranza's, to recover sophisticated tropes such as the skeleton, the deranged family, and the human who becomes nonhuman. In this archive, as in "The Famine Year," the skeleton appears at the feast. The Great Hunger in Ireland becomes a vital presence in their present, haunting and refusing to die, allowing Irish readers to recognize themselves in other starving people throughout the empire.

Endnotes

[1] Kevin Kenny, *The American Irish: A History* (Longman, 2000) and David Nally, *Human Encumbrances: Political Violence and the Great Irish Famine* (Notre Dame, 2011).

[2] Christine Kinealy, "Introduction: The Famine Killed Everything" in David Valone and Christine Kinealy (eds.), *Ireland's Great Hunger: Silence, memory, and commemoration* (University Press of America, 2000), p. 2.

[3] Kinealy, "The Famine Killed Everything," p. 3.

[4] Kenny, *The American Irish*, pp 89-90.

[5] Melissa Fegan, *Literature and the Irish Famine, 1845-1919* (Oxford, 2002), p. 2.

[6] Chris Morash, *The Hungry Voice: The Poetry of the Irish Famine* (Dublin, 1989), p. 37.

[7] For an account, see Charles Gavan Duffy, *Four Years of Irish History* (Cassell, Petter, Galpin, 1883), pp 70-84. For more on their relationship, see Karen Tipper, *A Critical Biography of Lady Jane Wilde, 1821?-1896, Irish Revolutionist, Humanist, Scholar and Poet* (New York, 2002), chapter 7. The question mark is in the original title of the source since Lady Wilde's birth year is unknown.

[8] Duffy, *Four Years of Irish History*, p. 95.

[9] Morash, *The Hungry Voice*, p. 18.

[10] Cornelia Pearsall, "Browning and the traumatic monologue: Deictic poetics in Childe Roland to the Dark Tower Came" (forthcoming), pp 5-9. I am grateful to Cornelia Pearsall for sharing this essay with me while it is in the publication process.

[11] For an excellent consideration of the idea of "trauma" in relation to the Famine in Ireland, see Oona Frawley, *Memory Ireland: The Famine and the Troubles* (Syracuse University Press, 2014), pp 7-9.

[12] This is a 19th-century spelling of corpses.

[13] Nally, *Human Encumbrances*, pp 1-56.

[14] Margaret Kelleher, *The Feminization of Famine: Expressions of the Inexpressible?* (Duke University Press, 1997), p. 19.

[15] Marjorie Howes, *Colonial Crossings: Figures in Irish Literary history* (Field Day, 2006), p. 10.

[16] Kelleher, *The Feminization of Famine*, p. 22.

[17] Ibid., p. 7. See also Stuart McLean, *The Event and its Terrors: Ireland, Famine, Modernity*, (Stanford University Press, 2004), pp 134-5.

[18] Kelleher, *The Feminization of Famine*, p. 71.

[19] Margot Backus, *The Gothic Family Romance: Heterosexuality, Child Sacrifice, and the Anglo-Irish Colonial Order* (Duke University Press, 1999).

[20] Chris Morash, *Writing the Irish Famine* (Oxford: Clarendon Press, 1995), p. 182.

[21] David Lloyd, "The Indigent Sublime: Specters of Irish Hunger" in Frawley, *Memory Ireland*, pp 22-23.

[22] See Howes, "Blood and Tears: Lady Wilde" in Howes, *Colonial Crossings*, pp 5-23, and Morash, *The Hungry Voice*, pp 22-30.

[23] See McLean's critique that Elgee figures vengeance as "deferred to an unspecified apocalyptic future" in *The Event and Its Terrors*, p. 88.

[24] "The Famine Year" would appear eventually in Irish school textbooks, specifically *Ballads of Irish History for Schools* in 1929. See Morash, *The Hungry Voice*, p. 30.

[25] Pierre Nora, "Between memory and history: Les Lieux de Memoire" in *Representations*, 26 (Spring, 1989), pp 7-24.

[26] *The Nation*, 5 Feb. 1875.

[27] Mike Davis, *Late Victorian Holocausts: El Nino Famines and the making of the Third World* (Verso, 2000), p. 7 & pp 110-12.

[28] Zahid Chaudhary, *Afterimage of Empire: Photography in Nineteenth Century India* (University of Minnesota Press, 2012), p. 172.

[29] Nally, *Human Encumbrances*, p. 3.

[30] *The Irishman*, 20 Jan. 1877.

[31] Gauri Viswanathan, *Masks of Conquest: Literary study and British Rule in India* (Columbia University Press, 1989) pp 7-8.

[32] David Nally, "The colonial dimensions of the Great Irish Famine" in John Crowley, William J. Smyth, and Mike Murphy (eds.), *Atlas of the Great Irish Famine* (Cork University Press, 2012), pp 67-9.

[33] *The Irishman*, 15 Dec. 1877.

[34] Davis, *Late Victorian Holocausts*, p. 9.

[35] *The Irishman*, 4 Aug. 1866.

[36] For a full account of the economic structures that led to the "Great Famine" in Madras and neighboring regions of India, see Mike Davis, *Late Victorian Holocausts*, chapter 1. See also Chaudhary, *Afterimage of Empire*, chapter 3.

[37] *Dublin Review of Books*, 3 Jan. 2015.

[38] *The Irishman*, 13 Jan. 1877.

Works Cited

Backus, Margot. *The Gothic Family Romance: Heterosexuality, Child Sacrifice, and the Anglo-Irish Colonial Order.* Durham NC: Duke University Press, 1999.

Beiner, Guy. "Memory Too Has A History". *Dublin Review of Books*, 3 January 2015.

Chaudhary, Zahid. *Afterimage of Empire: Photography in Nineteenth Century India.* Minneapolis: University of Minnesota Press, 2012.

Davis, Mike. *Late Victorian Holocausts: El Nino Famines and the making of the Third World.* London: Verso, 2000.

Duffy, Charles Gavan. *Four Years of Irish History.* Dublin: Cassell, Petter, Galpin, 1883.

Fegan, Melissa. *Literature and the Irish Famine, 1845-1919.* Oxford: Oxford University Press, 2002.

Frawley, Oona (ed.). *Memory Ireland: The Famine and the Troubles.* Syracuse: Syracuse University Press, 2014.

Howes, Marjorie. *Colonial Crossings: Figures in Irish Literary History.* Dublin: Field Day, 2006.

Kelleher, Margaret. *The Feminization of Famine: Expressions of the Inexpressible?* Durham NC: Duke University Press, 1997.

Kenny, Kevin. *The American Irish: A History.* New York: Longman, 2000.

Lloyd, David. "The Indigent Sublime: Specters of Irish Hunger" in Frawley ed., *Memory Ireland: the Famine and the Troubles.* Syracuse: Syracuse University Press, 2014.

McLean, Stuart. *The Event and Its Terrors: Ireland, Famine, Modernity.* Stanford: Stanford University Press, 2004.

Morash, Chris. *The Hungry Voice: the Poetry of the Irish Famine.* Dublin: Irish Academic Press, 1989.

Writing the Irish Famine. Oxford: Clarendon Press, 1995.

Nally, David. *Human Encumbrances: Political Violence and the Great Irish Famine.* University of Notre Dame Press, 2011.

"The colonial dimensions of the Great Irish Famine" in John Crowley, William J. Smyth, and Mike Murphy (eds.), *Atlas of the Great Irish Famine.* Cork University Press, 2012.

Nora, Pierre. "Between memory and history: *Les Lieux de Memoire.*" *Representations*, 26 Spring, 1989.

Pearsall, Cornelia. "Browning and the traumatic monologue: Deictic poetics in Childe Roland to the Dark Tower Came" (Unpublished manuscript, forthcoming).

Tipper, Karen. *A Critical Biography of Lady Jane Wilde, 1821?-1896, Irish Revolutionist, Humanist, Scholar and Poet.* New York: Edwin Mellen Press, 2002.

Valone, David and Christine Kinealy (eds.). *Ireland's Great Hunger: Silence, memory, and Commemoration.* Lanham Maryland: University Press of America, 2000.

Viswanathan, Gauri. *Masks of Conquest: Literary Study and British Rule in India.* New York: Columbia University Press, 1989.

Chapter Twelve

"Revolting scenes of famine":[1] Frances Power Cobbe and the Great Hunger

Maureen O'Connor

Every eminent writer, thinker, theologian, scientist and philosopher in the English-speaking world during the Victorian era not only knew of the Irishwoman Frances Power Cobbe—abolitionist, feminist and anti-vivisection campaigner—but likely knew her personally. In 1894, the founder of "New Journalism" in Britain, W.T. Stead, declared her the "oldest New Woman now living on the planet," as well as "one of the most remarkable women of the Victorian era ... [who] has every claim to be regarded as one of the most notable among the notable of her sex," while in that same year, the American critic Walter Lewin said of Cobbe that "excepting John Stuart Mill, she has done more than anyone else to give the dignity of principle to the women's movement."[2] Cobbe was born in 1822 at Newbridge House, Donabate, Co. Dublin, to a wealthy Anglo-Irish family with connections to the British aristocracy as well as other claims to distinction, having contributed distinguished officers to British military service (including a recipient of the Victoria Cross) and several archbishops to the Anglican Church. Cobbe, though virtually forgotten today, was at the center of the social, literary and intellectual circles of note of her time. She was ubiquitous in Victorian England's public discourse: the second edition of Charles Darwin's *Descent of man* cites her commentary on the first edition and dedicates a long footnote to her; Matthew Arnold refers disapprovingly to her defence of Colenso in *The function of criticism*; and John Ruskin foments against her regularly, once characterizing her as a "tinkling saucepan," but most famously in "Of Queen's gardens," where Cobbe is not named, though contemporary readers would have been in no doubt to whom he was referring in his complaint about women insolently "profaning" the science of theology. Perhaps her most impressive contribution to Victorian culture, however, was her influence on the passage of the Matrimonial Causes Act of 1878.[3] Having a number of prominent friends and relations in government, she was not only consulted as to the wording of the bill, but, thanks to these connections, she was also able to time the publication in *Contemporary Review* of her powerful essay, "Wife-torture in England," so that it appeared during parliamentary debate on the bill, a coincidence credited at the time—and since—with the final favorable vote. According to one of her recent biographers, Sally Mitchell, Cobbe published well over 100 articles in leading periodicals, 200 tracts for the anti-vivisection movement, and more than a thousand unsigned leaders for the *Echo*. She was a correspondent in Rome and Florence for the *Daily News* and the only woman to write regularly for the *Theological review*. She also wrote several books on theology and philosophy and lectured tirelessly until near the end of her long life. She championed the rights of black slaves, working girls, women of all classes, and of animals. According to Barbara Caine, "In her recognition of the connection between the many forms of female oppression evident within the family, the Church and the intellectual and professional worlds, Cobbe came closer to propounding a theory of patriarchy than did any other Victorian feminist."[4]

While no longer a household name, Cobbe has become a subject of increasing interest in the 21st century, with five monographs appearing between 2001 and 2006, and in more recent years a few PhD theses have taken her as their subject.[5] However, the fact of Cobbe's Irishness—the historic, political, cultural specificity and the potential impact of growing up and living in Ireland when she did—receives little attention from her biographers, who tend to identify her with her class and as "British," rather than as Irish in any fully developed way.[6] That she witnessed the Famine, taught "native" Irish children, and dedicates more than 200 pages of her autobiography to her time in Ireland, fails to register as particularly significant. As she says in the autobiography, however, while living on the family estate in Donabate, she was kept busy, especially during the 1840s:

> Teaching in my village school a mile from our house two or three times a week, and looking after all the sick and hungry in the two villages of Donabate and Dilisk. Those were the years of Famine and Fever in Ireland, and there was abundant call for all our energies to combat them.[7]

Even Deirdre Raftery, who claims in her 1995 essay that Cobbe's "feminism had its genesis" in her home in Donabate, does not locate that feminism or her subject's "philanthropic interests," or her ideological and intellectual formation, in any larger Irish context than the family estate.[8] And even then, Raftery's observations about the significance of Cobbe's philanthropic interests, which introduced her to the issue of women's rights, situate the first stirrings of that interest in Bristol, where Cobbe lived after leaving Ireland at the age of 35.[9] In fact, Cobbe's earliest exposure to the lives of the poor and the special struggles of women under straitened circumstances was in Ireland, particularly during the Famine, when she tended to the sick, starving and dying on the family estate, which included the town of Donabate, but especially in the nearby town of Dilisk, where material conditions were far worse than they were for the Cobbe family's tenants. The autobiography includes her striking recollection of the moment the potato blight struck:

> I happen to recall precisely the day, almost the hour, when the blight fell on the potatoes and caused the great calamity. A party of us were driving to a seven o'clock dinner at the house of our neighbour, Mrs. Evans, of Portrane. As we passed a remarkably fine field of potatoes in blossom, the scent came through the open windows of the carriage and we remarked to each other how splendid was the crop. Three or four hours later, as we returned home in the dark, a dreadful smell came from the same field and we exclaimed: "Something has happened to those potatoes; they do not smell at all as they did when we passed them on the way out." Next morning there was a wail from one end of Ireland to the other. Every field was black and every root rendered unfit for human food.[10]

The few biographical paragraphs typically devoted to her life in Ireland (if any) by those who write on Cobbe focus on her relationship with her family and the Anglo-Irish world, while her interactions with the larger Irish context and her contact with the "native" Irish go largely unexamined. A related aporia found in recent studies of Cobbe affects the strangely apologetic discussion of their subject's advocacy of animal rights, and especially her anti-vivisection campaign. Biographers seem compelled to explain away the passion with which Cobbe dedicated herself to this cause, a source of defeat and humiliation in her later years, in contrast to the many successes achieved by her work on behalf of women. It is often the case that in her rhetoric on behalf of animals Cobbe appears to betray her own highly valued rationalism and frequently voiced resistance to and critique of those weaknesses culturally determined to be "feminine," sentimentality chief among them. It is not only when talking about vivisection, however, that Cobbe obstinately forecloses the imposition of coherence or attempts at ideological recuperation. Even her most dedicated contemporary admirers found her maddeningly inconsistent.

As I have argued elsewhere, the discriminatory class and race affinities typical of a Victorian suffragist were complicated for Cobbe by a consciousness of belonging to an especially besieged class in late 19th-century Ireland, one marked by racialized sectarian difference.[11] In the context of her experiences of the Great Hunger, it is worth revisiting earlier positions. I have argued that Cobbe's experience as an Anglo-Irish woman at once stimulates and undermines her various modes of patriarchal resistance. In her study of 19th-century Englishwomen active in the cause of animal protection, Moira Ferguson observes that in a:

> revised vocabulary of rights the discourses against cruelty to animals, abuse of women, and enslavement overlapped and elided with one another, contributing at the same time to an updated definition of what constituted Englishness.[12]

The "Englishness" under construction in Ferguson's examination of the rhetorical imbrications among emancipatory causes is a national identity forming and reforming in reaction to imperial expansion. Ferguson contends that the depredations attendant on colonialism, which potentially allied the colonized in the peripheries with other powerless, marginalized communities, constituted a source of anxiety and ambivalence for the white, middle-class, English, Protestant activists in London who were championing women, animals and slaves at home. Ferguson includes Cobbe in this group, but Cobbe, though she took pride at times in being unidentifiable as "Irish," was at other times assertive about and protective of her Irish identity, lived in the colonial periphery for more than a third of her life, and was not middle class. Other complicating factors include the fact that she was brought up by a beloved Irish nurse, taught "native" Irish children, and in 1848 inadvertently contributed funds to the local "Cutthroat Club," which was threatening violent insurgence, targeting the Cobbe family. This occurred in one of the worst years of the Famine, and it was while ministering to victims of fever that Cobbe made this "accidental" contribution. It might be worth noting that elsewhere in her memoir Cobbe recalls that, as a child, she and her brothers often played "at rebellion."[13]

The potentially undermining contradictions subtending Cobbe's many advocacies animate the "Cutthroat Club" incident, an ironic, darkly comic diversion of relief funds, from immediate troubles—the provision of food for the sick and starving—to the elimination of the occupying population responsible for the conditions of penury and powerless that rendered the effects of the potato blight disastrous and drove millions from their homes in an unprecedented population displacement.[14] In the critique of domination Cobbe pursued over several decades, the points of intersection among her uneasy alliances with both the exploiters and the exploited are uniquely unstable. Thus it is that the strident and impassioned opponent of slavery, who was especially exercised about what she considered England's appallingly misplaced sympathies with slaveholders during the American Civil War, could, in an emancipation tract of 1863, *The red flag in John Bull's eyes*, speak pleadingly of negroes "displaying the peculiarly Christian virtues of placability and patience, in a matter hardly to be paralleled in the annals of the Caucasian race";[15] yet could also, in "The ethics of zoophily," an anti-vivisection article written in 1895, assert that "a Fuegian who eats his mother and can't count his fingers cannot be pigeon-holed a 'Person.'"[16] An often self-cancelling impulse to pigeon-holing leads to frequent lapses in Cobbe's reasoning, despite her vaunted rationalist ethos. For example, her position on the rights of animals can vacillate from essay to essay in her many works denouncing vivisection: on the one hand, she charges with base hypocrisy an English public that pampers and admires its pets but allows other animals to be tortured on the dissector's table, while on the other hand, she avails herself of a hierarchical "diminishing scale of sensibility" when she wants to distinguish between the justified killing of animals for sport and the inhuman practices of science.[17] This chapter will focus on two texts, contemporaneous with those cited above, in which Cobbe discusses her Famine experience. Her essay, "Ireland and her exhibition in 1865," was written in 1865, around the time she was writing urgently in the cause of abolition, as in *The red flag*. Her autobiography, *Life of Frances Power Cobbe: by herself*, was written toward the end of her life, in 1895, around the same times as she makes her disturbing assertion regarding the limits of non-white accession to personhood. The content of the 1865 essay provided the material for much of her recollection of the Famine in the autobiography, but some noteworthy changes were made in this 30-year span.

Unlike most 19th-century feminists who were animal advocates—a not unusual combination—Cobbe was not a vegetarian. While her declared revulsion against "vegetarian error" would seem to be of a piece with a scale of sensibility that privileges those avatars of the Irish Ascendancy, the hound and the horse, she supports her objection by citing her father's experience "during the Mahratta wars," where he witnessed:

> various revolting scenes of famine, wherein the sacred cows of the Hindoo temples were standing gorged to repletion beside huge vessels of rice devoted to their use, while the starving population lay dying and dead of hunger all around.[18]

The fact that Cobbe herself was witness to "revolting scenes of famine" in Donabate in the 1840s lends unacknowledged suggestive power to her condemnation of vegetarianism, a rejection of the kind of faddish self-denial available only to the privileged, an occluded expression of sympathy for those Irish peasants whose deaths she witnessed at close hand and whose brave and pious resignation under unbearable conditions she describes as offering her "a revelation of goodness."[19] Cobbe describes the Irish peasantry dying from hunger and fever in this way in "Ireland and her exhibition," in which she recalls the Famine 20 years previous. In 1895, half a century after the height of the Famine, when these memories are reconstructed again in her autobiography, this moving phrase is gone. In 1865 she poses a question to the reader:

> Shall we ask a man to train a rose when he needs to dig a potatoe, and when the space of his garden represented by the rose stands for a meal lost to him and his children?[20]

But by 1895, the desperate conditions precluding the maintenance of a decorative garden appear to have been forgotten when Cobbe complains of the lack of aesthetic sensibilities evident in the homes of the Irish peasantry where, "flowers in the gardens or against the walls were never to be seen."[21] This is not to say that there are not moving passages in her later recollections of what she witnessed. She tells us, for example, that "strong men fainted at their work in the fields, having left untasted for their little children the food they so sorely needed." This is followed by a description of the selflessness of a poor widow to whose door a desperately starving beggar appears:

> The traveller lay senseless, starved to the bone and utterly famine-stricken. The widow tried tenderly to make him swallow a spoonful of bread and water, but he seemed unable to make the exertion.[22]

The power of this scene is undermined somewhat when followed by the observation that "Of course all of the neighbouring gentry joined in extensive soup-kitchens and the like, and by one means or other the hard years of famine were passed over,"[23] though the use of the phrase "passed over" is not as dismissive or casual as some commentators interpret it to be. The touching piety Cobbe claims lay behind the brave resignation she saw among the suffering and dying in the 1865 essay is not identified as such in the autobiography. If Roman Catholicism is represented as possibly enabling virtue in 1865, it is simply a scourge by 1895. While Cobbe rarely expressed admiration for members of the Roman Catholic clergy, in the autobiography, she is particularly scathing. She describes ministering priests' purple and bloated cheeks indicating that they have gorged on a "too abundant of diet of bacon and whiskey punch."[24]

The priests' appetitive self-indulgence mark them out as different, body and soul, from their pious flock, whose simple fare Cobbe admires. The pre-Famine peasant's diet, she reports:

> consisted of oatmeal porridge, wheaten griddle-cake, potatoes and an abundance of buttermilk. The potatoes, before the Famine, were delicious tubers. Many of the best kind disappeared at that time (notable I recall the Black bangers) and the Irish housewife cooked them in a manner which no English or French *Cordon bleu* can approach. I remember constantly seeing little girls bringing the mid-day dinners to their fathers.... The cloth which carried the dinner being removed there appeared a plate of "smiling" potatoes and in the midst a well of about a sixth of a pound of butter. Along with the plate of potatoes was a big jug of milk, and a hunch of griddle bread.[25]

Cobbe's itemization of the elements of her own childhood diet, credited with contributing to the happiest time of her life, when she was "fed in body with the freshest milk and eggs and fruit, everything best for a child," and identified as "the best fare," significantly, does not include any meat.[26]

It may be worth noting that, in an 1877 essay, "The Celt of Ireland and the Celt of Wales," in which Cobbe says "happy is the child that has an Irish nurse," she also argues for the superiority of Irish children's wit. She uses the evocative phrase "*beef*-witted" to describe the slower English pupil—whom she first encountered in Bristol after extensive experience teaching "peasant" children—in comparison to the Celt, whose "mental machinery" she considers "better-oiled" than that of the English or the Scot.[27] Such observations are found in the autobiography as well:

> I have spoken of our village school, and must add that the boys and girls who attended it were exceedingly clever and bright. They caught up ideas, were moved by heroic or pathetic stories, and understood jokes to a degree quite unmatched by English children of the same humble class.[28]

> A fair amount of experience in teaching both [Irish and English children] has led us to the conclusion that the intellectual texture of an Irish child's mind is very much finer and more susceptible of impression than that of an English child of the working ranks. If there were but a little respite from poverty and the too early necessity to stop learning and turn to coarse field work, it is hard to say what might not be made of such noble stuff as the Irish peasant child, both as regards intellect and moral nature exhibition.[29]

In both the 1865 essay and the autobiography, Cobbe indicates that a meatless diet of "buttermilk and potatoes" may be what nourishes the sharpness of intellect amongst her native charges. It certainly is not detrimental to their physical health:

> Never did it happen to us to find a joke unappreciated by an audience of a score or two of little Irish imps, ignorant of the use of shoes, and rosy on a diet of buttermilk and potatoes.[30]

This sentiment recurs in the autobiography:

> [R]osy, bright, merry, children, who thrive with the smallest possible share of buttermilk and stirabout, are utterly innocent of shoes and stockings, and learn at school all that is taught to them at least half as fast again as a tribe of little Saxons.[31]

Cobbe certainly kept herself "rosy." Overweight most of her adult life, Cobbe is humorously self-deprecating in her autobiography about her lack of self-control when it comes to food, especially treats and dainties. She moved to Bristol to join Mary Carpenter's "Ragged School" movement, and to live with Carpenter, but the women fell out. The two main sources of contention between the women were Cobbe's inability to subsist on the ascetic food rations provided by Carpenter and the Irishwoman's treatment of her pet dog, indulgences Carpenter saw as tantamount to snatching the food from needy children's mouths. Both Carpenter and Cobbe witnessed hunger first-hand as well as the illnesses that accompany malnutrition and starvation, but Cobbe never came to regard self-denial as a rational or appropriate response.

Recalling Margot Backus's argument in *The gothic family romance*, I want to suggest that it is not only conflicted loyalties to the Anglo-Irish world of Cobbe's childhood and young adulthood, embodied in horse and dog, that informs the contradictions found in her writing, but more traumatically, what Backus calls the "Anglo-Irish child's ambivalent identification with the native Irish,"[32] and it is the necessarily repressed nature of such an attraction for someone like Cobbe that is particularly disabling for her rationalist ethos. There are recurring hints of a sneaking regard for and even occasional identification with the native Irish throughout her writing, which often uses the "wronged Celt" as a figure of oppressed victimhood when arguing in favor of abolition or against vivisection. Cobbe is certainly anxious to disassociate both herself and her parents from prevailing stereotypes of the self-indulgent and profligate Ascendancy, a phenomenon she wants to relegate to the past. She is at pains to distinguish her father's generation from what she calls the "Rackrent" Irish of previous times who, even in her own family were guilty of "the truly Irish principle of being generous before you are just," in the prodigality with which they opened their doors and furnished their tables. She recalls with clear distaste the legend around a large goblet in the family supposed to have been filled with claret, "calculated to hold *three bottles* of wine." According to tradition, "seven guineas were placed into the wine and he who drank it pocketed the coin."[33] She tries to imagine what "society" (meaning Anglo-Irish society) would have been like a hundred years earlier, based on her father's recollections of his own heavy-drinking father:

> Apparently it combined a considerable amount of aesthetic taste with traits of genuine barbarism; and high religious pretension with a disregard of every-day duties and a *penchant* for gambling and drinking that would now place the most avowedly worldly persons under a cloud of opprobrium.[34]

Cobbe contrasts the laxity of this earlier age with the wholesome simplicity of Ireland in the 1840s, a conscientious temperance to be distinguished from the dissolute habits of a younger, heedless generation, particularly the young people of the age in which she is writing her life story, the 1890s. Cobbe sets up a telling opposition between her father's upright generation and her brother's contemporaries, the generation that has produced unprecedented cruelties, including vivisection:

> When my father and his friends went on grouse-shooting expeditions to our mountain-lodge, I used to provide for the large parties only an abundance of plain food for

dinners, and for luncheons merely sandwiches, bread and cheese, with a keg of ale, and a basket of apples. By degrees it became necessary (to please my brother's guests) to provide the best of fish, fowl and flesh, champagne and peaches. The whole odious system of *battues*, rendering sport unmanly as well as cruel, with all its attendant waste and cost and disgusting butchery, has grown up within my recollection by the extension of luxury, laziness and ostentation.[35]

The virtuous grouse-hunting parties of Cobbe's father's time are remembered for their plain, vegetarian refreshment: bread and cheese and apples. The cruelty-free fare coincides with the "humane" pursuit of game, which, it is suggested, gives prey a sporting chance, unlike the "unmanly" practice of beating the bushes to drive helpless birds straight into the lazy hunters' guns. Such "disgusting butchery" is accompanied by ostentatious, carnivorous fare: "the best of fish, fowl and flesh."[36]

The perhaps unexpectedly conventional gendering of "fair play" here as "manly" is mirrored by another retreat to essentialized gender behavior later in the autobiography, once again in a passage about hunting. Cobbe nearly always defends hunting, the favored, if not defining, recreation of the Anglo-Irish, a defence that constitutes one of the most stubborn points of contradiction in her wide-ranging work. Her defences nearly always make recourse to the connection between hunting and providing food, often avoiding characterizing hunting as diversion or entertainment. One example occurs in "The Rights of man and the claims of brutes," in which she argues that:

> ...we may slay cattle for food, and take the fowls of the air and the fish of the sea to supply our table; but... we may not (for example) torture calves to produce white meat, nor slash living salmon to make them more delicate nor nail fowls to the fireside to give them diseased livers.[37]

Similar arguments are advanced in "Mr Lowe and the Vivisection Act," an essay of 1877, which includes a reference to cholera and diphtheria, diseases that affected victims of famine, as noted in Cobbe's autobiography:

> [O]f course it is nearly as rational to refer to fox-hunting, rabbit guns and Strasbourg geese as arguments against the endeavour to check the cutting up of living dogs and cats in a laboratory as it would have been when cholera or diphtheria first invaded us, to discountenance all efforts to stop their ravages until we had cured all the gouty and consumptive patients in the kingdom.[38]

She insists in the essay, "It would have been absurd and Quixotic to interfere with the vivisector if he never did nothing worse to animals than the sportsman or farmer do every day."[39]

In an article published just a few years earlier, however, Cobbe seems to contradict these positions when she suggests that

> ...the "savage" modern ailment of "heteropathy," or the taking of pleasure in others' suffering, can be traced to the cruelties of the slaughter house . . . bull-fights and dog-fights, and even among the field sports of a better kind.[40]

The competing allegiances that complicate and undo her defence of hunting become less abstract, more personal, if no less undermining, late in the autobiography:

When I was a little child, living in a house where hunting, coursing, shooting, and fishing, were carried on by all the men and boys, I took such field-sports as part of the order of things, and learned with delight from my father to fish in our ponds on my own account. Somehow it came to pass that when, at sixteen, my mind went through that strange process which Evangelicals call "Conversion," among the first things which my freshly-awakened moral sense pointed out was,—that I must give up fishing. I reflected that the poor fishes were happy in their way in their proper element; that we did not in the least need, or indeed often use them for food; and that I must no longer take pleasure in giving pain to any creature of God. It was a little effort to me to relinquish this amusement in my very quiet, uneventful life; but, as the good Quakers say, it was "borne in on me," that I had to do it, and from that time I have never held a rod or line (though I have been out in boats where large quantities of fish were caught on the Atlantic coast), and I freely admit that angling scarcely comes under the head of cruelty at all, and is perfectly right and justifiable when the fish are wanted for food and are killed quickly. I used to stand sometimes after I had ceased to fish, over one of the ponds in our park and watch the bright creatures dart hither and thither, and say in my heart a little thanksgiving on their behalf instead of trying to catch them.[41]

This tender extension of the hand of fellowship to "bright creatures," Cobbe's renunciation of fishing, a sport rarely considered as cruel as hare coursing or even grouse shooting, are followed by a brusque dismissal of any notion of placing blame on her own class, a dismissal that requires she retreat to an atypical assertion regarding the propriety of her womanly role, something she has represented her younger self as consistently defying in earlier sections of the text:

Of course, I disliked then, and always, hunting, coursing and shooting; but as a woman I was not expected to join in such pursuits, and I did not take on myself to blame those who followed them. I do not now allow of any comparison between the cruelty of such Field Sports and the deliberate Chamber-Sport of Vivisection.[42]

As already discussed, "The ethics of zoophily," from the same year as Cobbe's autobiography, is a vexed, frustratingly self-cancelling essay. It includes a dismissive argument regarding the morality of fox hunting, even while the persecuted Irish are compared to the despised animal in the course of an unexpectedly even-handed summary of the source of "Irish hatreds":

A very large share of human cruelty has, in all ages, arisen out of the persuasion of the cruel persons that they were God's favourites ... and the rancour of Irish hatreds, have had their roots in the conviction of one party that the other is under the curse of God.[43]

An earlier essay, published a year after "Exhibition," goes even further in expressing something like sympathy for the people her autobiography would come to see as ungrateful to their betters:

The real wrongs inflicted by England upon Ireland are probably as bad as ever disgraced the history of conquest—in itself without excuse. Not to speak of confiscations, and executions often taking the form of murderous raids into suspected districts ... a sad commentary on the boasted justice of English Parliaments. Irishmen lay under disabilities, political, social, and ecclesiastical, so severe and numerous that it really seems to have been a question what they were expected to do except to break some of these arbitrary laws, and so incur some cruel penalty.[44]

This piece, "The Fenian 'idea,'" in which Cobbe explicitly identifies as an Irishwoman, was written for a publication in the United States, where it may have seemed safer to express sympathy with the "native" Irish. In "Ireland and her Exhibition of 1865," traces of such sympathy, as well as hints of a criticism of the Ascendancy's position and privilege, are also to be found, as when early on Cobbe remarks on the "unnatural insulation of such wealth and cultivation as exist in the midst of dreary wastes of poverty and neglect."[45]

It is misleading, if not reductive, to place Cobbe in the company of later British first-wave feminists (Stead called her the *oldest* New Woman, after all), as Moira Ferguson and other commentators do. Beyond the fact of her landed background or even her hyphenated identity as Anglo-Irish, it is Cobbe's first-hand experience of the Famine that complicates her identity politics, not least for her own self-assessment. Cobbe repeatedly voiced concern about the heartless age she felt the coming 20th century augured. In her only novel, *The age of science: a newspaper of the twentieth-century* (written by "Merlin Nostradamus"), a dystopian text set in 1977, sympathy's antithesis, "heteropathy," has taken hold of public discourse and has replaced the life of the soul. Even the arts are judged "scientifically"; one book review that appears in the fictional newspaper applauds a novel's study of the effects of pity and sympathy on the relevant glands.[46] Cobbe's principled and determined stand against cruelty and abuse was established in Ireland, annealed by her experience of the Great Hunger, one important source of the many, if furtive, expressions of sympathy with the plight of the Irish found throughout her work.

Endnotes

[1] Frances Power Cobbe, "The rights of man and the claims of brutes" in *Fraser's Magazine* 68 (Nov. 1863), p. 598.

[2] W.T. Stead, "Character sketch" in *Review of reviews,* 10 (Oct. 1894), p. 329; Lewin quoted in Barbara Caine, *Victorian feminists* (Oxford, 1991), p. 105.

[3] Deirdre Raftery, "Frances Power Cobbe (1822-1904)" in Mary Cullen and Maria Luddy (eds.), *Women, power and consciousness in nineteenth-century Ireland* (Dublin, 1995).

[4] Caine, p. 3.

[5] Lori Williamson, *Power and protest: Frances Power Cobbe and Victorian society* (London and New York, 2001); Sandra J. Peacock, *The theological and ethical writings of Frances Power Cobbe: 1822-1904* (Lewiston, NY, 2002); Sally Mitchell, *Frances Power Cobbe: Victorian feminist, journalist, reformer* (Charlottesville, NC, 2004); Susan Hamilton, *Frances Power Cobbe and Victorian feminism* (New York, 2006).

[6] Kelly Cameron, *Imperial rhetorics: Frances Power Cobbe's answering of the Irish question in the nineteenth-century periodical press* represents a rare exception to this general trend (Ph.D thesis, Texas Christian University, 2012).

[7] Frances Power Cobbe, *Life of Frances Power Cobbe: by herself* (2 vols, London, 1895), i, p. 89.

[8] Raftery, p. 92.

[9] Ibid., p. 108.

[10] Cobbe, *Life,* i, pp 164-5.

[11] Maureen O'Connor, "Frances Power Cobbe and the patriarchs" in James Murphy (ed.), *Evangelicals and Catholics in nineteenth-century Ireland* (Dublin, 2005), pp 187-96; "Frances Power Cobbe: political animal" in *The female and the species: the animal in Irish women's writing* (Oxford, 2000), pp 31-58.

[12] Moira Ferguson, *Animal advocacy and Englishwomen, 1780-1900: patriots, nation, and empire* (MI, Ann Arbor, 1998), p. 6.

[13] Cobbe, *Life,* i, p. 141.

[14] Ciarán Ó Murchadha, *The great famine: Ireland's agony, 1845-1852* (London, 2011), p. 144.

[15] Frances Power Cobbe, *The red flag in John Bull's eyes,* Ladies' London Emancipation Society, tract 1 (London, 1863), p. 5.

[16] Frances Power Cobbe, "The ethics of zoophily" in *Contemporary review* (Oct. 1895), p. 504.

[17] Cobbe, "Ethics," p. 506.

[18] Frances Power Cobbe, "Brutes," p. 598.

[19] Frances Power Cobbe, "Ireland and her exhibition in 1865" in *Fraser's Magazine,* 27 (Oct. 1865), p. 408.

[20] Cobbe, "Exhibition," p. 418.

[21] Cobbe, *Life*, i, p. 127.

[22] Ibid., i, p. 138.

[23] Ibid., i, p. 139.

[24] Ibid., i, p. 144.

[25] Ibid., i, p. 124.

[26] Ibid., i, p. 27.

[27] Frances Power Cobbe, "The Celt of Wales and the Celt of Ireland" in *Cornhill Magazine* (Dec. 1877), p. 666.

[28] Cobbe, *Life*, i, p. 146.

[29] Ibid., ii, p. 405.

[30] Cobbe, "Exhibition," p. 416.

[31] Cobbe, *Life*, i, pp 149-50.

[32] Margot Gayle Backus, *The gothic family romance: heterosexuality, child sacrifice, and the Anglo-Irish colonial order* (NC, Durham, 1999), p. 76.

[33] Cobbe, *Life*, i, p. 117.

[34] Ibid.

[35] Ibid., i, p. 159.

[36] Ibid.

[37] Cobbe, "Brutes," p. 592.

[38] Frances Power Cobbe, "Mr Lowe and the Vivisection Act" in *Contemporary Review* (Feb. 1877), p. 342.

[39] Ibid., p. 345.

[40] Frances Power Cobbe, "The social sentiment, or heteropathy, aversion and sympathy" in *Theological Review,* 11 (Jan. 1874), p. 8.

[41] Cobbe, *Life*, ii, pp 618-19.

[42] Ibid., ii, pp 619-20.

[43] Cobbe, "Ethics," p. 507.

[44] Frances Power Cobbe, "The Fenian 'idea'" in *The Atlantic monthly* 17 (May 1866), p. 572.

[45] Cobbe, "Exhibit," p. 405.

[46] Frances Power Cobbe (as "Merlin Nostradamus"), *The age of science: a newspaper of the twentieth-century* (London, 1877), p. 22.

Works Cited

Backus, Margot Gayle. *The gothic family romance: heterosexuality, child sacrifice, and the Anglo-Irish colonial order*. Durham NC: Duke Press, 1999.

Caine, Barbara. *Victorian feminists.* Oxford University Press, 1991.

Cameron, Kelly. *Imperial rhetorics: Frances Power Cobbe's answering of the Irish question in the nineteenth-century periodical press*. PhD thesis, Texas Christian University, 2012.

Cobbe, Frances Power (as "Merlin Nostradamus"). *The age of science: a newspaper of the twentieth-century*. London: Ward, Lock and Tyler, 1877.

—— "The Celt of Wales and the Celt of Ireland." *Cornhill magazine* (Dec. 1877), 661-78.

—— "The ethics of zoophily: a reply." *Contemporary Review* (Oct. 1895), 498-502.

—— "The Fenian 'idea.'" *The Atlantic monthly,* 17 (May 1866), 572-7.

—— "Ireland and her exhibition in 1865." *Fraser's Magazine,* 27 (Oct. 1865), 403-22.

—— *Life of Frances Power Cobbe: by herself.* 2 vols, London, 1895.

—— "Mr Lowe and the Vivisection Act." *Contemporary Review* (Feb. 1877), 335-47.

—— *The red flag in John Bull's eyes*. Ladies' London Emancipation Society, tract 1. London, 1863.

—— "The rights of man and the claims of brutes." *Fraser's Magazine,* 68 (Nov. 1863), 586-602.

—— "The social sentiment, or heteropathy, aversion and sympathy." *Theological review* 11 (Jan. 1874), 1-35.

Ferguson, Moira. *Animal advocacy and Englishwomen, 1780-1900: patriots, nation, and empire*. MI: Ann Arbor, 1998.

Hamilton, Susan. *Frances Power Cobbe and Victorian feminism*. New York: Palgrave, 2006.

Mitchell, Sally. *Frances Power Cobbe: Victorian feminist, journalist, reformer*. Charlottesville, NC: University of Virginia Press, 2004.

O'Connor, Maureen. "Frances Power Cobbe and the patriarchs." James Murphy (ed.), *Evangelicals and Catholics in nineteenth-century Ireland*. Dublin, 2005, 187-96.

O'Connor, Maureen. "Frances Power Cobbe: political animal." *The female and the species: the animal in Irish women's writing*. Oxford, 2000, 31-58.

Ó Murchadha, Ciarán. *The great famine: Ireland's agony, 1845 -1852*. London: Bloomsbury, 2011.

Peacock, Sandra J. *The theological and ethical writings of Frances Power Cobbe: 1822-1904*. New York: Lewiston, 2002.

Raftery, Deirdre. "Frances Power Cobbe (1822-1904)" in Mary Cullen and Maria Luddy (eds.), *Women, power and consciousness in nineteenth-century Ireland*. Dublin: Attic Press, 1995, 89-124.

Stead, W.T. "Character sketch." *Review of reviews* 10 (Oct. 1894), 329-38.

Williamson, Lori. *Power and protest: Frances Power Cobbe and Victorian society*. London and New York: Rivers Oram Press, 2001.

⌘

Chapter Thirteen

"An invisible but inescapable trauma": epigenetics and the Great Famine

Oonagh Walsh

In May 2013, the British Psychological Society's Division of Clinical Psychology released a position paper entitled *Classification of behaviour and experience in relation to functional psychiatric diagnoses: Time for a paradigm shift*.[1] Released to coincide with the latest update to the American Psychiatry Association's *Diagnostic and Statistical Manual of Mental Disorders* (DSM), a widely used tool for the classification of mental illness in the developed world, the BPS paper took a robust stance against what it believed to be psychiatry's unswerving faith in the "disease" model.[2] The media were swift to seize on this promising controversy, with an *Observer* newspaper article declaring that "There is no scientific evidence that psychiatric diagnoses such as schizophrenia and bipolar disorder are valid or useful."[3] Quoting one of the paper's authors, the article declared that "there is now overwhelming evidence that people break down as a result of a complex mix of social and psychological circumstances—bereavement and loss, poverty and discrimination, trauma and abuse." The Society argued for the abandonment of what they regard as psychiatry's predominantly biomedical model of mental illness. The spat, which has been read as the latest manifestation of professional rivalry, is a depressing reminder of the contested nature of mental illness treatment, and the constantly shifting ground over which mental health practitioners battle.

In this chapter, I suggest that the psychological and physiological trauma of the Great Famine fundamentally altered health profiles in Ireland, leaving a mark upon survivors and their descendants that continued well into the 20th century. Both at home and as part of the diaspora worldwide, the Irish exhibited an unusual health profile (especially in relation to mental illness) that suggests impact on a communal rather than individual level, and impact that, moreover, was transgenerational.[4] This, combined with the unsettled social, political and economic circumstances of 19th century Ireland, may have led to higher levels of general stress in the population, and may go some way toward explaining our unique relationship with mental and physical ill health. Although this is a new direction in Irish historiography, there are some fascinating studies on other international cohorts that offer tantalizing clues as to how the great unanswered question in Irish health history—our high level of mental illness, as well as some chronic illnesses—might be addressed. I will, therefore, discuss a number of potential models for the Irish case that offer important points of comparison, and discuss how an Irish study might be developed.

Sadly, despite its inclusion in Martin Scorsese's 2006 Academy-Award winning film "The

Departed," it appears that Sigmund Freud never in fact said: "The Irish are the only race for whom psychoanalysis is of no use whatsoever."[5] However, the quote does reflect a widely held belief in the connection between the Irish and a compulsion to talk, and more importantly points up the importance of language and the manner in which it can conceal as much as it reveals: Seamus Heaney's poem, "Whatever you say, say nothing" springs to mind.[6] Irish garrulousness, and a love of language and its creative possibilities, do indeed suggest a potentially fruitful relationship with "talking therapies." Brendan Behan took the connection a step further when he declared: "Other people have a nationality. The Irish and the Jews have a psychosis."[7] We may flatter ourselves that our association with mental illness is a reflection of our national propensity toward genius, on the grounds that creativity and insanity have a long association. More pertinent perhaps is the issue of whether and how ethnicity may be linked with health and illness, and how far do imperatives entirely unrelated to mental health actually determine the levels and efficacy of health care?

Insanity casts a long shadow. Every European culture has its own representations of madness, and, in Ireland's case, they date back to the 6th century. There is an abundance of folk myths surrounding insanity, the best known of which is "Mad Sweeney," the tale of a pagan King driven to furious insanity when cursed by St. Ronan. In the best known account of his peregrinations, the medieval *Buile Suibhine*, he was condemned to wander Ireland until finally he was received into the Church on his deathbed. In the course of his meanderings, he came to a place in Kerry, near Tralee, called *Gleann na nGealt*. Its name—"Valley of the Mad"—derives from a belief that a cure for insanity exists in a well (*Tober na nGealt*), which is situated in the valley: the well can be accessed by a nearby river crossing named *Ath na Gealtan*, "The Fool's Crossing." In July 2012, a chemical analysis was carried out on the waters of *Tober na nGealt* and there was found to be 55.6 ppb of the chemical lithium in the water.[8] This was much higher than the content recorded in other water samples in the locality, and approximately 40 times the normal concentration of lithium in a naturally occurring water supply. Given lithium's well established place in the treatment of mental illness, especially bipolar disorder, it would seem that our forebears correctly recognized the power of the waters to effect a cure. This local peculiarity may be seen in other contexts. In 2010, Japanese researchers reported that low levels of naturally occurring lithium in drinking water supplies reduced suicide rates.[9] Earlier research had produced similar data in the American state of Texas.[10] So science and insanity have a long and well-established history, even if the mechanics by which cures were achieved were not fully understood. I suggest that we can learn a great deal about our mental health histories by applying the most recent scientific advances to our past, and using one of our most traumatic historical experiences to address modern health problems. But this work also may provide evidence for a reconsideration of modern health problems in areas still prone to famines, and help to direct the most effective relief efforts for vulnerable cohorts.

Ireland has a unique profile in terms of mental health and its treatment. From the start of a formal state system to care for the mentally ill at the beginning of the 19th century, the country has exhibited a heavy dependence upon institutional care that is unusual in the developed world. There are, of course, many social, economic and cultural factors that partly explain the profile, some of which include unique lunacy legislation, especially the Criminal Lunatics Act of 1838, which facilitated rapid committals of "dangerous lunatics"; a general poverty, that ensured people used the Act so that they could use the asylum without having to pay the costs of transporting and supporting their relatives; the use of institutions for respite care—people admitted patients for short periods of time, and then took them out against the asylum physician's advice; and the strategic use of asylums when families needed to emigrate.[11] But there are other elements that are not so easily explained. Ireland's District Asylum system, which became, largely unchanged, the modern psychiatric service, was inordinately large for the country's population. The Connaught District Lunatic Asylum in Ballinasloe, east Co. Galway is a case in point. From its modest beginnings in 1833, with beds for 150 patients (a figure it was believed was a gross over-estimate of the total number of lunatics in the province of Connaught, comprising the five counties of Galway, Mayo, Roscommon, Sligo and Leitrim, with a total of 1,348,077 souls), the Ballinasloe Asylum had expanded to offer accommodation for almost 1,200 individuals by the turn of the century, and was at that number turning away cases. Given that the asylum's catchment area had shrunk to the two counties of Galway and Roscommon, with a combined population of 284,015 in 1901, it would seem that mental illness was taking a disproportionate hold upon a population in steady decline. The accelerating rates of admission are truly shocking when set against demographic decline. In 1841, the population stood at just over eight million, and there were approximately 1,600 lunatics in the district asylums, and another 1,500 in jails, workhouses and houses of industry. The Famine years (c.1845-52) saw a sharp drop in the population of approximately two million, through a combination of famine-related mortality and emigration. By 1901, the general population numbered 4.4 million, reflecting the large-scale patterns of permanent migration consolidated by the Famine years. But as the population halved, the proportionate numbers of insanity cases rose sharply, with 17,000 patients in the District Asylum system in 1900, and an estimated 8,000 further insane people "at large," with no beds available for their care. This raises the great unanswered question in Irish medical history: why does the country have an alarmingly rapid and increasing admission rate, when the total population is dropping so sharply?

The Irish pattern is unique in mental health history, with no other country in the Western world in this period recording comparable levels of committals relative to the population, although many institutions did, indeed, share the Irish experience of overcrowded and inadequate facilities. If one argues that local factors are to blame for the Irish picture—poverty, familiarity with local sources of care, an increasing acceptance of medical authority—why then is this tendency carried to other parts of the world? Studies of admissions to asylums in Canada, Australia and Britain show that the Irish are disproportionately over-represented as inpatients in comparison with other migrant groups.[12] So this tendency is carried to all parts of the world with a substantial Irish diaspora, into a wide variety of environments, and across all socio-economic groups. Historians of medicine are inclined to look toward "nurture" in its broadest sense to explain such phenomena, and within the history of psychiatry in particular, there has been a loud and forceful rejection in some quarters of the possibility that mental illness has any biological basis.[13] But if we open ourselves to the possibility that some mental illnesses may originate in our bodies more than our minds, and be precipitated moreover by a complex response to excessively stressful conditions, might part of the answer to the puzzle lie in epigenetic change?

Epigenetics is the study of changes in gene expression, which do not involve alterations to the genetic code, but whose effects may persist over several generations. Epigenetic inheritance adds another, very subtle and sensitive, dimension to our understanding of the process of evolution. The genome changes slowly, through the processes of random mutation and natural selection. Thus, it takes many generations for a genetic trait to become common in a population, and many thousands of years for genetic change to take place in large, complex mammals that reproduce slowly like humans. The epigenome, on the other hand, can change rapidly in response to signals from the environment, and depending upon the changing environmental pressures also can change back within one or more generations. For non-scientists with a basic understanding of Darwinian evolutionary processes, this can be a puzzling concept, and it may be helpful to think of it in terms of music or drama. A printed music score (the genome) is unchanged regardless of the musician who plays it, but any performance of that score will vary largely depending upon the skill of the musician, the environment in which it is played (noisy or quiet, concert hall or village hall), and the quality and appropriateness of the instruments. Similarly, Marlon Brando's Stanley in *A Streetcar Named Desire* draws on the same Tennessee Williams's text as is available to any amateur dramatic group, but the performance is likely to be very different, with the respective actors bringing varying levels of skill and experience to the role. Crucially, epigenetic changes can happen in many individuals at once, and although the experiences that cause these changes may differ between persons, the effects may be experienced communally. Through epigenetic inheritance, some of the experiences of the parents—not, as was originally thought, only through the mother—may pass to future generations. At the same time, the epigenome remains flexible as environmental conditions continue to change. Epigenetic inheritance may allow an organism to continually adjust its gene expression to fit its environment, without changing its DNA code. This ensures that the offspring is prepared for specific environmental pressures before birth, and best placed to cope with, for example, food scarcity, or dangerous and volatile conditions. In 19th-century Ireland, large numbers of people underwent severe nutritional deprivation, as well as psychological stress, sustained over the lengthy duration of the Great Famine. As will be seen from the discussion of comparable international studies below, these factors provide the horrific conditions necessary to produce epigenetic change. We begin with what might fairly be described as the "gold standard" study of famine and epigenetic change: the Dutch Hunger Winter Cohort Study.

The winter of 1944–45 was particularly severe. All over Europe, already debilitated populations suffered from a lack of food and fuel, with thousands dying prematurely as a result. It is known as the "Hunger Winter" in the Netherlands which, in addition to the usual wartime privations suffered particularly severely in certain areas of German occupation. In September 1944, Allied troops had liberated most of the south of the country, but were halted at the Waal and Rhine rivers. The Dutch government in exile in London called for a national railway strike to hinder German operations and, in retaliation, the German authorities blocked all food supplies (from October) to the occupied West of the country. Up to this point, nutrition in the general population had generally been adequate but food supplies rapidly became increasingly scarce. By 26 November 1944, official rations, which eventually consisted of little more than bread and potatoes, had fallen below 1000 kcal per day, and by April 1945, they were as low as 500 kcal per day.[14] Within a few short months, starvation was widespread, and the excess death rate is estimated at between 18 and 20,000 persons.[15] Food supplies were restored immediately after liberation on 5 May 1945, so although the famine was horrifying, it was of limited duration. Its impact was, however, huge, imprinting itself upon all ages and stages, but with an especially pernicious influence upon mothers and their developing children. "The famine affected fertility, weight gain during pregnancy, maternal blood pressure, infant size at birth and central nervous system development."[16] Babies whose mothers were placed under severe nutritional stress in the third trimester of pregnancy were on average 300g lighter at birth, although subsequent birth weights rapidly returned to normal once food supplies were restored in the early summer of 1945. Indeed, the horrific experience might well have become a footnote in the history of World War II were it not for the fact that the Hunger Winter had occurred in a country that maintained excellent records relating to morbidity and mortality, and in a population that before and after the famine had been generally well nourished. It was a "natural experiment" and a unique opportunity to evaluate the impacts, short and long-term, of starvation on a modern, developed society.

The famine had a far reach. There were 3,307 babies born, in gestation, or conceived during the famine, and born after normal conditions had been restored. Owing to the high quality data from the period, researchers were able to pin-point the precise moments at which the foetus was under greatest strain, and link that with health and morbidity in adulthood. Invaluably, there were other cohorts with whom to compare these individuals. There were siblings born before and after the famine, as well as a non-effected control population outside the famine area, but with comparable profiles in terms of social class, access to food, health services and so on. As the famine survivors grew, their health was closely monitored, and by the 1970s, a large amount of data had been collected which began to be analyzed. The Dutch studies depend upon the Barker hypothesis, also known as the "Thrifty Phenotype Thesis."[17] This states that conditions during pregnancy will have long-term effects on adult health, and as the foetus develops it is programmed in response to factors such as the availability of nutrients: these determine several metabolic responses in adulthood. In layman's language, the foetus undergoes an epigenetic change to adapt to a hostile environment in which food is scarce. But if the environment changes, as in the Netherlands, and food is readily available, the adult is now unsuited for "excess" and is predisposed to an increased risk of disease. The lifelong diseases associated with epigenetic change linked to famine includes cardiovascular disease, type 2 diabetes, obesity and hypertension. These effects seem to be linked specifically to deprivation in mid to late gestation, which has the effect of reducing glucose tolerance.[18]

Similar observations have been made in other famines, and confirmed with animal experiments.[19] What the Dutch studies also revealed is that epigenetic change can persist for several generations, for a startling reason. As the ovum of a female foetus are being formed, they can, if placed under stress (psychological or nutritional), undergo a process known as cytosine methylation. This means that maternal starvation may affect not only the unborn child, but that child's own children, ensuring an impact upon three generations. A similar process also may occur in males during the period in which sperm is in formation (especially during the so-called "slow growth" period—see the Överkalix study below), widening the potential effect in a population.

If we take the Dutch findings and apply them to post-Famine Ireland, some interesting parallels emerge. In 1987, E.M. Crawford identified a steady rise in type 2 diabetes (diabetes mellitus) from the 1840s, which saw the death rate from the disease increase from 0.22 per 100,000 in 1840 to almost 10 per 100,000 by 1913.[20] Crawford posited that the rise might be linked to a change in diet (a greater consumption of fats and sugars), but the Dutch evidence suggests that epigenetic change may be a more compelling factor: although the Irish moved away from a predominantly potato-dependent diet, the change was toward high levels of consumption of nutritionally poor tea and white bread, as opposed to a wider ranging and richer variety of foods.[21] In terms of cardiovascular disease and hypertension, the Irish (especially Irishmen) have traditionally suffered from higher rates in comparison with other developed countries, with a lower life expectancy and poorer quality of life in later years.[22] This problem peaked in the early 20th century, with a noticeable improvement evident only from the 1980s onward.[23] But the Hunger Winter research has other implications for the Irish model, especially in relation to mental health. The Netherlands had a sophisticated mental health system with good records in the pre and post-war years, so there are reliable records against which to test the effects on what might be termed the "famine babies." The analysis of their long-term health showed a startling increase in mental illness in comparison with those who had not undergone the famine: "Early prenatal famine was found to be specifically and robustly associated with each of three conditions: (1) congenital anomalies of the central nervous system, (2) schizophrenia, and (3) schizophrenia spectrum personality disorders."[24] Thus, it seems, that the greatest risks to physical health occurs when the foetus is in mid to late pregnancy, but the risk to mental health occurs at a much earlier stage of foetal development, especially the first three months. There are also subtle gender impacts within this substantive rise in illness. The Dutch researchers found that the greatest increase in the risk of schizophrenia spectrum disorder occurred among children born in the famine cities in December 1945. These individuals had been conceived at the absolute peak of the famine in March–April 1945. However, the burden of this nutritional stress fell most heavily upon embryonic females. Adult women were adversely affected by severe deprivation in the first three months of their gestation, exhibiting much higher rates of hospitalized schizophrenia than both males, and the "normally-nourished" population. [25] This is especially interesting as a comparator for Ireland. Rates of mental illness rose inexorably in the second half of the 19th century, with a seemingly unstoppable flood of admissions to asylums that became increasingly overcrowded. Although male admissions consistently outnumbered female, men tended to die earlier than women, leaving a residual female asylum population that broadly equalled the male in most Irish district asylums. The asylum inspectors pointed to a variety of factors including intermarriage, the effects of poverty, poor levels of education (or in some individual cases excessive education), urbanization, and even, in slight desperation, excessive consumption of tea, to explain this rise. But could it in fact be the case that one of the Great Famine's most destructive legacies was literally bred into successive generations, leaving an invisible but inescapable trauma?

The case for epigenetic change linked to the Great Famine is further strengthened by a number of other studies. Recent research has shown that in addition to the impact of nutritional deprivation upon mental health, there is another means through which epigenetic change can manifest itself, and that is through exposure to severe stress in pregnancy. One such study concerns pregnant women who were affected by the Twin Tower attacks in New York on 11 September 2001. When the attacks occurred, there were 1,700 pregnant women in the area, some of whom went on to develop Post Traumatic Stress Disorder within weeks. Researchers took samples of saliva from these women and measured levels of the stress hormone cortisol. They found that those women who had developed PTSD following exposure to the attacks had significantly lower cortisol levels in their saliva than those who were similarly exposed but did not develop PTSD. [26] About a year later, the researchers measured cortisol levels in the children, and found that those born to the women who had developed PTSD had lower levels of the hormone than the others. Reduced cortisol levels were most apparent in those children whose mothers were in the third trimester of pregnancy when they were exposed to the attack. Associated studies by the team showed that lower cortisol levels are positively linked with a higher than normal risk of developing PTSD, and follow-up studies on these "9/11" offspring show increased distress responses to novel stimuli. Again, this was related to the stage of pregnancy—those with the greatest distress response were the ones born to mothers who were in their second or third trimester when exposed to the World Trade Center attacks. Thus the trauma suffered by the mother was transmitted through epigenetic change to her child, who in turn entered the world "primed for stress." When the environment changes—ironically to one that is largely without exceptional danger—the individual is less well adapted, and the affected New York children exhibited, and continue to exhibit, behavioral and mental health problems.

The mechanism through which this change occurs is an alteration to the expression of the glucocorticoid receptor, which plays a key role in the body's response to stress. [27] Animal studies have deepened our understanding of how traumatic events can alter both the relationship between mothers and their young, and cause the offspring to suffer long-term mental and physical problems. Experiments on rats have shown differences in DNA methylation that result in substantial impacts upon offspring. [28] This involved two litters of pups, one of which enjoyed a normal relationship with their mother, who fed, groomed and licked them at will. The other litter's mother was periodically removed at unpredictable intervals, and prevented from giving the same level of bonding and grooming. Analysis of the pup's brains showed substantive differences in DNA methylation, with the "loved" pups showing higher levels of methylation

"AN INVISIBLE BUT INESCAPABLE TRAUMA": EPIGENETICS AND THE GREAT FAMINE while the "unloved" pups had lower levels and subsequently lower glucocorticoid receptor levels as well. It is thought that this is the mechanism that accounts for the transmission of trauma from mother to unborn child.[29] The 9/11 researchers have seen similar results in the adult offspring of Nazi Holocaust survivors, another group that has exhibited the long-term damage that, as in Ireland, intense psychological stress and starvation can cause.[30] Ireland's Great Famine was a large-scale (one million directly related deaths, another million lost to emigration), long-term (six years) disaster. Although not a deliberate genocide like the Holocaust, there are clear comparisons in terms of proportionate loss of life and duration. But the two horrors have another link, I believe, and that lies in epigenetic change.

It has long been observed that major traumas can effect not merely the person who endures them, but their offspring. However, it has been suggested that this may be caused by the manner in which a traumatized parent treats their child, or how that child reacts to hearing of his or her parent's experience. This may well be true in many cases: a parent still suffering the effects of, for example, life in Auschwitz-Birkenau may be unable to bond with a child, or have difficulty in forming normal levels of attachment or detachment.[31] But recent work shows that the main element is epigenetic change, with researchers demonstrating the effect of the Holocaust on two generations of survivor offspring.[32] This manifests itself in greatly elevated levels of PTSD, as well as problems with addiction, behavioral issues and raised levels of mental illness including schizophrenia and depression.[33] In addition, the cohort also exhibit similar health profiles to the Dutch and Irish in terms of later-life obesity, heart disease and type 2 diabetes. The children and grandchildren of Holocaust survivors are three times more likely to suffer from PTSD following incidents such as car accidents, for example: events that may be traumatic in themselves, but that would not cause such an extreme response in other populations.[34] When one considers this evidence, it raises other, intangible but tantalizing, possibilities. Could the stereotypical image of the neurotic Jew actually have a biological foundation? Centuries of pogroms and anti-Semitism may have continually reinforced early epigenetic change, resulting in a population that may indeed be prone to the negative health consequences of such change, but that is also well adapted to life under pressure. Despite successive waves of expulsion and attempted annihilation, the international Jewish community is characterized by resilience. Is the same true of the Irish? First-hand accounts of the Great Famine all vividly attest to the horror that potato crop failure brought to Ireland. Travellers to the country wrote movingly of families walling themselves into their cabins to die, of mothers carrying their dead children in their arms, of the barely living, dead and dying mingling hopelessly, beseeching the affluent observers for help. The impacts of starvation were clear to see, but the psychological trauma, although less obvious, was nonetheless equally awful. To live for six years in a state of constant fear (interspersed with ill-founded hope that the blight would end) of starvation and death, and to see one's children die of hunger, had an impact comparable to that of the concentration camp inmates. One can only assume that the outcomes in terms of impaired mental and physical health are also comparable.

I want to turn to a final case that may offer a very specific comparator for Ireland. It is the Överkalix Cohort Study, one that is based to a substantial degree upon historical sources, as well as direct examination of blood and tissue samples (on which the Hunger Winter, Holocaust and Twin Towers projects are based).[35] Överkalix is in Northern Sweden, a remote and inaccessible area, and one like Ireland that had very little inward migration in the 19th century; this makes it a good subject for this kind of study, based on a defined population. It also has a body of records that are very similar to those available in Ireland, including material on crop yield and failure, data on food shortage and famine, grain prices and so on, which provides an important potential model for an Irish study. Överkalix has suffered periodic natural famines, interspersed with periods of food abundance, and so replicated the conditions observed (although with different precipitating causes) in the studies mentioned above, as well as in Ireland. The researchers examined the life cycles of almost a thousand individuals, born in 1890, 1905 and 1920 in this defined parish. The subjects were traced to their death, emigration or current residence, and the cause of death was recorded in approximately a quarter of the group.

The study has shown results similar to those I have mentioned in the earlier works. But the Överkalix findings include some other, very interesting results. As well as looking at embryonic impacts, the study included an examination of the impacts of preadolescent children, especially those in a stage of development known as the Slow Growth Period (usually about the age of 11). It seems that food supply for this age group has a direct impact upon offspring, and especially upon grandchildren. The strongest epigenetic effect is seen in the grandchildren of 19th-century children who were subjected to periods of famine and over-eating. This cohort died some 30 years prematurely, despite living in environments where the food supply was stable. But fascinatingly, the connection seems as strong for over-eating as it is for starvation. It is hardly surprising that populations tended to over-eat during times of abundance, when they are used to periodic food shortage. But this pattern lays down serious health problems for subsequent generations who exist in times of unbroken relative plenty. The consequences are, quite literally, huge. The grandchildren of "over-eaters" are four times more likely to die of diabetes and diabetes-related illness, and to suffer from high levels of adult obesity with all its associated health problems. The Överkalix study has made some interesting gender-specific findings too. It seems that the paternal (but not maternal) grandsons of Swedish boys who were exposed during preadolescence to famine in the 19th century were less likely to die of cardiovascular disease: it is thought that this is because at this age boy's sperm is still in formation, so very susceptible to change, which in this case has a positive effect on the health of subsequent generations. Another transgenerational study has confirmed this effect, showing that sons of men who smoke in pre-puberty were found to be at higher risk for obesity and other health problems than sons of non-smoking fathers.[36]

So what of Ireland? The studies briefly discussed above offer exciting and important models to explore our health history. The Great Famine changed Irish society forever, altering social, political, economic and religious life. I argue that it furthermore changed our basic biological makeup, laying down a specific mental and physical health profile in order to prepare whole communities for further famine and stress. Social and cultural factors are vital in understanding how Irish society developed in the second half of the 19th century, but I believe that epigenetic change provides us with another crucial piece of the picture.

Endnotes

[1] The British Psychological Society, *Classification of behaviour and experience in relation to functional psychiatric diagnoses: Time for a paradigm shift* (May 2013), pp 1-17.

[2] The DSM is now in its fifth edition, and has, somewhat controversially, continued to expand its range of diagnoses.

[3] "Psychiatrists under fire in mental health battle" in *The Observer,* 12 May 2013.

[4] This is defined as the transmittance of information from one generation of an organism to the next, that affects the traits of children without altering the primary structure of DNA.

[5] Along with "sometimes a cigar is just a cigar" and "time spent with cats is never wasted," the Irish quote is among the finest quips that Freud never uttered.

[6] Seamus Heaney, "Whatever you say, say nothing" in *North* (London, 1975).

[7] Brendan Behan, "Richard's Cork Leg" in *Behan: The Complete Plays* (London, 2014). This posthumously completed play ranges wildly across many Irish cultural preoccupations.

8 Ronan Foley, "Indigenous Narratives of Health: (Re)Placing Folk-Medicine within Irish Health Histories" in *Journal of Medical Humanities* (2015), vol. 36, Issue 1, p. 15.

9 Norio Sugawara *et al*, "Lithium in Tap Water and Suicide Mortality in Japan" in *International Journal of Environmental Research and Public Health* (2013), vol. 10, p. 6,046.

10 G.N. Schrauzer and K.P. Shrestha, "Lithium in drinking water and the incidences of crimes, suicides, and arrests related to drug addictions" in *Biological Trace Element Research Journal* (1990), vol. 25, p. 109.

11 One of the most poignant records in asylum archives is what I term the "Gone to America" letter. These are the notices sent to committing relatives of patients, stating that the latter has recovered and is ready to be discharged. These communications often bear several forwarded addresses, marking the last known places of residence of the patient's family. Eventually they return to the asylum with "Gone to America" written on the envelope, a sad testimony to the expedient committal of a vulnerable family member in order to facilitate the emigration of the remainder.

12 For discussions of Irish-born admissions to asylums in England, Canada and the Antipodes, see Elizabeth Malcolm, "'A Most Miserable Looking Object'—The Irish in English Asylums, 1851-1901: Migration, Poverty and Prejudice," in John Belchem and Klaus Tenfelde (eds), *Irish and Polish Migration in Comparative Perspective* (Klartext Verlag, 2003), pp 115-26; David Wright and Tom Themeles, "Migration, Madness, and the Celtic Fringe: A Comparison of Irish and Scottish Admissions to Four Canadian Mental Hospitals, c. 1841-91", in Angela McCarthy and Catharine Coleborne (eds.) *Migration, Ethnicity, and Mental Health: International Perspectives, 1840-2010* (New York: Routledge, 2012), and Angela McCarthy and Catharine Coleborne (eds.), *Migration, Ethnicity, and Mental Health* (Routledge, 2012).

13 Michael Foucault, of course, changed everything in terms of conceptualizing the role of the lunatic asylum in the social control of deviants, with *Madness and Civilisation: the Birth of the Asylum* his key work in this regard. Other influential texts include Andrew Scull's *The Most Solitary of Afflictions: Madness and Society in Britain, 1700-1900* (New Haven: Yale University Press, 1993); Thomas Szasz's *The Myth of Mental Illness. The Manufacture of Madness: A Comparative Study of the Inquisition and the Mental Health Movement* (New York, 1970).

14 L.H. Lumey, "Cohort Profile: The Dutch Hunger Winter Families Study" in *International Journal of Epidemiology* (2007), vol. 36, Issue 6, p. 1196.

15 Robert Scholte, Gerard van den Berg and Maarten Lindeboom, *Long-Run Effects of Gestation During the Dutch Hunger Winter Famine on Labor Market and Hospitalization Outcomes*, Institute for the Study of Labor Discussion Paper (Bonn, 2012), p. 27.

16 Lumey, "Cohort Profile," p. 1,196.

17 D.J.P. Barker and C.N. Hales, "Type 2 (non-insulin-dependent) diabetes mellitus: the thrifty phenotype hypothesis" in *Diabetologia* (1992), vol. 35, pp 595-601.

18 Impaired glucose tolerance does not in itself cause diabetes, but increases the risk. It also raises the risk of developing cardiovascular disease (heart disease, peripheral vascular disease and stroke).

19 W.Y. Kwong *et al*, "Support for Barker hypothesis upheld in rat model of maternal undernutrition during the preimplantation period: application of integrated 'random effects' statistical modeli" in *Reproductive BioMedicine Online* (2004), vol. 8, issue 5, pp 574-6.

20 E.M. Crawford, "Death Rates from Diabetes Mellitus in Ireland 1833-1983: a historical commentary" in *The Ulster Medical Journal*, vol. 56, no. 2, p. 110.

21 Ian Miller, "Nutritional decline in post-Famine Ireland, c. 1851-1922" in *Proceedings of the Royal Irish Academy*, vol. 115C, pp 1-17.

22 Emer Shelley, "The Changing Pattern of Cardiovascular Disease in Ireland: achievements and challenges" in *Heartwise*, Winter, 2006, p. 10.

23 Emer Shelley et al., "Trends in mortality from cardiovascular diseases in Ireland" in *Irish Journal of Medical Science*, January 1991, vol. 160, p. 5.

24 H.W. Hoek, A.S. Brown and E. Susser, "The Dutch famine and schizophrenia spectrum disorders" in *Social Psychiarty and Psychiatric Epidemiology* (1998), vol. 33, No. 8, p. 373.

25 Ezra Susser and Lin Shang, "Schizophrenia After Prenatal Exposure to the Dutch Hunger Winter of 1944-1945" in *Archives of General Psychiatry Journal* (1992), vol. 49, issue 12, pp 983-988.

26 Rachel Yehuda and Linda M. Bierer, "The Relevance of Epigenetics to PTSD: Implications for the DSM-V" in *Journal of Traumatic Stress* (2009), vol. 22, No. 5, p. 433.

27 These receptors are present in almost every cell, and regulate genes controlling development, metabolism and immune response.

28 Kathryn Gudsnuck and Frances Champagne, "Epigenetic Influence of Stress and the Social Environment" in *Institute for Laboratory Animal Research Journal* (2012), vol. 53, No. 3-4, pp 279-288.

[29] Frances Champagne and Michael Meaney, "Stress During Gestation Alters Postpartum Maternal Care and the Development of the Offspring in a Rodent Model" in *Biological Psychiatry* (2006), vol. 59, No. 12, pp 1,227-35.

[30] Rachel Yehuda et al., "Influences of maternal and paternal PTSD on epigenetic regulation of the glucocorticoid receptor gene in Holocaust survivor offspring" in *American Journal of Psychiatry* (2014), vol. 171, No. 8, pp 872-80.

[31] There is a fascinating body of work on other forms of trauma transmission. See for example Melissa Kahane-Nissenbaum, *Exploring Intergenerational Transmission of Trauma in Third –Generation Holocaust Survivors* (2011). Doctorate in Social Work (DSW) Dissertations. Paper 16, University of Pennsylvania.

[32] Natan Kellermann, "Epigenetic transmission of Holocaust trauma: can nightmares be inherited?" in *Israel Journal of Psychiatry and Related Sciences* (2013), vol. 50, No. 1, pp 33-9.

[33] Amy Lehrner et al, "Maternal PTSD associates with greater glucocorticoid sensitivity in offspring of Holocaust survivors" in *Journal of Psychoneuroendocrinology*, (2014), vol. 40, pp 213-220.

[34] David Samuels, "Do Jews Carry Trauma in Our Genes?" A conversation with Rachel Yehuda in *Tablet Magazine* (2014) December 11. www.tabletmag.com/jewish-arts-and-culture/books/187555/trauma-genes-q-a-rachel-yehuda Accessed 14 Feb. 2016.

[35] Lars Olov Bygren et al., "'Change in paternal grandmothers' early food supply influenced cardiovascular mortality of the female grandchildren" in *BMC Genetics* (2014). www.bmcgenet.biomedcentral.com/articles/10.1186/1471-2156-15-12 Accessed 16 Jan. 2016.

[36] This work draws upon the extensive data contained in the Avon Longitudinal Study of Parents and Children. Kate Northstone et al, "Prepubertal start of father's smoking and increased body fat in his sons: further characterisation of paternal transgenerational responses" in *European Journal of Human Genetics* (2014), vol. 22, No. 12, pp 1382-86.

Works Cited

Barker, D.J.P. and C.N. Hales. "Type 2 (non-insulin-dependent) diabetes mellitus: the thrifty phenotype hypothesis." *Diabetologia,*1992, vol. 35, pp 595-601.

Behan, Brendan. *Behan: The Complete Plays.* London: Bloomsbury, 2014.

The British Psychological Society. *Classification of behaviour and experience in relation to functional psychiatric diagnoses: Time for a paradigm shift.* May 2013.

Bygren, Lars Olov et al. "'Change in paternal grandmothers' early food supply influenced cardiovascular mortality of the female grandchildren." *BMC Genetics* (2014): http://bmcgenet.biomedcentral.com/articles/10.1186/1471-2156-15-12

Champagne Frances and Michael Meaney. "Stress During Gestation Alters Postpartum Maternal Care and the Development of the Offspring in a Rodent Model." *Biological Psychiatry.* 2006, vol. 59, No. 12, 1227-1235.

Crawford, E.M. "Death Rates from Diabetes Mellitus in Ireland 1833-1983: a historical commentary." *The Ulster Medical Journal.* Vol. 56, no. 2, 109-115.

Foley, Ronan. "Indigenous Narratives of Health: (Re)Placing Folk-Medicine within Irish Health Histories." *Journal of Medical Humanities,* 2015, vol. 36, issue 1.

Gudsnuck, Kathryn and Frances Champagne. "Epigenetic Influence of Stress and the Social Environment." *Institute for Laboratory Animal Research Journal,* 2012, vol. 53, no. 3-4, 279-288.

Heaney, Seamus. *North.* London: Faber and Faber, 1975.

Hoek, H.W., A.S. Brown and E. Susser. "The Dutch famine and schizophrenia spectrum disorders" in *Social Psychiatry and Psychiatric Epidemiology* (1998), vol. 33, no. 8, 373-79.

Kellermann, Natan. "Epigenetic transmission of Holocaust trauma: can nightmares be inherited?" *Israel Journal of Psychiatry and Related Sciences,* 2013, vol. 50, no. 1, 33-9.

Kwong W.Y. et al. "Support for Barker hypothesis upheld in rat model of maternal undernutrition during the preimplantation period: application of integrated 'random effects' statistical modeli." *Reproductive BioMedicine Online,* 2004, vol. 8, issue 5, 574-6.

Lehrner, Amy et al. "Maternal PTSD associates with greater glucocorticoid sensitivity in offspring of Holocaust survivors." *Journal of Psychoneuroendocrinology*, 2014, vol. 40, 213-220.

Lumey, L.H. "Cohort Profile: The Dutch Hunger Winter Families Study." *International Journal of Epidemiology.* 2007, vol. 36, issue 6.

McCarthy, Angela, and Catharine Coleborne (eds.). *Migration, Ethnicity, and Mental Health*. New York: Routledge, 2012.

"AN INVISIBLE BUT INESCAPABLE TRAUMA": EPIGENETICS AND THE GREAT FAMINE

Malcolm, Elizabeth. "'A Most Miserable Looking Object'—The Irish in English Asylums, 1851-1901: Migration, Poverty and Prejudice," in John Belchem and Klaus Tenfelde (eds.), *Irish and Polish Migration in Comparative Perspective.* Essen (Germany): Klartext Verlag, 2003.

Miller, Ian. "Nutritional decline in post-Famine Ireland, c. 1851-1922." *Proceedings of the Royal Irish Academy*, vol. 115 C, 1-17.

Northstone, Kate *et al.* "Prepubertal start of father's smoking and increased body fat in his sons: further characterisation of paternal transgenerational responses." *European Journal of Human Genetics,* 2014, vol. 22, No. 12, 1382-86.

Samuels, David. "Do Jews Carry Trauma in Our Genes?" A conversation with Rachel Yehuda. *Tablet Magazine* (2014) December 11. www.tabletmag.com/jewish-arts-and-culture/books/187555/trauma-genes-q-a-rachel-yehuda

Scholte, Robert, Gerard van den Berg and Maarten Lindeboom. *Long-Run Effects of Gestation During the Dutch Hunger Winter Famine on Labor Market and Hospitalization Outcomes.* Bonn: Institute for the Study of Labor Discussion Paper, 2012.

Schrauzer, G.N., and K.P. Shrestha. "Lithium in drinking water and the incidences of crimes, suicides, and arrests related to drug addictions." *Biological Trace Element Research Journal.* 1990), vol. 25.

Shelley, Emer. "The Changing Pattern of Cardiovascular Disease in Ireland: achievements and challenges." *Heartwise,* Winter, 2006.

Shelley, Emer, et al. "Trends in mortality from cardiovascular diseases in Ireland." *Irish Journal of Medical Science,* January 1991, vol. 160, 1-19.

Sugawara, Norio, et al. "Lithium in Tap Water and Suicide Mortality in Japan." *International Journal of Environmental Research and Public Health.* 2013, vol. 10.

Wright, David, and Tom Themeles. "Migration, Madness, and the Celtic Fringe: A Comparison of Irish and Scottish Admissions to Four Canadian Mental Hospitals, c.1841-91," in Angela McCarthy and Catharine Coleborne (eds.) *Migration, Ethnicity, and Mental Health: International Perspectives, 1840-2010.* New York: Routledge, 2012.

Yehuda, Rachel, and Linda M. Bierer. "The Relevance of Epigenetics to PTSD: Implications for the DSM-V." *Journal of Traumatic Stress,* 2009, vol. 22, no. 5, 427-434.

Yehuda, Rache, et al. "Influences of maternal and paternal PTSD on epigenetic regulation of the glucocorticoid receptor gene in Holocaust survivor offspring." *American Journal of Psychiatry,* 2014, vol. 171, no. 8, 872-80.

Chapter Fourteen

How the nuns of New York tamed the gangs of New York

Turlough McConnell

The enduring vision of America and New York as beacons of hope to immigrants worldwide can eclipse the heroism of the people who made it happen. The success of the hard-fought struggle to establish the nation and the city as centers of freedom and equality owes much to the transformative work of the Sisters of Charity of New York.

The story begins in 1774 in New York City, with the birth of Elizabeth Ann Bayley Seton to an established Episcopalian family. Elizabeth was raised to show compassion for the poor, a cause she championed after marriage and motherhood. When her husband contracted tuberculosis, Seton and her children traveled with him to Italy, where the Filicchi family befriended them. Impressed by their kindness and their Catholic faith, Seton converted to Catholicism when she returned to New York after her husband's death. Conversion presented problems for the young widow. To support her family, Seton, an educator, opened a private school for girls. However, when her Catholicism became known, Protestant New Yorkers withdrew their daughters and Seton fell upon hard times. In 1809, in a leap of faith, Seton moved to Emmitsburg, Maryland. That year, she took vows as a religious and, on 31 July, opened St. Joseph's Academy, the first American Catholic school for girls. The following year, she founded a religious community, the Sisters of Charity, dedicated to educating and caring for children, the sick, and the poor.[1]

In 1817, Seton sent a small group of Sisters to minister to the poor in New York City. New York was, as it is today, the center of the New World, of rich and poor, a place where cultures cohabited and collided. New York grew rapidly during the early 19th century, spurred mainly by emigration. In 1808, in response to this population growth, Pope Pius VII established the New York diocese, which included the entire state and much of neighboring New Jersey. Expansion continued with the construction of the first St. Patrick's Cathedral at the corner of Mott and Prince Streets. St. Patrick's opened in 1815 as the spiritual home for 35,000 Catholics, of French, Spanish, German and Irish origin.[2] Soon after their arrival, the Sisters opened the Roman Catholic Orphan Asylum on Mott Street. Known as the "Dead House," the orphanage had been a military hospital during the Revolutionary War and bore the telltale stains. Now, however, the house took on new life: after opening its doors to five orphans, the population multiplied. In 1822, to meet the educational needs of these children, the Sisters established St. Patrick's School, their first school in New York. Before long, the Sisters had opened seven schools in Manhattan and Brooklyn.[3]

Centuries of political dependence, augmented by exploitative agricultural practices and demographic changes in Ireland, had by the mid-1840s narrowed the food sources available to over one-third of its eight million people, who had become almost entirely dependent on the potato for sustenance. Between 1845 and 1847, blight caused by widespread fungal infection devastated the nation's potato crop and destroyed successive years' harvests; the crop failure put an entire nation's population at risk. Within seven years, over one million Irish had died and another two million starving men, women and children fled the country on "coffin ships," bound for any country that would take them. As many 30 percent of the passengers aboard these ships died.[4] The survivors included many orphaned children who disembarked in their new homeland weakened and susceptible to pestilence and disease.[5]

Many such immigrants flooded into New York City—some 50,000 in 1847 alone. At the time, the city was small, confined to an area below 14th Street where there was little housing, health care or social services. The immigrants disrupted the dominant Anglo-Protestant elite, who responded with nativist backlash that intensified as immigration swelled. The champion of Irish immigrants was Archbishop John Hughes, who had emigrated from Ulster a generation earlier. Hughes demanded an end to the persecution of newcomers struggling to survive in a nation dedicated to tolerance. It was Hughes's genius to turn the Catholic Church into a civic institution that would strengthen democratic ideals and support Irish-American ascendancy.[6] Hughes understood that support systems, such as education and child services, were essential if New York was to become a safe place for this new immigrant society. Most urgent was the need for medical care.[7] Once the Sisters of Charity established their motherhouse in 1847, plans for a Catholic hospital, in the works for more than a decade, could be realized. The Sisters were immediately pressed into service to provide medical services, as well as staffing schools and orphanages. The Sisters of Charity became the agents of the change that effected the transformation of the city.[8]

Over the succeeding decades, Irish-Catholic immigrants pouring into American society struggled to find their place. Their assimilation was a turbulent process before, during and after the Great Hunger. In 1835, more than 30,000 Irish arrived annually; during the years 1845 to 1855, when Famine-associated emigration peaked, the city's population grew from 371,000 to 630,000. Areas such as Five Points, near City Hall, overflowed with impoverished Irish, and exploded with crime and prostitution. In 1842, the English author, Charles Dickens, an authority on urban poverty, wrote in his travelogue, *American Notes for General Circulation*, that Five Points was "loathsome, drooping, and decayed." Indeed, Dickens had been accompanied by two policemen to ensure his safety when he visited America's first notorious slum. "The poorest and most wretched population . . . in the world—the scattered debris of the Irish nation"[9] were the words of Archbishop Hughes for the Irish residents of the Five Points in the wake of the Famine influx.

The combination of nativism and lawlessness was a lethal one. Thousands of abandoned and orphaned children of Irish parents roamed, or prowled, the city's streets. Violent Irish gangs, with names like the Forty Thieves, the B'boys, the Roach Guards, and the Chichesters, wreaked havoc. In 1844, as a massive anti-Catholic torchlight parade gathered in City Hall Park, ready to march up the Bowery, Hughes stationed sharpshooters on the protective walls surrounding St. Patrick's Cathedral.[10] Though a full-scale anti-Catholic uprising was averted, tensions persisted. In 1849, the Astor Street Riots erupted, which began over a dispute at who could play Macbeth better, the American actor, Edwin Forrest, or the Englishman, William Charles Macready. It developed into a violent conflict, with the anti-British sentiments of the Irish being appealed to in favor of Forrest. The riot left at least 25 dead.[11] Later, in 1857, the Dead Rabbits Riot on Bayard Street in the Five Points involved an estimated 800 to 1,000 gang members and completely overwhelmed New York's disorganized police force. The anger of these immigrants seemed ready to ignite a firestorm of rage.[12]

The Sisters of Charity prevailed in this atmosphere of urban terror. The situation grew increasingly dire and, in 1846, the Sisters made the difficult decision to break from their order in Maryland and start a new congregation so that they could concentrate their efforts on this desperate local population. In choosing to break with their order, these women had everything to lose and nothing to gain, but they knew what was at stake. One of those nuns, Sister Mary Angela, was Hughes's younger sister, who had entered Seton's novitiate in 1825 and had participated in nursing missions to Cincinnati and St. Louis before joining her brother in 1846 to found St. Joseph's Half Orphan Asylum for Children. The sisters were undaunted by the challenges of a refugee crisis in an unprepared city. Overcrowding and poor sanitation led to repeated epidemics of cholera, typhus, smallpox and tuberculosis, which the urban ill knew as "white lung." To care for the masses of suffering poor, the Sisters founded hospitals, sanatoriums and convalescent homes. To rescue parentless children from homelessness, they established orphanages and foundling homes. To ensure that the children were educated, they built and opened new schools.[13]

Through it all, the Sisters of Charity continued their mission of educating and caring for children and the sick. In 1847, the Sisters established a convent and school at McGowan's Pass, in what is now Central Park. In 1849, the Sisters founded St. Vincent's Hospital, which served generations of New Yorkers. In 1857, as Central Park expanded, the Sisters moved their motherhouse to its permanent location at Mount St. Vincent in the Bronx. The Mount, the building at McGowan's Pass, re-opened as St. Joseph's Military Hospital in 1862 to serve wounded New York soldiers of the Civil War. The 69th New York State Volunteers included many enthusiastic soldiers from the Irish-American community. These soldiers were treated at St. Joseph's, which accommodated up to 250 patients. Fifteen Sisters of Charity returned to St. Joseph's as nurses serving the wounded, those requiring amputations, and those who contracted the contagious diseases that killed more soldiers than fell in battle during the Civil War.[14]

The hospital administration found the nursing care provided by the Sisters to be exemplary. The nuns were fine nurses and efficient workers who did not waste time consorting with soldiers.[15] The Sisters established a ward for the younger patients, wounded boys as young as 13, who had served as buglers, flag-bearers and drummers. One Sister, known only as "the Irish Nightingale," brought in a guitar and often sang to comfort the boys.[16]

By 1863, hard times had arrived. New Yorkers had lost their enthusiasm for war, which had cut into the city's lifeblood, shipping. Prices for rent and other necessities rose. The Emancipation Proclamation fueled the suspicion that freed slaves would compete with the Irish for jobs. With enlistment down, Congress enacted military conscription that allowed men to escape service by paying $300. Though it raised funds for the Treasury, the fee exceeded what the average working man could pay. A draft lottery in July 1863 ignited protests, culminating in the notorious Draft Riots, in which more than 1,000 people were killed in three days. That riot targeted prominent draft supporters, the city's arsenal, the Colored Orphan Asylum, and African-American individuals. A mob threatened St. Joseph's Military Hospital but was turned back by Sister Mary Ulrica, the Sister Superior. She and her fellow sisters had refused orders to leave their patients and flee to safety.[17] By mid-month, soldiers who had fought in Gettysburg arrived to assist the police force in restoring order. But a mob that killed 120 people threatened to explode into citywide violence. Archbishop Hughes spoke to his congregants from the balcony of his sister's house, where he lay dying. In his last great public moment, he convinced the mob to disperse.[18]

After the Civil War, fortunes began to change for the Irish in New York as the U.S. economy and territory expanded. New railroads carried grain and goods from the country's interior to the port cities of the East. The discovery of gold in California in 1848 had launched boom times; over the next four years, the Gold Rush added $2 billion in wealth to the U.S. economy. New York became the Empire City, and the Irish opened groceries, shops and saloons. Jobs on the docks or in construction were available for anyone who wanted them. Continued poverty economic and political discrimination in Ireland produced ongoing waves of Irish emigration, usually consisting of equal numbers of men and women. Cities like New York were the destination for many immigrants, particularly women, who could find employment in domestic service. Tenements began to replace former shantytowns and slums until they too became overcrowded. As the need for a social safety net became ever more urgent, the Sisters of Charity, along with other Irish-Catholic institutions such as the Emigrant Savings Bank and the Mission at Holy Rosary Church, developed new strategies to provide compassionate assistance.[19]

The Sisters expanded their mission to include Long Island and upstate areas, New Jersey, Pennsylvania, Connecticut and Rhode Island. In addition to schools, orphanages and hospitals, the Sisters established convalescent homes, including the New York Foundling Hospital for parentless children needing medical care, and a home for the aged. Residential schools such as the New York Catholic Protectory were created to address the problem of homeless and wayward youth. In these environments, which were both secular and religious, young people from ages 7 to 21 were housed and educated. By 1909, the sisters had 540 girls under their care at the Protectory.

By the early 20th century, the Irish had cemented their position in New York City politics and business. Their success benefitted new immigrants from southern and Eastern Europe who were served by the safety net maintained by the Sisters of Charity. By the 1930s, in response to the Great Depression, the federal government had assumed greater responsibility for the task of providing social welfare for its destitute population. The Sisters of Charity had a reputation for excellence as educators, and Catholic parents looked to the Sisters for that excellence. The 20th century was a period of expansion for the city's parochial schools, including Cathedral High School (1905) and the College of Mount St. Vincent (1910). The Sisters were asked to serve as administrators and teachers at the Grace Institute (1897), a vocational school established by Mayor William R. Grace.[20]

The schools run by the Sisters of Charity would continue the tradition of educating New York's working class, including some of the nation's finest artists. One such student was the playwright Eugene O'Neill, born in 1888 in a New York City hotel room. O'Neill's morphine-addicted mother sent him to the Sisters of Charity in Riverdale. Another notable student was director Martin Scorsese, who attended Saint Patrick's School at 32 Prince Street, America's first parochial school. Scorsese's 2002 film, *The Gangs of New York*, tells a violent tale of gang warfare during those early New York days. City historian William J. Stern wrote in his essay "What Gangs of New York Misses," that the film ignored the real drama of the moment: the transformation of the city's Irish underclass into mainstream citizens.[21] Though the film's historical accuracy may be arguable, the storytelling expertise of the director is uncontested. "Martin loved to tell stories," says his eighth-grade teacher, Sister Marita Regina Bronner, when aged 91:

> In my English class Martin Scorsese was forever jumping up and asking if the class could act out the stories that we read. I told him to sit down. "Martin, the other children must first learn to read before they can act."[22]

Playwright John Patrick Shanley was also educated by the Sisters. Born in the Bronx in 1950, Shanley attended numerous city Catholic schools. He mentions that he was "thrown out of St. Helena's kindergarten, banned from St. Anthony's hot lunch program and expelled from Cardinal Spellman High School." However, it was at St. Patrick's School where Shanley first found pleasure in the written word. His teacher Sister Margaret McEntee recalls:

> John Patrick Shanley gave a marvelous wakeup call with the award-winning play and film *Doubt*, about the awareness, alertness and action of religious women in a school setting. His appreciation of consecrated religious women opened up the doors of dialogue.[23]

Vocations for religious orders continued to grow through two World Wars and peaked in the late 1950s. But major changes were on the horizon. In 1962, Second Vatican Council reformed the Mass and placed greater emphasis on lay participation. Feminism established new standards for women's behavior and expectations. Programs of the Great Society, like Medicare, Medicaid and the Voting Rights Act, strove to bring American freedom and prosperity to neglected groups and individuals. Always a religious order working among the people, the Sisters of Charity added their voice to the struggles. Sisters joined marches for civil rights for African Americans, assisted the poor in rural areas in Appalachia and the southwest, as well as in South and Central America, and they served in Vietnam during the war.

Post-Vatican II changes were also reflected in the day-to-day lives of the sisters. The traditional habit, modeled on early 19th century widows' dress worn by Mother Seton, was modified and then supplanted by "dress of the day," or civilian dress. Sisters were permitted to use their baptismal and family names. The term "Mother," which denoted the head of the order, was replaced by the more egalitarian "Sister." Though New Yorkers had long held the Sisters in high esteem, the ultimate honor was bestowed on 14 September 1975. On that day, hundreds of thousands of people gathered in St. Peter's Square in Vatican City for the canonization of the founder of the Sisters of Charity, Mother Elizabeth Ann Seton, as the first saint born in the U.S.[24] A person of divine holiness, St. Elizabeth Ann Seton remains an example to the women who dedicate their lives to helping those in need and calls attention to the inspiration behind the Sisters' work.

In the 21st century, the Sisters have become a public force for change, engaging in activism on behalf of the disenfranchised worldwide. The Sisters are visible and active participants on moral issues such as civil rights, income inequality, immigration and world hunger. Their mission of providing education, raising the orphaned, and delivering medical care now includes housing the homeless (Sisters of Charity Housing), feeding the hungry (Sisters Hill Farm and Part of the Solution), and all of the above, in a multi-service center (Casa de Esperanza). In Guatemala, the Barbara Ford Peace Center carries on the work of Sister Barbara Ford, who was murdered there in 2001. Today, the Sisters of Charity of New York, along with 12 other orders, form the Sisters of Charity Federation, which represents approximately 4,000 vowed members and 700 lay associates/affiliates from women religious congregations throughout North America. These member congregations follow the path set by St. Elizabeth Ann Seton, St. Vincent de Paul and St. Louise de Marillac. In 2009, the Sisters of Charity of New York honored the bicentennial of the founding of their order with a delegation in New York's St. Patrick's Parade. At the end of their second hundred years in New York, to be celebrated in 2017, the Sisters remain committed to the practice of God's work through varied ministries for all those in need, especially the poor.[25] As the great Eleanor Roosevelt once said: "One's philosophy is not best expressed in words; it is expressed in the choices one makes...and the choices we make are ultimately our responsibility."[26] In 1817, a New Yorker named Elizabeth Ann Bayley Seton made a choice, to send a small group of Sisters to minister to the poor in her native New York City, and that has made all the difference.

Endnotes

[1] Ellin Kelly, "The Vincentian Mission from Paris to the Mississippi: The American Sisters of Charity," in *Vincentian Heritage Journal*, xiv, 1 (1993), pp. 179-95.

[2] See http://oldcathedral.org/history.
Accessed 2 Nov 2015.

[3] Sisters of Charity of New York, *Sower-Seed-Soil* (Private publication: New York, 2013), pp 8-9.

[4] There are no precise numbers due to lack of complete passenger records, but as the examples of Grosse Ile and Montreal show, mortality was high even after arrival in the ports of destination. For more on this process, see Kerby A. Miller, *Emigrants and Exiles*: Ireland and the Irish Exodus to North America (Oxford University Press, 1988).

[5] Cecil Woodham-Smith, *The Great Hunger: Ireland 1845-1849* (London, 1962), pp 20-36, 246-69.

[6] William J. Stern, "How Dagger John Saved New York's Irish," *City Journal* (Spring 1997), 84-105.

[7] Some scholarship suggests that the relationship between Hughes and the Sisters was strained over the issue of priorities for institutional staffing (i.e., schools vs. hospital). It is likely that Hughes pressed the Emmitsburg order for more nuns than could be spared. But plans for a Catholic hospital were long deferred, and with the establishment of the New York order, there is evidence that the Sisters and Hughes had corresponding concerns. See Maureen Fitzgerald, *Habits of Compassion: Irish Catholic Nuns and the Origins of New York's Welfare System, 1830-1920* (University of Illinois Press, 2006), and Sr. Marie de Lourdes Walsh, *The Sisters of Charity of New York: 1809-1959* (Fordham University Press, 1960).

[8] Quoted in Ronald H. Bayor and Timothy Meagher, *The New York Irish* (Baltimore: Johns Hopkins University Press, 1997), p. 20.

[9] William J. Stern, "What *Gangs of New York* Misses," *City Journal*, 14 Jan. 2003.

[10] Sr. Elizabeth Ann, SJW, "Dagger John (1797-1864)," *Catholic Heritage Curricula*:
https://www.chcweb.com/catalog/files/daggerjohn.pdf
Accessed 1 Dec. 2015.

[11] For more, see http://boweryboyshistory.com/2014/05/the-astor-place-riot-massacre-at-busy.html
Accessed 29 Nov. 2015.

[12] Stern, "*Gangs*".

[13] Walsh, *The Sisters of Charity*, pp 137-57.

[14] See http://setonspath.tripod.com/civilwar.html
Accessed 30 Dec. 2015.

[15] Sisters of Charity of New York, *Sower-Seed-Soil*, pp. 11-12.

[16] See: http://famvin.org/en/2014/04/04/sisters-charity-ny-civilwar/
Accessed 4 Apr 2014.

[17] Iver Bernstein, *The New York City Draft Riots: Their Significance for American Society and Politics in the Age of the Civil War* (Lincoln, NE: University of Nebraska Press/Bison Books, 2010).

[18] Richard Daniel McCann, *Bishop John Hughes: His Church and the Coming of Age of New York's Catholic Irish* (E-BookTime, LLC 2012), pp. 118-23.

[19] Maureen Murphy, curator, "The Irish Mission at Watson House:" http://watsonhouse.org/exhibition/
Accessed 25 March 2013.

[20] Sisters of Charity of New York, *Sower-Seed-Soil*, pp 13-15.

[21] Stern, "*Gangs*".

[22] Interview with Sr. Maria Regina Bronner (22 Nov. 2015).

[23] Interview with Sr. Margaret McEntee (22 Nov. 2015).

[24] Joan Barthel and Maya Angelou (Foreword), *American Saint: The Life of Elizabeth Seton* (New York: Thomas Dunne Books, 2014).

[25] Sisters of Charity of New York, *Sower-Seed-Soil*.

[26] Eleanor Roosevelt. *You Learn by Living* (New York: Harper & Row, 1960), Foreword.

Works Cited

Barthel, Joan, and Maya Angelou. (Foreword), *American Saint: The Life of Elizabeth Seto*n. New York: Thomas Dunne Books, 2014.

Bayor, Ronald H., and Timothy Meagher. *The New York Irish*. Baltimore: Johns Hopkins University Press, 1997.

Bernstein, Iver. *The New York City Draft Riots: Their Significance for American Society and Politics in the Age of the Civil War*. Lincoln, NE: University of Nebraska Press/Bison Books, 2010.

Fitzgerald, Maureen. *Habits of Compassion: Irish Catholic Nuns and the Origins of New York's Welfare System, 1830-1920*. University of Illinois Press, 2006.

Kelly, Ellin. "The Vicentian Mission from Paris to the Mississippi: The American Sisters of Charity" in Vincentian Heritage Journal, xiv, 1 (1993).

McCann, Richard Daniel. *Bishop John J. Hughes, His Church and the Coming of Age of New York's Catholic Irish*. LLC 2012.

Miller, Kerby A. *Emigrants and Exiles: Ireland and the Irish Exodus to North America*. Oxford University Press, 1988.

Sister Elizabeth Ann, S.J.W. "Dagger John (1797-1864)," *Catholic Heritage Curricula*: www.chcweb.com/catalog/files/daggerjohn.pdf

Sisters of Charity of New York. *Sower-Seed-Soil*. Privately published, 2013.

Stern, William J. "How Dagger John Saved New York's Irish." *City Journal*, Spring 1997.

Stern, William J. "What *Gangs of New York* Misses." *City Journal*, 14 January 2003.

Walsh, Sister Marie de Lourdes. *The Sisters of Charity of New York: 1809-1959*. New York: Fordham University Press, 1960, 3 vols.

Woodham-Smith, Cecil. *The Great Hunger: Ireland 1845-1849*. London: Hamish Hamilton, 1962.

Chapter Fifteen

Lady Sligo and her letters: the mounting of an inaugural exhibition

Sandy Letourneau O'Hare and Robert A. Young Jr.

In 2014, the Arnold Bernhard Library at Quinnipiac University hosted an inaugural exhibition of materials contained in the *An Gorta Mór* Collection. The documents chosen were a sub-collection of personal correspondence written during the Famine period. A compelling reason for selecting the letters of Lady Hester Catherine Browne, second Marchioness of Sligo, for exhibition is that they provided a rare first-hand account of how an Anglo-Irish family responded to the catastrophe of the Great Hunger. Lady Sligo and her husband, Howe Peter Browne, second Marquess of Sligo, resided at Westport House, Co. Mayo, an estate in the west of Ireland. The title was granted in return for John Denis Browne's support for the 1800 Act of Union. As there was already an Earl of Mayo, the title Sligo was given.

The creation of this exhibition was a collaborative effort both in and outside the University—the Library, the newly created Ireland's Great Hunger Institute at Quinnipiac University, university faculty, Turlough McConnell Communications, and the Browne family of Westport House in Ireland came together to form the "Lady Sligo Committee." As preparations for the exhibition began, questions arose. How would the letters be presented? What additional research and documentation needed to be done? Were there other items in the Quinnipiac collection that could be utilized? And lastly, what considerations were needed regarding the physical space where the exhibition would be housed?

In 1997, Quinnipiac President John Lahey had served as Grand Marshall of the New York City St. Patrick's Day Parade. It was the 150th anniversary of "Black '47," possibly the deadliest year of the Famine, and so the parade was dedicated to the memory of the Great Hunger. Reading Christine Kinealy's *This Great Calamity: The Irish Famine 1845—1852*,[1] had had a significant impact on President Lahey's tenure as Grand Marshall and had also informed his decision to create a historical and cultural repository at Quinnipiac dedicated to *An Gorta Mór*.[2] He began to acquire books, manuscripts, and art of the period. Assisting him in the creation of this collection were brothers Murray (Quinnipiac 1950) and Marvin Lender. The brothers had been moved by President Lahey's talks on the Great Hunger. Although not Irish themselves, they identified with, and saw parallels between, their Jewish heritage, the Holocaust of World War II, and the 19th century catastrophe in Ireland.[3]

With the establishment of the Great Hunger Collection, Quinnipiac began a relationship with Kenny's Booksellers in Galway, Ireland. Kenny's actively sought out materials that specifically dealt with the Irish Famine on behalf of the University. From 1999-2000, the Arnold Bernhard Library was extensively renovated, and included in the plans was the construction of a room that would house this collection. The Lender Family Special Collection Room (also referred to as "The Great Hunger Room") was officially dedicated in 2000, and was described as having "the most extensive collection of art and literature in America devoted to Ireland's Great Famine..."[4]

In 2009, Conor Kenny visited the campus and met with the librarians. He presented over 200 Famine-era letters and a descriptive brochure that specifically highlighted their scholarly significance.[5] Approximately 120 of the letters touched directly upon various aspects of the Famine, and most of those letters were communications between Lady Sligo and her estate agent at Westport, George Hildebrand. The librarians understood the importance of the letters and thought they would be ideal additions to the collection, but they had some concerns. Factors to be considered included: proper archival storage, the indexing and dating of the collection, and creating transcriptions of the letters. Kenny realized that the letters were the type of primary documents that belonged in the *An Gorta Mór* collection and he insisted that they would not be returning with him to Ireland. After the meeting, the letters were secured in President Lahey's office until a final decision could be made regarding purchase. In 2011, the letters were added to the *An Gorta Mór* collection.

In 2013, Christine Kinealy joined the faculty at Quinnipiac as founding director of Ireland's Great Hunger Institute. She assessed the Great Hunger Collection's holdings and discovered the letters. Kinealy was the first historian to examine the collection, and quickly concluded that the letters provided unique insights into various aspects of Irish society in the mid-19th century. The letters spoke to the role and influence of women, the diverse response of the Big Houses to poor tenants during times of crisis, and the social and political difficulties faced by humane landlords during the Great Hunger. Most importantly, the letters provided a rare perspective by a woman on the Famine, in particular that of a woman of the Anglo-Irish landowning class. A reading of the letters shows that Lady Sligo possessed a keen awareness of contemporary politics and had compassionate concern for the poor, especially as the Famine unfolded in Co. Mayo, one of the worst affected regions.

One of the goals of the exhibition was to "breathe new life" into Lady Sligo and to restore her not only to her place in Irish history, but also to her place in the history of the Browne family. To do this, additional research had to be undertaken regarding the Browne family, the historical period and the Famine itself. As part of the preliminary work for the exhibition, the committee obtained permission to reproduce a painting of Hester Catherine Sligo. This painting was commissioned when she was only 16 and provides visual details related to her social status, as well as her personality.[6]

Hester Catherine de Burgh, daughter of the 13th Earl of Clanricarde, was born in 1800. In 1816, she married Howe Peter Browne, the second Marquess of Sligo, and together they had 14 children, 13 of whom lived to adulthood. By 1845, Lord Sligo was recovering from a stroke and the family was living in Tunbridge Wells in England. Lady Sligo had taken over the day-to-day running of the Westport estate by this point and was in almost daily communication with George Hildebrand, the agent. Upon her husband's death, early in 1845, she returned to Ireland. When her son, George John Browne, inherited the estate, Lady Sligo supported him through the difficult years of the Great Hunger and afterward, continuing to take an active part in the estate until her death in 1878.

The most important letters for exhibition purposes were those which Lady Sligo wrote to Hildebrand just as the crisis was unfolding. Out of the collection of 120 "Famine" letters, 20 were selected for the exhibition. From the letters, it is clear that Lady Sligo took seriously, but also enjoyed, her position as the Marchioness. She displayed firm control over the running of Westport House, regarding both major and minor concerns. For example, she instructed

Hildebrand on routine tasks, such as which garments to send her:

> I think you are mistaking the kind of fur I want. – I want white ermine fur with long black tails. – ...I want all the white fur, but I do not want any dark fur.[7]

However, she moved beyond the traditionally accepted role of a woman and commented on external things such as weather, politics, crop conditions and the state of the poor throughout the letters:

> We have a bad storm from the East here today – I hope it is not so bad at Westport...But there is a worse evil in this Country, which is the potatoes having had a blight about three weeks ago, which made all the Stalks turn black & wither before the potatoes were ripe, so that the potatoes will not keep long.[8]

And:

> I am afraid that Patrick Needham... is either careless or not honest, because I sent by him to Mr. John Browne some blankets, & he delivered 4 pair less than were sent by him... I am very glad to see that Lord Altamont has so good a feeling towards the poor on his estate, as the letter you sent me shows—I much fear there will be a greater scarcity of potatoes on his estate than you think – even if it will not be in the neighborhood of Westport, it may be about Lahinch, as I hear there was a great disease in the potatoes.[9]

Clearly, Lady Sligo was concerned about the local poor having the necessities needed to survive. The letters also provide evidence that she and the Browne family cared more about quality than price. They, at times, made it a point to eschew cost in favor of the best aid that they could provide for their tenants who were suffering from the effects of the potato blight:

> Which do you think best – that I should send you £25 to buy blankets for some of the very poor people at Westport or in the neighbourhood of Westport, or that I should buy the blankets here & send them to you – I can get blankets here from 6 to 8 shillings a pair – at 8 shillings they are very good & thick...[10]

And:

> As you do not think that there is at this moment a great want of blankets among the poor of Westport, I will, as you advise, keep what I can afford to give until it is more wanted – of course, food must be even more required, if there is to be a scarcity of their own produce, which I fear is almost certain in Ireland ... I send you five pounds to give away in blankets, or in other urgent cases of want now in the neighbourhood, amongst the very poor.[11]

It is through these letters that we learn firsthand what conditions were like and how intricately involved Lady Sligo was in the running of the estate.

Hester Catherine was a strong, dominant presence in her own right and, when she married Howe Peter, she joined a long line of formidable women in the family. Howe Peter was a direct descendant of Grace O'Malley, also known as the "Pirate Queen" or Granuaile. She was the daughter of a 16th Century Irish chieftain who defied Gaelic customs that barred women from clan leadership roles. She lived on through legend, books and a pirate-themed amusement park that was built during the 20th century on the grounds of Westport House. Until Lady Sligo's letters were brought to light, Grace was the only known female member of the Browne family. Until recently, the family knew nothing about Hester Catherine except, as Lady Sheelyn Browne said, "That she was one of the wives".[12] The most recent curators of Westport House were the daughters of the 11th Marquess of Sligo, Jeremy Altamont, who helped to break down barriers to female leadership. Under the terms of his inheritance, his estate had to pass to a male heir, but he had only daughters—five of them—and the future of the estate was uncertain. With his family facing a future battle to hold on to their historic home, in 1993 he challenged the succession laws and, with the assistance of another remarkable Mayo woman, Mary Robinson, won.[13] In 2014, when Lord Altamont died, his daughters inherited Westport House, continuing the family business and the tradition of strong women in the family. However, the title of Marquess continued to pass down the male line and was given to a cousin in Australia.

How could such a rich, multi-layered history, be told in a small exhibition area? The Lender Special Collection Room at Quinnipiac University is a small, uniquely designed space meant to replicate the steerage deck of a ship and evoke the feeling of being an immigrant traveling in steerage. The room has glass book cases on either side, and closed storage cases below. There is minimal enclosed display space for documents. There are maps and commemorative art on the walls, and sculptures placed throughout. This space needed to be transformed to tell the story of Lady Sligo and to be modified for the proper display of historical documents. In particular, the lighting was a major consideration. Before the exhibition, it did not meet display standards for historical documents. Filters were purchased to diffuse the light in the display cases and the overhead lights were adjusted so that they did not shine directly on the artifacts. Motion sensors were also installed to allow the documents to "rest" when visitors were not in the room.

A large fabric wall hanging, displaying the exterior of Westport House, was hung at the entrance to the exhibit, providing visitors with the impression of arriving at "The Big House." Passing through the door, visitors entered a simulation of Lady Sligo's study. Letters are personal and it was the intention to create an intimate feeling and connection between the visitors and the documents. White gloves, a string of pearls, writing quills, teacups, a candle and a writing desk were added to the room. Pictures of the family were reproduced, framed, and placed, much as Lady Sligo might have done. When considering putting the letters on display, one of the things to be taken into account was how they were written (quite literally). The penmanship was beautiful, but it was in script. Many millennials no longer read or write in script so typed transcripts were included for all of the displayed letters.

When the committee met, the first task was to figure out how to make a collection of letters into an interesting exhibition. Research revealed previously unknown aspects of the history of the family. For example, it was discovered that the "Busha Browne" brand of Jamaican hot sauce had a historical connection to the family, and this story was noted in an ancillary exhibit case.[14] The family members in Ireland were unaware of this family connection. In addition to the letters, other materials related to the Great Hunger were displayed elsewhere the library. One of the volumes of Parliamentary Papers owned by Quinnipiac includes a published letter by George Browne, 3rd Lord Sligo, requesting that the government adjust grain prices. The British government denied the request, stating that there could not be interference with the free market.[15] Also on display was a complete genealogy of the Browne family, constructed specifically for this exhibition. This traced the title line down to the 11th Marquess, Jeremy Altamont.[16] For the Browne family in Ireland, this family tree filled in some of the gaps in their knowledge.

As an introduction to the formal exhibition, a slideshow was created to reach a general audience. Bearing in mind that not everyone visiting the exhibition would have the same understanding of Irish history, the purpose was to impart some basic knowledge. The questions and topics covered included:

Who was this woman?

Who was her husband and what role did he play outside the Famine?

What was the role of an estate agent?

What was happening in Ireland during the Famine?

Why was their title "Sligo" if they were from Mayo?

What was the Poor Law?

Who are Lady Sligo's descendants?

How and why were the succession laws changed?

The "look" of the slides was also important. They had to relate to the letters without duplicating them. So, a ghost image of a letter was utilized as the background for all slides. Lady Sligo had a beautiful and unique signature. She signed her letters with "H Catherine Sligo", the H standing for Hester. This signature was captured and used on the welcome slide, and was subsequently adopted for use on the brochures and story boards. It literally became the signature of the exhibit.

Christine Kinealy reached out to the Browne family during the preliminary planning of the exhibition. The family had no idea that the letters existed and were excited to assist and contribute. This is how permission was granted to use Lady Sligo's portrait and other images from Westport House. Anne Anderson, Ambassador of Ireland to the United States, opened the exhibition, and Noel Kilkenny, counsel general of Ireland, and his wife, Hanora O'Dea, also attended. Anne Anderson was excited to be present since she was the first female ambassador from Ireland and this exhibition presented Irish history from a woman's perspective.[17]

Through the relationship that was established between the Browne family and Quinnipiac, the family learned of an ancestor about whom they knew little. They felt that it was important to share her story and requested that the exhibition move to Westport House, where it would remain permanently. Lady Sheelyn Browne explained:

> This exhibition truly belongs in Westport. It captures a very personal insight into one very privileged generation of the Browne family who unexpectedly landed in 1845 with a huge sense of duty. Thankfully they followed the family motto 'suivez raison' and did do the right thing. They rolled their beautifully ironed linen sleeves up and did their absolute best to ease the desperate situation in their hometown, both practically and financially.[18]

Facsimiles of the letters, transcripts and story boards were provided to Westport House by Ireland's Great Hunger Institute (with the original letters remaining at Quinnipiac).

The Westport exhibition was opened in April 2015 by the American Ambassador to Ireland, Kevin O'Malley, whose family had immigrated to America from Co. Mayo. The Westport opening occurred just one year after the original opening at Quinnipiac. The Lady had finally returned home after a long trip abroad.

Endnotes

1 Christine Kinealy, *This Great Calamity: The Irish Famine 1845-1852* (Gill and McMillan, 1994).

2 John T. Ridge, *Celebrating 250 Years of the New York City St. Patrick's Day Parade* (Quinnipiac University Press, 2011), p. 68.

3 Speech given by President John Lahey at Quinnipiac University, 29 April 2014.

4 The Lender Family Collection Description: www.thegreathunger.org/AboutCollection/CollectionDescription.asp Accessed 23 Nov. 2015.

5 *The Famine in Mayo: A View from the Big House* (n.p., n.d.).

6 Louis-Leopold Boilly, *Hester Catherine De Burgh, later second Marchioness of Sligo (1800-1878)*, in possession of Westport House, Co. Mayo, Ireland.

7 H. Catherine Sligo to George Hildebrand, n.d. (Arnold Bernhard Library, Lady Sligo Letters, Folder 29).

8 Ibid., 8 Oct. [1845] (Folder 64).

9 Ibid., 14 Jan. [1845] (Folder 34 part 1 and 2).

10 Ibid., 4 Dec. [1845] (Folder 24).

11 Ibid., 9 Dec. [1845] (Folder 14).

12 *Westport House and the Launch of the Great Famine Exhibition*. Mayo Matters. Irish TV. Westport, Co. Mayo, Ireland: 21 April 2015.

13 The Altamont (Amendment of Deed of Trust) Act, 1993 [Ire].

14 Busha Browne Story: www.bushabrowne.com/about_busha.php Accessed 23 Nov. 2015.

15 *Correspondence from July 1846 to January 1847 relating to the measures adopted for the relief of the distress in Ireland (Commissariat Series)*, BPP, 1847 [159-161], LI.

16 The Peerage: www.thepeerage.com/p3472.htm Accessed 23 Nov. 2015. Marble Hill: www.marble-hill.info/hester-catherine-de-burgh-lady/ Accessed 23 Nov. 2015. Craycroft's Peerage (http://www.cracroftspeerage.co.uk/online/content/sligo1800.htm) (23 Nov. 2015).

17 Speech given by Anne Anderson at opening of Lady Sligo exhibition, Quinnipiac University, 29 April 2014: www.quinnipiac.edu/prebuilt/pdf/Institutes/GreatHunger/AndersonRemarks42814.pdf   Accessed 30 Nov. 2015.

18 The Lady Sligo Exhibition: www.quinnipiac.edu/institutes-and-centers/irelands-great-hunger-institute/the-lady-sligo-letters-exhibition/ Accessed 23 Nov. 2015.

Works Cited

The Altamont (Amendment of Deed of Trust) Act, 1993 [Ire].

Boilly, Louis Leopold. *Hester Catherine De Burgh, later second Marchioness of Sligo (1800-1878)*. Westport House, Co. Mayo, Ireland.

Busha Browne website: www.bushabrowne.com/about_busha.php

Correspondence from July 1846 to January 1847 relating to the measures adopted for the relief of the distress in Ireland (Commissariat Series), BPP, 1847 [159-161], LI.

Craycroft's Peerage website: www.cracroftspeerage.co.uk/online/content/sligo1800.htm

The Great Hunger.org website: www.thegreathunger.org/AboutCollection/CollectionDescription.asp

Kinealy, Christine. *This Great Calamity: The Irish Famine 1845-1852*. Dublin: Gill and MacMillan, 1994.

Marble Hill website: www.marble-hill.info/hester-catherine-de-burgh-lady/

Ridge, John T., *Celebrating 250 Years of the New York City St. Patrick's Day Parade*. Hamden: Quinnipiac University Press, 2011.

Lady Sligo Letters. AB Library, Quinnipiac University.

The Famine in Mayo: A View from the Big House (n.p., n.d.)

The Lady Sligo Letters Exhibition website:
   www.quinnipiac.edu/institutes-and-centers/irelands-great-hunger-institute/the-lady-sligo-letters-exhibition/

The Peerage website: www.thepeerage.com/p3472.htm

Westport House and the Launch of the Great Famine Exhibition. Mayo Matters. Irish TV. Westport, Co. Mayo, Ireland, 21 April 2015.

Chapter Sixteen

The Earl Grey orphan scheme, 1848-1850, and the Irish diaspora in Australia

Rebecca Abbott

In 2012 I began work with a number of my colleagues researching the history of Ireland's Great Hunger, along with its impact both on those who left Ireland and those who remained. We were planning to make a documentary on this subject, and one of the very interesting—and less well known in North America—dimensions of the exodus from Ireland that we wished to explore was the story of the Earl Grey Girls, who emigrated to Australia between 1848 and 1850. While we failed in our initial plan to get funding support from the US National Endowment for the Humanities, I was able to continue the project through a series of small faculty research grants in 2013 from Quinnipiac University. These funds permitted travel not only to Ireland but to Grosse Île, Quebec, and to Sydney, Australia to gather interviews and documentary footage. My plan was to interview descendants of those who left Ireland during the Famine years, and let their engaging family stories make the dryer historical narrative more real and present and "bring it to life." The film that emerged from these efforts is titled *Ireland's Great Hunger and the Irish Diaspora* and it was completed in November, 2015.[1]

As I researched the documentary segment on the Earl Grey girls, I contacted Dr. Trevor McClaughlin, author and retired professor of history at Macquarie University, for whom the Earl Grey Female Orphan scheme was both his specialty and his passion. McClaughlin, in turn, connected me with the Australian historian, Dr. Perry McIntyre, who—among other posts—was chairperson of the organizing committee for the International Irish Famine Commemoration that, fortuitously, was taking place in Sydney that year. Delighted by my luck, I scheduled the trip to Australia in August of 2013 so that I could attend the commemoration, and the trip brought me in further contact with several noted historians of the Famine and the Earl Grey Girls, including Dr. Richard Reid, and Tom Power, retired chair of the Sydney Famine commemoration committee. All four graciously agreed to explain, on camera, the Earl Grey Orphan scheme, in addition to helping me connect with eight descendants of Earl Grey girls who also agreed to be interviewed for the documentary. It is hard to describe the thrilling sense of connection with history that I felt when I explored Hyde Park Barracks, and the beautiful and moving Famine memorial next to it, when I arrived in Sydney. That sense of awe only grew as I learned the histories that my interview subjects so generously shared with me, and so I could begin to picture their great, great, grandmothers landing on Australian soil where they began such dramatically new and, previously for them, unimaginable lives.

We chose the historic courtroom adjacent to Hyde Park Barracks as the site for Dr. McIntyre's interview. McIntyre explored the history and impact of the Earl Grey Orphan Scheme, which occurred between 1848 and 1850, and which brought 4,114 Irish orphan girls to Australia from Irish workhouses. The scheme was controversial for a number of reasons, not the least being the strikingly different expectations of the two groups. Australians hoped to welcome young women with experience in domestic service or other useful training, but most of the Irish orphans had little or no such experience, were illiterate to a fair degree, and were traveling with the desperate goal of fleeing from starvation, disease, loss of family, and absolute poverty. As Trevor McClaughlin explained in his interview:

> Earl Grey's female orphan scheme gets underway in 1848, and it is finished by mid-1850 largely because of opposition on the part of colonists who thought they wouldn't have to pay anything. But in fact they were paying for young women who weren't really trained in domestic service, but I mean, what did they expect?[2]

Yet, after their arrival and their struggle to find suitable placements and acceptance in their new home, one of the significant outcomes was that these orphan girls had an average of seven children each, and in many cases they had as many as 12 or 13 children. To quote McIntyre, "when you track that over five or six generations, which it is now, over 160 years ago, there are a lot of descendants."[3]

In fact, in the 2011 Australian census, which "asked respondents to provide a maximum of two ancestries with which they most closely identify," 9.7 percent of the country's residents indicated Irish heritage.[4] This does not include Australians with an Irish background, who chose to nominate themselves as "Australian" or who chose other ancestries. The Australian Embassy in Dublin claims that up to 30 percent of the Australian population identifies some degree of Irish ancestry.[5] Of course, these numbers include descendants of 40,000 Irish convicts transported to Australia from 1791 to 1867, migrants who came between the years of 1831 to 1850 on several different programs of government-assisted immigration (including the Irish female orphans who came between 1848 and 1850), and the Catholic Church-assisted migration of children from the 1870s through the 1950s. Nonetheless, the female orphans who left during the Great Hunger, and their many descendants, made a significant impact on the country.

To the question of why female orphans were preferred for emigration to Australia, it helps to note that during the decade following the founding of the Australian colony in 1788, those arriving were mostly male. This was due to reasons of exploration and commerce certainly, but also because of the large number of mostly male convicts sentenced to transportation from Britain, Scotland and Ireland to Australia. A "solution" of sorts was found by the Colonial Land and Emigration Commissioners and Earl Grey (the Secretary of State for the Colonies), suggesting that, "with a view of keeping up the supply of labour required, a free passage to New South Wales should be offered to certain classes of orphans..." and that, "by sending out a proportion of unmarried females, they are enabled to select good and useful labourers, who, from being unmarried, would otherwise have been ineligible."[6] The proposal initially included orphans of both sexes, but when it was finally implemented later in 1848 it included only females. These young women were chosen from workhouses across Ireland, and all—according to the definition of "orphan" at that time—had lost one or both parents. Details of this plan were articulated in The Colonial Land and Emigration Office report of 17 February 1848:

> ...having been informed that an eligible class of Irish emigrants may be found among the orphan children, now supported at the public expense in Ireland, will be prepared to offer to such of these persons as may, on inquiry, be approved, and as may be willing to emigrate, free passages to the above colonies. None will be accepted who are less than 14 or more than 18 years of age, and the nearest to 18 will be taken in preference.[7]

Such government reports, with their dry, bureaucratic, language, give no sense of who these orphan children were and how they might respond to being "chosen" by the British government for emigration away from the only life they had known to a continent half the world away, a place from which they likely never would return. McClaughlin has addressed the question of choice and the extent to which the young women selected for travel to Australia did so of free will:

> Our adolescent orphans were people who knew *an drochshaol*; they had first-hand experience of the 'bad life', the 'bitter time' of the Famine ... They had fallen on such hard times that they depended on the workhouse for their very survival. For them, the workhouse was the difference between life and death ... The *Sydney Morning Herald* later put it, they were: 'deprived, by death and pestilence, of their natural guardians.'[8]

McClaughlin also believes that "in the local media, and in the oral tradition to which the orphans belonged, Australia was an attractive destination."[9] That perspective can be confirmed in Mallow, Co. Cork, at least, where "the guardians found that orphan girls in service in the district were leaving their posts and endeavouring to be accepted in the workhouse so that they might be selected for emigration."[10] Clearly, for some young women this was an opportunity they could not ignore.

Dr. Richard Reid, speaking on camera in the historic New South Wales Parliament Building for the documentary, explained:

> These girls all had to be equipped with a box of clothing, it was a long voyage, three months, and there was a surgeon on board, and proper diet, so it was a very well organized kind of system.

The long passage was overseen by a ship's surgeon and a matron. As Reid explained, each girl was outfitted with a wardrobe suitable for such long travel, which was provided for them by the Board of Guardians of their Irish Poor Law Union. This included:

> six shifts, two flannel petticoats, six pair stockings, two pair shoes, two Gowns, one of which must be made warm material ... the Emigrants have to pass through very hot and very cold weather, and should therefore be prepared for both.[11]

Perry McIntyre elaborated further: "They're one of the few immigrant groups that come to Australia without having to pay anything."

As they began the long trip from Ireland to Australia, the young women first traveled from their respective workhouses to Plymouth, Liverpool, or Cork to board ship. The Irish part of the journey was undertaken by foot, by cart or by train, although "there was only about 120 miles of track in 1847."[12] The voyage from Dublin to Plymouth took nearly two days, on a steamer where the passengers traveled in the open on deck, unprotected from the elements. Still, given the special attention paid by organizers to safe travel, the mortality rate on the passage to Australia was exceptionally low, only 1 percent. This was a sharp contrast with the fates of many who traveled to America, especially those going by cargo ship. After their months at sea, McIntyre describes the sort of routine the girls followed:

> When they arrived ... they got their trunks up out of the hold, and they had three to five days on the ship getting themselves clean and respectable. Then they walked from the harbor up to Hyde Park Barracks, which is about a quarter of a mile, where they were housed and looked after until such time as they were hired out or in some cases where a relative may have come and collected them.[13]

From Hyde Park Barracks, potential employers of the girls were screened, and were encouraged to have them indentured. The young women's pay was set at £6 per year for those aged 14 to 15, £7 for those 15 to 16, and so on, up to £10 per year for those aged more than 18 years of age. To many of the young women this seemed generous, especially given the circumstances from which they came, but, by local standards it was actually quite low.

During the varied events of the International Famine Commemoration I met Neisha Wratten and learned of her delighted surprise, several years earlier, of discovering that she had an Earl Grey ancestor. The Famine Memorial at Hyde Park Barracks includes a glass wall on which are etched the names of the girls who traveled under the Earl Grey scheme. As I filmed, Wratten pointed to the name Bridget Cannon on the memorial's glass wall and said:

> There she is. She's my great, great, grandmother. And I suddenly discovered that my great great grandmother was an Earl Grey girl! She came across on the *Lady Peel*, third of July, 1849. The voyage lasted 110 days. She was apprenticed to a dealer in Sydney called Michael O'Brien. It only lasted for about two weeks, even though her indenture was for two years. But she ran away to Moreton Bay, where in January of the next year she met a man by the name of John Smith. And she had her first baby. She went on to have fourteen, fifteen children – the records differ – not all of them survived. And now I'm here, and I feel so proud of someone that I've never met.

As Wratten's account suggests, the young women's experiences in their new positions ranged across a spectrum, and sometimes they cancelled their indentures for a variety of reasons. This sometimes included abuse, as these examples from the *Registers and Indexes of applications for orphans* demonstrate:[14]

> ▪ No 967. October 1849. Sarah Cullins per *Lady Peel*, Parramatta Street, Sydney, complaining of ill-usage from her mistress and requesting to be removed from her service. Ask Dr. Gregory to investigate.
> - No 326. From Adelaide Forbes, Wooloomooloo 5 April 1849. Expresses desire to get rid of Mary Ann Galway (*Earl Grey*) who entered her service November last. Answer: could only get rid of her by bringing her up at the Police Office or by a regular transfer of indentures
> ▪ Eliza Taafe per *Inconstant* designated "insane" when she arrived in Adelaide. The Surgeon thought her strange behavior was caused by her Famine experience in Ireland. A local doctor predicted she was not permanently insane: simply in need of kindness and care.
> ▪ Margaret Cumins per *Pemberton* employed by Patrick Ryan at Salt Water River in 1849. "When her relative was out milking the cows, Ryan violated her forcibly and against her will: she did not tell this to her relative or to anyone else at the time, but went back again to live at Ryan's, and Ryan had frequently criminal connexion with her since that time."
> ▪ No 3708. Alice Ball, fourteen years old, orphan, Protestant, of Enniskillen workhouse. She and her sister Jane joined the *Diadem* at Plymouth for the voyage to Port Phillip Bay. Less than a year later, in April 1850, sixteen-year-old Alice, made pregnant by her employer, took her own life by throwing herself into Melbourne's River Yarra.[15]
> ▪ Seventeen year old Mary Colgan from Skibbereen arrived in Geelong in 1850. She married James Walton, a man "addicted to liquor and using violence to his wife," according to a judge. In 1857, at the Ballarat gold diggings, they were charged with

murder. James Walton was sentenced to eighteen months hard labour for manslaughter. Then in 1862, Mary was beaten and kicked by her drunken husband and suffered a miscarriage, the fifth child she had lost because of her husband's beatings. She died in the Ballarat District Hospital—"of typhoid fever and enteritis brought on by a miscarriage, occasioned by the ill-treatment of her husband"—according to the jury's verdict at her inquest. James Walton received seven years hard labour for his crime.[16]

Despite the many cases of hardship and struggle, there was also success, and even triumph. Ellen Parks, one of the Belfast girls from the infamous *Earl Grey*, married London-born George Clarke, a successful restaurant keeper and oyster merchant in Sydney. Despite difficulties in childbirth in the early years, due to malnutrition in her early life, she survived and eventually had nine children, six of whom were still alive at the time of Ellen's death in 1880. Ellen bequeathed to her children not only money but jewelry, books, glassware, furniture and fine engravings.[17]

McClaughlin introduced me to Dr. Eleanor Dawson, whose grandmother, Bridgette McMann, traveled with other Earl Grey girls on the ship *Maria* in 1850. Dawson learned her grandmother's story from her mother, who told her, "Grandmother was 16 when she came. She had I think eight children of whom she had lost two." Dawson's grandmother became a teacher, and her mother had seven children, of whom six survived. "Four graduated from Sydney University and they became quite a remarkable family in educational circles." Indeed, Eleanor Dawson's mother received:

> ... one of the first two Masters of Science degrees awarded at Sydney University. Her career resulted in her being awarded from Imperial College, London, one of two Dominion Fellowships and in 1924 she travelled in Lapland with a large group of European scientists.

Following in this new, family tradition, Eleanor Dawson decided to study medicine, and made her choice in an unusual way:

> I did very well at my school but I had tuberculosis. The doctors were young, handsome, swinging stethoscopes in their white coats, and I used to look out my window at other white-sheeted people being wheeled down a path. And so I asked what the building was that they were going to. It was the chapel, which was also the morgue. I got the sort of idea I'd rather be one of the ones who had a stethoscope, you know? [18]

Dawson received her own doctoral degree and practiced medicine for much of her life, and was a cancer researcher at the children's hospital in Sydney before becoming a practicing psychiatrist and published author for the second half of her long career.

There is little information about the girls' experiences during their months at sea, with one notable exception. Dr. Charles Strutt was ship's surgeon for the *Thomas Arbuthnot*, which sailed from Plymouth in 1849. Of all those accompanying the young women on their passage, Strutt alone kept a highly detailed, day-to-day diary of events on board ship, an account that not only provided a warmly human view of the girls in his care, but also revealed his unique efforts to offer education and training to his charges to improve their reception by their new hosts upon their arrival. Before my trip to Australia began, I had made contact—thanks to Perry McIntyre— with Peter Coll and his aunt Jude McBride, and also with Julie Evans, who had ancestors aboard the *Thomas Arbuthnot*. Peter Coll spoke with me in his home in Canberra, about a three-hour drive through mostly rural countryside from Sydney.

I'm Peter Coll, and my great, great, grandmother is Mary Ann Roughan, who is one of the famine orphans. My grandmother used to start talking about one of her ancestors, a young girl, who came out from Ireland, with a cousin, by themselves, and it wasn't until my uncle was contacted by a local parish priest and he said "I've got this stained glass window in the church, and apparently it belongs to your family." It was for Thomas Collins. His grandmother was Mary Ann Roughan. And so that actually verified what my grandmother was saying.

Peter's aunt, Jude McBride, met me at the church that Peter referred to, where I filmed her account of Mary Ann Roughan's story in front of the stained glass window that Peter had referred to.

Mary Ann Roughan was one of the orphan girls that came to Australia on the Thomas [*Arbuthnot*]. She was my great grandmother. The doctor in charge of their welfare on the ship really wanted to look after them, and after they landed in Australia, he made sure that they were all settled. Mary Ann Roughan was taken by dray out to Yass. And it would have taken a few weeks to get from Sydney out to Yass.

Roghan was indeed lucky to have joined the group on the *Thomas Arbuthnot* with Surgeon Strutt. Strutt's diary referred affectionately to the orphan girls as "my people" or "my girls." The matron working with Strutt was Mrs. Murphy, a 42-year-old widow from Dublin. Along with her daughter, Murphy and Strutt gave the young women the sort of structured existence they may have never before have experienced. Yet this supervision was always applied "with patience, kindness and care," that left room for dancing and singing. Strutt was pleased with the results: "Friday 7 December My girls have become much more orderly and tidy under the constant steady pressure I keep up against holes, rags, tatters and dirt."[19] After landing at Sydney, when the girls were asked if any would accompany him to Yass, which was an arduous, two- or three-week trip taken by ox cart, "130 at once expressed their wish to go any place that I might be going to."[20] McBride and Coll are intercut in the documentary imagining Roughan's trip:

Peter Coll: "To do that on an oxcart, you know, pretty poor roads, and it's a pretty mountainous area, too."

Jude McBride: "And there was little Mary Ann, seventeen, sixteen years old, on a cart and horse, going out in the country to a place that was quite unknown to her, and the terror of it must have been very high. She went straight into service in a family, and then she married John Collins."

Peter: "He was a local laborer. They were married in Saint Augustine's church, in Yass. They had their own farm, which was Fairy Hole Creek. They had six children, and one of those children was my great grandfather, Thomas Collins."

Jude: "And she died in childbirth with the last child. And the children came one a year. So she didn't have a very long life, little Mary Ann."

Julie Evans's great, great, grandmother was Bridget "Biddy" Ryan, who also traveled on the *Thomas Arbuthnot* in 1850. Bridget had left Bruff in Limerick and, after arrival at Hyde Park Barracks, she was hired by a master mariner from Balmain. Later she met James Murray, a Scott.

Within a year Bridget was married; very soon after that she had one baby, and they'd moved to the Manning Valley area. If you go by the records, her first baby was born when she was sixteen. She then proceeded to have thirteen children, one died as a baby, and there are still descendants all throughout New South Wales and throughout Australia.

When I met her, Julie Evans had done a considerable amount of research into her family history, much of it during previous travel to Ireland. She was rewarded with the discovery of a fascinating prelude to her great grandmother's exodus to Australia:

> The local parish priest, Dean Robert Carson, was the wealthy son of a tobacco millionaire who used his money to help his parish. He brought to Bruff a convent run by 'The Faithful Companions of Jesus' order of French nuns, along with its school called Laurel Hill. Accounts suggest that Carson paid for Bridget to be educated at this school.

Why was Bridget offered help? Julie believes it may have had something to do with the girl's father. Julie says: "Her father left the family, and Bridget must only have been three … when her father, Lancelot Ryan … was charged with bigamy. He had married Bridget's mother, and then he married a woman called Jane Huddy." Bridget Ryan's story is taken up in Kay Maloney Caball's book about the Earl Grey Orphans, titled *Kerry Girls*:

> Her father was called Lancelot (Lanty) Ryan. He had been a soldier but he had been convicted of being a bigamist and, aged 35, he was tried in July 1837 at Limerick Assizes and sentenced to seven years' transportation. In a report of the court case in the *Limerick Chronicle* of 12 July 1837, Fr. Halpin PP, Bruff, stated that he married 'the prisoner' to Mary Hynes (Biddy's mother) in Bruff and Fr. Lyddy PP, stated that he had married 'the prisoner' to Jane Huddy in Abbeyfeale at a later date. Jane Huddy deposed that she had married the prisoner and that six weeks later his former wife walked in with her family.[21]

Julie believes that part of the reason Biddy was the last to be added to the list of orphan girls on the *Thomas Arbuthnot* was because of Dean Carson's involvement. She imagines that Carson, concerned by Biddy's father's conviction, worried that it would ruin Biddy's future chances. Evans thinks that this led him to intervene by getting Biddy on the ship to Australia for a new start. Biddy's name appears last on the ship's list, out of alphabetical order, lending credence to Julie's interpretation.

Julie Evans found it remarkable to consider how Lancelot Ryan could be so romantically persuasive. "One of the most interesting things is his bodily state. Because when he was jailed, he had one arm, one eye, and many, many scars on his face and head. And we want to know what charm he had to attract two women!" As a postscript, Julie adds: "Lancelot ended up in Australia…and I have his ticket of leave and his certificate of freedom. And when Bridget arrived, she does say that her father is in Sydney. But whether they ever met up, I'll never know."

One of the people with whom Perry McIntyre put me in touch was retired police officer Collin Graham and his granddaughter, Teagan, whom I met in a southern suburb of Sydney. Despite the fact that his wife had recently become seriously ill, Col, as he is known, insisted on keeping the meeting for the interview. As with all the people I met and spoke with, it was a great pleasure to talk with Col and Teagen. And McIntyre had wisely known that seeing and hearing Teagan—who at the time of the interview was about the same age as the Irish orphans when they left their home country—would put the entire discussion into remarkable perspective.

Col and Teagan have not just one, but three Earl Grey girls in their heritage: Bridget Davis, or Davies, of Co. Clare; Margaret Reardon, from Croome, Limerick; and Bridget Mahon, from Headford, Co. Galway. "Within three years the three of them were married to people out here." Letters from Bridget Davis's uncle and aunt in Co. Clare, inform her that members of her family had left Ireland for America, South Africa, to England, because "they just had to get out of there, it was just too horrendous for them." Col explained that "Bridget Davies married a fellow named Amis Louis. His name should have been a French name Amie Louie Hughen, because his grandfather was a Frenchman from out here and his mother was an aboriginal girl." Col says, "Bridget actually died at the age of 29. She had had the 5 children with Amis and that's the line that I came down through, William Louis, her oldest boy."

Bridget Davies was also a passenger on the *Thomas Arbuthnot*. Col Graham was very familiar with Richard Reid's book *A Decent Set of Girls: The Irish Famine Orphans of the Thomas Arbuthnot, 1849-1850*, which presents Strutt's travel diary with historical commentary. Col said:

> Dr. Strutt also took them inland and had them placed all around the southwest area of New South Wales including Bridget, our girl Bridget Davis … They were living at a place called Blakney Creek, which is between Yass and Boorowa, and I don't know if she died out in the scrub or out in the bush or whether she died in town at Yass—she might have been in hospital and in Yass. It was several months after the birth of her youngest a girl Sarah Jane, so it might have been complications after the birth.

The following interviews are also from the documentary:

> Col: Margaret Reardon, she married John Cahoon, and Cahoon is my mother's maiden name. And he was a convict. He was sent out here for stealing a fowl, and his mother was sent out here for seven years for receiving a stolen fowl, so obviously he'd stolen it to give to his mother. You know I've tried to let Teagan know that they were much the same age as what she is now.

> Teagan: I think that would be so scary, like, as Papa said, you're leaving everyone that you know … And then it would just be a scary trip, like you don't know if you're even going to make it there or anything. And then you get there and it's a totally different place.

> Col: I'm really proud of the Irish ancestry that I've got, because it's just been fantastic to find these people and see the struggles that they put up with to come here to Australia and start a new life.

> Teagan: I'm quarter Chinese myself, my father's half Chinese and I'm quarter, but …

> Col: We've got Aboriginal ancestry, and Chinese, and French, and English, Irish, Scottish …

> Teagan: We embrace everything we've got.

It is my hope that these interview excerpts provide a degree of insight into the lives of some of the young women who survived the devastation of the Great Hunger. Their survival required them to leave the only life they had known in Ireland and to settle in a new and very different land, thousands of miles from home. Within Australia, these women are now honored for their bravery, their fortitude, and for their contributions to shaping the country. Their stories reinforce the diverse experience of Famine women, not only in Ireland, but in other parts of the world. As Jude McBride summarized, "their courage must have been extraordinary, I think. And Mary Ann, thank God, was able to produce children, those children produced children, and here we are today. And God bless us all."

Endnotes

[1] Rebecca Abbott, *Ireland's Great Hunger and The Irish Diaspora*, video documentary (2015).

[2] Ibid.

[3] Ibid.

[4] 2011 Census data shows more than 300 ancestries reported in Australia, 21 June 2012 *www.abs.gov.au/websitedbs/censushome.nsf/home/CO-62?opendocument&navpos=620* Accessed 1 Jan. 2015.

[5] *Wikipedia Irish Australian* http://en.wikipedia.org/wiki/Irish_Australian#cite_note-6 http://upload.wikimedia.org/wikipedia/commons/e/e6/Australian_Census_2011_demographic_map_-_Australia_by_SLA_-_BCP_field_1120_Irish_Total_Responses.svg

[6] Ibid., "Copy of a Despatch from Earl Grey to Governor Sir C. A. FitzRoy, Downing-street, 28 February 1848 (No. 35, p. 88) www.dippam.ac.uk/eppi/documents/12245/page/294969

[7] Ibid., Enclosure in No. 2, 17 Feb. 1848: www.dippam.ac.uk/eppi/documents/12245/page/294970 Accessed 13 Dec. 2014.

[8] This topic has generated so much popular interest in Australia that Dr. Trevor McClaughlin has created a personal blog to answer questions: "Trevo's Irish Famine Orphans," Trevo's Irish Famine Orphans, Earl Grey's Irish Famine Orphans (2) https://earlgreysfamineorphans.wordpress.com/2014/08/20/earl-greys-irish-famine-orphans-2/

[9] https://earlgreysfamineorphans.wordpress.com/2014/08/20/earl-greys-irish-famine-orphans-2/ Accessed 11 March 2015.

[10] Joseph Robins, *The Lost Children: A Study of Charity Children in Ireland, 1700-1900* (Dublin: Institute of Public Administration, 1980), p. 212.

[11] Enhanced British Parliamentary Papers on Ireland/EPPI, Emigration: papers relative to emigration to the Australian Colonies, Enclosure in No. 2, 17 Feb. 1848. www.dippam.ac.uk/eppi/documents/12245/page/294971

[12] Oliver MacDonagh, *A Pattern of Government Growth, 1800-60: The Passenger Acts and their Enforcement.* London: MacGibbon and Kee, 1961, pp 167-8 in https://earlgreysfamineorphans.wordpress.com/tag/keening/

[13] Perry McIntyre interview by Rebecca Abbott for *Ireland's Great Hunger and The Irish Diaspora*, timecode address: 09;28;26;27

[14] McClaughlin: https://earlgreysfamineorphans.wordpress.com/tag/eliza-taafe/ from: Registers and indexes of applications for orphans, State Records, New South Wales *http://search-cloudfront.records.nsw.gov.au/series/5240*

[15] www.historyireland.com/20th-century-contemporary-history/lost-children/ Accessed 3 April 2015.Sydney: ooks Australia, 2010..ofor 4919.n opportunity they could not ignore.g their posts and endeavouring to be accepted in theSydney: ooks Australia, 2010..ofor 4919.n opportunity they could not ignore.g their posts and endeavouring to be accepted in the

[16] Ibid.

[17] Ibid.

[18] Abbott, *Ireland's Great Hunger.*

[19] McClaughlin: https://earlgreysfamineorphans.wordpress.com/tag/keening/

[20] McClaughlin: https://earlgreysfamineorphans.wordpress.com/tag/voyage-to-australia-2/

[21] Caball, Kay Moloney: *The Kerry Girls: Emigration and the Earl Grey Scheme,* Dublin: The History Press, 2014. Kindle edition, location 1974 of 4919.

Works Cited

Caball, Kay Moloney. *The Kerry Girls: Emigration and the Earl Grey Scheme.* Dublin: The History Press, 2014.

—— *Farewell My Children: Irish Assisted Emigration to Australia 1848-1870.* Sydney: Anchor Books Australia, 2011.

McClaughlin, Trevor. *Barefoot and Pregnant?: Irish Famine Orphans in Australia: Documents and Register.* Victoria, Australia: Genealogical Society of Victoria, 1991.

—— Web blog—*Trevo's Irish Famine Orphans – Earl Grey's Irish Famine Orphans* https://earlgreysfamineorphans.wordpress.com/2014/08/20/earl-greys-irish-famine-orphans-2/

MacDonagh, Oliver. *The Passenger Acts: A Pattern of Government Growth.* London: MacGibbon and Kee, 1961.

McIntyre, Perry. *Fair Game: Australia's First Immigrant Women.* Sydney: Anchor Books Australia, 2010.

Reid, Richard. *A Decent Set of Girls: The Irish Famine Orphans of the Thomas Arbuthnot.* Yass, Australia: Yass Heritage Project, 1996.

Robins, Joseph. *The Lost Children: A Study of Charity Children in Ireland, 1700-1900.* Dublin: Institute of Public Administration, 1980.

Postscript and a Personal Reflection.

The editors and Ruth Riddick

The Great Hunger of 1845 to 1852 did not mark an end to famines in Ireland. Sadly, poverty and hunger, with all their contingent sorrows, continued throughout the late nineteenth century and into the twentieth. While the importance of women as care-givers and as emigrants in the 19th century has received some attention,[1] relatively little attention has been paid to women's other roles during periods of shortage and famine. What is the place of Irish women in the historiography of famine and in the curriculum?

During Michael D. Higgins' keynote speech at the National Famine Commemoration in 2013, he paid tribute to a recent generation of women for recovering the memory of the Great Famine, using a variety of mediums:

> In the 150th commemoration of the Famine in the 1990s, the visible presence of women was striking. From Mary Robinson and Eavan Boland, to Nuala Ní Dhomhnaill, Sinéad Ó Connor, Christine Kinealy, Medbh McGuckian and many others, Irish women actively involved themselves in an act of cultural recuperation. This generation of women drew attention to their marginalisation within the writing of Irish history. They understood that the Famine dead and Irish women emigrants were each characterised by silence and invisibility – both were victims of an historical erasure.[2]

These women, however, are part of a longer continuum of women who have written about the terrors of the Great Hunger, starting with the forthright Asenath Nicholson, herself an eye-witness to the unfolding tragedy, to Mildred Derby's gothic account, aptly named "The Hunger," and published in 1910,[3] to the pioneering research of Cecil Woodham-Smith in 1962.

The relationship between the Famine and art is more complex.[4] According to art historian Catherine Marshall, "For well over a century the horror of the event and the guilt of the survivors meant that the Famine was rarely represented visually."[5] There are notable exceptions, where women artists have captured the awfulness of hunger and eviction, ranging from Lady Elizabeth Butler's, *Evicted* (1890),[6] to Lilian Lucy Davidson's, *Gorta* (1946),[7] to Alanna O'Kelly's The Country Blooms, a Garden and a Grave (1990).[8] These various representations raises a further question, do women experience, and thus represent, famine differently from men?[9]

Clearly, women have been significant in helping to recover and reimagine the memory and the tragedy of the Great Famine, yet their various stories during periods of famine still remain under-represented. Their marginalisation is even more stark when examining the famines that occurred in Ireland prior to 1845 and after 1852. In 1741, for example, during what came to be known as 'Bliadhain an Air' (the year of slaughter), Katherine, the widow of William "Speaker" Conolly of Castletown House, Celbridge in Co. Kildare, constructed an obelisk to help relieve the effects of famine. During the famine of 1822, women in both Ireland and Britain undertook successful fund-raising activities on behalf of the starving poor, a role that has been omitted in the (admittedly still sparse) historiography.[10]

To highlight one further example: during the so-called forgotten famine of 1879-80, Constance Gore-Booth assisted her father Sir Henry Gore-Booth in alleviating hunger and providing aid for the tenants on their estate at Lissadell in Co. Sligo. This proved to be one of her formative experiences that helped shape her political temperament. Constance Markievicz would become one of Ireland's most influential women—as a feminist, suffragette, revolutionary nationalist leader during the Easter Rising in 1916, Sinn Féin politician and Fianna Fáil politician, the first woman elected to the British House of Commons in 1918, and one of the world's first cabinet ministers as Minister for Labour of the Irish Republic in 1919-1922. Despite her political legacy, however, she is all too often remembered (like Maud Gonne) as a source of poetic inspiration for W.B. Yeats. In Yeats's canonical poem, "In Memory of Eva Gore-Booth and Con Markievicz" (1933), the sisters are described as "two girls in silk kimonos, both beautiful, one a gazelle." In spite of her role as a revolutionary leader during the Easter Rebellion of 1916, Constance Markievicz is recalled by Yeats as having been "condemned to death / Pardoned, drags out lonely years / Conspiring among the ignorant... withered old, and skeleton-gaunt / An image of such politics." Her formative experience of providing famine relief, and the political legacy it inspired, seems long forgotten in Yeats's transformation of Constance Markievicz into a cautionary figure made "withered old, and skeleton-gaunt" from her revolutionary zeal. Moreover, Yeats's dismissive attitude to "such politics" appears symptomatic of a still widespread indifference to women's political activities in contemporary Ireland.[11] In a similar fashion, both Fanny Parnell and Maud Gonne have been largely written out of famine historiography,[12] while their considerable political contributions have been overshadowed, or even defined, by those of men who were close to them (Charles Stewart Parnell and W.B. Yeats, respectively).[13] *Women and the Great Hunger* seeks to recover the experiences of a small number of women during the Great Famine. This closing section recognizes that much still remains to be done. If the role of well-known women, including Countess Markievicz in providing famine relief in Lissadel, Fanny Parnell's fund-raising efforts in the U.S. in 1879 and 1880, and Maud Gonne's work in distributing food in the west the 1890s, still remain little recognized, inevitably, the contributions of many lesser-known women in other times and places, are still not well understood or sufficiently appreciated.

What insights do these omissions provide into the status of famine studies after 20 years of intense publishing activity, into the position of the women's movement in Ireland, 50 years since second-wave feminism ignited, and, more generally, into women's place in the curriculum overall? This book concludes with a personal reflection—which is, simultaneously, a heartfelt appeal.[14]

An Irish woman's place is on the curriculum:
A short overview of women's history in Ireland

At a recent Countess Markievicz School in Dublin, itself a project of feminist reclamation, this writer opined that:

> Our stories are purposefully lost in projects of ideological forgetting. [For example] filmmaker Lelia Doolan speaks of the difficulty in securing funds for her exemplary 2012 documentary on "forgotten" Bernadette Devlin, once among the most famous people on the planet – a mere forty years ago. These truths demand that we document our history in our own time. That history, in turn, contextualizes present struggles: we don't look back to marinate but to understand that we carry our foremothers incomplete and imperfect work forward into new challenges.[15]

Women of what has become known as second-wave feminism were radicalized not by formal education, which, thanks to a previous generation's activism, many had and in unprecedented numbers, but by recognizing ourselves in non-academic books, specifically in *The Feminine Mystique* (1963) and *The Female Eunuch* (1970).[16] Both Betty Friedan and Germaine Greer, respectively, spoke to the subjective, but as yet unarticulated, life experience of their readers— women who, in their time, had not previously been addressed as a primary audience. Let us pause to consider just what we did know of, and in, Ireland at the dawn of this second-wave. Did we know, for example, what is behind the lasting resonance of the Cúchulainn myth? (Clue: it is not related to the massive bronze in Dublin's General Post Office, historic as this piece may be.) Why is the Christian Church (both Roman Catholic and Church of Ireland, traditional sectarian enemies since the Reformation) headquartered in a small Northern Ireland town? Who was Anne Devlin? (Hint: Housekeeper is not an answer.) Was there a feminist campaign against adoption of the 1937 Constitution in what was then the Irish Free State? (Closed question: yes or no.) What is the single line that led to banning of Kate O'Brien's 1941 novel, *The Land of Spices*?

A mid-century Irish schooling would have prepared us for these questions but might not have supplied the following answers: Cuchulainn was the male warrior who prevailed over Queen Maeve. All patriarchal cultures have some form of this overthrow myth. We are invited to approve. The stories are, in fact, heartbreaking in their chauvinism and contempt. Armagh is an anglicization of "Ard Mhaca," named for Macha, an ancient goddess. The townland is sacred to her. The Christian Church in Ireland, usurping her religious and geographic place and notwithstanding its internal enmities, may be said to nestle in the goddess's bosom. Anne Devlin was full participant in the rebellion of 1803, a revolutionary celebrated in feminist Pat Murphy's eponymous film from 1984. Devlin was captured, interrogated and jailed. The biopic is based on her prison diaries. Murphy, meanwhile, has also filmed Brenda Maddox's life of Nora Barnacle Joyce (*Nora* from 2000). Yes, and, although it is hard to believe, Taoiseach Éamon de Valera is known to have compromised on some provisions to ensure adoption of the conservative 1937 constitution. Nearly 50 years later, in parallel circumstances, Taoiseach Garrett Fitzgerald added the phrase "with due regard to the equal right to life of the mother" to the proposed wording of what became the Constitution's problematic Article 40.3.3 (the 8th amendment guaranteeing the "right to life of the unborn," which, in turn, became the subject of a vigorous grassroots repeal movement). Finally, Kate O'Brien's heroine espies her father in "the embrace of love" with another man. This beautiful phrase was too much for the prurient moralists of the Irish Censorship Board.

Second-wave feminists, in Ireland as surely as in America, were quick to rise to the opportunity presented by Friedan and Greer's manifestos. In Ireland, the activism of the 1970s yielded revolutionary change in consciousness, services and social attitudes. Indeed, the genesis of the 2015 marriage equality vote lies in an early 1970s meeting of the self-styled "Sexual Liberation Movement," itself a consciously parallel initiative to the pre-existing Women's Liberation Movement. Held at Trinity College Dublin, this meeting was addressed by legendary gay-rights activist, David Norris, later a long serving member of the Irish Senate. As a new-minted feminist, awash with youthful optimism, I attended in solidarity. Immediately, Irish feminists established services responding to and naming previously hidden, occasionally deadly, issues facing women in our daily lives. These services included Women's Aid for domestic violence survivors, Cherish for one-parent families (subsequently known as One Family), the Dublin Rape Crisis Center, the Dublin Well Woman Center, and the Irish Pregnancy Counselling Center. By the 1980s, these voluntary organizations started becoming mainstream NGOs; their feminist founders serving on public policy boards and participating in international conferences. A government position at non-cabinet level was created for "Women's Affairs" and inaugurated by activist Nuala Fennell, since deceased. Less than a decade prior, Fennell had exposed the scandalous practice of involuntarily committing inconvenient wives to mental hospitals on dubious male authority led by the inconvenienced husband; an Irish divorce. In 1990, Ireland elected the legal champion of social justice issues, Mary Robinson, as Ireland's first female President. Nineteen years later, Robinson was presented with the U.S. Presidential Medal of Freedom, the country's highest civilian honor. Did we feel somehow "patronized" by so speedily coming in from the margins? We did not.

Contemporaneously, the major Irish universities began adopting women's studies curricula mostly devised and developed by academic women. These departments were generally headed by prominent feminists whose names lent both academic legitimacy and ideological urgency to the courses on offer, such as: The Centre for Women's Studies established at Dublin's historic Trinity College in 1988 (TCD itself was founded by the English queen, Elizabeth I); the University of Limerick, created in 1989, offered an MA in women's studies. In 1996, the Kathleen Lonsdale Building, honoring a groundbreaking Irish scientist, was opened on campus; the high-profile Women's Education Research and Resource Centre (WERRC) at University College Dublin was launched in 1990; University College Cork's first MA in women's studies was offered in 1991 and formed in 1997, at the former Roman Catholic seminary, the National University of Ireland Maynooth, offered a women's studies PhD in applied social studies. In addition, the feminist principles and procedures of non-directive pregnancy counselling, developed in the 1980s by this writer, are taught in master-classes given here by current practitioners. Through a number of complementary initiatives in this period, women's history also became a formal academic discipline under the leadership of many notable female academics and activists: in 1987, the Feminist History Forum was established in Dublin; in 1988, the Society for the History of Women was established by postgraduate students at University College Dublin and in 1989, historian Mary Cullen, a founder of the discipline, became the first president of the Women's History Association of Ireland (WHAI).

However, the record is not without its reversals. From the early 1980s, Attic Press published contemporary women's polemic. Among an exemplary catalogue, *A Dozen Lips* is a selection of essays commissioned and edited by UCD-WERRC's Ailbhe Smyth, which presents a thoughtful and well-argued snapshot of the era's feminist agenda and its calls to action. This volume is practically unavailable today, even as an historical artifact. Now merged with Cork University Press, Attic's back list is effectively unavailable and no new polemic has appeared under this imprint in more than 10 years. Meanwhile, bowing to vociferous feminist demands for inclusion, the much-praised *Field Day Anthology of Irish Writing*, which had first appeared in 1991 under all-male editorship, finally recognized women's work through important additional volumes published (grudgingly?) a decade later. These volumes, prohibitively priced and essentially available only to academic or other libraries, are described by publisher, Cork University Press, as "the most comprehensive corpus of Irish women's writing ever published."[17] Likewise, Arlen House Press—now primarily identified with New York's Syracuse University—inaugurated, in 1983, the annual Kate O'Brien Weekend in her native Limerick city; the first major Irish literary event to be named for a woman. In 2014, the event was renamed the Limerick Literary Festival, all but eliding the city's most famous female writer. Finally, as recently as 2015, WHAI scholars edited a collection of essays, *Sexual Politics in Modern Ireland*, in which they argued that some mainstream historians still regard women's history as incidental rather than crucial.

In the momentous flurry of second-wave achievement, feminists did not recognize how the mainstreaming of our projects paradoxically leaves these projects vulnerable to external pressures and priorities impacting our sustainability in ways beyond our control, as per processes such as the following. Taking my own case, the Dublin-based service, Open Door Counselling (successor in 1983 to the Irish Pregnancy Counselling Center), openly espoused a feminist commitment to "women's right to choose." Strategically, in order to extend service access through a more sustainable organizational model, I actively pursued a relationship with the national Irish Family Planning Association, an organization belonging to a more liberal, mainstream tradition. In 1993, with my direct involvement, the IFPA launched a nationwide, publicly-funded network of non-directive pregnancy counselling centers, effectively subsuming Open Door. I acted as consultant to this initiative, establishing service protocols and supplying senior staff who later served on the governmental Crisis Pregnancy Agency, founded in 2002. That is, I consciously traded ideological independence for mainstream service stability—a decision not without controversy in feminist circles—confident that the IFPA's tested mission and ethos would prove politically resilient even as its service provision reached further and deeper into the community. For a period of more than 20 years and counting, the IFPA has implemented Open Door's protocols in a wholly ethical manner guaranteeing a level of access unachievable under the previous service model. And the IFPA's advocacy for women has been impeccable throughout. I am fortunate; the process could have turned out very differently.

The second vulnerability for mainstreamed initiatives is that this "disappearing" of women is particularly noticeable in Irish academia where pioneering women's studies curricula are now buried within less assertive departmental rubrics. For example, the Women's Education Research and Resource Centre no longer appears on University College Dublin's homepage. Yet, in its day, the WERRC brand appeared ubiquitously and powerfully in Irish public life. (Diligent digging reveals that WERRC still exists at UCD, but within the Department of Social Justice, founded in 2005.) This case, and others like it, raises three key questions for the country's current academic leadership: To what extent has women's studies as a discipline been co-opted by patriarchal structures, narratives and priorities in the academy? To what extent has women's studies, together with the discipline's feminist roots and agenda, been disappeared into larger, more generic frameworks such as politics, history and law departments? And to what extent do those institutions with women's studies curricula engage with contemporary history as it develops in the public square?

The Trinity College Dublin website is succinct: "In 1999, in order to reflect the increasing diversity of its interests in areas such as sexualities and masculinities, the Centre for Women's Studies expanded its title and remit to become the Centre for Gender and Women's Studies. In 2005, the Centre became a full member of the School of Histories and Humanities."[18] Meanwhile, the National University of Ireland, Galway is pleased to discuss women in the context of "globalization" per its stated academic commitment to "build cross-disciplinary knowledge and understanding of gender and global issues through a critical human rights lens."[19] Thus, what started as a feminist initiative is now subsumed within a framework which favors multiple "histories" and "humanities". In the process, women's studies became interested in—surprise!— "masculinities" and, elsewhere, morphed into considerations of multi-dimensional "equalities," "globalization" and "human rights." You can still find "women," but it is an archaeological dig; we are not so much dead as buried.

In 2011, female students at UCD's School of Social Justice (the new institutional "parent" of women's studies) founded the *Countess Markievicz School*. A recognizably feminist project arising from concern about the declining numbers of women in Irish public and political life, the school is an annual discussion forum on women in Ireland named in honor of Ireland's first female Member of Parliament (M.P.) in Britain and Cabinet Minister in Ireland. At Quinnipiac University, the Ireland's Great Hunger Institute's founding director appears to be engaged in a reversal process of her own. In 2014, her first year at this generically titled department, she mounted an electrifying exhibition on the multi-faceted life of Hester, Lady Sligo, thereby restoring the voice of women to our previously partial record of Ireland's single greatest national trauma. Opening formalities for this exhibition were performed by Ireland's first female ambassador to the United States, the formidable Anne Anderson, allowing for a photo-op highlighting three history-making women. Ireland's Great Hunger Institute is continuing the work by presenting this groundbreaking academic conference about—*women*! (and publishing its findings). This is leadership. I offer my deepest appreciation and thanks.

Endnotes

[1] For example, Maria Luddy, *Women and Philanthropy in Nineteenth-Century Ireland* (Cambridge University Press, 1995); Margaret Preston, *Charitable Words: Women, Philanthropy, and the Language of Charity in Nineteenth-Century Dublin* (California: Praeger Press, 2004); Janet A. Nolan, *Ourselves Alone: Women's Emigration from Ireland, 1885-1920* (University Press of Kentucky, 2009).

[2] President Michael D. Higgins, Remarks at the National Famine Commemoration, Kilrush, Co. Clare, 12 May 2013: http://www.president.ie/en/media-library/speeches/remarks-by-president-michael-d.-higgins-at-the-national-famine-commemoratio
Accessed 26 September 2016.

[3] *The Hunger, being the realities of the Famine years in Ireland 1845 to 1849* (London: Andrew Melrose, 1910) by Andrew Merry – the pseudonym of Mildred Darby (1867-1932).

[4] A number of prominent art historians have lamented the lack of paintings that depict the Famine, see, Catherine Marshall, "Painting Irish History: The Famine," *History Ireland*, vol. 4, no. 3 (Autumn 1996), pp 47, 48-9.

[5] Catherine Marshall, Representations of the Famine at the Irish Museum of Modern Art: http://www.imma.ie/en/page_19233.htm Accessed 24 September 2016.

[6] This painting is on display in the Folklore Archive in University College, Dublin.

[7] This work is owned by Quinnipiac University and is displayed in Ireland's Great Hunger Museum in Hamden, CT. This photomontage is part of the permanent exhibition at the Crawford Art Gallery in Cork: http://www.crawfordartgallery.ie/pages/Other/Alannah_OKelly.html Accessed 15 July 2016.

[9] This question was raised by Melissa Fegan, *Literature and the Irish Famine 1845-1919* (Oxford: Clarendon Press, 2002), p. 212.

[10] *Report of the Committee for the Relief of the Distressed Districts in Ireland: appointed at a general meeting held at the City of London Tavern, on the 7th of May, 1822, with an appendix* (London: William Phillips, 1823), pp 320-346.

[11] The centenary commemorations of 1916 have helped to recover the important role that many women played in the Easter Rising.

[12] Gonne, who lived until 1953, included a whole chapter on the famine of 1897-1898 in her autobiography, *A Servant of the Queen. Reminiscences* (London; Victor Gollancz, 1974), 226-246.

[13] Jane Côté, "Writing Women out of History: Fanny and Anna Parnell and the Irish Ladies' Land League," *Études irlandaises*, Année 1992, vol. 17, Numéro 2, pp 123-134.

[14] The lead in to the Postscript was written by the editors.

[15] The Summer School was founded in 2011 by students in the School of Social Justice in University College Dublin. For details of the 23 May 2015 School, see www.countessmarkieviczschool.ie/2015-school.html Accessed 30 May 2015.

[16] Betty Friedan, *The Feminine Mystique* (New York: W.W. Norton and Co., 1963) and Germaine Greer, *The Female Eunuch* (Colorado: Paladin Press, 1970).

[17] *Field Day Anthology of Irish Writing: Irish Women's Writing and Traditions* (Cork University Press, 2002). This volume, in turn, provoked a feminist response, Patricia Boyle Haberstroh and Christine St. Peter, *Opening the Field: Irish Women, Texts and Contexts* (Cork University Press, 2007).

[18] "School of Histories and Humanities" at TCD: www.histories-humanities.tcd.ie/ Accessed 31 March 2016.

[19] "Centre for Global Women's Studies," at NUIG: www.nuigalway.ie/womens_studies/ Accessed 31 March 2016.

A PERSONAL REFLECTION

Works Cited

Côté, Jane. "Writing Women out of History: Fanny and Anna Parnell and the Irish Ladies' Land League." *Études irlandaises*, 123-134.

Fegan, Melissa. *Literature and the Irish Famine 1845-1919*. Oxford: Clarendon Press, 2002.

Friedan, Betty. *The Feminine Mystique*. New York: W.W. Norton and Co., 1963.

Greer, Germaine. *The Female Eunuch*. Colorado: Paladin Press, 1970.

Haberstroh, Patricia Boyle and Christine St. Peter. *Opening the Field: Irish Women, Texts and Contexts*. Cork University Press, 2007.

Luddy, Maria. *Women and Philanthropy in Nineteenth-Century Ireland*. Cambridge University Press, 1995.

Marshall, Catherine *"Painting Irish History: The Famine,"* History Ireland, vol. 4, no. 3 (Autumn 1996), 47-50.

Merry, Andrew. *The Hunger, being the realities of the Famine years in Ireland 1845 to 1849*. London: Andrew Melrose, 1910.

Nolan, Janet A. *Ourselves Alone: Women's Emigration from Ireland*, 1885-1920. University Press of Kentucky, 2009.

Various editors. Field Day *Anthology of Irish Writing: Irish Women's Writing and Traditions*. Cork University Press, 2002.

Illustrations

Source: Irish Photo Archive
Caption: "Cecil Woodham-Smith receiving an Honorary Doctorate."
Chapter Author: Dr. Christine Kinealy

Credit: Photo courtesy of *The Bookman*, Vol 1 (November 1926) 103.
Caption: "Drawing of Asenath Nicholson by the artist, Anna Maria Howitt."
Chapter Author: Dr. Maureen Murphy

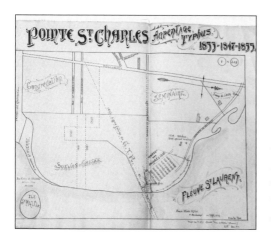

Credit/Caption: Image courtesy of Soeurs
Grises de Montréal
"Montréal Plans, Tabl.4, No.2B [2F]"
Chapter Author: Dr. Jason King

Bring me before a Court
Maria Monk

Credit: frontispiece, *Confirmation of Maria Monk's disclosures concerning the Hotel Dieu nunnery*, J.J. Slocum
(London: James S. Hodson, 1837).
Engraving by W.L. Ormsby
Caption: "Maria Monk and her child"
Chapter Author: Dr. Jason King

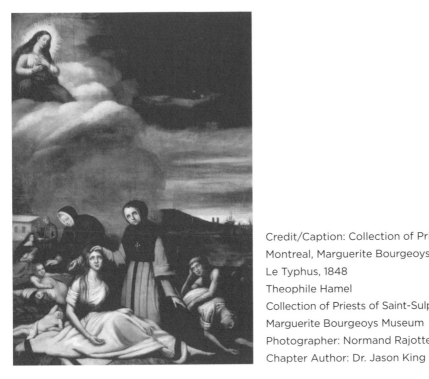

Credit/Caption: Collection of Priests of Saint-Sulpice of
Montreal, Marguerite Bourgeoys
Le Typhus, 1848
Theophile Hamel
Collection of Priests of Saint-Sulpice of Montreal,
Marguerite Bourgeoys Museum
Photographer: Normand Rajotte
Chapter Author: Dr. Jason King

"Speranza": Lady Wilde as a Young Woman

Credit: Illustration of Chapter XVIII in the
book "Oscar Wilde, His Life and Confessions",
by Frank Harris.
Caption: "Speranza of the Nation"
Chapter Author: Matthew Skwiat

Credit: Courtesy of Sandy O'Hare

Caption: "Introduction to Lady Sligo Exhibition Slideshow, created by Sandy O'Hare"

Chapter Authors: Sandy O'Hare; Robert Young

Credit: Sligo Collection, Quinnipiac University

Caption: "Lady Sligo to her estate agent, George Hildebrand."

Chapter Authors: Sandy O'Hare; Robert Young

Credit: Photo courtesy of Westport House. Photo credit: Michael McLaughlin
Caption: "Portrait of Lady Hester Catherine de Burgh, later Lady Sligo"
Chapter Authors: Sandy O'Hare; Robert Young

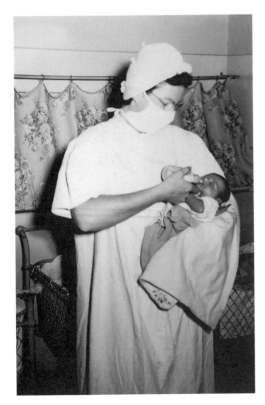

Credit: Photo courtesy of Eleanor Dawson
Caption: "Dr. Eleanor Dawson, great grand-daughter of Earl Grey girl, Bridget McMann."
Chapter Author: Rebecca Abbott

Credit: Photo courtesy of Eleanor Dawson

Caption: "Marjorie Collins, mother of Eleanor Dawson and grand-daughter of Earl Grey girl, Bridget McMann."

Chapter Author: Rebecca Abbott

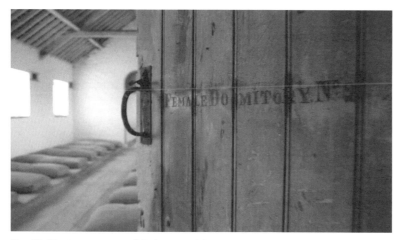

Credit: Photo courtesy of Rebecca Abbott

Caption: "Female dormitory, Portumna workhouse, Galway"

Chapter Author: Rebecca Abbott

IRELAND'S GREAT HUNGER INSTITUTE AT QUINNIPIAC UNIVERSITY

Ireland's Great Hunger Institute is a scholarly resource for the study of the Great Hunger, which is also known as *An Gorta Mór*. Through a program of lectures, conferences, course offerings and publications, the institute fosters a deeper understanding of this tragedy and its causes and consequences.

To encourage original scholarship and meaningful engagement, the institute develops and makes available the Great Hunger Collection, a unique array of primary, secondary and cultural sources, to students and scholars.

Ireland's Great Hunger Institute was established in September 2013 and its founding director was Professor Christine Kinealy.

CORK UNIVERSITY PRESS www.corkuniversitypress.com

Contributor Biographies:

Rebecca Abbott is Professor of Communications at Quinnipiac University and an independent film producer, director and editor. Abbott's recent films include the Emmy award winning documentaries *Albert Schweitzer: My Life is My Argument* on the life of humanitarian Albert Schweitzer, and *Aeromedical*, which tells the story of aeromedical rescue in the US Air Force. Abbott's latest work, *Ireland's Great Hunger and the Irish Diaspora* (2015) is narrated by actor Gabriel Byrne, and explores the historical and socio-political circumstances of the Great Famine and its lasting legacy.

Cara Delay, Associate Professor of History and Director of the Women's and Gender Studies Program at the College of Charleston, holds degrees from Boston College and Brandeis University. Her research analyzes women, gender, and culture in 19th- and 20th-century Ireland, with a particular focus on the history of reproduction, pregnancy, and childbirth. She has published in *The Journal of British Studies*; *Lilith: A Feminist History Journal*; *Feminist Studies*; *Études Irlandaises*; *New Hibernia Review* and *Éire-Ireland* and has written blogs for Nursing Clio and broadsheet.ie.

Christine Kinealy has worked in educational and research institutes in Dublin, Belfast and England and, more recently, in the USA. In September 2013, she was appointed the founding Director of Ireland's Great Hunger Institute at Quinnipiac University. Professor Kinealy has published extensively, her most recent books including "Charity and the Great Hunger: The Kindness of Strangers" (Bloomsbury, 2013), and *An Drochshaol* (with John Walsh, Dublin, 2016).

Jason King has been a Postdoctoral Researcher, Assistant Professor, and Lecturer at the National University of Ireland, Galway, the University of Limerick, Concordia University, the Université de Montréal, Maynooth University, and University College Cork. His recent publications include *Interculturalism and Performance Now: New Directions?* (with Charlotte McIvor, Palgrave, 2017), *Irish Global Migration and Memory: Transatlantic Perspectives of Ireland's Famine Exodus* (with Marguérite Corporaal, Routledge, 2016), *Irish Famine Migration Narratives* in the *History of the Irish Famine: Primary Sources* series (with Christine Kinealy and Gerard Moran, Routledge, 2017), and a special issue of *Irish Studies Review* on "Irish Multiculturalism in Crisis" (with Pilar Vilar-Árgaiz, 2016). He is the curator of the Digital Irish Famine Archive: http://faminearchive.nuigalway.ie/.

Gerard MacAtasney is an independent historian based in Belfast. He has written a number of books on famine studies as well as biographies of Tom Clarke and Seán MacDiarmada.

Turlough McConnell is a creative director specializing in Irish-American history and culture. He has written and produced exhibitions, multi-media projects, documentary films and live events for over 30 years. He was Special Advisor for the Ireland's Great Hunger Museum and Ireland's Great Hunger Institute at Quinnipiac. Turlough is a regular contributor to *Irish America Magazine*.

E. Moore Quinn, Professor of Anthropology, is Associate Chair of the Department of Sociology and Anthropology at the College of Charleston, South Carolina. Quinn is the author of "Walking the Path to the Unbaptized Children of Ireland: A Case Study of *Crucán na bPáiste*" (Inter-Disciplinary Press 2015). Other recent articles appear in *New Hibernia Review*; *Irish Studies Review*; *Women, Reform, and Resistance in Ireland, 1850-1950* (Delay and Brophy eds., 2015); and *Consuming St. Patrick's Day* (Bryan and Skinner eds., 2015). Quinn's co-edited volume, *Dynamic Paths: Pilgrimages on the World Stage*, was published in 2016.

Gerard Moran is a researcher at the SSRC at NUI Galway, where he has lectured in the Dept. of History. His areas of research include Irish emigration and the diaspora, the Great Famine and land and political agitation in 19th century Ireland. He is author of *Sending Out Ireland's Poor: Assisted Emigration to North America in the Nineteenth Century* (Dublin, 2004 and 2014) and joint editor of *Mayo—History and Society* (Dublin, 2014).

Maureen Murphy holds the Joseph L. Dionne Chair of Teacher Education at Hofstra University. She is the author of "Compassionate Stranger. Asenath Nicholson and the Great Irish Famine" (Syracuse, 2015), is a former Director of the New York State Great Irish Famine Curriculum and the historian of The Irish Hunger Memorial at Battery Park City. She is the Past President of the American Conference for Irish Studies and the Past Chair of the International Association for the Study of Irish Literatures.

Maureen O'Connor is a lecturer in the School of English, University College Cork. She has published widely in Irish Studies, especially women's writing, and is the author of *The Female and the Species: The Animal in Irish Women's Writing* (2010). She has edited and co-edited a number of volumes, most recently, with Derek Gladwin, a forthcoming special issue of *The Canadian Journal of Irish Studies*.

Sandy Letourneau O'Hare holds a Master of Library Science degree and is Head of Access and Document Services at the Arnold Bernhard Library, Quinnipiac University where she is also an instructor in the First Year Seminar Program. In addition, Sandy participates in information literacy instruction, reference services, is the Library Liaison to the English Department, serves as personal librarian to all student veterans on campus and collaborates with Ireland's Great Hunger Institute on various projects and exhibitions.

Ciarán Reilly is a historian of nineteenth and twentieth century Ireland. He is author of The Irish Land Agent, 1830-1860: the case of King's County (Dublin, 2014); *Strokestown and the Great Irish Famine* (Dublin, 2014) and *John Plunket Joly and the Great Famine in King's County* (Dublin, 2012).

Ruth Riddick is a reproductive rights activist and service provider who led a successful appeal at the European Court of Human Rights against Ireland's restriction on information about extra-territorial legal abortion (Open Door Counselling 1992), resulting in Irish constitutional and legal reform. Her polemic on "Women's right to choose" is featured in the *Field Day Anthology of Irish Writing*. Her occasional essays are published in *Conscience*, the news journal of Catholics for Choice.

Mathew Skwiat is a graduate at the University of Rochester studying late 19th and early 20th century British, Irish and American Literature. He currently works in the William Blake Digital Archive at the University of Rochester and has taught courses in history, writing, and literature at a number of universities in New York and New Jersey. He has contributed to *Irish America Magazine*, the *Oscholars*, and *Irish Economic and Social History,* as well as presenting at conferences in the United States, England, Ireland, and France.

Oonagh Walsh is Associate Dean for Research in the Glasgow School for Business and Society at Glasgow Caledonian University, Scotland. A Co. Galway native, she was educated at Trinity College, Dublin and Nottingham University, and has held academic appointments at University of Southampton (New College), Aberdeen University and University College Cork. Her research interests lie in medical history, especially mental health history, and epigenetic change linked to the Great Famine.

Daphne Dyer Wolf is a PhD candidate in the History and Culture program at Drew University, Madison, NJ, where her dissertation will explore the history of collective action on the De Freyne Estate in County Roscommon. Her essay, "A Beggar's Gabardine: Thomas Carlyle and the Irish Famine," published in the *Australasian Journal of Irish Studies,* was the winner of the Irish Studies Association of Australia and New Zealand 2015 Postgraduate Essay Prize. In 2013, she was a co-curator of an exhibit, "Labor & Dignity: James Connolly in America," sponsored by the Irish Department of Foreign Affairs and Glucksman Ireland House at New York University, where she received an MA in Irish Studies in 2011.

Robert Young is Public Services Librarian at the Arnold Bernhard Library at Quinnipiac University. He provides assistance to scholars and researchers who wish to access materials in The Great Hunger Special Collection, and is the contact for individuals who would like to donate new materials to the collection. In addition, he assists the campus community with questions related to copyright and Fair Use, serves as library liaison to several academic departments, and has collaborated with Ireland's Great Hunger Institute on various projects and exhibitions. In his spare time, he is an avid collector of vintage photographs and is currently researching the history behind a collection of snapshots that document the life of a gay male couple in the 1950s.

Index. Women and Great Hunger